PARENTS WITHOUT PAPERS

PARENTS WITHOUT PAPERS

THE PROGRESS AND PITFALLS OF MEXICAN AMERICAN INTEGRATION

FRANK D. BEAN, SUSAN K. BROWN, AND JAMES D. BACHMEIER

Russell Sage Foundation • New York

6/6/16
LB
$37.50

The Russell Sage Foundation

Library of Congress Cataloging-in-Publication Data

Bean, Frank D.
  Parents without papers : the progress and pitfalls of Mexican American integration / Frank D. Bean, Susan K. Brown, James D. Bachmeier.
    pages cm
  Includes bibliographical references and index.
  ISBN 978-0-87154-042-3 (pbk. : alk. paper) — ISBN 978-1-61044-851-2 (ebook)
  1. Immigrants—Cultural assimilation. 2. Mexican Americans—Cultural assimilation. 3. Children of immigrants—United States. 4. Social integration—United States. 5. Hispanic American parents. 6. Mexico—Emigration and immigration. 7. United States—Emigration and immigration. I. Title.
  JV6342.B43 2015
  305.868'72073—dc23

2015006864

Text design by Suzanne Nichols

Cover Artwork
Artist: Carmen LOMAS GARZA
Title: Barbacoa para Cumpleaños (barbeque birthday party)
Medium: Alkyds on canvas; Size: 36 × 48 inches
©1993 Carmen Lomas Garza

RUSSELL SAGE FOUNDATION
112 East 64th Street, New York, New York 10065
10 9 8 7 6 5 4 3 2 1

In memory of Carolyn P. Boyd

══ Contents ══

List of Figures and Tables

═ About the Authors ═

Frank D. Bean is Distinguished Professor of Sociology and director, Center for Research on International Migration, at the University of California, Irvine.

Susan K. Brown is associate professor of sociology and director, program in Demographic and Social Analysis, at the University of California, Irvine.

James D. Bachmeier is assistant professor of sociology at Temple University.

$=$ Acknowledgments $=$

P robably more often than not, the main idea for a book occurs long before the final product is completed. Certainly that's true for this book and the project behind it. The two senior authors first started talking about doing a study of Mexican American integration in Los Angeles shortly after Susan arrived on the campus of the University of California, Irvine (UCI), in 2001. We joined with other immigration colleagues (Leo Chavez, Louis DeSipio, Jennifer Lee, and Rubén Rumbaut) at UCI and another (Min Zhou) at the University of California, Los Angeles, to apply for a grant to examine the mobility of the children of several different groups of immigrants in Los Angeles. Although all the members of the team were interested in what happens to immigrants and their children in the United States, we each had specialized interests beyond that, sometimes in certain groups, sometimes in certain aspects of integration, or sometimes in both, which eventually led us to develop multiple studies on the large subject of immigrant integration. In the beginning, we obtained a grant from the Russell Sage Foundation (RSF) to conduct an omnibus study in metropolitan Los Angeles focusing on five second-generation groups (Chinese, Guatemalan/Salvadorans, Koreans, Filipinos, and Vietnamese) and another group, Mexicans, for whom we obtained interviews through four or more generations of descendants. The present book is a study of both immigrant integration in general and the recent integration experiences of Mexican Americans in particular. Our first acknowledged debt for help in this endeavor is to our colleagues who worked with us to launch the initial overall study.

We owe special thanks to Eric Wanner, the president of RSF at the time the study was instigated and funded. He offered wise counsel about our project and enthusiastically supported the early suggestion of the senior author to collect information on Mexican American generations beyond the second, the one group for whom such data were possible to collect. Eric also conceived and led a longstanding program of research at the foundation on immigration, from which several studies constituted part of the inspiration for the Los Angeles Study. These studies included the

Children of Immigrants Longitudinal Studies (CILS) in Miami and San Diego, conducted by Alejandro Portes and Rubén Rumbaut, and the New York Second Generation Study, conducted by Philip Kasinitz, John Mollenkopf, and Mary Waters. These researchers were not only our intellectual models but also sources of a great deal of practical advice about key research details that guided our decision-making for the Los Angeles data collection. We owe them all a debt of gratitude. Sheldon Danziger, current president of RSF, and Suzanne Nichols, RSF's director of publications, were both patient and supportive, providing useful guidance that strengthened the manuscript. Similarly, three anonymous reviewers made numerous suggestions for revision that helped improve the final product.

Mark DiCamillo of the Field Research Corporation of San Francisco, the professional survey organization that conducted the data collection, not only provided a veritable fount of research and technical expertise, which immeasurably improved the quality of the data, but also, perhaps because he was the offspring of Italian immigrants, was genuinely interested in the topic. He thus also made substantive suggestions that benefited the project.

UCI also supported the project in many ways, particularly through its establishment and support of the Center for Research on Immigration, Population and Public Policy. Carolynn Bramlett deserves a special acknowledgment for the long hours and years she worked on the manuscript without once losing her cheerfulness. Several graduate students in the Department of Sociology or in the master's program in Demographic and Social Analysis at UCI also worked as research assistants on the project. Some of them are coauthors of chapters, but we also want to thank Heather Arata, Ann Fefferman, Yader Lanuza, Shila Patel, Carolyn Zambrano, and Karina Zavaleta-Abel for what was often painstaking work. Jennifer Van Hook, director of the Population Research Institute at Pennsylvania University, also contributed demographic analyses that showed the contributions of various sources of demographic change to shifts over several decades in those who self-identify as belonging to the Mexican-origin population in the United States.

We also want to thank Rudy and Patricia Speier-Torres for their long-time support of this project and for suggesting the family-based artwork of Carmen Lomas Garza for the book cover. We thank the artist as well for allowing us to reproduce her heartwarming *Barbacoa para Cumpleaños*. Finally, we express our deepest gratitude and love to the family members who put up with the demands of our research: our spouses Carolyn Boyd, who passed away while the manuscript was in production, and Jennifer Havelock Bachmeier, and the three daughters who have grown up with this project, Helene and Eva Wierzbicki and Kaia Bachmeier. They are the unsung heroines behind our work.

= Chapter 1 =

Introduction

Three general questions have long driven debates in social science and public policy about immigration to the United States: How many and what kinds of immigrants are (or should be) coming to the country? How do new arrivals affect both the country and the persons already here? And how rapidly and how well are immigrants being integrated into the economy and American society as a whole?[1] The last of these questions is arguably the most important in the long run. The success or failure of immigrant integration lays bare the values of contemporary American society by showing how the country treats one of its most vulnerable (and increasingly needed) groups. As immigrants constitute ever larger components of the U.S. workforce, the stakes associated with immigrant integration rise ever higher. Because arrivals from Mexico make up the largest single immigrant group, and because so many enter without much education and without legal status, their presence has created the most significant integration challenge now facing the country.[2] This book analyzes how that challenge is being met. Although many immigration issues (such as the country's need for high-skilled immigrants) deserve extended study, research into Mexican American integration arguably addresses the single most significant piece of the U.S. immigration-policy puzzle.

Would the United States benefit from adopting new immigrant policies? Answering this question must take into account how well current policies are working. To what degree has the recent integration of Mexican immigrants and their descendants been successful? If current kinds and levels of integration are satisfactory, new policies might not be needed. But if current integration could be improved, thus suggesting a need for alternative policies, what should these policies be? In such a case, an important corollary question also arises: How important is it for the country to adopt such new policies? This book assesses overall integration among Mexican Americans, strives to understand the causal origins of their integration patterns, and, based on the results of our analyses, makes recommendations

1

about immigrant integration policies. Note that we speak here of immigrant policies, not immigration policies. The latter refer to laws and practices pertaining to which immigrants come; the former refer to laws and practices affecting immigrants after they arrive. Although conceptually distinct, these two policy domains are interrelated: certain immigration policies often contribute to inadequate immigrant integration outcomes, which in turn point to the need for new immigrant policies.

The number of Mexican migrants entering this country in recent decades has eclipsed the totals from any other country. From 2003 to 2013, the United States granted legal permanent residency to nearly 1.7 million Mexican immigrants, more than twice the total from the next-largest sending country, China.[3] Also, during the 1990s until 2009, more of the unauthorized persons who established de facto residency came from Mexico than from any other country.[4] Despite a dramatic drop-off in migration since the Great Recession, the total number of unauthorized Mexicans in the country by 2012 was about 6.1 million people (or 56 percent of all unauthorized residents). Most of these migrants came as laborers, and their skill level is generally low. The schooling level of recent Mexican immigrants is 9.2 years on average (authors' calculations from IPUMS data), the lowest of any major entry group.[5] But if these migrants can nevertheless find plenty of work, the implication for policy is that their labor is necessary for the economy and that their integration also should matter for the strength of the larger social fabric.

Although the full integration of Mexican immigrants and their descendants is clearly desirable, social science research has not yet generated consensus about the nature and degree of this integration. Even when agreement exists on such matters as, say, second-generation education being higher than that of the first generation, or third-generation schooling still lagging behind that of white natives, disagreement arises about the reasons for such patterns. Thus it remains unclear why integration is incomplete. This unfortunate dissensus sometimes comes about simply because researchers assess integration in different ways. Depending on the angle from which they approach the matter, researchers can appear to generate different results, leading some to conclude with guarded optimism that many of today's less-skilled Mexican migrant workers will become tomorrow's prosperous U.S. citizens,[6] while others remain pessimistic about Latino integration.[7] As the literature has noted, optimistic or pessimistic conclusions can simply depend in part on whether researchers exclude the least-integrated immigrant (or first) generation in analyses of Mexican American mobility.[8]

But more substantive factors underlie the various interpretations of research results. The main controversy concerns the role of ethnoracial discrimination in forestalling Mexican American integration. Scholars of assimilation have envisioned such discrimination as diminishing across generations, especially when institutional structures exist to support attainment for nonwhite minorities.[9] The research findings emanating from this neo-assimilationist tradition tend to suggest little need for further policy reform, beyond maintaining civil rights laws and affirmative-action programs to sustain schooling and labor-market opportunities for immigrants who belong to disadvantaged minority groups. Another research approach emphasizes the persistence of discrimination, which thwarts even third-generation integration.[10] Ironically, the short-term policy recommendations from such studies are similarly minimal, because the prejudice undergirding discrimination is seen as so deeply embedded in culture and institutions that only long-term policies such as improving education have been recommended as ways to ameliorate the problem.

Our emphasis is on altogether different factors and falls between the neo-assimilation and racial-discrimination extremes. It offers the prospect of results that imply concrete and immediate policy needs. We focus on the effects of unauthorized migration status on integration, both for the children and the grandchildren of Mexican immigrants, examined separately by gender. Although the role of unauthorized status has previously been recognized as an integration handicap for first-generation Mexican immigrants, its legacy influence on the children and grandchildren of immigrants has not been sufficiently examined in integration research, either theoretically or empirically. On the theory side, unauthorized status has often been noted by scholars as something likely to constitute an important limiting influence on integration,[11] but it has tended to be viewed mainly as a factor to be considered in analyses rather than as a phenomenon with broader theoretical significance deriving from its institutional embeddedness in official definitions of societal membership.[12] On the empirical side, the lack of data about unauthorized status, especially for the parents and even the grandparents of the U.S.-born second and third generations, respectively, has foreclosed the possibility of examining how much difference unauthorized status makes for integration. Also largely yet unexamined but nonetheless important are assessments of the effects of changes in migration status, by which newcomers to the United States successfully transition from unauthorized to legal status.[13]

The integration patterns of this latter group of migrants may especially matter for policy. If migrants who were able to legalize could subsequently (and relatively quickly) find steadier and higher-paying jobs, and if their children in turn benefited from this status change and from the ensuing incentives to obtain more schooling, this would imply that unauthorized migration status per se plays a substantial role in holding back migrants and their children. However, if such legalized migrants and their children showed levels of schooling and income little different from those of migrants who come to the country illegally and remain unauthorized, it would suggest that legalization provides few benefits and that some other factor, such as ethnoracial status, limits Mexican Americans' integration. In contrast, if those who were able to legalize exhibited substantially higher integration, so that they ended up on a par with those who come legally, the policy implications would be dramatically different. If changes in migration status of parents allowed their children to learn more and earn more, good policy would emphasize providing opportunities for legalization.

Understanding the integration of Mexican Americans thus involves conceptualizing what unauthorized status means, gauging to what degree it handicaps Mexican Americans, and unraveling how this and other forces govern economic and social successes and shortfalls. Integration encompasses multiple dimensions and crosses multiple generations, and unless research tries to cover their sizable scope rather thoroughly, it risks drawing conclusions based on either partial data or unfinished processes. To develop a logic for how unauthorized status, and more broadly lack of early societal membership, hampers many other aspects of advancement, we draw on several theoretical approaches about immigrant integration. Because theoretical perspectives are often not mutually exclusive, more than one may apply. Also, some may pertain to certain kinds of integration better than others, and some may describe certain subgroups more than others. In short, hybrid perspectives may be needed to account for Mexican American integration.

At the level of specific research goals, we seek to assess the effects of unauthorized entry and subsequent changes in migration status on multiple kinds of integration across three generations. We first gauge the effect of unauthorized migration status in the immigrant generation, looking at its relationship with key labor-market indicators (including education and income). Then we ascertain how such parental status affects both the socioeconomic and sociocultural integration of their children, including those born in the United States. But it is crucial not to limit our analyses to the first two generations. We could focus only on mobility from the first to the second generation (that is, on how much integration occurs comparing immigrants with the children of immigrants). Indeed, doing so would constitute a self-contained endeavor in its own right. Instead, we trace out such differences through a third-only generation (not a third-plus generation, as we emphasize later in this chapter) to capture longer-term integration processes. Because the mobility literature has long shown the importance of parents' socioeconomic status on children's outcomes,[14] looking at integration across three generations without considering the legacy effects of unauthorized migration would omit a crucial factor that may influence the overall process. Thus we do both in what follows, using unique data collected in the metropolitan Los Angeles area that provide information on both respondents and their parents.

Definitions and Use of Certain Terms

Before proceeding further, some terminological clarification may be useful. First, we often use the terms *Hispanic* and *Latino* interchangeably, as well as the terms *Mexican-origin population* and *Mexican Americans*. In each case, we do so with the understanding that we are referring to persons living in the United States who came from Mexico or whose ancestors at one time lived in Mexico, including the period when Mexico extended to much of today's American Southwest. In our usage, these terms are meant to cover unauthorized Mexican immigrants, most of whom are included to a certain extent (although not identified as such) in official U.S. government sources of data such as the decennial census. Our specific focus is the integration of Mexican Americans, although we may introduce heuristic theoretical comparisons involving other immigrant or ethnoracial groups to clarify and sharpen understanding. When we speak of Mexican Americans, we thus mean not only those who live in the United States by dint of geographic annexation or who have moved to the United States from Mexico (either temporarily or permanently) but also their children, their grandchildren, and other descendants further removed.

Although only those who initially moved to the United States from today's Mexico are technically immigrants, to assess the integration experience of the Mexican-origin group in its entirety (a phenomenon that may take place over several generations), we need to go beyond just the experiences of the immigrant generation and consider those of the children and grandchildren of immigrants as well. It might even be helpful to study the great-grandchildren of immigrants, but information on the birthplaces of great-grandparents (which would be required to define who falls into a fourth-generation category) is generally lacking or sketchy. So as a matter of first approximation, we concentrate on three main groups of Mexican Americans, referring to immigrants as the first generation, the children of immigrants as the second generation, and the grandchildren of immigrants as the third generation. We further subdivide these groups, depending on the age at arrival of the immigrants or the nativity of parents and grandparents in the cases of the second and third generations, respectively. Following convention, we may refer to the Mexican-born children of immigrants as the 1.5 generation if they came to the United States before the age of fourteen. We refer to respondents with one foreign-born parent and one native-born parent as the 2.5 generation.

Considerable potential also exists for confusion about the racial and ethnic status of today's immigrant groups.[15] Contemporary social science views racial and ethnic labels as social constructions, meaning that these labels come not from immutable physical or biological characteristics but from the social meanings (often pejorative and stereotypical) that have been attached to these and other characteristics. Despite this, and all too often consistent with past stereotypes, the concept of race is still often treated as more fixed and immutable than is the concept of ethnicity.[16] In other instances, *race* is often used synonymously with national origin (that is, as in the more "fixed" sense that terms like *African American* are often employed to refer to persons whose ancestors came to the United States from Africa), whereas the term *ethnicity* is often applied to cultural characteristics associated with members of a particular group. In the context of racial and ethnic terminologies used in the United States, especially those constituting the basis for official government classifications, the term *Hispanic* (often used in a national-origin sense) is applied to those persons who self-report themselves in such terms, even though data collection agencies are careful to note that Hispanics "can be of any race" (as the term *race* is used by the U.S. government).

Here, we do not belabor these distinctions, although we recognize their importance. Rather, we mean that both self-reports and attributions of racial or ethnic status may be markers that correlate with other characteristics. The issue for this study is what term we use to designate such statuses. We adopt the term *ethnoracial status* to refer to any "racial" or "ethnic" status that may constitute a basis for self- or other-classification.[17] Thus we speak of both Mexican Americans and African Americans as members of ethnoracial groups. We leave as an empirical matter the determination of the extent to which any two groups are similar or dissimilar in the ways they see themselves and are treated by others rather than beginning with a terminology that presupposes some underlying basis of racial or ethnic group membership.

Features of This Investigation

This study has numerous distinctive features. Most important, it has a two-pronged focus. It both develops a new approach for analyzing immigrant integration in general and, relying on this approach, assesses the extent of integration for the most important immigrant group in the United States at the moment, Mexican Americans. Within these two broad emphases, four particular features of the book are especially notable.

The Meaning and Effects of Unauthorized Status

The first distinctive feature is that the book develops a new theoretical perspective about why and how unauthorized status, reinforced by immigration and immigrant policies of the United States over the past fifty years, hinders the integration of Mexican Americans. Even as recent demographic changes in the United States have ensured a growing need for labor migrants, migration policies have all but guaranteed that most of those entrants will be unable to attain the status of legal permanent resident. Furthermore, as enforcement policies have become harsher, such migrants now must live even more on the margins of society than their predecessors may have had to. Although unauthorized Mexican migrants have always lacked full societal membership, the gap between their experiences and full membership has worsened, thereby exacerbating their lack of integration. In any case, studying the adverse effects on today's second and third generations of unauthorized parents or grandparents probably understates the current magnitude of such effects because conditions may now be even harsher than thirty or forty years ago.

We contend that right from the beginning, legal status—or, more generally, societal membership—is crucial for integration, especially socioeconomic integration. The harder the social boundary that delineates who is deemed suitable for social (and particularly legal) citizenship in a given society, the more likely immigrants are to experience formal and informal exclusion and stigmatization to the point of being deemed socially illegitimate.[18] We call this absence of societal membership *membership exclusion.* The nature of membership exclusion can and does vary from country to country, involving variously religion (for example, being Islamic in many European countries);[19] origins in a former colony (for example, Algerians in France during the 1960s and 1970s);[20] race (for example, African Americans before the civil rights era and to a considerable extent even afterward);[21] residency restrictions (for example, Chinese of rural origin living without official papers in a large city);[22] and citizenship restrictions (for example, Turkish and other guest workers in Germany during the 1960s and 1970s)[23] or just second-class citizenship (many Arabs in Israel today).[24] Whatever the particular basis for the existence of a strong exclusionary boundary, its effect in the receiving society is to stigmatize migrants falling outside the boundary and to reinforce the view that their presence and status are illegitimate.

In the United States historically, notable cases of denials of social citizenship include African Americans in the South during slavery, Mexican Americans in Texas in the second half of the nineteenth and the first half of the twentieth centuries, the forced relocation of Native Americans, as in the Trail of Tears, and Chinese exclusion.[25] All these groups were either dislocated or subjected to apartheid-like restrictions that were not officially eliminated until the landmark civil rights legislation of the mid 1960s.[26] Immigrants who face such exclusions today, like these ethnoracial minorities earlier, experience social and psychological distress[27] as the strain and tension stemming from a lack of membership dampen structural forms of immigrant incorporation, such as educational attainment.[28]

Since the Immigration Reform and Control Act of 1986 made it illegal to hire unauthorized workers,[29] migration status in the United States has increasingly constituted this kind of strong boundary, especially for Mexicans, who make up the bulk of the U.S. unauthorized population.[30] Because so many Mexicans have come to the United States as unauthorized entrants and then remained in marginal statuses for long periods of time, their individual geographic and social mobility has been restricted by such social and legal exclusions as the inability in most states to get a driver's license and the risk of apprehension and deportation. The effects of these burdens extend to their children, undercutting their access to opportunities in school, heightening stress, undermining motivations to achieve, and slowing cognitive and emotional development.[31] The membership-exclusion conceptualization thus explicitly emphasizes that structural integration depends on this earliest form of political incorporation. In the case of Mexicans, structured integration depends on having or obtaining legal status or official indication that legal status is imminent.

Empirically, we develop and present an estimate of the education penalty among the children of Mexican immigrants that results from their parents residing in the country as unauthorized migrants. We also evaluate the extent to which the penalty disappears, if at all, when migrant parents are able to legalize. In addition, we assess the relative importance of this penalty compared with other factors affecting incorporation. To our knowledge, this is the first time such relative magnitudes have been calculated and comparatively examined for the second generation. The results provide a basis for developing quantitative assessments of the human-capital gains that could be attained if immigration policy reforms were to provide pathways to legalization.

Gender Differences in Integration

A second distinctive feature of the book involves explicit attention to the role that gender plays in shaping integration. Theories of why migration takes place in the first place have often noted how decisions to migrate emerge from family or household contexts that differentially affect males and females.[32] However, in seeking explanations of immigrant integration after migration, researchers have less often explicitly considered how family and household factors may influence males and females differently, a somewhat surprising underemphasis given that migration itself often both strengthens family bonds and occurs among more cohesive families.[33] Of course, rather than fostering cohesion, migration may also involve family separation and disruption, outcomes that hamper integration.[34] Such different effects of migration on family cohesion point to the possibility that migration itself, especially unauthorized labor migration, may be associated with family-based orientations and cultural frames and repertoires that facilitate integration in some instances and retard it in others, and differentially so for males and females.

An example comes from recent research findings showing that resource-poor unauthorized Mexican labor migrants develop short-term, family-oriented strategies, both among the immigrants themselves and among their children, as ways to minimize economic risk. Such tendencies may fruitfully be viewed as family-based cultural frames and repertoires that affect not only integration behaviors among unauthorized labor migrants[35] but also behaviors that spill over to their offspring.[36] They include, for example, emphases among both fathers and sons on finding and keeping jobs to maintain stability of income flows and the imposition of protective orientations toward daughters to maintain their marriageability and capacity for caring for parents in old age. Such cultural tendencies may limit investment in the education of sons, sacrificing longer-term maximization of sons' earnings while ironically leading to gains in daughters' education because parents view school activities as providing safe supervision for daughters.[37] Evidence suggests these tendencies do not carry over strongly to the third generation.[38]

Different Kinds of Integration for Both Groups and Individuals

A third feature of the study is that it explicitly conceptualizes how the multidimensionality of integration corresponds with theoretical perspectives on incorporation. Theoretical approaches about integration differ in what they imply about the components of migration, with some (such as classic assimilation) suggesting that integration tends to be a more one-dimensional process. On the other hand, more-pluralist approaches (such as multicultural frameworks) imply a more multidimensional process. If pluralistic perspectives that emphasize sociocultural differences either among groups or across individuals within groups better fit the experiences of many of today's immigrant groups, including Mexican Americans, this would suggest that more than one theoretical approach to integration may be useful in explaining Mexican American integration outcomes.

Multidimensionality of integration thus implies that a given group's experience cannot be adequately assessed without examining each of the several dimensions involved in that experience. Moreover, multidimensionality suggests that individuals can show markedly higher integration on one dimension than another. Observers who focus on assessing integration through only one dimension may misconstrue a given group's progress because a preponderance of group members fare less well on that one dimension than others. Such observers also risk overlooking important individual heterogeneity across individuals within groups. To reach meaningful conclusions about the overall integration experience of Mexican Americans, it is important to conceptualize the salient dimensions (that is, kinds) of integration and their relationships to one another. We try to do this by not only specifying what various theoretical perspectives imply about the number of integration dimensions but also examining empirically a large number of indicators to ascertain how many dimensions emerge in the data. We can thereby more meaningfully assess which dimensions show cross-generational patterns consistent with the forces implied by various theoretical perspectives.

Data for the Third-Only Generation

A fourth feature is that we assess integration using a measure to isolate the third generation. This helps to overcome the limitations of studies that stop with the second generation and others that include information on a so-called third-plus generation in their comparisons. Using third-only generation data offers two benefits. First, it is predicated on the importance of examining mobility across at least three generations, to the grandchildren of the immigrants, rather than across just two generations of Mexican Americans. This is crucial if for no other reason than that the membership-exclusion theoretical emphasis predicts that unauthorized parental entry will curtail progress among the children of Mexican immigrants in particular. To the extent that such limitations occur, studies comparing only the first and second generations will by definition be unable to reveal the level of integration of subsequent generations.

Second, the approach relies on information specifically for third-generation persons, not third-and-later-generation persons. Some studies attempt to assess integration by making comparisons using a third-plus generation group, but this creates problems. A wealth of recent research shows that notable numbers of later-generation Mexican Americans of higher socioeconomic status marry outside their ethnic group, and many of these (and many of their children) thereby no longer identify themselves as members of the ethnic group. That is, sufficient selective attrition out of the ethnic group occurs to cast considerable doubt on aggregate information on third-plus (that is, third- and later-) generation Mexican Americans.[39] In effect, third-plus generation data provide a faulty foundation for gauging multigenerational individual mobility.[40] In the empirical work presented here, we estimate roughly the aggregate magnitude of this bias using demographic analysis and use a third-only measure in our analyses of individual mobility.

We do this by undertaking multigenerational comparisons using unique data collected as part of a two-decade-long immigrant-integration research initiative begun in 1990 by the Russell Sage Foundation in selected major U.S. gateway cities. One of the target cities, which also included New

York, Miami, and San Diego, was Los Angeles, where we and other colleagues undertook a project called Immigration and Intergenerational Mobility in Metropolitan Los Angeles (IIMMLA).[41] The study collected from Mexican Americans information on the birthplaces of their grandparents, which we use to identify a third-generation-only group (defined as those for whom two or more grandparents were born in Mexico). This enables a much cleaner third-generation comparison than can be obtained from official U.S. data that are often the only kind available—for example, from Current Population Survey data. Because the latter do not collect information about the birthplaces of grandparents, they do not allow the isolation of a true third-generation group, which means multigeneration comparisons using such data must rely on a third-generation proxy made up of an aggregate of third, fourth, fifth, and later generations. As noted, this inevitably causes to misleading results owing to substantial downward bias in integration measures from selective attrition. For this reason we use a third-only measure based on the IIMMLA data.

These data provide the major source of information for both our analyses of the effects of first-generation unauthorized status on integration measures among their own adult children and our multigenerational analyses of other integration outcomes. In addition, we also rely on national data sets to conduct analyses that set the context for the Los Angeles work and provide findings that supplement the Los Angeles results. Thus besides the IIMMLA data, we also make use of the American Community Survey, the Current Population Survey, and the Survey of Income and Program Participation data for certain purposes. But the core of our empirical work, assessing the effects of unauthorized status on multigenerational integration, uses the data from Los Angeles.

Studying Mexican American Integration in Los Angeles

These considerations indicate that assessing the effects of immigrant unauthorized status (and subsequent legalization) on integration requires both having data containing an adequate measure of unauthorized status in the immigrant generation and looking at the effects of such status and its change on outcomes examined across three generations of Mexican American experience. To gauge effects on important human capital and labor market factors such as education and income, and to enable comparisons with the new immigrant groups covered in an East Coast project that was a companion to this one (the New York study, noted later in this chapter), these data need to be obtained for adults who are not far past their formative years of experience.[42] Young adults fit this prerequisite, so this study focuses on persons between the ages of twenty and forty.

But if we seek to examine effects on young adults who are the off-spring of unauthorized immigrants, their parents could have migrated fifty years ago or more. In what city is there a large enough concentration of second-generation Mexican Americans whose parents migrated during the late 1960s on up through the 1980s and were substantially unauthorized? The answer is Los Angeles. Indeed, it may be the only large city that meets these criteria. As we elaborate later, unauthorized Mexican migration began to increase notably as the U.S. economy rapidly expanded during the decades after World War II and after the end of the Bracero Program in 1964. Enormous growth in agriculture, manufacturing, and defense and aerospace contracting made California the major destination for such migration.[43] Unauthorized migrants emerged conspicuously in official U.S. data for the first time when their large numbers in the 1980 totals initially led the technical experts at the U.S. Bureau of the Census to think that there had been an overcount in that year's census. A substantially disproportionate share of such migrants concentrated in California, especially in Los Angeles.[44] The Los Angeles metropolitan area is thus the best locale in the country in which to conduct interviews of the young adult children (aged twenty to forty) of unauthorized immigrants. There, a large population of unauthorized Mexicans lived in the city some forty to fifty years ago, and there appeared to be no other city at that time that contained anywhere close to as large a concentration of unauthorized Mexicans, and certainly not a large enough population to make it feasible to screen respondents for parental migration background as a prerequisite for survey participation. Thus Los Angeles is probably uniquely qualified for a study of the legacy effects of unauthorized status on the integration of the children and grandchildren of such immigrants.

Studying Mexican American integration in the five-county metropolitan area of Los Angeles offers other advantages as well. For one thing, Los Angeles is the preeminent West Coast gateway for immigrants. With a population of 18 million people, greater Los Angeles approaches the New York metropolitan area in the size and scale of immigration, providing an important counterpoint to the East Coast immigrant experience: about 30 percent of Los Angeles's population is foreign born, more than 6.5 million Angelenos are of Mexican origin, and nearly 44 percent of the city's immigrants were born in Mexico.[45] Also, California was the state in which more people legalized their migration status through the 1986 Immigration Reform and Control Act than any other state.[46]

Los Angeles also provides a good example of the range and degree of opportunities for U.S. social mobility in the latter half of the twentieth century. A jobs powerhouse during this time, the city kept its manufacturing base longer than other major cities such as New York and Chicago.[47] Whereas Mexican Americans in the Southwest were isolated for decades, those in California enjoyed better access to education and more opportunity than elsewhere, especially compared with Mexican Americans in Texas.[48] This is not to diminish the historical extent of exclusion in Los Angeles. Ricardo Romo notes that the development of a Mexican American barrio in East Los Angeles constituted a mixed blessing, something caused by discrimination but also ultimately a place that fostered ethnic identity and provided a supportive haven for immigrant workers flocking to the city in search of employment opportunities.[49]

The Los Angeles metropolitan area is also a propitious site for studying Mexican American integration because the education and labor-market opportunities available there to Mexican Americans, although less extensive than those afforded non-Hispanic whites, were still superior to those available to Mexican-origin persons outside California (most notably in Texas).[50] This background enables an upper-bound assessment of the mobility experienced by different generations of Mexican Americans. In addition, in recent decades Los Angeles has been a magnet for college graduates of all ethnoracial backgrounds even as it has lost native-born less-educated populations.[51] In this sense, the choice of Los Angeles as the site for the study may furnish a good approximation of the degree of maximal integration of this important group into the fabric of U.S. society. Of course, relatively strong integration in Los Angeles does not mean that similar integration exists elsewhere, but it certainly would imply that such integration is possible. Better opportunities for Mexican immigrants in Los Angeles (and California more broadly) help explain why the studies of Mexican Americans that rely on respondents from Texas as well as California may show less overall mobility.[52]

Preview of Our Findings

It is useful here to preview our findings, at least briefly. When we are able to measure certain key variables more adequately than they have been in most past research (especially third-generation status), and when we examine multiple dimensions of integration, including the key economic indicators of both education and income, together, many Mexican Americans appear to be achieving appreciable integration by the third generation. However, others, because of unauthorized migration among many of their ancestors, show attainment levels that fall below those of non-Hispanic whites. Among males, even those whose parents or grandparents came legally, progress is slow. Offsetting education deficits in the second and third generations are marked spikes in achievement among both men and women whose parents or grandparents were all born in Mexico. Also, absent the limiting effects of unauthorized status, third-generation Mexican American women show attainments nearly identical to or surpassing those of non-Hispanic whites. We argue that these results, especially those for males, reflect the influence of both membership exclusion and working-class delay. Membership exclusion constitutes an important new complement to other theoretical perspectives on integration. Slower integration results from membership exclusion in both the first and the second generations and from third-generation working-class delay, which emphasizes how working-class opportunities to improve income, combined with the high cost of college, limit the attractiveness of attending college among the grandsons of immigrants. These constraints on educational attainment point to the crucial need for the country to provide attainable (that is, not prohibitively costly) and reasonably quick pathways to legalization and citizenship for less-skilled Mexican immigrant workers and their families, especially because the nation increasingly depends heavily on their labor, and to develop affordable ways for the children of working- and lower-middle-class parents, including those of Mexican immigrants, to attend and graduate from college.

Our results also suggest that most Mexican immigrants and their descendants are integrating into American society linguistically and spatially, although the latter is also slowed by unauthorized migration. Overall then, Mexican American integration is slower than it is for many other contemporary groups, especially Asians.[53] But Mexican American integration has nonetheless been occurring steadily and surely over the past half century or so, since roughly the end of World War II, especially for women, although recently the acute stigmatization of unauthorized migrants and the prohibitively high cost of college for working-class families threaten to derail the process. The culmination of integration is thus not inevitable, especially if pathways to legalization and citizenship remain cut off and if current policies allow only for poor-quality schooling and little means of affording higher education for the descendants of immigrants.

In the rest of the book, we elaborate these themes, organizing our treatment of topics as follows. In chapter 2 we outline the major theoretical perspectives on immigrant integration, focusing on their strengths and weaknesses. We also assess theoretically the importance of unauthorized labor migration and its significance for integration, formulating in the process the theoretical perspective on integration we call membership exclusion. The foundational principle of the framework is that initial denial of social citizenship based on migration status puts immigrants in such marginal social and economic positions that their and their children's material integration is hampered. We also outline how family and migration-based cultural repertoires associated with unauthorized status promote work over schooling and thereby retard integration. We also note that membership exclusion envisions legalization as a life-course turning point, the attainment of which may mark the weakening if not end of the inhibiting mechanisms of unauthorized status, whereas several other theoretical perspectives envision sources of cumulative disadvantage as persisting beyond the point of legalization. The chapter also specifies how cross-generational patterns of integration may vary for males and females.

In chapter 3 we outline specific research hypotheses and important research issues for analyses of immigrant-group integration, including those that affect choice of data, comparisons, and measures. We also describe how a very low level of Mexican American integration in Texas decades ago partly explains overall integration deficits today. In chapter 4 we explore how unauthorized migration relates to socioeconomic attainment in the first generation and to less education attainment among young second-generation adults who come from unauthorized migrant backgrounds, thus also limiting later-generation patterns of schooling. We also investigate a selective acculturation hypothesis that suggests that those with parental or ethnic homogeneity are more likely to become education overachievers. We examine whether this tendency is greater for women than men, and we assess its relative size compared with negative unauthorized migrant background effects.

In chapter 5 we conduct a multigenerational examination of education and income, key aspects of the crucially important dimension of economic integration. We find that income follows a discontinuous pattern consistent with membership exclusion, with notable jumps in attainment among the grandchildren of immigrants. We also find that generational and ethnic differences in education help explain generational and ethnic differences in income, but that the relative increases in income among third-generation over second-generation males substantially exceed their relative increases in education. We suggest that this finding is compatible with the working-class-delay theoretical perspective because it implies that income mobility remains attainable for many working-class males despite minimal increases in schooling, thus ironically possibly dampening motivations to pursue higher education when opportunities to do so are limited and costly.

Chapter 6 examines spatial integration, noting the multiple reasons the different dimensions of incorporation may not vary with spatial mobility. In general, the findings show patterns consistent with membership exclusion (specifically, improved tendencies to live in better neighborhoods in the third generation compared with the second) but with an interesting twist. Those children of Mexican migrants who move to the Inland Empire, where housing costs are much lower than in the rest of the Los Angeles metropolitan area, exhibit quicker improvement in ethnoracial outcomes across generations, suggesting that spatial opportunity in the form of affordable housing may counterbalance some of the constraining effects of initial unauthorized status. In chapter 7 we examine various indicators of sociocultural integration separately because, as predicted by what we call a postindustrial-individualistic theoretical perspective on immigrant integration, such measures are only weakly related with one another.

In chapter 8 we trace trends in Mexican migration to the United States and outline how public policy, changing demographics, and shifts in the labor market have contributed to the increase in unauthorized and less-skilled migrants since 1990. Specifically, we show that over the past twenty-five years, the decline of U.S. native-born fertility, the aging of baby boomers, and rising education levels in the U.S.-born population have appreciably reduced the availability less-skilled native-born workers and thus probably contributed to the rise in Mexican migration since 1990 in particular. This demographic void constitutes a new kind of "pull" factor for migration and adds a new urgency to the need for the country to facilitate legalization to foster immigrant integration. In chapter 9 we argue that our findings illustrate the crucial importance of adopting immigration policy reforms that provide sensible, realistic, and inexpensive pathways to legalization for Mexican immigrants, whose workforce contributions to American society are becoming ever more important. We also argue for education and economic policies that provide increased and less costly education opportunities for middle- and working-class families.

= Chapter 2 =

Theoretical Perspectives on Immigrant Integration and Beyond: Introducing Membership Exclusion

E mpirical assessments of the nature and extent of integration are enhanced when they consider issues of conceptualization and theory. Here we begin by defining the concepts of assimilation, incorporation, and integration. By assimilation, we mean the process by which the characteristics of members of immigrant groups and the members of a given receiving society come to resemble one another.[1] As Richard Alba and Victor Nee note, assimilation proceeds via a two-way process leading to convergence between immigrants and natives, not just a one-way street on which newcomers move toward natives over time.[2] The concept of incorporation, however, refers to a broader range of processes, including those that can involve difference as well as greater similarity in immigrant and native group characteristics.[3] When such differences grow larger over time or undermine social cohesion, negative incorporation ensues. The enslavement of African involuntary migrants in the South constitutes an example. But when sociocultural differences are tolerated and persist over time without undermining social solidarity, the resulting diversity can strengthen the receiving society by exposing natives to new ways of thinking and doing things, thus fostering resilience, creativity, and innovation.[4]

Although the idea of incorporation encompasses the possibility of both positive and negative outcomes arising from the sociocultural differences that may emerge as a result of immigration, it does not explicitly specify that such differences can lead to favorable consequences, especially under certain conditions, either for the larger society or for the immigrant group. The concept of integration, however, more explicitly suggests such possibilities through its postulation that individual structural assimilation may occur with greater facility and lead to more positive social outcomes when it takes place in contexts that tolerate sociocultural difference.[5] The idea of integration has thus tended to emerge from contexts in places where official multicultural policies have either been considered or adopted, which means it occupies more prominent standing in Canadian and European scholarship on immigrants than it does in the United States.[6] Here, while we recognize and acknowledge the nuances involved in the concepts of assimilation, incorporation, and integration, and while we use the terms interchangeably at times, we generally prefer the idea of integration. The reason is not just that it better acknowledges the possible beneficial consequences of ethnoracial and sociocultural diversity but also that its logic entails greater allowance for flexibility, fluidity, and broader ranges of outcomes in regard to sociocultural phenomena among individuals. It thus better accords with the fact of growing individual heterogeneity in postindustrial societies.[7]

Different aspects of integration may thus proceed differently among different immigrant groups. Although rapid advancement in structural integration with minimal sociocultural integration (or vice versa) may seem incongruous, examples abound among groups that have been in the United States for many generations. For instance, even though their religion and ethnicity are distinctively different from mainstream Anglos, Jews in the United States have achieved levels of education and income that are higher than those of the general population.[8] The Hutterites in Canada and the upper Great Plains have controlled their acculturation through self-segregation in agricultural enclaves, adopting such outside practices as the use of modern technology and birth control as they deem consonant with their religious beliefs even while eschewing socioeconomic mobility.[9] African Americans still lag whites in education and income even though they are socioculturally similar in many ways, particularly in religious denominational affiliation.[10] Such divergent outcomes are real occurrences that point to the need to consider not only the overall process but also its constituent parts, as well as how these parts relate to one another. This is what we call the dimensionality question in conceptualizing immigrant integration.

Such apparently incongruous combinations are consistent with theoretical perspectives on integration that emphasize the operation of forces other than the main assimilation ones of exposure and time. Hypotheses about the existence of cross-generational differences in sociocultural integration do not follow readily from the idea that all aspects of assimilation move in the same direction or at roughly the same pace. This is the case even though some analysts have modified the assimilation theoretical perspective to depict the process as one often occurring in an irregular way.[11] In other words, to a considerable extent, classic assimilation implies a bundling together of different kinds of integration. To be sure, approaches like segmented assimilation implicitly suggest different degrees of integration for immigrant subgroups, although this perspective does not emphasize differences by kind (or dimension) of integration. However, recognition that integration consists of multiple parts, and that many of these can occur relatively independently of one another, is increasingly emerging in the literature.[12] Thus a crucial task for theory building involves searching for perspectives that explicitly conceptualize different kinds and degrees of integration. To what extent do particular theoretical approaches include conceptualizations of such differences and specify their differing degrees of cross-generation mobility, and what forces do they envision as driving such differences? We call this the theoretical expectations question.

Dimensionality thus matters for theory, and vice versa. Acknowledging the possibility of multiple and relatively independent kinds of integration is consistent with the development of new more pluralist-based theoretical approaches to integration. Perspectives such as segmented assimilation, which embrace the idea of different incorporation dynamics for different segments of a given immigrant group, nonetheless begin (and end) with the notion that assimilation, involving a roughly monolithic convergence with natives, occurs for many groups, and for some members of all groups, albeit at times with a twist for some. The internal logic of such relatively unitary approaches is theoretically limiting because it fosters agnosticism with regard to the content of incorporation. That is, perspectives that start with the assumption of eventual assimilation for all or many members of a group tend not to highlight, depend on, nor care much about what kind of integration is taking place. Their presupposition is that all aspects of integration will ultimately take place, even if in "fits and starts," or in "bumpy-line" ways.[13] As a result, there is little need for such perspectives to examine or attempt to uncover different kinds of integration, either across or within groups. The logic of other approaches, however, alerts us more to ideas of difference and are more likely adequately to emphasize group differences across dimensions, differences across subgroups (for example, men and women), or differences among individuals within a group.

In this chapter we present the outlines of nine distinct theoretical perspectives. We call six of these assimilation-based approaches, although they vary in the degree to which they exclusively imply assimilation processes. These are the classic assimilation, ethnic-resource-advantage, ethnic-disadvantage, racialization, segmented-assimilation, and working-class stagnation-or-delay perspectives. Second, we classify two additional approaches as more pluralist based because each explicitly emphasizes (and allows for) differences. These are the multicultural and postindustrial-individualistic perspectives. In the multicultural case, the differences envisioned occur across groups. In the postindustrial-individualistic case, they occur across both groups and individuals. We also introduce a third perspective, which we label membership exclusion. It explicitly emphasizes the curtailment of structural kinds of mobility owing to formal societal exclusion. Such a perspective highlights the negative forces that factors such as unauthorized migration status can impose on the mobility prospects of migrants and their descendants. Because it is better formulated to allow for both individual and group heterogeneity, we suggest it fits under the pluralist-based rubric. To illuminate what all nine of the perspectives imply about the question of dimensionality, or the "what" of integration, we scrutinize and assess them in terms of their suggestions about independent components of integration.

To address the question of theoretical expectations, we outline what the various perspectives, including membership exclusion, imply concerning cross-generation degrees of immigrant mobility. The reader may wonder why we focus on so many theoretical approaches, especially since some have not been much in vogue in recent years. The answer is that examining all for both their dimensionality and their expectations about mobility provides a clearer and more coherent basis for discerning hybrid patterns of integration. By a hybrid pattern we mean one that involves applying more than one theoretical perspective to different dimensions of mobility (or to different subgroups of an immigrant group). That is, different perspectives may better apply in the cases of some kinds of mobility than others. And different perspectives may better apply to women than men. In other words, because we are assessing multiple kinds of mobility, combinations of perspectives may fit the data best (that is, with one perspective working better for a certain dimension than others, and another better for another dimension). In the next chapter we explicate the mechanisms through which we think membership exclusion, in particular, applies in the Mexican American case, suggesting also why we think distinct mixtures of theoretical perspectives are likely to characterize men and women.

Theoretical Perspectives on Integration

Theoretical ideas that have proved useful for understanding integration are best viewed as approaches or perspectives rather than theories. They less involve axiomatically derived general postulates about social behavior than systematic middle-range rationales for why certain phenomena occur.[14] Such formulations can make sense of what happens to immigrants and their families over time and can imply different patterns and degrees of cross-generation mobility. Without the orientation of theoretical frameworks, researchers are able to talk about their results only in terms of particularities, making it more difficult to connect their findings to overall integration, broader social change, or legislative proposals for policy reform.

Assimilation-Based Frameworks

The perspectives that have been most often relied on to guide empirical research investigations, especially in the United States, are assimilation-based approaches. We next discuss the six approaches that have been most influential in such research.

Classic and New Assimilation Models   The notion of the United States as a melting pot has permeated public consciousness for a century or more. The sociological paradigm that constitutes the lodestar for perspectives on immigrant-group mobility is classic assimilation, which dates to the 1920s. Most recently elaborated in the work of sociologists Alba and Nee, it has been especially prominent in the United States.[15] Although its treatment at the hands of early exponents is more complex than often recognized, in general, classic assimilation theory envisions immigrant-ethnic and majority groups as roughly following "straight-line" convergence, becoming more similar over time in norms, values, behaviors, and characteristics. The theory expects those immigrants who reside the longest in the host society, as well as the members of later generations, to show greater similarities with the majority group than immigrants who have spent less time in the receiving society.

As Peter Kivisto and Thomas Faist note, however, assimilation processes are difficult to conceptualize but easy to caricature, leading analysts frequently to misconstrue assimilation as following only a straight-line pathway.[16] Such straw-man depictions tend to misrepresent the views of prominent early immigration-assimilation theorists, such as Robert Park of the Chicago School. Park, for example, devoted considerable emphasis on spatial relationships of immigrant groups and how these affect incorporation. Overly simplistic critiques also tend to overlook that the Chicago School's best-known conception of assimilation stresses culture over spatial or structural position, defining it as "a process of interpenetration and fusion in which persons and groups acquire the memories, sentiments, and attitudes of other persons or groups, and by sharing their experience and history, are incorporated with them in a common cultural life."[17]

In the post-Depression era, the work of Lloyd Warner and Leo Srole, whose research covered multiple generations of European immigrant groups (as well as parents and children within these groups), is often depicted as epitomizing the unilineal nature of assimilation.[18] Based on data from the first half of the 1930s, when the economic mobility of all groups (including the native born) faced the headwinds of the Great Depression, their approach yielded nuanced assessments of social mobility across time and multiple dimensions, charting each immigrant group beginning its journey at the bottom of the social ladder and then gradually climbing upward, so that at a given point in time the oldest groups stood highest on the ladder. They explicitly emphasized the steepness of assimilation's straight line and its variation by ethnoracial status, culture, skin color, and the strength of coethnic communities. Thus even this early vision of what many observers have viewed as prototypical classic assimilation hints at some of the kinds of differences that recent perspectives have started to recognize and theorize about.

Such nuances notwithstanding, assimilation as represented in the work of Milton Gordon is widely viewed as having achieved preeminent and canonical status in post–World War II social science.[19] Gordon envisioned integration as containing three major variants: a "melting-pot" tendency, after the popular eponymous play of 1908; an Anglo-conformity tendency, ranging from mere promotion of the English language and middle-class cultural patterns to embracement of discredited theories of racial superiority; and a cultural-pluralist tendency, emphasizing the maintenance of origin-country culture and institutions despite economic and civic incorporation into the destination country. Of these different strands, Gordon suggested that a moderate version of Anglo-conformity appeared to predominate, although he personally did not embrace this variant over others. According to Gordon, several stages follow the acquisition of culture and language. First comes structural assimilation (close social relations with the host society), followed by large-scale intermarriage, ethnic identification with the host society, and the ending of prejudice, discrimination, and value conflict. Nonetheless, Gordon appears to view these not as different kinds of incorporation but rather as different phases of one general process, parts of which may occur at different points in time.

In what they call new assimilation theory, Alba and Nee refine Gordon's account by arguing that certain institutions, including those bolstered by civil rights law, play important roles in achieving assimilation.[20] They give the example of Jewish organizations that persuaded the New York City Council in 1946 to eliminate the tax-exempt status of colleges or universities that discriminated on the basis of race or religion. More so than in earlier versions of this theory, Alba and Nee stress that the incorporation of immigrant groups also involves change and acceptance by the mainstream population. Classic assimilation theory as a whole works best, however, when the mainstream can be easily defined. While Alba and Nee acknowledge that assimilation takes place within racially and economically heterogeneous contexts, their approach is subject to the limitation that in postindustrial societies, particularly those with relatively large sectors of their economies involved in high-tech knowledge-based activities, it is increasingly difficult to delineate a single "mainstream," especially in regard to many sociocultural domains of life.[21]

Ethnic Resource and Advantage Models   While granting the existence and force of assimilation mechanisms, other U.S. scholars emphasize ethnic family and community resources as a means of both facilitating and handicapping integration. Such writers call attention to the benefits of ethnic retention and difference rather than focusing on discrimination. For example, Nathan Glazer and Daniel P. Moynihan's *Beyond the Melting Pot* argues that ethnicity can constitute a benefit as well as a burden in achieving upward economic mobility.[22] One way this occurs is through ethnic enclaves and economies (geographic concentrations of ethnic enterprises or businesses that consist of coethnic workers and that cater to coethnic markets), which foster entrepreneurship and provide opportunities for economic mobility.[23] Alejandro Portes and Min Zhou use a concept they call selective acculturation to contend that immigrant parents nurture and emphasize ethnicity to preserve traditional values and thereby protect children from the temptations of instant gratification and countercultural excesses in receiving societies that are more consumption oriented and individualistic than origin societies.[24] As a result, second-generation children are better equipped to focus on education without being distracted. What has remained somewhat unclear, however, is the extent to which the goal of educational achievement differs from that of many white middle-class parents.[25] In other words, when the research focus is on relatively highly educated Asian immigrants, is the operative factor boosting strong second-generation achievement ethnicity or social class?

Recently, the ethnic-advantage perspective has focused on various kinds of cultural resources in neighborhoods and ethnic communities that support mobility among the children of immigrants.[26] Jennifer Lee and Zhou suggest that cultural frames and network resources available in the ethnic community are particularly valuable in fostering mobility aspirations and high achievement among the children of immigrants.[27] To assess this, they conduct in-depth interviews with second-generation Chinese, Vietnamese, and Mexican immigrants in Los Angeles. The Asian immigrants and their children define doing extremely well in secondary school and going to a prestigious college as objectives that are automatically expected of children, whereas Mexican immigrants and their children often see finishing high school as a substantial achievement, which, relative to the parents' education, is indeed a major accomplishment. Moreover, Lee and Zhou find that these kinds of frames are reinforced by networks and other cultural resources in the ethnic community, as does Silvia Domínguez.[28] Particularly in the case of the Asian groups, they note the prevalence of successful role models and the sharing of information about strategies for finding good schools and taking the best types of courses to gain college acceptance help even the children of Asian parents with relatively low levels of education do as well as peers whose parents have more education.

The ethnic-advantage perspective represents a variant of the classic assimilation perspective, despite its emphasis on the persistence of ethnic culture. Rather than seeing the maintenance of ethnic cultural orientations as an impediment to education, it views cultural frames, repertoires, networks, and resources in the ethnic community as reinforcing socioeconomic attainment. An important remaining research question, however, is still the extent to which selective acculturation reflects social class as opposed to ethnicity, or perhaps other kinds of effects. In the Mexican American case, differences in cultural repertoires and family structure within and across generations may indeed influence mobility, but these may often emerge from and reflect lower social-class backgrounds.[29] By contrast, Asians generally immigrate legally and with much higher levels of education and more intact families;[30] thus they start with more resources enabling families to focus on children's achievement. Mexicans, by contrast, navigate a much more complex migration with more potential for family disruption and fragmentation. Many not only must undergo the transition from temporary to permanent migration but often also contend with unauthorized status. Moreover, husbands and wives often come at different times rather than migrating as couples.[31] Such impediments may hamper mobility.

Ethnic-Disadvantage Models   Other scholars argue, by contrast, that some groups' ethnic distinctiveness impedes their assimilation. This stream of thought, which we call the ethnic-disadvantage point of view, is also reflected in the writings of Glazer and Moynihan and sometimes in those of Portes and his colleagues.[32] In general, this line of theoretical development, especially its more recent versions, argues that language and cultural familiarity are often not sufficient for much assimilation at all, let alone reasonably rapid assimilation. Lingering ethnic discrimination (especially episodic periods of nativism) and institutional barriers to employment and access to other opportunities stemming from ethnic and cultural differences may delay integration, especially in contexts of reception lacking supportive policies for newcomers.[33] Because immigrants may favorably compare socioeconomic opportunities in the host country with those in their countries of origin, they initially may not perceive such barriers to incorporation. However, by the second or third generation, they may realize that the goal of full integration may be more difficult and take longer than originally presumed. Such realizations can have social and cultural consequences, including the reemergence of ethnic consciousness.

The European groups coming to the United States during the nineteenth and early twentieth centuries illustrate the long-term persistence of ethnic distinctiveness even as economic mobility occurs. For example, in Austin, Texas, a city where sizable numbers of Lutherans from Germany and Sweden arrived beginning in the middle of the nineteenth century, it was not until 1938 that any Lutheran congregation held religious services exclusively in English.[34] Because we can conceptualize many immigrant groups as more like ethnic than racial groups, their ethnic distinctiveness, while often associated with sufficient obstacles to retard social and economic mobility for a while, does not appear to have blocked integration permanently. Thus at least in the American context so strongly characterized by the dynamics of the stark black-white color line, ethnicity appears often to be associated with delayed immigrant incorporation more than permanently blocked integration.[35] With the eventual disappearance of structural differences, as in the case of European groups, later generations often then manifest what some scholars have called symbolic ethnicity, meaning that such ethnic identifications become optional for the members of these groups.[36]

Racialization Models   Other perspectives see group boundaries as harder to cross. They acknowledge that theories constructed on the basis of ethnic distinctiveness in the context of black-white models of racial relations may apply less forcefully to today's new arrivals from Latin America and Asia, whose histories and contemporary experiences differ considerably from those of both blacks and European immigrants. But they also contend that such theories fail to recognize the extent to which the new immigrant groups are treated in many instances more like racial groups than ethnic groups.[37] Such racialization perspectives give greater weight to race as a factor that blocks rather than just temporarily retards mobility. While social scientists generally agree that both race and ethnicity are social constructions, these perspectives conceptualize race as a harder, more deeply embedded construct that is considerably more difficult to overcome and change than ethnicity. For racialization scholars, a key question is whether the new Asian and Latino immigrant groups are seen, and see themselves, as more like ethnic groups or more like racial groups. Stated differently, do they see themselves as part of a hierarchical social system based on race in which those in the middle or bottom have worse outcomes than those at the top?

Such perceptions may occur irrespective of official statistical categories of race and ethnicity.[38] Racial disadvantage perspectives tend to perceive the new immigrant groups as nonwhite minorities who are subject to a kind and degree of discrimination that is similar to that experienced by African Americans. By contrast, classic assimilation, ethnic-resource, and ethnic-disadvantage perspectives tend to assume, or to stress, that the new immigrants (except in the cases of those with substantial African origins, like some Caribbean groups) tend to see themselves and be seen by others as nonblack.[39] Thus classic assimilation and the two ethnic-based perspectives envision newcomers gradually becoming accepted and integrated into American society across time and generations, whereas the racialization perspective tends at a minimum to see this as taking much longer.

Segmented-Assimilation Models   Still other scholars combine elements of all four of the previously mentioned perspectives. Even though assimilation appears to be only partial for many descendants of immigrants, even as late as the third generation, uneven patterns of convergence do not necessarily indicate lack of assimilation but rather may reflect a "bumpy" rather than "straight-line" course, as Gans pointed out.[40] Others have noted that just as some members of immigrant groups become cut off from economic mobility, others find multiple pathways to assimilation, depending on their national origins, socioeconomic status, contexts of reception in the United States, and family resources, both social and financial.[41] As a result, the assimilation experiences of recent immigrants show more variegated and diverse scenarios than those provided by the classic assimilation, ethnic-resource, ethnic-disadvantage, or racialization perspectives alone. To state this possibility and to describe the particularities of a given group's experience, however, leaves little basis for discerning policy implications unless analysts also specify what such alternatives are in broader theoretical terms.

This approach began with the work of Portes and Zhou, who combine straight-line assimilation, ethnic resource/advantage, and racialization/disadvantage perspectives into a framework they call segmented assimilation.[42] They theorize that structural barriers, such as poor urban schools, cut off access to employment and other opportunities—obstacles that often are particularly severe in the case of the most disadvantaged members of immigrant groups. Such impediments can lead to stagnant or downward mobility, even as the children of other immigrants follow different paths toward classic straight-line assimilation. Heavily disadvantaged children of immigrants may even reject assimilation altogether and embrace attitudes, orientations, and behaviors considered oppositional in nature, such as joining street gangs. Other more advantaged groups take advantage of selective acculturation and embrace traditional home-country attitudes to inspire their children to achieve, a process similar to Glazer and Moynihan's ethnic-resource hypothesis. In general, segmented assimilation focuses on identifying the contextual, structural, and cultural factors that separate successful from unsuccessful, or even negative, assimilation.

Portes and his various collaborators often note that it is especially important to identify such factors in the case of the second generation, because obstacles facing the children of immigrants can thwart assimilation at perhaps its most critical juncture. Racial discrimination, in particular, is given considerable weight. While some children of immigrants will find ways to move toward mainstream status, others will find such pathways blocked, particularly as a consequence of racialization. Thus for example, Portes, Fernández-Kelly, and Haller argue: "Children of Asian, black, mulatto, and mestizo immigrants cannot escape their ethnicity and race, as defined by the mainstream. Their enduring physical differences from whites and the equally persistent strong effects of discrimination based on those differences . . . throw a barrier in the path of occupational mobility and social acceptance. Immigrant children's identities, their aspirations, and their academic performance are affected accordingly."[43] Because of the relative newness of these migration streams, this perspective has not been empirically tested widely beyond the current second generation (the members of which are often still adolescents). For that reason, some researchers have questioned whether segmented assimilation may misinterpret oppositional attitudes historically found among adolescents or young adults and misconstrue the pace of assimilation.[44]

Working-Class-Assimilation or Delayed-Integration Models   There is one final perspective that we also place in the assimilation set, primarily because its expositors themselves have labeled it working-class, or delayed, assimilation.[45] Veronica Terriquez terms a modified version of this approach "working-class stagnation,"[46] but we use the phrase working-class delayed integration for this hypothesis for reasons we note that follow. In general, this perspective is more compatible with pluralist-based approaches because of its inherent emphasis on multidimensionality in structural integration. We do not give this perspective as full-fledged a treatment as some of the others we have discussed, because it envisions integration as an unfinished process, one that is only partial and involves assimilation into the U.S. working-class in a manner similar to that of Italian and Polish immigrants in the early twentieth century. Delay can occur for various reasons. For example, Susan K. Brown and Frank D. Bean suggest that in the Mexican American case, intergenerational integration is slow because so many immigrants started from such a low structural point.[47] Although many studies have noted slow integration into even the third generation or beyond, in general, this perspective is more open ended than others because it leaves unaddressed what the nature and extent of further integration processes may be, even though the unstated assumption is that these will eventually occur. The approach also devotes less attention to the sociocultural aspects of integration.

The basic tenets of the working-class delay perspective are that Mexican immigrants, through at least the second generation and likely beyond, undergo a process in which mobility takes place not only across generations but also within generations and within U.S. blue-collar occupations and industries. This has occurred especially in the American Southwest, although since 1990, Mexican immigrants, of course, have been fanning out into other parts of the country.[48] Importantly, this within-generation mobility can be multidimensional. For instance, it may occur more for income than for education, and it may be most evident in the second and third (especially) generations, particularly among Mexican American males as they increasingly gain work experience, acquire tacit skills, and take advantage of the availability of better-paying jobs that do not require more formal schooling. Awareness of the availability of such jobs itself thus often provides an incentive to forgo investment in higher education in favor of the more immediate monetary rewards of working.

The twist that Veronica Terriquez adds to this depiction is that she conceptualizes (and finds in her research) that substantial movement out of blue-collar positions and into those requiring college degrees appears to have stalled (or, more accurately, never much to have taken place) in the Mexican American third-plus generation, an outcome she attributes to the erosion of well-paying manufacturing jobs and wage declines (after adjusting for inflation) for much of the U.S. population since the 1970s.[49] In short, she explicitly conceptualizes a lack of middle-class opportunities as a major factor contributing to such stagnation among Mexican Americans. In addition to a relative lack of external middle-class opportunities requiring college, however, the relative availability of better working-class opportunities may also delay the pursuit of higher education. Given the low point from which most Mexican immigrants start the mobility process, the working-class perspective reminds us that uneven and substantial amounts of structural mobility can occur within generations up through at least the third generation, without this being sufficient for the group to reach parity with non-Hispanic whites in important aspects of mobility, such as education.

Several recent research studies support this idea. The findings of Jacqueline Hagan, Rubén Hernández-León, and Jean Luc Demonsant that Mexican members of the first generation often increase their earnings significantly by moving to better-paying types of work within the same industry (for example, within construction) provides one example of this.[50] Roger Waldinger, Nelson Lim, and David Cort observe something similar within the second generation, namely transitions to jobs of higher quality (that is, higher paying) without other characteristics of the second generation changing much.[51] Similarly, were we to find here among third-generation Mexican Americans higher earnings compared with the second generation without observing much difference in education between these two generations, this would suggest that the availability of higher-paying working-class jobs may itself deter third-generation Mexican Americans from pursuing more schooling, especially given the rapidly escalating cost of attending college in recent decades.

Pluralist-Based Frameworks

Integration perspectives that are not based on assimilation—while often more prescriptive than analytical—tend to imply that various aspects of integration can and do occur at different times and in different ways. We identify two categories of such approaches, multicultural and postindustrial-individualistic perspectives, and develop in the next section a third, membership exclusion. As noted, the first two of these have typically been used more in European and Canadian contexts than in the United States and thus have rarely served in the United States as explicit guides for empirical assessments of integration.[52] In general, the models invoked in Europe have emphasized differences more than assimilation. Perhaps iron-ically, some European countries and Canada have more quickly adopted "integration" settlement policies that provide assistance and support to immigrants than has the United States,[53] whose settlement policies (or lack thereof) can most accurately be described as laissez-faire.[54] Europeans thus often use the term *integration policy* to mean the adoption of policies that provide assistance to immigrants in such matters as housing and labor-market entry while at the same time assuming that the immigrants and their children seek to (and do) maintain distinctive sociocultural ori-entations. As a result, such settlement policies assume that satisfactory integration is desirable and achievable in certain arenas without being necessary in others.

Multicultural Models   Multicultural perspectives in particular postulate that the retention of specific ethnic values, customs, and practices on the part of a given group is not necessarily inimical to other kinds of integra-tion.[55] Fundamentally, and broadly, the multicultural perspective implies a two-dimensional approach to integration. Immigrant-group advance-ment can occur along more instrumental and material dimensions of incorporation (for example, employment, jobs, earnings, housing) even as many sociocultural aspects (for example, religion, ethnic identity, fam-ily forms, marriage patterns, gender roles) continue to distinguish the immigrant group from the host society. Stated differently, greater dif-ferentiation is likely between these two different incorporation domains than is likely within them. The goal of settlement policies is equivalence with respect to structural but not necessarily sociocultural domains, differences in the latter being conceptualized as acceptable features of pluralist societies. The multicultural approach has sometimes generated backlashes in Europe.[56]

Postindustrial-Individualistic Models   Another perspective, which repre-sents a synthesis of several more general social-science theoretical per-spectives and which we call a postindustrial-individualistic perspective, takes this a step further.[57] Although the multicultural approach tends to assume relative homogeneity among sociocultural aspects of incorporation (that is, it envisions considerable similarity of sociocultural facets of integration within immigrant groups but not between immigrant and native groups), the postindustrial-individualistic approach does not tend to specify this (that is, it envisions heterogeneity in the sociocultural facets of sociocultural integration both across groups and across individuals within groups). As Rogers Brubaker might state the matter, it involves "ethnicity without groups."[58] Moreover, it tends to see such heterogeneity as increasing, especially in postindustrial societies, at least in part as a result of rising individualism in such societies.[59] This perspective thus combines elements of a number of alternative social theoretical approaches, including social psychological theories of individualism,[60] second-demographic-transition theoretical perspectives emphasizing reduced fertility and increased individualism in postindustrial societies,[61] theories of postindustrial changes in cultural values,[62] and various postmodern and critical theories.[63]

All of these models imply that more developed postindustrial societies have evolved in ways that foster considerably greater sociocultural heterogeneity and individualism in social life today. They also emphasize fluidity and contingency of sociocultural identities, processes, and behaviors, thus suggesting multidimensionality in both sociocultural indicators and other kinds of incorporation across both groups and individuals within groups. This follows from the observation that advanced societies increasingly do not require that given ethnoracial identities, sexual orientations, marital statuses, religious preferences, or family behaviors align closely with one another, even within the same individual.[64] In effect, these approaches stress that in many instances, a single mainstream (or even two or three identifiable "mainstreams") is much less characteristic of many Western countries than would have been the case fifty years ago. To the extent that such greater sociocultural fragmentation has emerged in a given country, we would expect greater differentiation—that is, more independent sociocultural dimensions—in regard to sociocultural incorporation than we would with respect to structural incorporation. That is, what matters to people may increasingly depend less on their ethnic or religious group, or even the social class to which they belong, and more on their own individual interests, preferences, and proclivities.[65]

The Membership-Exclusion Model

None of the theoretical perspectives outlined above concentrate primarily on the implications of societal membership for integration, although the racialization model argues that the experiences of many of today's immigrant groups, including Mexican Americans in the United States, are exclusionary, similar to those of African Americans in certain respects.[66] However, even proponents of a racialization model for explaining the Mexican American experience also emphasize that the "persistent low status of Mexican Americans is also *clearly not* the rigid caste-like type predicted by . . . theories predicated on the African American example."[67] To draw attention to the possibility that the lack of formal social membership may strongly condition structural integration, we introduce the complementary theoretical perspective of membership exclusion. It would be an exaggeration to claim this perspective is entirely new, since other perspectives, such as segmented assimilation, note that various contexts of reception, including some that involve membership withholding, can negatively influence integration. And other scholars have noted the importance of membership.[68] However, formal lack of societal membership in many respects reflects such a powerful force adversely influencing integration, as we elaborate later in this chapter, that we suggest it warrants its own designated perspective to underscore the signature role it plays in the integration process. Certain kinds of integration, most notably structural integration, are simply often not attainable, or not easily attainable, without formal societal membership.

Because there is nothing in its tenets that requires a unitary representation of structural integration, we place the membership-exclusion perspective squarely in the pluralist-based category. It posits that all kinds of structural integration (including those aspects of political incorporation that may be conceptualized as structural rather than somewhat sociocultural) are contingent on formal societal membership, one of the earliest, if not the earliest, form of political incorporation.[69] In this regard, the membership-exclusion perspective is inherently multidimensional. Moreover, it also envisions nonmonolithic sociocultural integration, which also makes it pluralist based in emphasis. To clarify further, we envision membership exclusion as a framework that is most likely to apply in advanced postindustrial societies such as the United States. Thus it would overlap with the postindustrial-individualistic perspective in its expectation for considerable relative independence among individuals in sociocultural aspects of integration. But it further would explicitly expect that one aspect of early political incorporation, namely official societal membership (especially membership in the formal sense of the term), would condition both other aspects of political incorporation and aspects of structural incorporation. Thus it postulates that societal membership is necessary, if not sufficient, for many other aspects of integration. To state the matter precisely in the language of statistics, it expects both an interaction effect between societal membership and structural incorporation and also relative independence both among aspects of sociocultural integration and between aspects of sociocultural integration and structural incorporation.

Societal Membership

Societal membership refers to both legal and social citizenship in the sense that T. H. Marshall uses the term, encompassing not only who is eligible to vote but also membership in a broader sense.[70] This latter idea holds that citizenship rights can and should extend to inclusion in civic and social institutions, especially insofar as such rights provide access to opportunity (and thus social mobility) and a social safety net. Indeed, after World War II, Marshall and others argued for policies extending civic and social rights to the lower social classes as a way of forestalling social conflict in Western countries.[71] Subsequently, Brubaker, in his now classic study, drew attention to the role of immigration in such policies, noting that social citizenship in modern Western societies, in both practice and law, was almost always "internally inclusive" but "externally exclusive."[72] That is, residents born within a nation-state whose ancestors had been born there generally received civic and social rights, whereas those born elsewhere or of other descent often were excluded. His analyses implied that the status of immigrants in the social welfare state was ambiguous.

Immigration complicates the idea and practice of social citizenship. Societies differ on whom they designate as social citizens, with newcomers often being excluded to various degrees and for different reasons in different places.[73] Whatever the particular criterion of inclusion or exclusion, such practices may stymie immigrant integration for a host of reasons.[74] Thus the official exclusion of new immigrants limits achievement on structural dimensions of integration that hinge on that membership. This drawback should have less effect on sociocultural dimensions of integration, such as language acquisition, because they are likely to depend more on the length of exposure to the host society.

Unauthorized Migration and Membership Exclusion

At one level, such exclusionary processes may seem reminiscent of the mechanisms advanced by the segmented-assimilation and racialization perspectives with respect to racial status, in that racial or ethnic discrimination may lead to the same kind of structural blockages as unauthorized status. Many scholars have examined the extent to which racialization and immigration policy have been intertwined, concluding that exclusions to the United States have historically fallen harder on Asian immigrants, whereas Europeans have found individual access to status adjustment easier to navigate.[75] While national civil rights legislation in the United States has reduced the likelihood of race-based immigration legislation, between statutes drafted in general terms and their day-to-day enforcement, especially at the local level, lies a gulf of discretion that creates space for racial profiling and other discriminatory actions. In recent years, enforcement of deportation laws has fallen disproportionately not just on Latinos but particularly on working-class male Latinos.[76] Even though discourses of racism may be held in check, nativist narratives have proliferated, lending a certain public acceptability to mechanisms for promoting the exclusion of immigrants.[77] Indeed, Linda Bosniak suggests that immigration scholars examine how mechanisms based not only on ethnoracial status but also on gender, sexual identity, disability, and poverty shape practices of exclusion when newcomers are defined officially as "aliens."[78]

In the United States, race has constituted a relatively long-lasting and permanent criterion of exclusion, even when civil rights legislation bars discrimination. By contrast, migration status can be and has been changed as a matter of public policy. Once the stigmatized migration status disappears, then so too might its effects. Thus while unauthorized status has since the 1990s constituted grounds for withholding social citizenship in the United States,[79] many persons in that category have been able to legalize, and more could do so, were U.S. policy to open wider pathways to legalization. This mutability also suggests that race, which in the United States is applied much more rigidly than migration status, constitutes a qualitatively different criterion of exclusion.

Current empirical and theoretical work also clearly distinguishes legal status from racialization. Multiple studies of immigrants show the increasing salience of legal status.[80] While the brightest boundary in studies of membership may lie between authorized and unauthorized immigrants, that brightness varies across immigrants from different countries and over time. Moreover, bureaucratic policies at the local level can mitigate or exacerbate the effect of national laws.[81] The importance of local context thus matters, because that is where much of integration occurs.[82] Unauthorized immigrants are, by their very presence, somewhat incorporated into the host society, though their dimensions of greatest incorporation are likely to be sociocultural, where legal restrictions have less reach. Even though unauthorized immigrants may feel as if they exist in a liminal status or "borderland,"[83] they nevertheless have some rights, such as free access to secondary education in the United States, and thus may be considered more like subcitizens that noncitizens.[84] There is, in fact, a paradox in their situations. The more they seek integration, the more contact they have with formal institutions and the more vulnerable they thus become.[85] As this risk rises, because immigration law has become more like criminal law, the possibility of deportation increases.[86]

The case of unauthorized Mexican migrants in the United States provides a particularly illustrative example of membership exclusion. The tendency for U.S. scholars to focus on race rather than giving membership special emphasis in integration studies occurs in part because the major models of integration for today's new immigrants have been assimilation models based on the experiences of the European immigrants of a century ago.[87] The tendency to focus on race as the counterexample to assimilation also derives in part from America's exclusionary practices involving Native Americans and the Chinese in the nineteenth century and the Japanese and Mexicans in the early decades of the twentieth century, exclusions based on what was viewed as race at the time, when race and national origin were conflated in the public mind. Observers now often extend the idea of race, perhaps in this former sense of the term, to include today's Mexican immigrants. However, while both unauthorized Mexicans and African Americans today experience membership exclusion, an important difference between them is that the children of Mexican immigrants in the United States are not subject to formal exclusion themselves by dint of birthright citizenship. This guarantees that an unauthorized immigrant's U.S.-born children are not also unauthorized. After the Bracero Program ended in 1964, unauthorized migrants could work for a period of time in the country and find pathways to legal status. As their trips recurred over time, they eventually became longer-term settlers, were often able to become legal, and could close the earnings gap between themselves and migrants who had come legally, and they were able to do this precisely because they could find pathways to legalization.[88]

However, unauthorized migrants today are much more subject to fears of deportation (and thus exploitation) because enforcement levels have been vastly increased and because the collateral penalties for being caught are much more severe than they were twenty years ago.[89] Now they are more permanently consigned to outsider status, to the legal purgatory of societal nonmembership.[90] Most immigrant newcomers during the nineteenth and early twentieth centuries were treated more inclusively, as persons who were considered settlers and "citizens in waiting," even if they were not always liked and frequently discriminated against.[91] The severity of nonmembership among the unauthorized today cannot help but have negative implications not only for the integration of the Mexican immigrants themselves but also for their children.

The Dimensionality of Integration

To assess immigrant-group integration, it is necessary to decide what needs to be assessed. That is, what is the content of integration? What are its various dimensions? What are its constituent parts? In a world in which social, cultural, and economic life appear to have grown ever more differentiated and complex,[92] the preeminence, even roughly, of a single monolithic "mainstream" that receiving societies aspire to make immigrants a part of, and that immigrants in turn strive to emulate and join, seems less and less plausible. Integration seems more likely to involve multiple processes, or dimensions. By dimension we mean a kind of integration that may occur relatively independently of others. Sociocultural dimensions in particular may vary more because immigrant groups come from different national origins and cultural backgrounds, the persistence of these reflecting group differences more than integration failures. Independence may also occur within groups as individuals become increasingly distinctive socially and culturally over time.[93]

It is thus not surprising that immigration scholars such as Charles Hirschman have trenchantly criticized the assimilation literature for "lack of a clear specification showing how the various dimensions are related to one another."[94] Here we seek theoretically to shed light on what kinds of integration are most important, that is, to assess integration's dimensionality. We do this mainly by reviewing the theoretical perspectives on integration and what they imply about the number and types of dimensions and by briefly examining integration research studies relevant to the connections among dimensions. We have already indicated why societal membership may condition structural integration. This in itself imparts a nonunitary quality to early political integration. Thus logic and evidence that this kind of integration conditions others and that multiple dimensions of incorporation are only weakly associated with one another would lend support to the idea that pluralist-based approaches characterize today's integration experiences. This pluralism in turn would imply a greater possibility that multiple ethnic groups can coexist in the same place and that various kinds of sociocultural differences can occur both across and within groups, although none of these should be viewed as inevitable outcomes, only tendencies. By contrast, evidence of more unidimensionality among multiple incorporation indicators would be less consistent with the possibility of coexistence.

The Dimensionality Implied by Theoretical Perspectives on Integration

What do the various theoretical perspectives on integration imply about the dimensionality of integration? The classic assimilation perspective and its five major variants—ethnic advantage, ethnic disadvantage, racialization, segmented assimilation, and working-class delay[95]—share the idea that the various aspects of integration tend to progress together over time,[96] although four of the five corollary perspectives envision incomplete assimilation. The pluralist-based perspectives—the multicultural, the postindustrial-individualistic, and the membership-exclusion frameworks—emphasize that various aspects of integration (such as economic, sociocultural, spatial, and political) can and do occur at different times and in different ways.[97] The multicultural perspective in particular postulates that the retention of specific ethnic-group sociocultural tendencies—values, customs, and behavioral practices—is not necessarily anomalous with respect to other kinds of incorporation. The approach envisions the possibility that immigrant groups can and do embrace religious behaviors, patterns of sexual orientations, family forms, and other ethnic values and behaviors that may be distinctive from those of a native comparison group. However, it does not tend to imply that these various sociocultural tendencies vary much within the group. That is, the multicultural framework suggests a tendency toward sociocultural homogeneity within immigrant groups, while theorizing that this does not necessarily preclude economic or other kinds of incorporation. In places where mainstream society tolerates and respects ethnic identity and culture, little reason exists to think ethnic sociocultural distinctiveness will thwart economic or political integration.[98]

The postindustrial-individualistic approach, in light of its emphasis on the fluidity and contingency of sociocultural identities, processes, and outcomes across individuals, implies still more sociocultural variation and thus even more multidimensionality of sociocultural integration. This follows from its notions that advanced societies increasingly do not require that given ethnoracial identities, sexual orientations, marital statuses, religious preferences, and family behaviors bundle closely together to be intertwined for economic integration to take place.[99] In short, variation in sociocultural indicators is likely to be highly individualistic and independent of other kinds of integration. This implies that structural but not sociocultural facets of integration will be subject to the constraints on cross-generation integration predicted by membership exclusion.

Kinds of Integration Implied by Research

The organization and findings of scholarly research also suggest that it is fruitful to conceptualize integration as involving multiple dimensions. At a prima facie level, this is evident in the fact that academia involves a division of labor among economics, sociology and anthropology, geography, and political science around four broad domains of subject matter that also reflect four kinds of individual-level immigrant incorporation: economic, sociocultural, spatial, and political. Similarly, that scholars often draw sharp distinctions between structural and sociocultural incorporation[100] suggests that various aspects of each of these (for example, human capital and labor-market outcomes in the former case and such phenomena as group identity, linguistic patterns, and family and religious orientations and behaviors in the latter) may vary independently of one another (that is, they can occur separately and not necessarily together). While this seems reasonable, it is less clear that economic and sociocultural integration occur independently of spatial and political incorporation. Spatial assimilation is often thought to be a direct function of sociocultural adaptation and economic mobility,[101] though recent studies question this connection.[102] Several new Asian groups in the United States (Chinese, Koreans, and to a lesser extent Filipinos) include many highly educated immigrants; some settle in coethnic communities when they arrive, but many do not.[103] The extent to which economically successful members of a group continue to live in its enclaves suggests a loose association between spatial and economic incorporation. Chapter 6 elaborates these points.

The picture is even more complicated in the case of political incorporation, because this domain encompasses so many parts as to be almost intractable.[104] In recognition of this, and in an effort to bring some conceptual order to the area's unwieldy subject matter, Jennifer Hochschild and John Mollenkopf have developed a conceptual schema that seeks to clarify systematically the key constituent parts of the process.[105] Their approach underscores that different kinds of political incorporation are likely to take place at different times in the process. Thus, for example, immigrants cannot vote until they become naturalized citizens, meaning that in the United States voting behavior is not a relevant aspect of political incorporation until immigrants have lived here long enough to become eligible to apply for citizenship. This sequence alone prefigures the particular theoretical importance that we think needs to be assigned to societal membership as a factor conditioning the occurrence of other incorporation outcomes. Just as one cannot vote without becoming a citizen, neither can unauthorized newcomers get on track to becoming citizens, let alone apply for many kinds of jobs that require legal status, if not citizenship. Lack of social membership, or suffering the status of being an unauthorized immigrant, results in exclusion from many arenas of societal participation, some by law, others by dint of social disapprobation, and often by dint of both. Unauthorized immigrant residents of the United States lack effective membership in so many different sectors of American life that their integration with respect to many other kinds of incorporation is problematic. Integration can at best be partial without formal membership.[106]

Integration's Greater Dimensionality in More Inclusionary Places

Another reason to conceptualize integration as multidimensional comes from research suggesting greater dimensionality in more inclusionary places. Classifications of countries based on their incorporation regimes all tend to find that the German-speaking countries of Austria, Germany, and Switzerland traditionally have shown more exclusionary policies compared with other Western countries. Moreover, despite social change, differences between these countries and more inclusionary places have remained surprisingly stable.[107] Recent research finds that immigrants in cities in the more inclusionary contexts show more independent dimensions of integration.[108] Conversely, exclusionary policies mean that immigrants have fewer pathways for advancement and thus fewer potential dimensions along which independent integration might occur. A key example involves citizenship, which exclusionary countries until recently had made impossible or very difficult for immigrants and their children to attain.[109] This formally limits other advancement, because citizenship often is required for access to many services and labor-market opportunities. Inclusionary places allow and foster more economic advancement that does not require political or sociocultural uniformity.[110]

Theory, logic, and research findings together thus suggest that immigrant integration involves multidimensional and relatively independent processes, especially in more inclusionary places. This multidimensionality is hinted at in the unbundling of dimensions implied by the theoretical off-shoots of classic assimilation, such as segmented assimilation; by the multidimensionality explicitly embedded in the multicultural and postindustrial-individualistic theoretical perspectives; and by the greater multidimensionality that has been hypothesized and observed more in inclusionary countries than in exclusionary ones.[111] Multidimensionality with respect to sociocultural factors is also implied by the fact that liberal nation-states over the past half century have become increasingly tolerant of racial and ethnic differences as a matter of public policy, especially immigration policy. As Christian Joppke notes, "An epistemic shift after World War II outlawed race as a legitimate principle of ordering the social world."[112] As a result, Waldinger observes, "neutrality is required of the liberal state when it comes to the ethnic or cultural differences among the *existing* people of the state; the same principle applies to *potential* members of the state."[113] From such emphases, greater multidimensionality of integration tends to follow, if for no other reason than that economic mobility and other kinds of integration do not have to be accompanied by sociocultural uniformity.

Theoretical Expectations about Cross-Generational Mobility

What would the various theoretical perspectives predict regarding differences in degrees of mobility across generations? They are not always explicit about this. However, all contain emphases and logic that suggest certain patterns. We depict these here in terms of expected levels of integration relative to the first generation, starting with the so-called 1.5 generation and running across subsequent generations. By the

1.5 generation we mean persons who immigrated to the United States before the age of fourteen; by the 2.0 generation we mean those persons with at least one Mexican-born parent; and by the 3.0 generation, we refer to persons with at least two Mexican-born grandparents. (Later in this chapter we discuss other definitions of the 3.0 generation in more detail.) The classic assimilation approach would imply a pattern across generations showing the 2.0 generation with advancement compared with the 1.5 generation, and the 3.0 generation with even more still. Moreover, the third generation might close in on parity or equivalence with mainstream natives on whatever dimension of comparison is under examination (see table 2.1). In other words, classic assimilation predicts with regard to some factor such as, say, education that successive generations will exhibit steadily rising levels of schooling such that, in the best case, the third generation might end up on a par with the schooling levels of the mainstream group. Similar patterns would also be expected for other kinds of integration.

The expectations of the ethnic-resources-and-advantage perspective differ little from those of classic assimilation, except in one important respect. Although both imply steadily greater integration gains across generations, because the ethnic-resources-and-advantage perspective sees ethnic distinctiveness as fostering social and cultural factors that lead to integration enhancements, it implies that by the third generation, integration could reach levels high enough to exceed the level of the mainstream group (see column 2 of table 2.1). Ethnic disadvantage, by contrast, expects something entirely different, namely, not much in the way of rising levels of integration across generations, even though these could increase slightly relative to the immigrant generation for each later-generation group. In general, the ethnic-disadvantage framework expects constrained but not a total forestalling of integration, with the result that the third-generation members of the group might still show deficits relative to the mainstream (see column 3). Racialization perspectives are more different still. Because of the harder boundaries envisioned by racialization approaches, the limited integration predicted by an ethnic-disadvantage hypothesis would not be expected. Rather little if any integration would be expected owing to relatively permanently blocked mobility from difficult-to-eradicate discrimination against the group. As a result, integration would not increase much across generations but instead would remain stuck at fairly low levels until such time as racial discrimination and other barriers to racial advancement disappeared. This approach would not expect parity with mainstream natives even well after the third generation (see column 4). The perspective of working-class delay would expect uneven mobility because some aspects of structural mobility (for example, income) can often be achieved without others (for example, education) occurring. This perspective thus sees the structure of mobility opportunities rather

Table 2.1 Cross-Generational Mobility and Third-Generation Gap Relative to Non-Hispanic White Attainment, as Implied by Eight Theoretical Approaches to Integration

| | Assimilation-Based | | | | | | Pluralist-Based | | | | |
| | (1) | (2) | (3) | (4) | (5) | (6) | (7) MC[b] | | (8) PII[c] | | |
Pattern of Mobility[a]	CA	EA	ED	R	SA	WCD	S	C	S	C1	C2
Generation 1.5	+	+	0	0	0	0	+	0	+	0	+
Generation 2.0	++	++	+	+	+	+	++	0	++	+	0
Generation 3.0	+++	+++	++	+	++	+ or ++	+++	0	+++	0	+
Gap between generation 3.0 and majority	0	0 to +	–	– –	–	– or – –	0	– –	0	–	– –

Source: Authors' compilations.

Note: Mobility key: 0 = no mobility; "+" = slight mobility; "++" = moderate mobility; "+++" = considerable mobility; "–" = some deficit; "– –" = considerable deficit. Perspective code: CA = classical assimilation; EA = ethnic advantage; ED = ethnic disadvantage; R = racialization; SA = segmented assimilation; WCD = working-class delay; MC = multicultural; PII = postindustrial individualistic; S = structural; C = cultural.

[a]Generation 1.0 is the reference category.

[b]This approach implies a distinctive sociocultural profile between the mainstream and immigrant groups.

[c]This approach implies a distinctive sociocultural profile between groups and among individuals within groups, heuristically represented as two group sociocultural profiles distinctive relative to each other and a majority group.

than prejudice and discrimination targeted toward the group as the key driver (or limiter) of mobility.

Segmented assimilation allows that a sizable portion of many immigrant groups will experience similar degrees of integration to those expected by the classic assimilation approach. However, unlike classic assimilation, it takes more explicitly into account the possibility of variegated forms of integration. This theory would see some members of the group as experiencing conventional assimilation, some as experiencing ethnic-advantage integration (through selective acculturation), and some as experiencing disadvantage or racialization. Overall, this perspective would expect results like those shown in column 5 (of table 2.1). The overall pattern would consist of moderately rising average integration across generations (owing to the group undergoing assimilation and selective acculturation), but because other members of the group experience disadvantage or racialization, not enough integration emerging overall for the group to achieve parity with the mainstream by the third generation. As previously noted, this perspective also begins to consider multidimensionality of integration in that it contends that some groups selectively retain aspects of ethnicity (especially certain family values and practices) that support higher educational achievement in the second generation whereas others are sufficiently blocked from mobility that advancement does not occur (an outcome called downward mobility in this framework).

The hypotheses implied by the multicultural and postindustrial-individualistic perspectives are more complex than the assimilation-based ones because they entail the explicit idea that sociocultural aspects of mobility can (and often do) occur independently of structural aspects. Moreover, in the case of the postindustrial-individualistic approach, sociocultural aspects are also seen as often occurring independently of one another. Different patterns of intergenerational integration are thus possible across sociocultural indicators. While both perspectives allow for (and in their prescriptive forms seek to promote) integration that would reflect the assimilation pattern of increasing integration across generations, they allow departures from this pattern in the cases of at least some sociocultural indicators. The multicultural approach tends to focus not on distinctions across different kinds of cultural dimensions within the ethnoracial immigrant group but rather on differences between this group and a mainstream group. The postindustrial-individualistic approach explicitly suggests that various sociocultural indicators are not necessarily related to one another even within the group. Thus, in its view, sociocultural aspects such as religious affiliation, church attendance, and the importance of ethnicity do not necessarily strongly covary, or even covary at all. To reflect these tendencies, we delineate the expected patterns for these two perspectives in table 2.1 in terms of both structural

Table 2.2   Cross-Generational Mobility and Third-Generation Gap
Relative to Non-Hispanic White Attainment, as Implied
by the Membership-Exclusion Theoretical Approach

Pattern of Mobility[a]	Membership Exclusion[b]			
	Structural	Cultural 1	Cultural 2	Cultural 3
Generation 1.5	+	0	+	0
Generation 2.0	+	+	0	0
Generation 3.0	+++	0	+	0
Gap between generation 3.0 and the majority	0, –	–	–	– –

Source: Authors' compilations.
Note: Mobility key: 0 = no mobility; "+" = slight mobility; "++" = moderate mobility; "+++" = considerable mobility; "–" = some deficit; "– –" = considerable deficit.
[a]As implied by the membership exclusion theoretical approach to integration. Generation 1.0 is the reference group.
[b]The cultural approach implies distinctive sociocultural profiles both between groups and among individuals within groups, here heuristically represented as three sociocultural profiles that are distinctive relative to each other and to that of a hypothetical majority group.

and cultural dimensions, one cultural dimension in the case of the multi-cultural approach and two in the case of the postindustrial-individualistic approach (although the latter perspective would be expected to show as many "dimensions" as aspects examined).

It is important to note that pluralist-based theoretical approaches to integration do not preclude the possibility of assimilation or other patterns of cross-generation integration occurring with respect to structural aspects of integration. This is why we show such a pattern for them in table 2.1. However, pluralist-based approaches (unlike assimilation-based approaches) emphasize that either group-based sociocultural dimensions will be distinctive and important (that is, the multicultural perspective) or individual-based ones (for example, the postindustrial-individualistic perspective) will be. Membership-exclusion dynamics are particularly likely to apply to the economic, spatial, and perhaps linguistic dimensions of incorporation but not necessarily to sociocultural facets, for the reasons noted earlier. Immigrants incurring membership exclusion may show mobility on sociocultural facets of integration because of their aspirations to belong to the receiving society, although the perspective also implies that there will be individual variation in these. Thus the perspective would not expect correlations across individuals in aspects of socio-cultural integration (that is, someone high on secularism might not be weak on ethnic identity), even though the group as a whole would be expected to show cross-generational variation in such aspects (that is, higher secularism and weaker ethnic identity) (see table 2.2). That is, in many respects they may show evidence of acculturation, even though they may be cut off from enjoying some of the material benefits the society has to offer mainstream citizens.

Conclusion

The classic assimilation perspective, so dominant in the United States in the first half of the twentieth century, came under fire in the wake of the civil rights movement for failing to account for the plight of African Americans. The backlash arguments stressed racial disadvantage and the persistence of racial and ethnic identities so much that in 1993, Nathan Glazer published an influential essay titled "Is Assimilation Dead?" Glazer argued that, in general, the answer was no.[114] That same year, Portes and Zhou introduced the concept of segmented assimilation, which stressed a three-part path: assimilation for those with advantages in human capital, ethnic disadvantage and racialization for some because of poverty and discrimination, and the reliance on ethnic resources and the selective retention of ethnicity for yet others. Thus began a reexamination of assimilation theory, with a new stress on institutional roles and the contingent nature of ethnic identification. Recent research shows that rising U.S. immigration and greater diversity of national origins are resulting in new modes of incorporation,[115] weakening ethnoracial boundaries,[116] and more sociocultural differentiation, both across groups and individuals, tendencies increasingly characteristic of postindustrial societies.

These trends imply that new pluralist (or pluralist-based, as we discuss here) models of integration are more apt for understanding the experiences of new U.S. immigrant groups. To begin moving in this direction, we have examined in this chapter eight theoretical approaches that provide different bases for understanding the integration of immigrants and their descendants. We have introduced an additional perspective, the membership-exclusion approach, whose tenets and emphases are different from but complementary to these. We compare the approaches in regard to their conceptualizations and the forces they see as driving incorporation. We also assess the various perspectives in terms of what they imply about the kinds of integration, or the dimensionality of incorporation. Thus we classify several as generally assimilation based and suggested that they imply that integration tends roughly to follow a unitary course, even though some of these, most notably segmented assimilation, also specify supplementary processes, such as selective acculturation and downward mobility.[117] These perspectives begin to acknowledge dynamics that lead to different degrees of integration for various kinds of incorporation and for some subgroups within an ethnic group compared to others. We also classify other approaches as pluralist based, including the membership-exclusion perspective, which we suggest explicitly underscores the likelihood that integration varies among dimensions, subgroups, and individuals.

Although these approaches entail different emphases and imply different cross-generational patterns of mobility, they are complementary rather than contradictory perspectives. In this regard, they show the same character as theories of migration, the complementarity of which Douglas S. Massey has so cogently outlined, noting that they stress different mechanisms as drivers of migration.[118] But the growth in unauthorized migration, a status that in the United States has become more stigmatized over the past twenty years, suggests that the theoretical emphases of membership exclusion are needed to highlight the handicaps caused by this type of marginalization. Many immigrants are formally excluded from social membership at their destinations and thereby prevented from achieving tangible mobility. The next chapter addresses how membership exclusion and the factors emphasized by other theoretical perspectives on immigrant integration might combine to generate distinctive Mexican American patterns of integration across generations.

= Chapter 3 =

Gauging Mexican American Integration: Research Hypotheses and Methodological Considerations

everal major studies of Mexican American integration have examined at least three generations of mobility experience.[1] Integration studies of other more recently arriving national-origin groups, however, have concentrated mostly on the children of immigrants and their parents because so few members of a third generation had even been born.[2] Most U.S. immigrants since 1965 came from countries that previously had sent few immigrants. The important second-generation projects undertaken by Alejandro Portes and Rubén Rumbaut and by Mary Waters, John Mollenkopf, and Philip Kasinitz, although yielding valuable insights on the integration of the adolescent and young adult members of several second-generation groups, especially Cubans and Nicaraguans in Miami and Filipinos and Vietnamese in San Diego, as well as Chinese, Dominicans, South Americans (Colombians, Ecuadorians, and Peruvians), West Indians, and Russian Jews in New York City, have not been able to study the third generation.[3] They nonetheless have shown that most of the members of these groups develop resilience and navigate schooling and young-adult transitions fairly well, although some members of certain groups falter for various reasons.

Compared with these more recent groups, Mexican Americans constitute an entirely different case. For one thing, the third generation is large, because Mexicans have been migrating continuously to the United States for a long time. For another, Mexican Americans have historically faced substantial obstacles to integration, especially in Texas, where more than half of that population lived before 1950.[4] Because notable numbers of Mexican Americans who grew up in Texas (or whose parents did) now live in other states, especially California, the handicaps from their Texas backgrounds may offset more positive integration experiences in their new destinations. This legacy effect can skew estimates of their recent progress. Also, although studying first- and second-generation Mexican Americans would provide useful information about the extent of integration up to a point, ignoring the third generation would virtually guarantee an incomplete assessment of Mexican American integration.

For Mexican Americans, a strong case thus exists for carrying out a three-generational examination of integration. We do this here in two ways: by gauging Mexican American integration across three generations on the dimensions identified in chapter 2—economic (especially education and income), spatial, linguistic, and sociocultural—and by comparing third-generation Mexican Americans with "mainstream" non-Hispanic whites. In the first half of this chapter, we develop specific research hypotheses, based on ideas coming from the membership-exclusion theoretical perspective and on ideas from gender and sociology of development theoretical perspectives,[5] predicting different cross-generation integration patterns for men and women by legalization trajectory among Mexican Americans. In the second half of the chapter, we discuss several important methodological issues that impinge on empirical results involving three-generation Mexican American comparisons, and we note how we deal with these in this research.

In developing expectations derived from membership-exclusion considerations, we also revisit what other theoretical perspectives on integration, particularly ethnic-disadvantage approaches, would expect. Based on the membership-exclusion perspective, we would expect in general to find socioeconomic mobility rising across generations as Mexican Americans accumulate more exposure to the United States, especially between the first and second generations, because the immigrants start from such a low entry point. Because the U.S.-born second generation has birthright citizenship, its handicaps are the legacy of its parents. When the parents entered the country legally or became legal after arrival, the second generation should be better off than those with unauthorized parents who remained unauthorized. The offspring of legal parents would be expected to start their U.S. experience from a higher status level than those whose parents did not or could not obtain legalization, and this latter group would lower the average attainment of the second generation. To the extent that the effects of parental status are transmitted to children, the grandchildren (the children of the second generation) may also show evidence of legacy effects of unauthorized migration if for no other reason than that some of their parents will have been held back the generation before. But if legalization enables complete catch-up, then the structural integration of those third-generation persons whose family backgrounds involved grandparents who legalized after arrival should end up close to that of persons whose grandparents entered the country legally in the first place. All of these tendencies should be more pronounced among females than males for reasons we explain later in this chapter.

Certain other theoretical approaches—notably, ethnic disadvantage, racialization, and segmented assimilation—imply lower degrees of mobility across generations, with minimal advancement and a lack of parity with non-Hispanic whites by the third generation. By contrast, membership exclusion implies that once immigrants attain legal status, they and their children should be as likely to advance as those who came legally, although the third generation may still be held back by the intergenerational transmission of lower education levels from their parents, whose own parents were unauthorized. Perspectives emphasizing racialization and ethnic disadvantage generally imply mechanisms such as discrimination and stigmatization that create more-enduring disadvantages across generations, irrespective of migration status and its changes.[6] To the extent that such factors are operating, we would expect Mexican Americans to show minimal increases in mobility across generations.

Research Hypotheses

What have we learned about long-run Mexican American integration from prior research? Although a plethora of studies have relied on the use of a so-called third-plus generation (that is, third and later generations), the results of such research are inconsistent at best and invalid at worst. A growing body of evidence indicates that such third-plus-generation studies are seriously flawed. Third-plus-generation categories involve negative selectivity, which results in downward bias that masks the level of third-generation integration.[7] Because of this problem, our review of the results of recent research omits third-plus-generation studies. To our knowledge, this leaves only four notable recent research projects on Mexican Americans. After discussing these, we introduce the research hypotheses of the present research.

Previous Studies

The first previous study, by Susan K. Brown, examines spatial mobility, finding that the tendency to live in Anglo neighborhoods in Los Angeles did not increase much between the first and second generations. However, it then rose sharply from the second to the third generations.[8] This pattern of early stagnation followed by greater mobility in the third generation is not implied by any of the seven theoretical frameworks on integration, but it does appear consistent with the predictions of membership exclusion. A second research example comes from the landmark project carried out by Edward Telles and Vilma Ortiz, who in 2000 reinterviewed the original respondents (and their children) who were part of the classic assessment of Mexican American incorporation conducted by Leo Grebler, Joan Moore, and Ralph Guzman in Los Angeles and San Antonio in 1964.[9] In regard to what they see as the fundamental integration yardstick, namely educational attainment, Telles and Ortiz interpret their findings as reflecting minimal integration because their statistical analyses uncovered little net individual education mobility in the third generation after controlling for the effects of parental education. Other scholars have noted, however, that their findings show notable rises in actual education for the children compared with those of their own parents, leading them to argue that more integration may have taken place than Telles and Ortiz conclude.[10]

A third project by Tomás Jiménez, focusing on later-generation Mexican American identity, comes up with results that support neither a standard assimilation perspective (in which case ethnicity for third-generation respondents might become symbolic or optional) nor a disadvantage perspective (in which case reactive ethnicity develops, that is, strong Mexican ethnicity as a consequence of perceptions of having been mistreated).[11] Rather, the respondents reflected substantial hybridity, meaning they saw themselves as Mexican Americans who were both American and Mexican and middle-class persons whose ethnicity remained salient because continuing Mexican immigration into the areas where they lived replenished the supply of ethnic cultural practices. In particular, they did not view themselves as "an aggrieved minority," although they indicated they had encountered nativism, but more as a "permanent immigrant group."[12] A fourth study using General Social Survey data from 1972 to 2002 finds evidence of cross-generational mobility when using a third-only generation measure, but not as much mobility as when respondents were compared with their own parents.[13]

None of these studies provides strong evidence either for complete assimilation or for enough disadvantage to suggest thwarted integration. Among other things, incomplete integration could result from multiple offsetting processes taking place. Interestingly, none of the studies strongly emphasized unauthorized status as something that itself might lead to different integration outcomes in the immigrant and subsequent generations. Although some indicate that unauthorized migrants may be exploited and their mobility stymied, none explicitly conceptualized such disadvantage within a social-citizenship nexus that offers a basis for understanding how this kind of deprivation limits incorporation, especially compared with persons whose families have legal backgrounds. Finally, and also interestingly, none of the projects systematically took gender into account. Although they sometimes controlled for gender statistically in focusing on other factors that might affect structural integration, gender differences, if expressed at all, were treated as compositional complications that needed to be removed before examining the independent influence of other variables. In considering integration, none of the studies conceptualized the effects of gender dynamics as these might be shaped in part by the cultural milieu emerging in and reinforced by processes of migration and settlement.

Unauthorized Labor Migration and Structural Integration

Good reasons exist to think that unauthorized migration will limit the structural integration of such immigrants and exert effects that are likely to carry over to the U.S.-born children and perhaps even the grandchildren of such immigrants. These consequences are likely to show up particularly in regard to education,[14] the success of which depends substantially on the structural integration of parents, especially mothers, whose roles in shaping children's adjustment, aspirations, and schooling are vitally important.[15] If the structural integration of parents is limited by migration status, they will be less able to help their children because they will be afraid to engage with institutions outside the home, such as neighborhood organizations and schools.[16] A negative relationship between unauthorized migration in the first generation and educational attainment in the second generation thus seems likely.

But other perspectives also predict low educational attainment and emphasize that lack of access to opportunity and social isolation are factors causing severe poverty. The perspectives on ethnic disadvantage, segmented assimilation, and racialization focus on endemic cumulative disadvantage resulting from ethnoracial discrimination that they suggest does not appreciably abate across generations. Membership exclusion, however, suggests the slowing of integration is rooted more in the lack of legal status, leading to more transitory dampening effects.

Membership Exclusion   The effects of unauthorized status work both through the lack of structural opportunity and through cultural repertoires that arise as part of the migration and settlement process, especially for unauthorized immigrants. Cultural repertoires consist of ideas, customs, and orientations that, while originating in materialist conditions, take on a force of their own and help people establish priorities, cope with life necessities, and resolve day-to-day work and family dilemmas,[17] although the strength of such tendencies may fluctuate across situational contexts.[18] In any case, Mexican labor migrants arriving in the United States are likely to place an unusually strong emphasis on finding and sustaining employment and on working hard. Such tendencies emerge in part from their status as migrants who are self-selected for initiative and optimism about success.[19] As Amy Hsin and Yu Xie note, "The very decision to migrate in search of better opportunities can be seen as a sign of this optimism."[20]

Deciding to migrate also originates in social conditions that encourage moving for purposes of seeking work.[21] More than other types of immigrants (for example, refugees or high-skilled employment immigrants), Mexican migrants tend to lack papers and have few skills but nevertheless need and expect to provide for their families.[22] Not only do they face usually bleak labor-market prospects in their towns, villages, and cities of origin,[23] they also shoulder the expectations of both their families and their communities of origin that they migrate to the United States expressly to work.[24] Because such young migrants are embedded in familial and social contexts with interests in their migration, they are likely to view finding a job in social-insurance terms, that is, as a way to minimize family financial risk as opposed to a way to achieve individual upward mobility.[25]

Being unauthorized only accentuates the imperative to work and the development of family-related cultural repertoires in the immigrant generation. Moreover, such strong needs to support one's family carry over even into the second generation, encouraging teenage children of immigrants to seek employment instead of staying in school. Such cultural repertoires are particularly directed at boys.[26] Given the socially structured underpinnings of labor migration and the reliance of migrants on social networks to obtain employment (the need for which is increased by unauthorized status), it is unsurprising that Mexican immigrants generally find work more quickly in the United States than do members of other immigrant groups.[27] But because unauthorized migrants generally earn low wages and hold unstable jobs, even multiple jobs may not be enough to alleviate family poverty.[28] Unauthorized workers are also vulnerable to exploitation, which further contributes to the prevalence of poverty. All of these factors combine to create an overwhelming need to rely on and provide for one's family, all else being equal.

Not surprisingly, such social-insurance motifs (that is, risk-minimization strategies) among unauthorized Mexican labor migrants are similar to U.S. working-class cultural orientations in general,[29] although the tendencies are likely to be even stronger among those with unauthorized labor-migration backgrounds than among native working-class Mexican Americans. As conceptualized by social psychologists engaged in studying the cultural orientations associated with social class, members of the U.S. middle class tend to adopt understandings of normatively appropriate actions that are "independent from others and the social context; freely chosen, personally controllable, and contingent on one's preferences, intentions, and goals; and directed toward influencing and standing out from others."[30] In short, such actions reflect an independent model of agency. By contrast, members of the working class tend to embrace an

interdependent model of agency, or one in which normatively appropriate actions are "interdependent with others; responsive to and contingent
on expectations of others, social roles, situations, and the larger social
context; and directed toward adjusting to and fitting in with others."[31]
Among unauthorized Mexican labor migrants, the drive to seek employment and to work hard derives in part from family- and household-
induced social-insurance-seeking orientations and behaviors that are
generally consistent with the working-class cultural milieu in the United
States, although stronger in the case of immigrants because their life situations entail greater risk. All of this is not to imply that Mexican immigrants and their children move in lockstep, particularly on sociocultural
dimensions such as language acquisition or self-identity. Even members
of the same family may well diverge without losing sight of their economic
interdependency.

Disadvantage Perspectives   Perspectives emphasizing ethnic disadvantage, segmented assimilation (through its downward-mobility hypothesis), and racialization, however, envision Mexican immigrants as
encountering sufficient ethnoracial discrimination and hostility through
host-society institutions (such as labor markets and schools) that opportunities for structural mobility and integration are blocked.[32] Moreover,
the hardships resulting from discrimination toward Mexican immigrants
are not seen as involving temporary conditions but rather are viewed
as obstacles of more permanent duration whose force accumulates over
time. Because they are based on prejudice toward the entire group
as a category, they persist across generations and impinge on both
men and women. In such perspectives, the birthright citizenship of
the U.S.-born second generation is viewed as unlikely to begin to ameliorate disadvantage because the root of the discrimination is seen as
stemming from prejudice and phenotype, qualities that are more enduring. This is in contrast to the membership-exclusion approach, which
suggests that, in the case of the U.S.-born children of unauthorized immigrants, integration will proceed without being hindered by migration status per se, although second-generation attainment may still be somewhat
indirectly affected by the migration status of their parents.

Although disadvantage perspectives allow for small degrees of intergenerational advancement, they generally posit that ethnoracial discrimination curtails the possibility of notable structural integration across
generations. This tends to foreclose life-course mobility patterns because
persistent ethnoracial discrimination and the cumulative disadvantage it
fosters lead to scarring in subsequent generations.[33] The enduring negative effects of such forces imply a generally flat cross-generational pattern
of mobility. The membership-exclusion perspective, by contrast, envisions
more mobility taking place once turning points (such as legalization) are

reached, after which structural integration can rise appreciably. This perspective would see obtaining legal status as an important and positive life-course event that carries significant positive implications for subsequent structural integration.[34]

Gender Variations

The dynamics of unauthorized Mexican labor migration may also lead to behavior patterns that often seem to reflect traditional Mexican emphases on gender role specialization in the family. Even though the movement of families to the United States may in general work to make Mexican American gender roles more egalitarian,[35] the more immediate exigencies of labor migration can sometimes reinforce traditional gender patterns to meet family needs. Thus some research finds greater marital stability[36] and a greater prevalence of extended family living arrangements among Mexican immigrants than among U.S.-born Mexican Americans.[37] These findings appear to suggest that traditional Mexican family values have been transported to the United States. But this impression dissolves in the light of findings of these and other studies that document higher marital instability and a lower prevalence of extended-family living arrangements in Mexico. Thus what often may seem to reflect traditional Mexican family values being transported to the United States can instead represent manifestations of meso-level migration-induced cultural repertoires that encourage migrants to be more cautious and interdependent the better to provide for the larger family unit.

The consequences of such cultural repertoires become manifest in various ways. For example, adolescent sons of Mexican immigrants adopt bifurcated (mutually exclusive) cultural orientations in regard to education and work because doing so provides greater social insurance for the family. That is, because of the strong commitment to work among Mexican migrants, coupled with their low-wage jobs, sons tend to specialize in either work or schooling.[38] Such inclinations imply different patterns of cross-generation integration than those predicted by disadvantage perspectives, such as segmented assimilation's downward-mobility hypothesis, which would expect high proportions of second-generation young men to be neither in school nor in the labor force, with the result that poor Mexican youth become more and more like an underclass. The membership-exclusion perspective, however, would imply that to reduce risk, second-generation Mexican American teenage boys from unauthorized family migration backgrounds are strongly encouraged to work to help support their families (either their own or their parents'). If they were enrolled in school, this would be seen as an investment in their family's future; if they were working, this would be an investment in the present.[39] In short, risk-minimization supports expectations that they do one or the other and not be idle. In fact, research has found that such a bifurcated school-work pattern is more evident among Mexican Americans than Anglos or blacks, among the second-generation than later-generation Mexican Americans, and among Mexican American boys than girls.[40]

First-generation cultural repertoires reflecting social-insurance imperatives may also affect second-generation daughters. The female children of Mexican immigrants often grow up in highly protective environments.[41] Although this emphasis partly reflects traditional gender roles, it can also reasonably be interpreted as derived from and buttressed by migration. Strong protection of girls constitutes a means of strengthening daughters' loyalty to parents and family, increasing the likelihood they marry well and are better able to care for elderly parents. Such tendencies can also have ironic consequences. Research shows that such protectiveness, which allows girls to attend chaperoned extracurricular school activities but not other nonchaperoned activities outside the home, exposes them relatively more to teachers and educational activities and options than their brothers so encounter. They thus become more familiar with the U.S. education system, devote more time to schoolwork, learn more about postsecondary educational opportunities, and—like American girls as a whole—are more likely to attend some form of college than boys.[42]

Strong family- and migration-related cultural repertoires among first-generation Mexican immigrants thus affect boys and girls differently. The emphasis on the necessity of working falls disproportionately on boys.[43] Given the poverty of many unauthorized Mexican immigrants, and given that males earn more than females,[44] pressuring sons to join the workforce at an early age represents a social-insurance strategy for supplementing household income. Not every son will feel obligated to work as early as possible, of course, but the tendency is likely to occur often enough to make a difference. Thus we would expect the sons more than the daughters of unauthorized migrants to show stronger initial effects of migration status on indicators of structural integration. Specifically, we would expect the sons of immigrants more than the daughters to obtain less education when their parents are unauthorized. Although second-generation girls may start some form of college more often than boys, many may also cohabit or marry and quickly have children, which then limits their further education. But in general, all else being equal, both Mexican immigrants and U.S.-born Mexican American girls encounter a society that for nearly four decades has been characterized by women more rapidly increasing their levels of schooling over time than men.[45] Thus we would expect females to evince a steeper upward pattern of increasing education compared with males.

More than one kind of dynamic may also limit education increases to a greater degree among males relative to females across generations. One would be the dampening effects of ethnoracial prejudice and discrimination, which plausibly may fall more heavily on minority males than females.[46] Another might be working-class delay, which, when combined with residues of cultural expectation that encourage males to forgo higher education to work to support their families, may limit levels of educational attainment even in the third generation. Clues about which of these might be exerting the stronger influence may lie in income patterns. If the forces of prejudice and discrimination are the main limiters of attainment, both education and income should be about the same for third-generation males as for the second generation. But if working-class delay is the stronger force, we might see higher incomes among third-generation males than second-generation males even without much change in their education levels. That is to say, unless discrimination across generations precludes third-generation Mexican American males from becoming more familiar with American job opportunities and finding higher-paying working-class jobs, the third generation might earn higher incomes than the second-generation even while showing little difference in education.

Social and Cultural Capital Effects

Although both membership exclusion and other theoretical perspectives may help to explain cross-generational patterns of Mexican American integration, other approaches may also be relevant. Specifically, the perspective on selective acculturation (here termed also ethnic advantage) highlights the importance of coethnic social and cultural capital for mobility. This perspective seems relevant because the same cultural repertoires leading to employment strategies that minimize risk and emphasize hard work are reinforced by social capital and are likely to operate more strongly under certain family circumstances than others. Considerable research shows that Mexican immigrant families evince obligations to family by spending time with family members, sharing with siblings, helping with chores, respecting elders, and even staying in school.[47] Such tendencies contribute to cultural repertoires that encourage children's and grandchildren's high achievement, in part through exhortations to work hard to compensate for the immigrant generation's sacrifices.

Familial support for achievement among the children of immigrants thus seems likely to be stronger the greater the generational ethnic density of the family. That is, in the second generation, if both immigrant parents, rather than only one, were born in Mexico, or if in the third generation all four grandparents, rather than only one or two, were born in Mexico, then it seems reasonable to think that stronger pressures might emerge in the second and third generations, respectively, to work hard, whatever particular form that might take. In other words, ethnic density in the immediate family network may reinforce the importance of strong efforts to make something of oneself in order to compensate the sacrifices of the migrant generation, a common theme in Mexican American culture.[48]

This suggests the hypothesis that second-generation respondents with two parents who were born in Mexico and third-generation respondents with four grandparents who were born in Mexico will show even higher degrees of structural integration compared with Mexican Americans with less ethnically dense family backgrounds.[49]

Specific Research Hypotheses

Our theoretical and empirical investigations of integration's dimensionality presented in the previous chapter indicated two structural dimensions—economic and spatial—that would be expected to reflect the influence of unauthorized migration status background (here we treat linguistic integration as primarily a sociocultural indicator, which we examine in chapter 7). As previously noted, membership-exclusion considerations would lead to the expectation that sociocultural integration would increase across generations but not generally be limited by unauthorized background. We also theorized that membership exclusion would involve individual variation with respect to sociocultural aspects of integration. Thus we expect sociocultural indicators not to bundle together into a single dimension. In fact, when we examine this empirically, no multiple-indicator components emerge for sociocultural indicators in principal components analyses (these results are reported in appendix B), as would be expected by an individualistic-pluralist theoretical approach. This suggests that individuals, not just groups, are characterized by heterogeneous profiles with respect to sociocultural phenomena.

Membership exclusion thus would predict only limited structural integration among the sons of unauthorized Mexican immigrants, including those sons who are U.S.-born (that is, among the members of the second generation). Greater cross-generation mobility would be expected among the daughters of unauthorized immigrants, with even higher levels among females up to and including the third generation (that is, the grandchildren of the immigrants). Those members of the second and third generations whose grandparents were not unauthorized would benefit from their families' having started from higher positions, so on average they would be more likely to achieve socioeconomic parity with mainstream whites by the third generation. On the other hand, even though a notable increase might also occur between the second and third generations among girls whose grandparents stayed unauthorized, this may be insufficient to raise their overall position to parity with mainstream whites. Whatever the case, we suggest that full integration of Mexican Americans is contingent on the legal membership status of the first generation. Without such membership, integration falls short; with it, integration can proceed.

Membership exclusion also implies that the effects of unauthorized background on immigrants and their children will not depend solely on unauthorized entry but rather also on the trajectory of migration status. That is, those who migrate in an unauthorized status may largely stop experiencing the debilitating effects of unauthorized status when they become legal permanent residents. Thus the elimination of unauthorized status may forestall the scarring of immigrant families with the effects of disadvantage that accumulate well beyond the point of legalization.[50] Life-course theoretical approaches would conceptualize the cessation of unauthorized status as a turning point that represents the beginning of increasing cumulative advantage.[51] As here conceptualized, the membership-exclusion approach explicitly posits that legalization constitutes a significant life-course turning point that breaks the force of disadvantage, with doors to opportunity increasingly opening from that point on. Insofar as migration-status trajectories are concerned, membership exclusion would thus expect that the children of immigrants whose parents came as unauthorized entrants and who then subsequently legalized to exhibit greater structural integration than those whose parents came as unauthorized entrants, but remained unauthorized. Although greater pressures on males than on females to work in the 1.5 and 2.0 generations would suggest initially smaller intergenerational gains for males, those males and females whose parents or grandparents legalized should show similar degrees of mobility from the second to the third generation, all else being equal.

Methodological Issues

Before moving on to the results of the analyses that assess these ideas, it is important to address several crucial methodological issues concerning the measurement of key integration indicators or other factors that can cloud the interpretation of research results on integration, especially in the case of Mexican Americans. Each of these can influence conclusions about integration. We also need to make clear how we deal with these. The most relevant are the issue of defining integration and specifying an appropriate comparison group given that definition; the problem of generation-cohort heterogeneity; the question of cross-generational versus intergenerational measures of difference or mobility; the problem of measurement error in third-generation classifications of Mexican Americans; the need to make comparison groups similar on factors that affect incorporation; and the need to take geographic differences in historical discrimination and selective ethnic attrition into account in measuring and interpreting integration indicators.

Defining Appropriate Comparison Groups

In drawing conclusions about immigrant-group integration, it is important to specify what the most appropriate comparison group is. This is in part a theoretical issue. Perhaps the most basic decision integration researchers must make involves whether to examine the experiences of immigrants, including unauthorized migrants, in comparison with the situations of people in the country of destination or in the country of origin.[52] Because the very concept of incorporation (or assimilation or integration) is framed in terms of country-of-destination dynamics, comparisons of interest are usually made between immigrants and others in the destination society. If the United States is the destination country, this could mean asking any of several questions: To what extent are immigrants like natives in general, like native coethnics, like native majority-group members, or like native members of minority groups?

But if the research focuses on reasons for leaving an origin country (as might be the case if one were examining how economic development influences emigration), then the comparison group might instead be those left behind in the origin country, either when the migrant group leaves or after some time away. For example, research could show that Mexican immigrants see themselves as not doing well in the United States relative to native-born Americans but as still faring better than nonmigrants in Mexico. Having an ill-paying job in the United States may be seen as better than having no job in Mexico. Some researchers term the process of becoming less like those who stayed in the origin country "dissimilation" because it involves ever-growing dissimilarities over time between emigrants and natives of the origin country.[53]

Comparisons of groups within the United States are also more relevant to assessing some theoretical perspectives than others. For example, a classical assimilation perspective implies that immigrants and native whites converge with one another.[54] This perspective suggests focusing on comparisons of later-generation immigrant-group members with later-generation whites, whereas an assimilation-as-intergenerational process perspective implies that the later-generation members of the immigrant group do considerably better than the early-generation members even if full convergence with whites is not yet complete. This would suggest comparisons among the first, second, and third generations.[55] Similarly, a segmented-assimilation perspective would imply that at least some members of the immigrant group become like the most disadvantaged native minority group (which suggests a comparison of third-or-later-generation immigrants with third-or-later-generation African Americans).[56] Thus the kind of comparisons researchers make can lead them to different conclusions about the degree of integration. Here we focus explicitly on multigenerational dynamics to make assessments of the classical intergenerational assimilation and membership exclusion hypotheses (that is, we compare Mexican-origin generations with one another and we compare the Mexican-origin third generation with third-or-later-generation whites).

The Problem of Generation-Cohort Heterogeneity

Because Mexicans have migrated continuously to the United States for at least a century, generational groups may contain different birth cohorts, or birth cohort heterogeneity within generational groups. As Tomás Jiménez and David FitzGerald note, "Using only generation as a temporal marker of assimilation is not enough. Each generation of Mexican-origin individuals is made of people from a mix of birth cohorts, and each birth cohort contains individuals from many immigrant generations."[57] And, in particular, different birth cohorts in the first generation may be heterogeneous with respect to important factors affecting integration. Thus a cross-section of the first generation may include persons who were born a long time ago and who came to the United States some time ago, along with persons who are younger or came more recently.[58] The older (and earlier) cohorts include people from Mexico who came at a time when the extent of education in that country was very low (less than six years), and thus their schooling levels are low. Those coming more recently, though they have little education by U.S. standards, have higher schooling levels (around ten years). The average for the first generation will thus reflect the generation's mix of birth cohorts. Another example involves looking at the first generation by the length of time its members have been in the country. This can appear to show that integration varies positively with age, whereas in fact this variation owes to differences in birth cohort composition within the generation. We see an example of this in the next chapter. Two ways to help overcome this problem consist of controlling for age or making generational comparisons within relatively narrow age ranges, both of which we do here.

Cross-Generational versus Historical-Family-Generational Confusion

We also need to clarify our use of terminology in regard to generation and note what our cross-generation measures capture and what they may not. The term *generation* is often used to refer to two different concepts. Following Telles and Ortiz, we use the term *historical-family-generation* when we are speaking of kin lineages.[59] Thus comparisons between children and their biological parents and grandparents yield mobility information for individuals across time for family generations. An example would be comparisons between the education of an individual and the education of that person's parents. Such measures reflect intergenerational mobility since they show actual change within one's own family. In contrast, we use the term *immigration-generation,* or *cross-generational difference,* when speaking of the generational time elapsed since either the individual's or his or her family's migration. In this framework, those who themselves are immigrants are referred to as first-generation persons, those who are the children of parents who were immigrants as second-generation persons, and those who are the grandchildren of those who were immigrants as third generation.[60] Comparisons made across immigrant generations using cross-sectional survey data can examine, for example, the education levels of first-generation respondents relative to those of second-generation respondents, and those of the second generation relative to those of the third generation and so forth. Because such measures reflect cross-generational differences at a given point in time, not individual change within a family lineage, we refer to them as cross-generational differences.

The immigrants from various European countries coming to the United States in large numbers during the early part of the twentieth century almost entirely stopped coming in 1924. This cessation lasted for nearly half a century because of the changes in U.S. immigration policy, followed by the Great Depression and World War II. This stoppage creates the fortunate consequence that examination of the average characteristics of first-, second-, and third-generation Americans from Eastern and Southern European origins using 1970 U.S. census data yields cross-generation results closely approximating family-generation mobility. Almost all the first-generation persons in the data would have come in the first two decades of the twentieth century and would have been aged fifty or older. Those in the second generation, the children of those in the first generation, would have been, on average, between twenty and fifty (allowing thirty years for each generation). Those in the third generation would have been mostly their grandchildren. This is less the case among Mexican immigrants, however, who have been coming to the United States continuously for more than a century and in notably large numbers since at least the beginning of World War II, when the Bracero Program began.[61] The implications for studies that make cross-generation comparisons are discussed later in this chapter.

This matter is similar in certain respects to the first issue, though it does not raise a question about whether capturing the process of integration (for example, as indicated by intergenerational differences between parents and their children within the immigrant ethnic group) reflects integration just as much as does the final result (for example, closing the gap between the advanced generation and an appropriate mainstream society group like non-Hispanic whites). Rather, it raises the question of whether mobility achieved across immigration generations reflects as much as mobility between family generations. As a practical matter, studies of assimilation as intragenerational mobility have almost entirely been conducted within the first generation (that is, on the immigrants themselves) rather than within the second, third, or later generations. To the extent that the indicator of integration being measured consists of something that has been changing over time in a secular sense (that is, for everyone, as would be the case if one were studying, say, income in a country experiencing an extended economic surge), the measures of intragenerational and intergenerational growth could be highly conflated. But to our knowledge no such long-term longitudinal studies have ever been carried out because appropriate data have not been available (that is, data following those within a generation for long enough—twenty-five to thirty years—to be equivalent to the length of a generation or the rough time between generations). Partial exceptions may be James Smith's aggregate cross-sectional time series investigations that provide an approximation of such generations or Telles and Ortiz's follow-up of a study from the 1960s.[62]

These issues are relevant for the present research in a particular way. We examine in the next chapter the degree to which having unauthorized parents who stay unauthorized after migrating affects the schooling of the second generation. That is, based on the data we collected on young adult second-generation respondents in 2004, we assess how much unauthorized status among parents who migrated anywhere from twenty to fifty or more years ago limited their children's education. This limitation derives from the degree to which such status stigmatized their parents and curtailed their access to structural opportunities then. Things may be different now. Although this is true, the significantly harsher climate facing unauthorized Mexican migrants today seems likely to be generating even stronger negative effects on migrants and their children now than was true some decades ago. Hence in estimating unauthorization effects based on dynamics occurring decades ago, we are probably underestimating how large they are now.

The Problem of Selective Attrition

Making multigenerational comparisons also requires dealing with selectivity. Taking schooling as an example, from the second to later generations, the education trajectory among the descendants of Mexican immigrants can yield ambiguous results. Numerous cross-sectional studies have shown little difference in educational attainment between second- and third-plus-generation Mexican Americans.[63] Others have found notable and sometimes significantly lower educational attainment for third-plus-generation Mexican Americans (or Latinos) compared with second-generation Mexican Americans.[64] Moreover, lower attainment of the third-plus generation compared with the second generation has also often emerged for groups that are non-Hispanic,[65] suggesting that this particular kind of problem is not unique to the Mexican case. Whatever its causes, that this pattern has also occurred for other groups than Mexicans implies that the seeming stagnation of educational attainment between second- and third-plus-generation Mexican Americans may not result from contemporary disadvantage dynamics alone.

Ambiguity in the findings of cross-sectional studies may thus occur because of the aggregation of the third or later generations. As a result, the third-plus-generational measures typically available in national level data include fourth, fifth, sixth, and even later generations, which are quite subject to selective attrition, especially by education. Such selectivity will bias downward the observed educational attainments of later-generation Mexican-origin persons. Because information on birthplace of grandparents is required to isolate the third generation, it is rare to be able to distinguish a true third, or third-only, generation (which we here define as consisting of those with at least one Mexican-born grandparent) from later generations (consisting of those whose grandparents were all born in the United States). One study that has made such a distinction used General Social Survey data from 1972 to 2002.[66] When these surveys were examined cross-sectionally, only a slightly higher level of educational attainment emerged for third-plus-generation Mexican Americans compared with the second generation. But when the education of respondents was directly compared with that of their own parents, the data indicated substantially greater increases in education for whites and for Mexican Americans, whose parents' education was particularly low. Most crucially, when this study directly examined the education difference that emerged based on using a third-only measure compared with a third-plus measure, the third-only generation was found to have attained more education than the third-plus group.

It is likely that third-only-generation results, such as those we report here based on the Immigration and Intergenerational Mobility in Metropolitan Los Angeles (IIMMLA) data, are less biased by such selective attrition because the grandchildren of immigrants (as opposed to the great-grandchildren or the great-great-grandchildren, and so on) will have had less time to lose their ethnic identity. They are also likely to know the birthplace of their grandparents. In the IIMMLA sample, respondents in the pool of third-generation Mexican Americans were chosen on the basis of either self-identity or having one or more grandparents born in Mexico, not only self-identification. These data show a deficit of −0.4 years of school for third-plus-generation males compared with third-only males (see table 3.1). For females, a similar deficit emerged. In sum, when researchers have no alternative than to rely on third-plus measures, as is the case with research using Current Population Survey data, assessments of the third-plus generation education gap in relation to non-Hispanic whites are biased. Moreover, as a percentage of the gap between the third generation and non-Hispanic whites, a deficit of −0.4 years can constitute a substantial part of the difference. Similarly, calculations of education gain from the second to the third-plus generation

Table 3.1   **Average Years-of-Schooling Deficits for Third-Plus and Third-Only Measures of Generation, Males and Females of Mexican Origin, Aged Twenty to Forty, Los Angeles, 2004**

	Generation Measure		
Gender	Third Plus	Third Only	Deficit
Males	13.1	13.5	−0.4
Females	13.4	13.8	−0.4

Source: Data from Immigration and Intergenerational Mobility in Metropolitan Los Angeles (see Bean, Leach et al. 2011).

substantially understate percentage advancements in schooling. We deal with this problem in the present research by examining third-only-generation groups for males and females separately.

What accounts for the distortion? Recent research suggests it results mostly from selective attrition. Errors in defining the Mexican-origin group become more numerous the more generations are included since immigration. Any sampling frame that depends on ethnic self-identification for inclusion in the sample misses those people who no longer identify as either Hispanic or Mexican. This is particularly true for people with only one or two Mexican-born grandparents. For example, nearly 30 percent of the third-generation children of Mexican-origin parents are not identified as Mexican under the Hispanic question in the Current Population Survey.[67] In a separate study of U.S. censuses from 1980 to 2000, Richard Alba and Tariqul Islam also find substantial apparent attrition from the Mexican-origin group.[68] Moreover, those who no longer identify as Mexican appear to be highly selected among those whose parents have out-married. Not only is out-marriage fairly commonplace among Mexican Americans, but it occurs more often among the more highly educated.[69] Selective attrition thus produces substantial downward bias in measures of socioeconomic attainment in samples selected on the basis of ethnic self-identification.

Making the Reference Group Comparable

A final issue to consider involves making the reference group (the one being compared with an immigrant generational group for purposes of gauging the degree of incorporation) comparable to the immigrant group in terms of differences in other factors that could affect the education levels of the two groups. In national-level studies, this can be achieved through multivariate analyses employing appropriate controls if the study includes measures of all relevant factors that matter. In other instances, this may be more difficult. For example, because their economies involve sectors that rely heavily on technology and knowledge, Los Angeles, along with New York and several other major metropolises in the country, attracts disproportionate numbers of college graduates and experiences out-migration of persons with only high school diplomas or less (the latter for cost-of-living reasons if nothing else). Moreover, this selective migration occurs to a greater relative degree among non-Hispanic whites than among the Mexican-origin population, because the former group contains a higher proportion of college graduates. Stated differently, selective in-migration among educated whites and out-migration among less-educated whites in Los Angeles could mean that the gap in educational attainment between whites and Mexican Americans will substantially exceed this same education gap in the rest of the country. For example, among males, the schooling gap between whites and Mexican Americans is 1.9 years in Los Angeles versus only 1.2 years for the rest of the country. One way to adjust roughly for such distortions is to examine a difference-in-difference estimator, obtained by subtracting from non-Hispanic white levels the average net differential between Los Angeles and the rest of the country for both men and women.

Taking Geography into Account

Adult members of today's third and later generations of the Mexican American population are the grandchildren of first-, second-, and third-generation immigrants who came of age in the United States well before the civil rights era.[70] This is crucial on several fronts. First, the forebears of today's third-plus generation were in their schooling years at a time when the American public school system was less developed than it is today and when there existed substantial regional variation in the development and formalization of this system.[71] This means that the public school system overall was less capable of meeting one of its fundamental motivating objectives: ensuring equality of educational opportunity, especially in southern states, including Texas, where the majority of the Mexican-origin population was concentrated before 1960 and where the development and formalization of a public schooling apparatus was particularly slow to develop.[72]

Almost universally, educational orientations and attainments among children are determined in large part by those of their parents.[73] The education legacy inherited by third-plus-generation Mexican Americans was forged at a time when strong, equality-promoting institutions that might counterbalance the virulent racism endured by Mexicans in Texas especially were largely absent. Access to education was especially limited for Mexican-origin children residing in Texas during the first half of the twentieth century.[74] The Progressive movement, which sought the Americanization of the nation's diverse immigrant ethnic groups through increases in public school enrollment, was influential and intertwined with the rapid development and formalization of public schooling in northeastern and midwestern states as well as in California.[75] Progressives, however, had little influence in southern states, including Texas, which were, as a result, far slower to develop a formalized public school system.

In 1940, 41 percent of the nation's 512,000 school-age U.S.-born Mexican-origin children resided in Texas. At that time, the second largest concentration, 27 percent, lived in California. Recent work by James Bachmeier suggests that today's third-plus-generation Mexican-origin population has inherited a disadvantaged education legacy growing out of their grandparents' experiences in Texas.[76] He finds that among U.S.-born Mexican-origin women aged thirty-five to forty-seven in 1970, those born in Texas averaged just 6.8 years of schooling, a mere half year of schooling more than similarly aged Mexican immigrant women (6.3 years). By contrast, their Mexican-origin peers born in California averaged 9.7 years of schooling. Moreover, Bachmeier finds that fertility among Texas-born Mexican-origin women was substantially higher than among similarly aged Mexican immigrant women (5.6 births per woman among Texas-born Mexican American women compared with 5.1 births among Mexican immigrants). Thus a disproportionate share of today's nationwide third-plus generation traces its U.S. origins to Texas-born grandparents whose educational attainments barely surpassed those of Mexican immigrants. The implication is that the education legacy passed down to the third-plus-generation Mexican-origin population was shaped by historical and regional forces that are largely absent from the contexts of reception for today's Mexican immigrants and their children. Such legacy effects must be considered when interpreting cross-sectional comparisons in Mexican American educational attainment across immigrant generations because, unlike nearly every other contemporary immigrant group in the United States, large portions of the Mexican-origin population have been subjected to historical forces that predate the civil rights era.

Finally, the IIMMLA sample and other Mexican American data sets are most likely affected by these historical forces, which have presented particular education disadvantages for Mexican Americans residing in Texas. Beginning in about 1960, California became the preferred destination for immigrants from Mexico, and the state also experienced considerable inflows of Texas-born Mexican Americans. In 1970 census data, in which it is possible to observe the third-plus generation, 15 percent of adult third-and-later-generation Mexican Americans residing in California were born in Texas, a number that probably increased after 1970. Thus while it is not possible to determine which members of the third-only or the fourth-plus generations in the IIMMLA data trace their origins to Texas, a similar drag effect on the educational attainment of this group may be present in the IIMMLA sample. This needs to be kept in mind when interpreting our results.

To demonstrate further how large the effect of selective attrition and other factors may be in biasing the results of studies relying on third-plus-generation measures, we report in appendix C the results of a simulation study that assessed the degree of the bias. The results from the simulation exercise provide substantial empirical support for the notion that third-plus-generation educational attainment among Mexican Americans is appreciably affected by a pre–civil rights era historical legacy in Texas, demographic change, and ethnic attrition processes that unfold as more highly educated members of the population intermarry and their offspring no longer report Mexican ancestry in survey data. Today's second generation of Mexican origin comes of age within an education system that, while still imperfect, offers considerably more in education opportunity than that available to the grandparents of the third-and later-generation Mexican Americans, who were concentrated largely in Texas. Moreover, the educational attainment of the second generation is practically unaffected by ethnic attrition, as nearly all members of the second-generation identify as Mexican or Mexican American. Because the education profile of the third-plus generation is pulled down by its Texas legacy, demographic change, and selective ethnic attrition, extreme caution in inferring the extent of contemporary integration from third-plus-generation data is warranted.

Conclusions

We expect the membership-exclusion theoretical perspective to help explain what appears to be low structural mobility and integration for the children of Mexican immigrants. Focusing on educational attainment in particular, we anticipate that the schooling of those children of immigrants who have unauthorized parents who stay unauthorized will be decidedly lower than the attainment of those children of Mexican immigrants who have parents who legalized. We also expect an initial deficit (for first-generation persons) to emerge more strongly for females than for males but that this gender pattern will reverse in the second generation. In addition, we expect what might be called a selective acculturation effect associated with high ethnic density in the immediate ancestral family. That is, in our three-generation cases, we expect those children and grandchildren of Mexican immigrants with more homogeneous Mexican backgrounds (with parents or grandparents all born in Mexico) to show greater mobility (for example, higher educational attainment) than those without such homogeneous backgrounds. Moreover, we expect this pattern to emerge more strongly for females because their gender role socialization tends more to emphasize sociocultural loyalty to family, thus imparting a stronger impetus for them to compensate in their own lives for the sacrifices their parents or grandparents made in coming to the United States. Finally, we also expect a steady upward integration effect on sociocultural indicators across generations. We suggest such a pattern reflects individual pluralism as much as group pluralism because of the multidimensionality among sociocultural indicators we observed in principal components analyses (see chapter 2 and appendix B). That is, the facets of sociocultural incorporation tended not to correlate highly with one another, thus reflecting more the expectations of a pluralist-based postindustrial-individualistic theoretical model of integration compared with assimilation or multicultural models.

Also, to assess the hypothesis of membership exclusion compared with other hypotheses, it is necessary to examine differences between late-generation Mexican Americans and Anglos. Following the discussion presented in this chapter about the heterogeneity and likely distorting effects of attrition in so-called third-plus-generation data, we take advantage of the fact that we can isolate a clear-cut third-only generation in the IIMMLA data. Our comparisons thus concentrate on examining educational attainment and other integration measures for young adults (age twenty to forty) in Los Angeles who are the children of Mexican immigrants (the first generation) and for two groups of Mexican Americans: the second generation, including some who migrated to the United States as young children, and the third-only generation. Our comparisons here of third-only and third-plus Mexican Americans suggest that the education levels of the latter are biased downward by about 4 to 5 percent, an amount consistent with the results of the historical demographic projections showing that the degree to which the proportion of Mexican Americans today with high school educations or more is biased downward because of attrition. In chapter 5, we estimate in the aggregate the lingering depressive effects on the educational attainment of the third generation after removing the effects of some of them having had unauthorized grandparents. This enables us to approximate what would happen to education outcomes for the second and third-only generations were unauthorized Mexican immigrants able to legalize.

═ Chapter 4 ═

The Implications of Unauthorized Migration for the Schooling of Immigrants and Their Offspring

For both theoretical and empirical reasons, economic factors constitute one of the main dimensions of integration, as discussed in chapter 2. And such factors are often seen as the first priority for social-scientific assessment of incorporation.[1] Policy analysts and lawmakers considering changes in immigration policy are particularly interested in learning how well immigrants and their offspring are faring in regard to education and earnings, often seen as the key aspects of structural integration.[2] It is thus appropriate to start our empirical analyses of economic integration with a focus on these important labor-market outcomes. Because our ultimate objective, for reasons noted in the previous chapter, is to assess overall Mexican American integration comprehensively and completely, we examine such measures through the third generation in the next chapter. But before we can analyze mobility into the third generation, we must assess whether and to what degree unauthorized migration status affects Mexican immigrants themselves and then, in turn, whether and how much unauthorized status and its change after immigration to the United States affect the children of Mexican migrants.

This chapter thus looks at the implications for labor-market indicators of being unauthorized, both for Mexican immigrants and for their adult offspring. In the case of the immigrants, however, because they obtain little schooling after they migrate, we first assess relationships between their migration status and a wider array of selected labor-market indicators using national-level data. This provides a broader picture of the employment-related disadvantages facing unauthorized immigrants (and by extension their offspring). When we turn to the case of the adult children of immigrants (the second generation), owing to schooling's crucial role in affecting mobility, we concentrate only on how and how much coming from a family with unauthorized status in its background affects educational attainment.[3] This requires that we use the IIMMLA data set because it contains information on parental legal status.

In the next chapter, we shift from two- to three-generational analyses of education and income for Mexican Americans. Differences in education have repeatedly been found to account for almost all of the income gap between later-generation Mexican Americans and majority whites, findings that contrast with the results of comparable research on U.S. African American males, for whom a large earnings residual remains after taking black-white education differences into account.[4] Such patterns are incompatible with the idea that U.S.-born Mexican Americans have confronted (at least in recent decades) as much negative discrimination in the labor market as blacks with respect to employment and earnings. However, Mexican Americans, especially immigrants, may face discrimination in schooling, which constitutes another reason for emphasizing education in this and the next chapter.[5]

To begin to address the impacts of legal status on Mexican-immigrant human capital and labor-market outcomes, we first review the findings of past research. Then we examine results from our own analyses of recent data on the relationship between unauthorized status and the labor-market positions of first-generation Mexican Americans compared with those of legal permanent residents (LPRs), naturalized citizens, and all U.S.-born workers. To accomplish this, we use multiple-imputation techniques to develop measures of migration status for the Mexican born in the 2012 American Community Survey.[6] Then, to estimate the magnitude of the effects of unauthorized status on children's schooling (including that of U.S.-born offspring), we present the results of research using data from the Immigration and Intergenerational Mobility in Metropolitan Los Angeles (IIMMLA) survey to assess how much parents' unauthorized migration status handicaps the educational attainment of the children of Mexican immigrants. One of the major benefits of these analyses is that they help ascertain whether membership-exclusion or disadvantage dynamics (including racialization) better account for slow integration among Mexican Americans. They thus enable us to assess the role that actual legalization trajectories, and the important life-course turning points they represent, play in affecting educational attainment as opposed to more continuous and enduring cumulative-disadvantage processes. As we show below, the results are more compatible with the turning-point hypothesis.

Research on Immigrants

Various small-scale surveys and qualitative studies suggest that unauthorized migration is associated with diminished cognitive and socio-emotional development among children,[7] implying that their parents endure considerable hardship and insecurity in the labor market. Also, previous research using data for migrants who have returned to Mexico after coming to the United States confirms inferior labor-market outcomes for those who are unauthorized migrants compared with those who are legal.[8] Only limited up-to-date empirical evidence from large U.S. data sets exists, however, for the education and labor-market disadvantages of unauthorized Mexican migrants, mostly owing to a dearth of survey information on immigrants' legal status.[9] Moreover, the majority of studies on legal status and earnings use data collected before 2000 and thus do not reflect what today's situation might look like.

Studies of unauthorized immigrants who legalized under the provisions of the 1986 Immigration Reform and Control Act (IRCA), however, although somewhat dated, provide useful information on this subject. This body of work suggests that immigrants who were able to adjust their status experienced significant wage increases as a result. Using Legalized Population Survey (LPS) data, for example, a panel study of a representative sample of IRCA adjustees found that the earnings penalty associated with unauthorized status ranged from 14 to 24 percent.[10] George Borjas and Marta Tienda observed an even larger wage deficit of 30 percent in their analyses of administrative data of IRCA legalization applications pooled with data from the 1983, 1986, and 1989 samples of the Current Population Survey.[11] And in another analysis of the LPS data, Francisco Rivera-Batiz calculated a 40 percent hourly wage disadvantage associated with unauthorized status, with differences in human capital and other characteristics explaining only between 43 and 48 percent of this gap.[12]

A number of additional studies have been conducted using data from the Mexican Migration Project (MMP), a community-based sample of Mexican migrants to the United States, the overwhelming majority of whom have been interviewed on their return to Mexico. Using MMP data from 1982 to 1983, Massey found no significant wage penalty associated directly with unauthorized status.[13] However, Massey and colleagues suggest on the basis of several post-IRCA MMP-based studies that the penalty associated with unauthorized status in the U.S. labor market has increased since IRCA because the hiring of undocumented workers became illegal and federal enforcement efforts increased after the law was enacted.[14] After accounting for other determinants of earnings, Katharine Donato and Douglas Massey observed a significant wage penalty of 19 percent among unauthorized migrants in the MMP sample but only among those whose trips to the United States occurred after 1986.[15] Net of other explanatory variables, the same study also found that post-1986 unauthorized Mexican migrants were significantly more likely than migrants with legal documents to be paid below the minimum wage, a finding that does not hold for migrants making U.S. trips before IRCA. Massey and Kerstin Gentsch also estimated in regression models of logged wages earned by Mexican migrants to the U.S. between 1970 and 2009 that unauthorized migrants incur a net wage penalty of about 20 percent relative to those with documents.[16]

To our knowledge, only one study has examined the association between legal status and earnings among Mexican immigrants using nationally representative survey data. Using the 1996 and 2001 panels of the Survey of Income and Program Participation (SIPP), Matthew Hall, Emily Greenman, and George Farkas observed that the average hourly wage for unauthorized Mexican immigrant men was 17 percent lower than that of their legally resident male counterparts and that this gap declined to 8 percent when accounting for differences in human capital, and other characteristics associated with earnings.[17] The corresponding wage penalty associated with unauthorized status among Mexican immigrant women was 9 percent (unadjusted) and 4 percent (adjusted). Their analyses also found that undocumented immigrant men show significantly lower earnings returns to educational attainment.

To summarize, estimates of the association between immigrants' legal status and earnings vary widely depending on the source of data and period of data collection. The estimated adjusted wage penalty associated with unauthorized status tends to be relatively large in studies of immigrants who legalized under the provisions of IRCA in 1986, which range from 14 to 40 percent.[18] Studies using MMP data tend to place the post-IRCA unauthorized wage penalty at around 20 percent.[19] And while Hall, Greenman, and Farkas also find significant net wage penalties associated with unauthorized status, these penalties are more modest than those found in previous studies, at 8 and 4 percent among Mexican immigrant men and women, respectively.[20]

As we have noted, empirical estimates of the association between unauthorized status and immigrants' earnings are limited in several ways. Legalized Population Survey data are now more than two decades old and are representative only of unauthorized immigrants who legalized through IRCA. This population was heavily concentrated in the Southwest, was disproportionately male, consisted of large numbers of agricultural workers, and was made up disproportionately of Mexican immigrants from the traditional sending region of West Central Mexico.[21] Since IRCA, Mexican immigrants have dispersed considerably to non-traditional receiving states in the United States.[22] At the same time, unauthorized immigrants from Mexico increasingly originate in non-traditional sending regions within Mexico.[23] Also, more recently, the unauthorized immigrant female population has grown[24] and the share of Mexican unauthorized immigrants working in agricultural occupations has declined.[25] As a result of these changing patterns of unauthorized migration, studies based on the Legalized Population Survey may not be instructive for drawing inferences about the current association between legal status and the earnings of immigrants.

Similar concerns attend research based on MMP data. Earnings analyses using MMP data are based overwhelmingly on the reports of legal and unauthorized immigrants who have returned to Mexico after trips to the United States. Post-IRCA border enforcement appears to have disrupted circular flows of unauthorized migration, which in turn has caused unauthorized migrants to settle permanently more often in the United States.[26] This raises important questions about the degree to which returnees are comparable to Mexican immigrants residing in the United States and, in turn, the extent to which estimates of the association between legal status and earnings among returnees can be generalized to the population of Mexican immigrants in the United States. Finally, the wage analyses of Hall, Greenman, and Farkas are based on nationally representative data of Mexican immigrants working in the United States during the late 1990s and early years of the twenty-first century.[27] Because these data were collected during a period of robust economic growth and before the deep economic recession that began in 2008, their estimates of unauthorized wage penalties may not apply to the postrecession wages of Mexican immigrants.

Here we examine the association between legal status and the earnings of Mexican immigrants using 2012 American Community Survey data. While the survey does not collect information on immigrants' legal status, we employ recently developed methodological strategies for imputing the legal status of noncitizens to estimate zero-order and adjusted differences in wages, by legal status and citizenship.[28] Van Hook et al. have demonstrated that the imputation method, which uses nationally representative data collected in 2009 to impute the legal status of noncitizens in the 2012 American Community Survey, produces unbiased estimates of the association between legal status and a given outcome as long as certain conditions are met. The methodology of the imputation strategy is described in detail elsewhere.[29]

We limit our comparisons to Mexican immigrants arriving in the United States after the age of fourteen (the 1.0 generation), who are much less likely ever to enroll in U.S. schools as their dominant motive for migrating is to seek employment.[30] Because such migrants are more likely to complete all of their education in Mexico, one might reasonably assume that their legal status in the United States is unrelated to the amount of education obtained in Mexico, a key determinant of earnings and other labor-market outcomes, and as a result, we can conclude with greater certainty that legal-status differences in labor-market outcomes derive from legal status as opposed to other factors.[31]

The characteristics of unauthorized, legally resident noncitizen and naturalized Mexican immigrant adult (aged twenty-five to sixty-four) men and women are presented in table 4.1. Unauthorized immigrants average four years younger than their legal noncitizen counterparts, who

Table 4.1   Descriptive Characteristics of Mexican Immigrants in the United States, Aged Twenty-five to Sixty-four, by Gender, Citizenship, and Imputed Legal Status, 2012 (percentage)

Variable	Unauthorized		Legal Noncitizens		Naturalized Citizens	
	Men	Women	Men	Women	Men	Women
Mean age	38.3	39.4	42.5	43.2	48.2	48.0
Mean age-squared	1,547.2	1,630.4	1,908.8	1,962.3	2,402.1	2,390.5
Birth-cohort distribution (percentage)						
1978 to 1987	38.4	34.3	24.2	21.5	8.8	9.6
1968 to 1977	38.3	39.0	35.4	35.7	24.9	27.0
1958 to 1967	17.4	19.4	25.6	27.0	38.8	34.6
1948 to 1957	5.9	7.3	14.8	15.8	27.4	28.8
Mean years in the United States	13.7	13.6	19.2	17.9	25.7	25.0
English-language proficiency (percentage)						
Speaks only English	2.8	2.7	2.4	2.5	3.7	4.4
Speaks English very well	10.9	7.4	17.3	10.4	29.2	26.2
Speaks English well	24.3	15.7	28.7	18.5	38.8	31.9
Speaks English, but not well	40.3	42.0	35.9	40.3	23.5	29.8
Does not speak English	21.6	32.1	15.6	28.4	4.8	7.8
Mean years of schooling completed[a]	8.5	8.4	8.8	8.8	10.8	11.3

Source: Data from 2012 American Community Survey (Ruggles et al. 2010) with the legal status of immigrants imputed using information from the 2009 Survey of Income and Program Participation (SIPP) and combined-sample multiple imputation (Van Hook et al. 2015).
[a]Adjusted for differences in age and duration of U.S. residence between legal and citizenship statuses, assuming that each gender-specific status group has the same average age and duration of residence.

in turn, show a mean age approximately five years younger than naturalized Mexican immigrants. Unauthorized Mexican immigrants also report fewer years in the United States relative to legal noncitizens and naturalized citizens. Both unauthorized men and women average nearly fourteen years of U.S. residence, compared with about nineteen and eighteen years of residence among LPR men and women, respectively. As one would expect, Mexican immigrants who have obtained U.S. citizenship have been in the country the longest, averaging twenty-six years among naturalized males and twenty-five among naturalized females.

As a result of less experience in the country, unauthorized Mexican immigrants are not as likely to report proficiency in English. Sixty-two percent of unauthorized men and 74 percent of unauthorized women report little or no proficiency in English (those who speak it "not well" or not at all). Among legally resident noncitizens born in Mexico, 69 percent of women report limited English proficiency, which falls between the percentages for unauthorized men and women. About 51 percent of legally resident noncitizen men report limited English proficiency. The majority of naturalized Mexican immigrants—72 percent of men and 62 percent of women—are proficient in English.

We also show legal status and citizenship comparisons with respect to educational attainment, reported as age-adjusted years of completed schooling. We make this correction because substantial heterogeneity in birth and arrival cohorts across legal and citizenship statuses biases unadjusted measures in educational attainment. Because unauthorized immigrants were born later than legal noncitizens and naturalized citizens, they benefit from structural improvements in educational opportunities in Mexico that were unavailable to earlier birth cohorts. Thus we present years of schooling measures that assume the same average age and duration of U.S. residence for each of the three legal and citizenship status groups, separately by gender. By this measure, unauthorized Mexican immigrant men and women have the lowest mean years of schooling, at 8.5 and 8.4 years, respectively. The mean educational attainment among legal noncitizens is slightly higher at 8.8 years for both men and women, and schooling is substantially higher among naturalized men and women, 10.8 and 11.3 years, respectively.

We turn now to labor-market outcomes among Mexican immigrant men and women across legal and citizenship status categories (table 4.2). With respect to employment, there are few notable differences between these groups. Unauthorized immigrant men are slightly more likely than legal noncitizen and naturalized men to be employed, and they participate at somewhat higher rates in the labor force. The one notable difference in employment is for Mexican immigrant women, among whom naturalized citizens participate in the labor force at a substantially higher rate than unauthorized and legally resident noncitizen women. Fifty-three and 52 percent of unauthorized and legal noncitizen Mexican immigrant women, respectively, were in the labor force in 2012, compared with 66 percent among Mexican immigrant women who are naturalized citizens.

Although unauthorized immigrants tend to be disadvantaged with respect to several dimensions of immigrant incorporation, the distribution of unauthorized immigrants across broad occupational categories is nearly identical to that of legally resident noncitizens. Moreover, naturalized citizens tend to be concentrated in similar occupational categories, though to a lesser degree. Among men, the leading occupation for

Table 4.2   Labor Market Outcomes among Mexican Immigrants in the United States, Aged Twenty-five to Sixty-four, by Gender, Citizenship, and Imputed Legal Status, 2012 (percentage)

Variable	Unauthorized		Legal Noncitizens		Naturalized Citizens	
	Men	Women	Men	Women	Men	Women
Employment status						
Employed	87.1	45.9	84.4	45.9	83.7	60.1
Unemployed	5.2	7.4	5.6	6.3	5.7	5.9
Not in the labor force	7.7	46.7	10.1	47.8	10.7	34.0
Occupation[a]						
Management, business, science, and arts	3.8	4.3	6.2	6.6	10.9	15.5
Healthcare	0.2	1.9	0.4	3.0	0.9	6.1
Protective services	0.3	0.1	0.3	0.2	0.7	0.4
Food preparation	12.0	17.7	10.0	15.3	6.5	10.0
Building grounds cleaning and maintenance	14.1	25.6	12.9	23.7	10.9	15.0
Personal care and services	0.4	6.0	0.5	7.8	0.8	8.9
Sales and related	2.6	6.1	2.9	6.3	4.9	9.1
Office and administrative support	2.4	5.2	2.6	6.7	4.9	11.5
Agriculture	9.0	8.5	7.3	6.7	3.5	2.2
Construction and extraction	27.3	1.1	27.3	0.8	18.0	0.5
Installation, maintenance, and repair	4.8	0.2	5.3	0.2	6.9	0.3
Production	12.8	16.1	12.8	15.8	15.2	15.2
Transportation and material moving	10.3	7.2	11.3	7.0	15.9	5.3
Mean hours worked per week[b]	40.2	34.5	40.8	35.0	42.3	36.5
Part time[c]	14.3	34.9	13.0	31.8	8.8	26.4
Mean annual earnings[d]	23,564	14,866	27,859	17,012	37,852	24,200
Median annual earnings[d]	20,000	13,060	23,960	14,920	31,200	20,000
Mean annual earnings (natural log)[d]	9.8	9.3	10.0	9.4	10.3	9.7

Source: Data from 2012 American Community Survey (Ruggles et al. 2010) with the legal status of immigrants imputed using information from the 2009 Survey of Income and Program Participation (SIPP) and combined-sample multiple imputation (Van Hook et al. 2015).
[a]Among persons who are currently employed or have worked within the previous five years.
[b]Among persons who worked during the previous year.
[c]Among persons who worked fewer than thirty-five hours a week.
[d]Among persons with positive earned income during the previous year.

all three groups is construction. Twenty-seven percent of unauthorized and legally resident noncitizen men are in construction occupations compared with 18 percent of Mexican-born men who are naturalized citizens. Among Mexican immigrant women, the leading occupation for the unauthorized and legal noncitizens is building and grounds cleaning and maintenance; 26 and 24 percent of unauthorized and legal noncitizen women, respectively, are in this occupational category, compared with 15 percent of naturalized women.

As with occupational categories, unauthorized Mexican men and women work, on average, a similar number of hours per week as their legally resident noncitizen counterparts. Men of both legal status groups average about forty hours per week, and 14 percent of unauthorized men and 13 percent of legal noncitizen men do not work full time (that is, average less than thirty-five hours of work per week). Unauthorized and legal noncitizen women who work report an average of about thirty-five hours worked per week, with unauthorized women being slightly more likely to work part time (35 versus 32 percent). Possibly owing to the fact that they are likely to be engaged in steadier employment arrangements, naturalized Mexican men and women report significantly more average hours worked per week and a sizable advantage in full-time employment. Naturalized men average more than 42 hours in a usual workweek, and just 9 percent report part-time employment, while their naturalized female counterparts average 37 hours per week and 26 percent work part-time. Turning to earnings, expressed in natural log form, unauthorized Mexican immigrant men report earnings (that is, all forms of earned income reported in the American Community Survey) that are 14 percent lower than those of legally resident noncitizen men and 43 percent lower than those of male naturalized citizens. Female unauthorized workers report earnings that are just under 14 percent lower than those of legal noncitizen women (13.7) and 50 percent lower than those of Mexican immigrant women who are naturalized citizens.

Figure 4.1 presents unadjusted and adjusted earnings of unauthorized Mexican immigrant men and women and naturalized men and women relative to legally resident noncitizens (the omitted category). The unadjusted earnings gaps are based on the averages of logged earnings reported in the final row of table 4.2 and thus reflect the same 14 percent earnings disadvantage among unauthorized men and women relative to legal noncitizens. Moreover, the unadjusted earnings advantage among naturalized citizens relative to legal noncitizens is 29 and 36 percent for men and women, respectively. The adjusted earnings differences are based on ordinary least-squares regression models, estimated for men and women separately, in which we include as controls all of the variables listed in tables 4.1 and 4.2, as well as state dummy variables. Among men, when adjusting for legal and citizenship status differences in background

Figure 4.1   **Earnings of Mexican Immigrants in the United States, Aged Twenty-five to Sixty-four, Los Angeles, 2012**

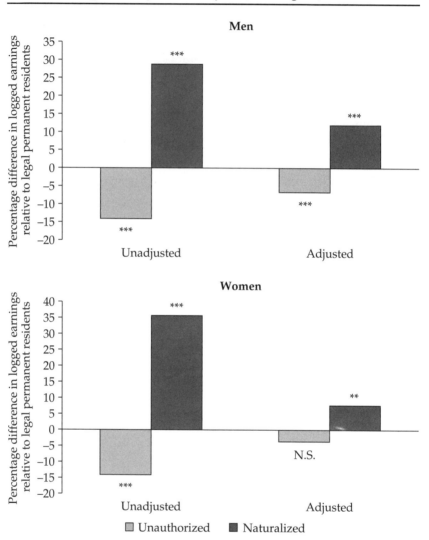

Source: Data from 2012 American Community Survey (Ruggles et al. 2010) with the legal status of immigrants imputed using information from the 2009 Survey of Income and Program Participation (SIPP) and combined-sample multiple imputation (Van Hook et al. 2015).
Note: Adjusted estimates are from regression models of logged annual earnings regressed on legal and citizenship status, age, age-squared, English-language proficiency, duration of U.S. residence (years), educational attainment (in years), usual hours worked per week, occupation, and state of residence.
*** $p < .001$; ** $p < .01$; N.S.: not significantly different from legal permanent residents at the $p < .10$ threshold.

characteristics, the earnings disadvantage among the unauthorized relative to legal noncitizens is reduced to 6.6 percent, still a statistically significant difference. The earnings advantage of naturalized immigrant men relative to legal noncitizens also diminishes to 11.9 percent.

Among unauthorized Mexican immigrant women, the relative earnings disadvantage of unauthorized Mexican immigrants is entirely explained by background variables, as the remaining 3.5 percent earnings disadvantage relative to legally resident noncitizen women is not statistically significant. A significant earnings advantage over legal noncitizens remains for naturalized Mexican immigrant women after including controls in the model. In short, the unauthorized show considerable earnings disadvantages compared with both LPRs and the naturalized, although these differences largely disappear when other variables are controlled, a pattern the meaning of which we return to in the next chapter.

Parental Migration Status and Gender Differences in Education among the Adult Offspring of Mexican Immigrants

Now we turn to parental unauthorized status effects on the children of immigrants, the second generation. Although numerous case studies portray the heartrending difficulties the unauthorized and their children face in navigating school and work, no research to our knowledge has addressed the question of how unauthorized status differentially harms the male and female children and grandchildren of immigrants, especially their schooling.[32] To ascertain whether a life-course turning point perspective or a long-term cumulative disadvantage framework best depicts the negative effects of unauthorized status, we first present evidence on combinations of parental legalization trajectories, which enable us to distinguish the influence of changing status (that is, legalization) from the effects of continuous disadvantage (that is, staying unauthorized). We use such trajectories to examine the schooling of the offspring of immigrants. As noted earlier, Mexican immigrants are by far the largest U.S.-immigrant group. Because so many come without papers, Mexican-origin children account for a large majority of the children in the United States with an unauthorized immigrant parent. According to current estimates, 70 percent of the 5.5 million children of unauthorized immigrants in the United States have a Mexican-born parent.[33]

Such estimates imply that in 2010 more than half of the 7.3 million children of Mexican immigrants residing in the country had an unauthorized parent.[34] Moreover, most children of unauthorized parents, about 80 percent as of 2009, are born in the United States and thus are U.S. citizens.[35] Even though U.S.-born children of immigrants presumably enjoy access to the same education and jobs as any other citizen, their parents' migration-status histories reflect the first societal-membership experiences of their families in the host society. Such experiences may have lasting effects on second-generation children.[36] While targeted policies such as the Dream Act may address the situations of children who are themselves unauthorized, policies directed at the unauthorized population as a whole can affect both immigrants and their native-born children.

Because of Mexico's proximity to the United States and the unauthorized status and poverty of most migrants, Mexican immigrants exhibit a greater variety of pathways to legal status and citizenship than other groups.[37] Mexican migrants to the United States have traditionally circulated back and forth between the two countries,[38] often changing frames of reference and gradually becoming permanent migrants,[39] in a process that may occur over many years.[40] Hence as migrants move from being sojourners to settlers,[41] their orientations shift from the society of origin toward the society of destination. Thus when poor, unskilled laborers (especially males), who initially migrate for temporary employment, find permanent work, they often seek ways to legalize. Because the family reunification provisions of U.S. immigration laws provide the bulk of opportunities for legalization, they encourage the development of complex family-based strategies for achieving legalization.[42]

Individual Migration-Status Trajectories

The high prevalence of unauthorized status in the Mexican first generation forces many Mexican immigrants and their children to the margins of society, causing their incorporation perhaps to take longer than that of other immigrant groups.[43] Beyond this, it may not just be initial membership exclusion that matters but rather whether a transition to legalization occurs. That is, those who come as unauthorized entrants and subsequently legalize are likely to fare better in general than those who stay unauthorized,[44] and such trajectories may differ for the mother and the father. Thus combinations of parents' legal status trajectories are what children actually confront and what are likely to be consequential for their lives. At the individual level, we can assess these by examining entry, legalization, and citizenship statuses at two points in time for each parent separately. Such parental trajectories may vary considerably within and across couples, both because immigrant parents may not have arrived together in the United States at the same time and because the high costs of legalization and naturalization often require the family to choose which parent should legalize first.

Scarcely any national-level or other data sets provide information on both the migration status of immigrants and the characteristics of their adult children. However, the IIMMLA survey includes such data.[45] The survey consists of a large sample of second-generation Mexican

Table 4.3   Various Nativity-Migration and Legalization-Citizenship Trajectories of Mexican-Origin Parents, 2012 (percentage) (N = 935)

Trajectory	Mothers	Fathers
Unknown	1.0	6.4
Never migrated to the United States	8.7	12.7
Authorized to naturalized	32.1	25.6
Authorized to legal permanent resident	13.7	12.6
Unauthorized (or unknown) to naturalized	14.8	16.3
Unauthorized (or unknown) to legal permanent resident	15.2	12.2
Unauthorized (or unknown) to unauthorized	4.2	4.3
U.S. born	10.5	9.9

Source: Data from Immigration and Intergenerational Mobility in Metropolitan Los Angeles (see Bean, Leach et al. 2011).
Note: These trajectories include some mothers or fathers who after entry spent some time as unauthorized migrants but whose entry status was unknown by the respondent. They became legal permanent residents and in most instances naturalized. Most likely, these persons entered initially as students or tourists, overstayed their visas, subsequently were able to adjust to legal permanent resident status, and finally naturalized.

respondents, aged twenty to forty, and information on their parents. The study offers valuable information for a random sample of the children of younger adults in the U.S. city with the largest number of Mexican immigrants in the country (see appendix A for further details about the IIMMLA survey). The data contain questions about the migration status of each parent when that person first entered the United States, as well as the parent's legal and citizenship status at the time of the interview. The information obtained enables the comparison of migration statuses for each parent at time of entry and at time of interview. In some cases respondents either had never known one of their parents or did not know their parents' initial migration status. Other parents had never lived in the United States. Still others had come as unauthorized entrants and then had become legal permanent residents. Some of these eventually naturalized.

The percentage of parents experiencing various individual trajectories are shown in table 4.3. Mexican parents are highly likely to have been unauthorized when they came to the country: 34.2 percent of Mexican mothers and 32.8 percent of Mexican fathers in the sample were unauthorized at entry. Because a high proportion of Mexican immigrant parents at any particular moment may still be making the transition from temporary to permanent immigrant, and because U.S. immigration policy is so complicated that it encourages multiple legal entry strategies,[46] Mexicans show more parental trajectory combinations of entry and subsequent legalization or citizenship statuses than other immigrant

Table 4.4   **Means and Standard Deviations for Respondents'
and Parents' Characteristics, 2004**

	Respondents	
Variable	Mean	SD
Age	27.80	5.93
Years of education completed	13.00	2.35
Male	0.50	0.50
Second generation	0.67	0.47
Spoke Spanish at home while growing up	0.91	0.29
Enrolled in school at interview	0.30	0.46
Lived with both parents while growing up	0.72	0.45

	Mothers		Fathers	
	Mean	SD	Mean	SD
Years of education	8.70	3.81	8.60	4.07
Held laborer occupation in home country	0.24	0.43	0.50	0.50
Worked in white-collar occupation in home country	0.21	0.41	0.17	0.38
Migrated from West Central region of Mexico	0.52	0.50	0.51	0.50
Returned to home country for more than six months after migration to U.S.	0.15	0.36	0.15	0.36

Source: Data from Immigration and Intergenerational Mobility in Metropolitan Los Angeles (see Bean, Leach et al. 2011).

groups, particularly those of Asian origin.[47] Here we examine how Mexican American parental trajectories relate to educational attainment for the male and female children of immigrants separately. We do this by gauging the extent to which children's schooling varies across parental combinations of migration status categories, controlling for parents' antecedent and respondent's characteristics.

Parental Combinations of Migration Status Trajectories

The members of the Mexican immigrant generation and their children show characteristics typical of unskilled labor migrants and their offspring. For example, nearly three decades or more after migrating to the United States, the Mexican parents still have mostly not finished high school, averaging only a little more than eight-and-a-half years of schooling (see table 4.4). The Mexican American young adult respondents, by contrast, are much better educated than their parents, having completed thirteen years of schooling on average. Many of these respondents did not speak English at home while growing up (although most also learned English), and nearly three-fourths lived with both parents. Also, a noticeable proportion of their parents had returned to Mexico after migrating and living in the United States for at least six months, a pattern consistent with sojourner migration.[48]

Following Frank Bean et al., we conduct latent class analyses for parental couples, in which the individual migration status trajectories for each parent of the second-generation respondents are included, to ascertain how various combinations of couple trajectories cluster together.[49] In the absence of theory about what kinds of combinations to expect, we want to avoid predetermining the combinations of parental trajectories among couples, which would risk imposition of arbitrary a priori categorizations on subsequent analyses. Rather, the latent class analysis allows those that occur together naturally in the data to emerge. The results show that the couples can be characterized by seven migration-status trajectory combinations that indicate considerable diversity in mother-father migration-status patterns. For example, two of the combinations involve either all of the fathers (but not all of the mothers) being citizens (either being born in the United States or having naturalized) or all of the mothers (but not all of the fathers) being citizens. We label these father-driven, all citizens; and mother-driven, all citizens, respectively. Twenty-four and 13.9 percent, respectively, of the Mexican parental combinations fall into these groups (figure 4.2).

Two additional combinations involve both parents becoming legal permanent residents with many (slightly less than half) having naturalized, although not quickly. In one of these groups, many of the parents had entered legally, and in the other almost none of them had. We term these the legal permanent residents (17.0 percent) and the unauthorized entrants who legalized (17.1 percent). Two other classes also show mother-father differentiation, each involving substantial unauthorized entry and subsequent universal attainment for one parent of LPR status with some naturalization. But in each of these classes, the other parent remained unauthorized, either the father or the mother. We label these groups fathers unauthorized, mothers legalized (4.5 percent) and mothers unauthorized, fathers legalized (14.1 percent). The remaining group (9.3 percent of the sample) consists of parents who had entered or remained unauthorized or parents whose status was unknown (both parents unauthorized).[50]

The last three classes include couple trajectories that involve at least one parent having entered the country and remained unauthorized, whereas the first two classes include virtually no transitions from unauthorized to legal status. In the middle two classes, almost all the couple trajectories involve at least one parent who made the transition from unauthorized to legal status. Recall that the dynamics emphasized

**Figure 4.2   Distribution of Parental Combinations
                  of Migration-Status Trajectories**

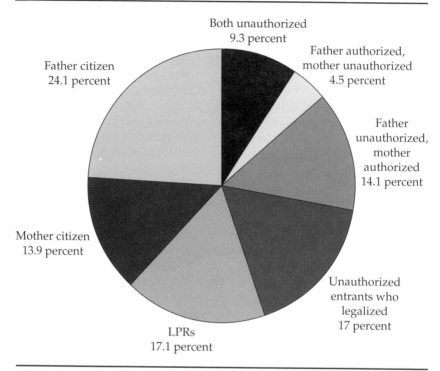

Source: Data from Immigration and Intergenerational Mobility in Metropolitan Los Angeles (see Bean, Leach et al. 2011).

by membership exclusion imply that it is the lack of membership itself that most handicaps immigrants, suggesting that once membership is obtained, integration processes are likely to proceed more rapidly. Such dynamics would lead us to expect that those whose parents' trajectory classes involve transitions from unauthorized to legal status will show schooling levels as high as those of persons whose parents came to the country legally to begin with. That is, we would expect the educational attainment of second-generation persons whose parents fall in the two middle trajectory classes (having made the transition from unauthorized entry to legal membership) to rise close to the levels of those with parents in the top two classes. As noted earlier, membership-exclusion dynamics imply that legalization constitutes a turning point after which deficiencies in schooling resulting from parental unauthorized status start to be made up. By contrast, if initial unauthorized status leads to second-generation scarring that persists well beyond the point of legalization, we would not expect to find evidence of catch-up schooling among the sons or daughters of the parents exhibiting postentry legalization.

Results: How Trajectory Combinations
Actually Relate to Children's Education

To ascertain how antecedent factors relate to parental clusters of migration-status trajectory combinations (that is, the latent classes), we also conduct multinomial logistical regression analyses relating membership in one of the seven trajectory combinations to variables characterizing mother's and father's backgrounds. The background indicators include each immigrant parent's education and occupation in Mexico; the region of origin in Mexico; whether the parent had returned to Mexico; and whether the parents had lived together for most of the respondent's childhood. The results reveal patterns consistent with the trajectory combinations in the classes (see appendix D for detailed results of the analyses). For example, when parents (especially fathers) are better educated and had never worked in Mexico as laborers, both parents lived with the child while the child was growing up, and the parents had never returned to Mexico, respondents were are more likely to fall into the mother-citizen or father-citizen combinations.

How do the trajectory combinations actually relate to children's schooling? To assess this, we regress the second-generation respondents' education (measured as years of schooling) on dummy variables for the seven parental mixed-trajectory combinations (with the omitted reference category consisting of those respondents both of whose parents had entered and remained unauthorized). We estimate these models for the entire sample and separately for men and women, both with and without control variables for respondents' and parents' antecedent characteristics. The results are expressed in terms of the differences in schooling levels for each of the six couple trajectory classes relative to the "both parents unauthorized" category (see table 4.5). Looking at results for the entire sample (top panel), we see that those respondents with parents who were unauthorized at entry and remained unauthorized exhibit considerably fewer years of schooling than do the children of immigrants whose parents either entered legally or became legalized. The only exception to this pattern involves the trajectory combination containing fathers who became legal and mothers who remained unauthorized, whose offspring also have little education. In other words, the only trajectory combinations that show significant unadjusted second-generation schooling deficits compared with the others are the two involving mothers who entered the United States without papers and subsequently stayed unauthorized.

Among those classes showing schooling premiums (the remaining five), and without adjusting for other differences (model 1), one combination in

Table 4.5   Regressions of Years of Schooling on Combinations of Parental Migration-Status Trajectories, 2004

Migration Trajectory Class	Model 1	Model 2	Model 3	Model 4
All				
Father-driven, all citizens	2.60***	1.21***	2.08***	1.15***
Mother-driven, all citizens	2.47***	1.20***	1.97***	1.18***
Authorized entrants, often naturalized	2.19***	1.28***	1.92***	1.34***
Unauthorized, legalized, often naturalized	2.31***	1.62***	2.01***	1.60***
Fathers unauthorized, mothers legalized	2.03***	1.24***	1.69***	1.15***
Mothers unauthorized, fathers legalized	0.87**	−0.09	0.86**	0.16
Both parents unauthorized (omitted)				
R-squared	0.10	0.15	0.18	0.22
Males				
Father-driven, all citizens	2.46***	1.12**	2.15***	1.24**
Mother-driven, all citizens	2.38***	1.10**	2.04***	1.21**
Authorized entrants, often naturalized	2.07***	1.08**	1.89***	1.21**
Unauthorized, legalized, often naturalized	2.13***	1.29**	1.96***	1.41***
Fathers unauthorized, mothers legalized	1.83***	1.04**	1.64***	1.09**
Mothers unauthorized, fathers legalized	1.78**	0.62	1.53***	0.67
Both parents unauthorized (omitted)				
R-squared	0.11	0.16	0.18	0.21
Females				
Father-driven, all citizens	2.81***	1.38**	2.16***	1.21*
Mother-driven, all citizens	2.59***	1.37**	1.98***	1.26**
Authorized entrants, often naturalized	2.35***	1.54***	2.06***	1.58***
Unauthorized, legalized, often naturalized	2.51***	1.92***	2.11***	1.81***
Fathers unauthorized, mothers legalized	2.24***	1.45**		1.33**
Mothers unauthorized, fathers legalized	0.09	−0.64		−0.27
Both parents unauthorized (omitted)				
R-squared	0.11	0.17	0.2	0.25

Source: Data from Immigration and Intergenerational Mobility in Metropolitan Los Angeles (see Bean, Leach et al. 2011).
Note: Model 1: unadjusted; model 2: adjusted for parental antecedent characteristics (see appendix C); model 3: adjusted for respondent characteristics (see appendix D); model 4: adjusted for both parental antecedent and respondent characteristics.

particular stands out for the schooling advantage it conveys: the mother-citizen group. However, closer inspection of the characteristics of the parents in this group reveals that two-thirds of the mothers in the class are native born (see appendix D). The other third entered the country as LPRs (none illegally), and all quickly naturalized. And while many of these mothers (40 percent) married unauthorized males, a figure that testifies both to the ubiquity of unauthorized Mexican male labor migration and to the fact that when such migrants marry natives they gain eligibility for green-card status, it is not surprising that adult children with parents like these show the highest levels of education. With so many native-born mothers, this group starts from a high attainment level that provides an upper-bound benchmark for how parents' advantages become transmitted to their children. However, after adjusting for either parental antecedent or respondent characteristics (see models 2 and 3 results in table 4.5), we note that this category differs little from the other trajectories containing either the mother or both parents having legalized. In general, and not distinguishing between men and women, those second-generation persons with mothers who legalized show on average a schooling advantage of about one and one-quarter years compared with those from families in which the mother remained unauthorized.

What do the results indicate about support for the turning-points and the scarring hypotheses, and by extension for membership exclusion and cumulative disadvantage theoretical perspectives? Here it is notable that respondents whose parents fall into the two trajectory combinations containing sizable proportions of mothers who entered as unauthorized migrants but subsequently become legal permanent residents, the unauthorized, entrants who legalized, and the unauthorized fathers and legalized mothers combination classes show schooling premiums that are virtually identical to those whose parents were in one of the first three categories (that is, to those whose parents are in the mother citizen, father citizen, or LPR classes). In other words, if membership-exclusion dynamics are driving these results and the life-course turning-points hypothesis is supported, we would expect second-generation persons whose parents started out as unauthorized migrants but then legalized to have caught up educationally with those whose parents were always legal. The scarring hypothesis, which is more compatible with the dynamics involved in racialization and disadvantage perspectives, would expect those entering as unauthorized migrants to show smaller schooling premiums even if they eventually legalized. What we see in the actual results is that those respondents with the fewest years of schooling completed are those with mothers who entered the country and remained unauthorized. By contrast, those whose parents legalized show evidence of catch-up schooling. Thus the trajectory results support membership exclusion dynamics more than they do cumulative disadvantage, or racialization dynamics.

The results for the entire sample indicate that the educational attainment of the second generation (the children of Mexican parents who entered the United States as unauthorized migrants and then either did not or were unable to legalize) is appreciably hampered by parental migration status.[51] After controlling for a wide variety of parental background and respondent characteristics that might plausibly affect the tendency to acquire more schooling and to find pathways to legalization, a sizable premium of 1.24 years of schooling relative to the children of those staying unauthorized still attaches to virtually all of the legalization trajectory combinations that involve one or both parents having legalized their status. We conclude that this deficit derives more from the dynamics of membership exclusion than from racialization and the scarring associated with cumulative disadvantage. Again, the reason is that those whose parents showed transitions from unauthorized status to legalization, especially when this trajectory characterized the mother, exhibit schooling levels as high as or higher than those for persons whose parents had always been legal. This is more compatible with the dynamics of membership exclusion and ideas about life-course turning points than with long-term cumulative-disadvantage or racialization perspectives.

Gender Differences

What are the findings for men and women separately? Recall that membership exclusion dynamics imply that migration and family exigencies will be more likely, at least across the first two generations, to encourage males more than females to sacrifice postsecondary education for employment. If so, males in the second generation would be more likely than females to work rather than start college, and this will constrain their schooling attainment even among those whose parents successfully navigate the transition of postentry legalization. This would have the consequence that their legalization premiums will be smaller than those of females. In fact, this appears to be evident in the data. Females in the IIMMLA data show a slightly greater tendency than males to graduate from high school (80.2 percent for males versus 83.0 percent for females), but among those graduating from high school, females are decidedly more likely to start college than males (62.6 percent versus 57.1 percent). Along these same lines, females whose parents underwent postentry legalization transitions show higher schooling levels relative to those whose parents stayed unauthorized (see the bottom two panels of table 4.5).

Thus as expected by membership-exclusion ideas, migration-status trajectories that include immigrant-parent legalization appear to involve legalization turning points that foster further educational attainment more for women than men. This notion is further reinforced by the fact that respondents with parents in the one parental trajectory class involving two significant turning points (that is, the one in which parents go from unauthorized to legal status and then from legal to naturalized status) show the highest schooling premium of all over those with parents who continued in an unauthorized status. This is also stronger for these particular females than for males (for example, a premium of 1.81 years of schooling for such females and one of 1.41 years for such males, fourth row of bottom panels of table 4.5).

Table 4.6   Schooling Premiums to Maternal Legalization with and without Adjustments for Background and Personal Characteristics, by Gender, 2004

Maternal Trajectory	Model 1	Model 2	Model 3	Model 4
All				
Entered or became legal	2.07***	1.39***	1.65***	1.24***
Stayed unauthorized (omitted)				
Male				
Entered or became legal	1.72***	0.87**	1.48***	0.94***
Stayed unauthorized (omitted)				
Female				
Entered or became legal	2.48***	1.96***	1.92***	1.68***
Stayed unauthorized (omitted)				

Source: Data from Immigration and Intergenerational Mobility in Metropolitan Los Angeles (see Bean, Leach et al. 2011).
Note: Model 1: unadjusted; model 2: adjusted for parental antecedent characteristics (see appendix C); model 3: adjusted for respondent characteristics (see appendix D); model 4: adjusted for both parental antecedent and respondent characteristics.

In sum, the most noteworthy second-generation schooling attainments occur for those whose parental trajectory classes involve the mother either having entered the country legally or having become legal after entry. Moreover, for the five classes like this, the differences among them in schooling premiums are minimal (with the exception of the class involving two turning points, whose schooling premium is even higher, as would be expected by the life-course framework),[52] thus supporting the idea of "catch-up" integration implied by membership exclusion. This result also suggests the possibility of consolidating classes in subsequent analyses. Hence in the analyses of the IIMMLA data presented in the rest of the book, we combine into one category those five classes in which a mother's legal entry or legalization trajectory occurs, and we combine into another single category the two classes containing mothers whose unauthorized status persisted across time. Henceforth, when we refer to respondents' "unauthorized background" or "parental unauthorized status," we mean those respondents whose mothers entered the country and stayed unauthorized.

Summary indications of how far the schooling levels of the legalized fall above those with unauthorized backgrounds are displayed in table 4.6, for males and females. As the membership-exclusion theoretical perspective would expect, both male and female children of immigrants with legal backgrounds show higher schooling premiums over those whose parents remained unauthorized, at 0.94 years of education for males and 1.68 years of schooling for females. The latter value is higher than that for males because females benefit more from parental legalization than do males, on whom pressures to work persist into the second generation.

Conclusions

Unauthorized Mexican migrants and their children live difficult lives and face many challenges, including pressures to help their families deal with migration and earn a living, the social isolation of unauthorized mothers,[53] and long work hours and demanding jobs that keep parents away from home a lot and drain their energies.[54] All of these contribute to their children's educational deficiencies. This chapter documents both the extent of the labor-market hardships unauthorized Mexicans endure and the magnitude of the schooling deficits shown by adult second-generation children of such immigrants. Males in particular face pressures to work to help their parents, which hampers their pursuit of postsecondary schooling. Females whose parents legalize are less hindered in attaining further education, resulting in greater premiums from legalization for women than for men, a result consistent with the hypothesis in the sociology of gender literature that the greater role separation and gender segregation in Mexico, especially rural Mexico, results in women coming to the United States with lower levels of schooling (a pattern we see in the findings presented in this chapter) and then having the most to gain from the relatively more egalitarian gender roles in the United States.[55] The result is more rapid advancement in regard to educational attainment among women in the second generation. In a subsequent chapter, we assess whether this continues through the third generation.

The findings we present for how the parental legal status trajectories of the second-generation men and women affect their schooling also help in selecting among the various theoretical perspectives about integration outlined early in this chapter. In particular, the results are more compatible with the ideas of membership exclusion than they are with perspectives emphasizing the negative impact of cumulative disadvantage: the ethnic-disadvantage, segmented-assimilation, and racialization perspectives. Such approaches emphasize the long-term scarring effects from prejudice and discrimination, handicaps that would persist long beyond the point of parental legalization. Membership exclusion, by contrast, envisions the possibility that once legalization occurs, the hindrances from parental unauthorized status begin to dissolve, reflecting that legalization constitutes a major life-course turning point for immigrants that carries substantial benefits.

That this is the case is evident in the research findings for the Mexican American second-generation young adults whose mothers came to the

United States as unauthorized migrants and then subsequently legalized. These persons show schooling attainments on a par with those of legal second-generation persons (that is, schooling levels as high as those for persons one or both of whose parents were either U.S.-born or initially came as a legal migrant). In short, legalization appears to act as a life-course turning point that enables even those second-generation persons whose parents experience some time in unauthorized statuses to catch up with their legal peers after their parents are able to legalize. In subsequent chapters, we present additional evidence based on three-generational analyses that further assist us in making distinctions among which of the various theoretical perspectives provide the most helpful portrayals of the Mexican American integration experience.

= Chapter 5 =

Three-Generational Analyses of Structural Integration: Education and Income Patterns

The results in the previous chapter showed that when Mexicans come to the United States as unauthorized immigrants and are unable to legalize, their children (even those who are have been born in the United States) suffer substantial education penalties. Conversely, when unauthorized immigrants are able to legalize, their adult children show evidence of having attained schooling levels that place them on a par with the offspring of those who migrated legally, those who came legally and naturalized, and those who came legally and were married to native citizens. This chapter, after first expanding our focus on educational attainment in the second generation, moves on to assess the education and income levels of third-only generation Mexican Americans. This involves estimating in the aggregate the degree to which the second-generation schooling deficits associated with having unauthorized migrant parents spill over into the third generation. Thus we ask, how large is the legacy effect on schooling for the grandchildren of unauthorized Mexican migrants? Such three-generational analyses enable us to examine evidence that helps ascertain which of the various theoretical perspectives outlined in earlier chapters best accounts for the generational changes, distinguishing between men and women within generations. This helps in assessing empirical support for hypotheses about gender in particular, including the idea that greater background ethnic density boosts integration, more so among women than men.

We work with five generational categories, starting with the 1.5 generation and then the 2.0, 2.5, 3.0, and 3.5 generations. We define the 1.0 generation as those who immigrated as adults, and the 1.5 generation as persons who migrated before the age of fifteen. Using this latter group as a baseline instead of the first generation enables us to avoid comparisons across the two national school systems arising from the greater availability and lower cost of secondary school in the United States.[1] Thus although the 1.5 generation consists of immigrants, their young age at arrival gives them the opportunity to take advantage of free U.S. schooling through high school.[2] They thus have backgrounds that provide better bases of comparison with those of later-generation Mexican American groups than do first-generation immigrants, who were schooled in Mexico. We define the 2.0 and 3.0 generations, respectively, as those who had two parents born in Mexico and those who had all four grandparents born in Mexico. The 2.5 and 3.5 generations are those with one U.S.-born parent and those with two U.S.-born parents and two grandparents born in Mexico, respectively.[3]

The membership-exclusion perspective lends us to expect notably higher educational attainment for those second-generation persons whose parents have authorized backgrounds (that is, who either came legally or legalized sometime after arrival). This framework also expects less such attainment for second-generation men than women because of pressures on males to work instead of pursuing higher education. Here, in looking at the third generation and recalling the generally more favorable societal context for female educational attainment in the United States over the past several decades, we also expect Mexican American women to show higher schooling levels than males in the third generation.[4] Alternatively, if Mexican Americans were appreciably held back because of prejudice and discrimination, as racialization perspectives suggest, then we would not expect to find higher levels of schooling in third-generation relative to second-generation groups or to find such a pattern emerges for women but not men. In addition, because of selective acculturation, we expect an extramotivational dynamic to boost education and income the greater the ethnic density of second- and third-generation parental and grandparental ties back to the initial migration experience, all else being equal. Hence we anticipate disproportionately higher structural integration (evinced by schooling or income levels) among those children of immigrants with two parents born in Mexico than among those with only one such parent, as well as higher levels among the grandchildren of immigrants with four grandparents born in Mexico as opposed to only two. Because the membership-exclusion perspective postulates that having an unauthorized background mostly exacerbates work pressures among the male children of Mexican immigrants, we expect the extramotivational boost in schooling to emerge less prominently among men than among women.

Income is also a key aspect of structural integration. Thus we also examine cross-generational patterns in annual earnings, including the effects of migration-status background on generational patterns of difference, looking again at results separately for men and women. Working-class delay ideas envision the availability of mobility in working-class earnings for the third generation within the Mexican American working class but limited movement out of the working class into jobs that require college in part because of its high cost. While the expositors of this hypothesis do not fully spell out the reasons why such opportunities might be reasonably plentiful, an important one is the shrinkage since 1990 of the U.S.-born working-age population under the age of forty-five, a phenomenon we examine in more detail in chapter 8, where we elaborate on the increasing importance of less-skilled Mexican immigration for bolstering the less-skilled U.S. workforce. In any case, even though such changes may also make it easier for blue-collar Mexican Americans to find work, all working-class Americans have had to grapple with growing economic inequality, an important aspect of which deters upward mobility, namely, the rapidly rising cost of college.[5] The greater unaffordability of higher education seems likely to constitute a key factor holding back the educational mobility of the working class (Mexican American as well as others).

If this is true, it should be evident in our data in the form of minimally higher schooling levels for the third generation compared with the second. This pattern may particularly apply to men, because even though third-generation males may find working-class jobs that pay reasonably well, fewer women may enjoy the option of finding a high-paying job without some college-level education.[6] Thus if income mobility opportunities are still available to the working class, especially males, without their having to acquire more schooling, we would expect third-generation Mexican Americans to show higher incomes than their second-generation counterparts. In short, even absent higher schooling levels compared with the second generation, third-generation men may be able to find jobs that pay more or are more likely to be full-time than those held by the second generation, thus raising incomes and providing incentives not to make the sacrifices necessary to pursue higher education.

Such jobs and mobility dynamics have been observed for both first- and second-generation Mexican immigrants.[7] They may also characterize third-generation Mexican American males, leading to the expectation of minimal differences in education between third- and second-generation men but notably higher third-generation incomes. By contrast, third-generation Mexican American women may have fewer disincentives to starting higher education. They thus may show better outcomes than males in secondary school (that is, they may be more likely to complete high school and start college) and may live in a general secular context in which women are outstripping men in educational attainment, especially among the working class.[8] Racialization as opposed to working-class incorporation dynamics would not expect third-generation income gains. We outline the different expectations of working-class delay and racialization perspectives in table 5.1.

A few methodology issues that require explication arise in considering education outcomes for third-generation Mexican Americans. First, how

Table 5.1   Expected Direction of Education and Income Differences Between the Second and Third Generation under Three Theoretical Perspectives

	Males		Females	
Theoretical Perspective	Education Difference	Income Difference	Education Difference	Income Difference
Working-class stagnation	0	+	0 or +	+
Male racialization	0	0	+	+
Male and female racialization	0	0	0	0

Source: Authors' heuristic summary.

is it possible to examine the legacy effects of unauthorized migration on third-generation men and women when we do not know which individual third-generation respondents had grandparents who were unauthorized? In fact we did not collect such information in the Immigration and Intergenerational Mobility in Metropolitan Los Angeles (IIMMLA) survey because pretests showed that many respondents did not know the legal status of their grandparents. Despite this, it is important to estimate such legacy effects if possible, because they are likely to exist. We know this from the research literature on intergenerational transmission of inequality, which has recently emphasized the importance of taking multiple-generational sources of influence into account.[9] We do this by estimating at the individual level the effects of first-generation unauthorized status on the second generation, the results of which are presented in the previous chapter. Now, in turn, we estimate at the aggregate or group level the effects on the third generation that derive from those second-generation deficits. We can calculate these because we have a concrete idea of the degree to which second-generation schooling is dampened by unauthorized status, meaning we can extrapolate into the third generation as a group the extent to which such deficits are intergenerationally transmitted. We present the details of these estimations in appendix E.

Second, how do we know how many of the grandparents' generation were unauthorized immigrants? While we have no direct measure, accounts of Mexican migration from the 1950s through the 1970s are explicit about the large proportion of the Mexican immigrant population that was unauthorized.[10] We take a range of conservative estimates, the most conservative of which is that the proportion unauthorized among the grandparents' generation equaled the proportion unauthorized in the parents' generation.

Third, how can we gauge the experience of being unauthorized two generations ago to that of the parents of the second generation? If anything, the grandparents of the current respondents may have faced greater ethnic discrimination because they had fewer protections of civil rights. But they also faced discrimination on account of their legal status. Operation Wetback in the 1950s led to nearly 4 million expulsions.[11] Nor did they have the protections of *Plyler v. Doe* to ensure schooling for their own children.[12] We are implicitly assuming that unauthorized status in the 1960s and 1970s carried at least as much education penalty for offspring as in the 1990s and the early years of the present century. In fact, the penalty is now likely to be larger, which means that our estimates are probably conservative.

Generational Differences in Schooling by Gender

We begin by assessing some of the ideas developed in chapter 3 about differences in gender patterns emerging out of the risk minimization strategies adopted by Mexican immigrant families and their differential application to daughters and sons. We could not do this in the previous chapter, where we look at a single category of second-generation "persons." Now we break such persons into two groups, the 2.0 and 2.5 generations, along with a 1.5 generation group. The different implications for males and females of risk-minimization strategies lead to the expectation of a crisscross pattern of schooling levels by gender across these three groups that cannot be seen when all are lumped together.

Male and Female Patterns among the Children of Immigrants

Sociology of development and gender-role-specialization perspectives suggest that less developed countries are often characterized by sharper gender divisions of labor and greater role specializations for males and females than is the case in more developed societies. Traditionally, female migrants from countries like Mexico have been likely to show greater socioeconomic disadvantages relative to males. They also often stand to gain more from migration than do males,[13] although the degree and pattern of gain often depends to some degree on other factors.[14] This implies that women in the immigrant generation will show lower levels of schooling than males but surpass them by the second generation. In addition, the pressure on men to work, and the more protective socialization of daughters, as elaborated in chapter 3, impart an education advantage to women. Those two factors may operate more strongly among parents with unauthorized backgrounds because their family situations are more precarious. In addition, recent research on schooling shows that girls are more likely to earn good grades and boys are more prone to falling into a peer culture that resists schooling when they attend poor schools.[15] While this study focuses more on family than on school factors, the schooling patterns are likely to reinforce gender-based family patterns.

Table 5.2   **Educational Attainment of Mexican American Adults,
Aged Twenty to Forty, by Gender, Los Angeles, 2004**

	Generation		
Category	1.5	2.0	2.5
Women			
A. Completing high school	.71	.87	.89
B. Starting postsecondary schooling (among high school completers)	.53	.66	.69
C. Completing college (among college starters)	.32	.46	.30
Men			
A. Completing high school	.64	.82	.87
B. Starting postsecondary schooling (among high school completers)	.59	.59	.59
C. Completing college (among college starters)	.33	.39	.39

Source: Data from Immigration and Intergenerational Mobility in Metropolitan Los Angeles (see Bean, Leach et al. 2011).
Note: Conditional on prior attainment.

Examining key grade-level transitions and mean completed years of schooling by gender for the 1.5 to 2.5 generations, we find that these theoretical expectations are generally borne out. Among persons in the 1.5 generation, the lower proportion of females versus males graduating from high school, starting college, and finishing college are consistent with the idea that more traditional gender roles characterized Mexico when the parents migrated (see table 5.2). In the 2.0 generation, however, among those who have graduated from high school, women show higher proportions on each of these three probabilities, results that are consistent with the advantages that accrue to daughters in the United States.

These transition probabilities also translate into similar differences in average years of schooling completed. Thus 1.5 generation females exhibit lower average age-adjusted levels of schooling than males (12.2 years on average compared with 12.4 years for males) (figure 5.1) but higher levels in the 2.0 generation (13.6 years compared with 13.3 years) and then lower levels in the 2.5 generation (13.0 versus 13.2 years). This crossover pattern by gender is consistent with the theoretical expectations previously outlined. When we break the results down further by whether persons come from legal or unauthorized backgrounds, the expected sharper pattern for women from unauthorized backgrounds does not emerge (see figure 5.2). Instead, the pattern is evident for those from both authorized and unauthorized backgrounds, with a crossover occurring only for the former. The socialization pressures on males and females deriving

Figure 5.1   Age-Adjusted Years of Schooling Completed by Mexican
Americans, Aged Twenty to Forty, by Generation and Gender,
Los Angeles, 2004

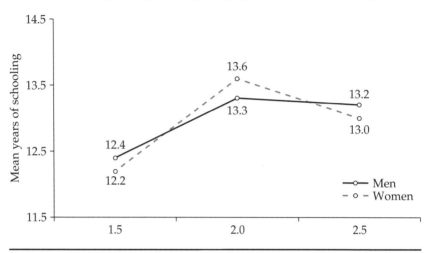

Source: Data from Immigration and Intergenerational Mobility in Metropolitan
Los Angeles (see Bean, Leach et al. 2011).

from migration status and family-related cultural repertoires appear to
impinge on the male and female children of Mexican immigrants in ways
that boost female education in the entire 2.0 generation, making for a
crisscross pattern by gender of advancing education mobility across these
generation categories.

Three-Generational Patterns by Migration Status

Four notable patterns emerge when all five generation categories are
disaggregated by both gender and legal status background. First, in
keeping with the statistically significant and sizable adverse effects of
unauthorized background on second-generation schooling shown in the
previous chapter, education levels for young adult second-generation
persons with unauthorized backgrounds are markedly lower than those
for persons with authorized backgrounds (we operationalize unauthorized background as having mothers who came illegally and did not subsequently legalize). The second notable pattern, as expected based on our
ideas about migration and family-based cultural repertoires, is that the
differences across generations are larger for women than for men because
many families encourage boys to work more rather than pursue additional schooling, especially in the 2.0 and 2.5 generations.

Figure 5.2   Age-Adjusted Years of Schooling Across Two Generations of Mexican Americans, Aged Twenty to Forty, by Generation and Migration-Status Background, Los Angeles, 2004

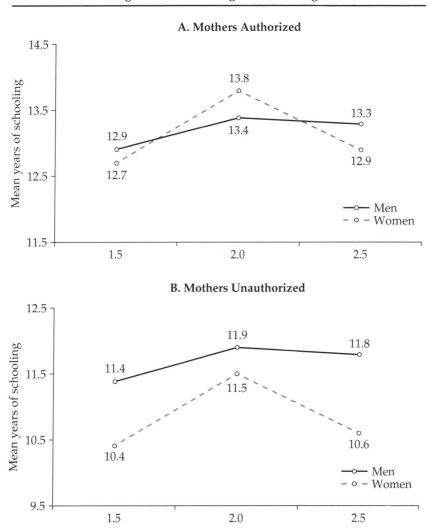

A. Mothers Authorized

B. Mothers Unauthorized

Source: Data from Immigration and Intergenerational Mobility in Metropolitan Los Angeles (see Bean, Leach et al. 2011).

Figure 5.3   Age-Adjusted Years of Schooling Completed by Mexican
              Americans, Aged Twenty to Forty, by Generation,
              Los Angeles, 2004

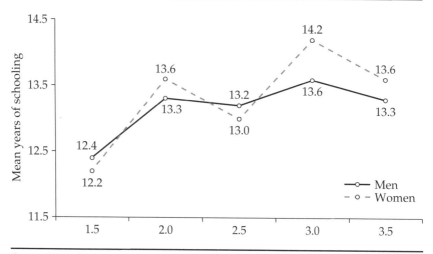

Source: Data from Immigration and Intergenerational Mobility in Metropolitan Los Angeles (see Bean, Leach et al. 2011).

The third notable result is that even though males from families with legal migration backgrounds attain more years of schooling than those from unauthorized backgrounds, the differences in schooling from the second to the third generation for legal-background males are not sizable. Even looking at third-only generation respondents to eliminate any negative effects of selective attrition, the education gains are small (13.6 years of schooling among the 3.0 generation males compared with 13.3 in the 2.0 generation) (figure 5.3). Further analyses on income, presented later in this chapter, suggest that an important reason for this may be that third-generation males, as the working-class-delay theoretical perspective would expect, find ways to increase income without acquiring much additional schooling, implying that opportunities to earn more remain possible even without much education mobility between the second and third generations.

The fourth significant pattern involves Mexican Americans from ethnically dense family backgrounds (operationalized here for the 2.0 generation as both parents having been born in Mexico and for the 3.0 generation as all four grandparents being born in Mexico), who show disproportionately large increments in educational attainment compared with the 2.5 or 3.5 generations, that is, those who have one U.S.-born parent or one U.S.-born grandparent (who might or might not have Mexican ancestry), respectively. Again, according to labor-migration and family-based cultural repertoire ideas, women should exhibit this pattern more strongly than men, and, in fact, they do. Among women, the positive ethnic-density effect (which we interpret as stemming from their working extra hard to compensate for the immigration-related sacrifices and expectations of parents and grand-parents) is in fact larger than it is for males. For example, women's aver-age years of schooling rises from 12.2 years in the 1.5 generation to 13.0 years in the 2.5 generation (for those with only one parent born in Mexico) (figure 5.3). But for those with two parents born in Mexico (the 2.0 generation), it rises from 12.2 to 13.6 years of schooling. By the third genera-tion (that is, the grandchildren of immigrants), female attainment for the 3.0 generation increases still more notably, rising to 14.2 years of schooling, whereas for the 3.5 generation, it increases only to 13.6 years. Thus though schooling across generations generally rises for females, it jumps particu-larly for the women with the most ethnic background ties. We argue this pattern is consistent with ethnic-advantage or selective-acculturation ideas.

What impact does having an unauthorized background exert on three-generational patterns? As noted earlier, we can calculate aggregate-level 3.0 and 3.5 generation schooling levels for persons with unauthorized and authorized backgrounds even though we do not have individual-level data identifying which individual persons have such backgrounds. The approach used in making these calculations is outlined in appendix E. The resulting adjusted means for all generations, including those for the 3.0 and 3.5 generations, are presented in figure 5.4. Again, for both males and females, those with unauthorized Mexican immigrant mothers who never legalized (or who were never able to) show lower levels of education than those with authorized mothers. In the 2.0 and 3.0 generations from unauthorized backgrounds, we would expect females to show evidence of extra effort. This is indeed the case for these women, who exhibit larger and more-positive schooling jumps compared with men, but ones that still leave them below their legal counterparts. Nonetheless, both of the female third-generation groups exceed their second-generation counter-parts to a notable degree, but this gain in schooling is especially sizable for those with four Mexican-born grandparents (rising from 11.5 years in the 2.0 generation to 13.7 years for those with unauthorized backgrounds). Thus as expected by combined membership-exclusion and ethnic-density hypotheses, the gains for this group are the largest of any two generational groups that can be compared. Finally, it is notable that increases for males from authorized backgrounds into the third-generation groups are small, all averaging less than one-half a year of schooling.

These same patterns emerge when we regress schooling levels on the generational categories, controlling for age (see table 5.3 for descriptive statistics on variables in the regressions). In this case, we see that the 2.0 generation schooling levels for males and females respectively range from nearly a year (0.90) to 1.42 years above the 1.5 generation's levels (model 1, table 5.4), reflecting the substantial

(Text continues on p. 103.)

Figure 5.4   Age-Adjusted Years of Schooling Across Three Generations of Mexican Americans, Aged Twenty to Forty, by Migration-Status Background, Los Angeles, 2004

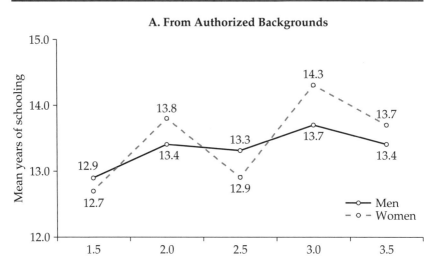

A. From Authorized Backgrounds

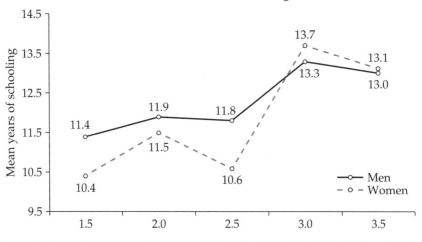

B. From Unauthorized Backgrounds

Source: Data from Immigration and Intergenerational Mobility in Metropolitan Los Angeles (see Bean, Leach et al. 2011).

Table 5.3 Means and Standard Deviations for Socioeconomic and Control Variables Used in Income Regressions, by Gender and Generational Status, 2004

| | Generation | | | | | | | | | | | 3+ Non-Hispanic White | |
| | 1.5 | | 2.0 | | 2.5 | | 3.0 | | 3.5 | | | | |
Variable	Mean	SD	Mean	SD	Mean	SD	Mean	SD	Mean	SD		Mean	SD
					Men								
Annual income	28,674	26,889	29,547	27,939	29,715	20,027	47,370	32,811	36,323	28,656		43,686	43,156
Age	28.89	6.47	26.67	5.31	28.83	6.68	31.96	6.92	29.06	4.93		30.60	5.81
In school	0.23	0.42	0.33	0.47	0.29	0.46	0.09	0.29	0.26	0.44		0.18	0.39
Works full time	0.73	0.44	0.59	0.49	0.68	0.47	0.96	0.21	0.81	0.40		0.69	0.46
Education (yrs.)	12.55	2.50	13.33	2.03	13.39	1.95	13.78	2.13	13.61	1.94		14.43	2.18
					Women								
Annual income	23,396	15,378	20,974	19,520	22,826	16,383	35,615	22,366	29,543	29,195		26,716	23,631
Age	29.29	7.07	29.26	6.14	27.44	5.33	29.93	6.06	30.46	6.29		30.98	6.16
In school	0.25	0.44	0.25	0.44	0.40	0.49	0.29	0.46	0.15	0.38		0.27	0.45
Works full time	0.58	0.50	0.51	0.50	0.58	0.49	0.57	0.50	0.62	0.51		0.50	0.50
Education (yrs.)	12.53	2.95	13.80	2.00	13.07	2.09	14.23	2.83	13.54	1.74		14.99	2.30

Source: Data from Immigration and Intergenerational Mobility in Metropolitan Los Angeles (see Bean, Leach et al. 2011).
Note: Generations are weighted to represent the Mexican-origin generational distribution in Los Angeles and adjusted for generational age differences.

Table 5.4   Effect of Migration-Background Status on Years of Schooling Completed, Mexican Americans, Aged Twenty to Forty, by Gender and Generation, Los Angeles, 2004

| | Men | | | | | | Women | | | | | |
| | Model 1 | | Model 2 | | Model 3 | | Model 1 | | Model 2 | | Model 3 | |
Category	B	SE	B	SE	B	SE	B	SE	B	SE	B	SE
Mother unauthorized			-1.54***	0.289	-1.88***	0.36			-2.30**	0.33	-2.91+	0.43
Generation 1.5												
Generation 2.0	0.90***	0.23	0.49*	0.23	0.35	0.26	1.42***	0.25	1.11***	0.24	0.88***	0.26
Generation 2.5	0.80**	0.29	0.38	0.29	0.18	0.31	0.79*	0.32	0.26	0.32	0.12	0.32
Generation 3.0	1.16*	0.47	0.65	0.47	0.55	0.47	2.02**	0.69	1.48*	0.66	1.34*	0.66
Generation 3.5	0.91*	0.41	0.39	0.41	0.28	0.42	1.38**	0.45	0.85+	0.43	0.71	0.44
Unauthorized × 2.0					0.64+	0.52					1.46*	0.67
Unauthorized × 2.5					1.85	1.14						
Age (mean-centered)	0.05**	0.02	0.05**	0.02	0.05**	0.02	0.03	0.02	0.03+	0.02	0.03+	0.02
Constant	12.41***	0.17	12.93***	0.20	13.04***	0.20	12.15	0.19	12.68***	0.20	12.82	0.21
N	523		523		523		518		518		518	
R-squared	0.049		0.099		0.105		0.069		0.150		0.157	

Source: Data from Immigration and Intergenerational Mobility in Metropolitan Los Angeles (see Bean, Leach et al. 2011).
Note: The 1.5 generation is the reference category.
***$p < .001$; **$p < .01$; *$p < .05$; +$p < .10$

ethnic-density effects picked up by this generation group. Adding un-authorized background (in models 2 and 3), however, shows that the generational differences are predominantly a function of unauthorized background for men (the statistically significant ones shown in model 1 are no longer statistically significant in models 2 and 3) after unauthorized background status is added to the model, whereas they remain statistically significant in the female cases, consistent with the idea that the selective acculturation and ethnic density effects are larger for women than men. The patterns here, and their shift, are thus compatible with the ideas that unauthorized backgrounds discourage boys from exchanging their work responsibilities for more schooling, whereas girls remain freer to do so. Of course, schools and peer groups can exert influences over education levels as well, but we have no reason to expect schools or peers to operate differently for children of families depending on their ethnic density.

Assessing the Relative Magnitude of Ethnic-Density Effects

Indeed, one of the challenges in interpreting what kinds of forces are driving such patterns is unraveling the relative influence of other factors whose effects may run in opposite directions. For example, we see evidence in the graphs in figure 5.4 of both a positive generation effect over time, although one not as large for males as females, and also a substantial negative effect of unauthorized background in the case of both males and females. In addition, having parents or grandparents born in Mexico is also associated for both genders with obtaining more schooling, although appreciably more so for women than men, as expected. As a heuristic for gauging the relative magnitudes of these opposite-direction effects, we regress years of schooling completed on generation (treated as a linear-coded variable), age, gender, unauthorized background, and ethnic homogeneity (coded 1 if either both of one's parents or all of one's grandparents were born in Mexico).[16] The reason for specifying such a simplified model is to estimate the magnitude of unauthorized background's effect compared with that of ethnic-density, given that these are somewhat obscured when generational dummies are used. Tests for all possible two-way interaction effects among independent variables showed that only one was significant, that involving a difference by gender in the effects of homogeneity on schooling (women with high ethnic-family densities obtained more than twice as much additional schooling as similar men, as hypothesized).

The results represent average effects across all respondents. Although only a heuristic distillation, they nonetheless provide useful indications of the relative magnitude of certain effects. For example, the average linear effect of generation across the five generational groups involves an

Figure 5.5   **Average Educational Attainment, Mexican-Origin Adults, by Gender, Generation, and Mother's Migration-Status Background, Los Angeles, 2004**

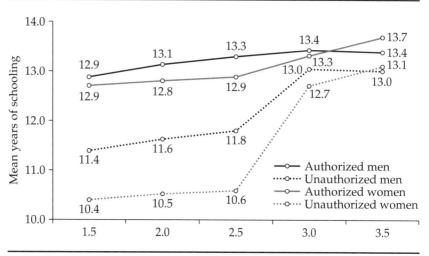

Source: Data from Immigration and Intergenerational Mobility in Metropolitan Los Angeles (see Bean, Leach et al. 2011).
Note: Adjusted for age and ethnic density differences between generations.

increase of about one-seventh of a year's schooling for each adjacent generation group. In other words, comparing the 2.5 generation group with the 3.0 group (and all such similar adjacent pairs) yields an average education difference of 0.151 years of schooling. The most important result is that for authorized background status, which here can be evaluated in terms of its relative importance compared with the family-related ethnic-density variable. Parents being able to legalize raises children's schooling by almost two years on average ($b = 1.85$). This is more than six times as large as the ethnic-homogeneity effect for males ($b_m = 0.26$) and almost twice this effect for females ($b_f = 0.26 + 0.73 = 0.98$). In short, legalization results in the largest consistent positive effect on education, one that increases the schooling premium for both males and females, especially the latter, even in comparison with the sizes of other positive effects.

These results can be illustrated by graphing the generations' linear effects after removing the positive ethnic-density bumps occurring in the 2.0 and the 3.0 generations for each of the four migration status and gender combinations.[17] The graph reveals three patterns (figure 5.5). The first, as we have already seen, is that the schooling levels of both men and women coming from unauthorized backgrounds are lower than those of persons from authorized backgrounds. The second is that those from unauthorized backgrounds show notable increases from the 2.5 to the 3.0 generation. In the female case, there is also a notable increase among those with authorized backgrounds from the 2.5 through the 3.5 generation, a pattern in keeping with society-wide increases in education among women. The third, however, is that even males from authorized backgrounds do not achieve as much in the way of improvement in educational attainment across generations as women, a pattern noted earlier in this chapter but one that bears repeating. The average schooling level of 13.4 years for third-generation authorized-background males with two grandparents born in the United States reflects that many of the men in this group still have only a high school education and do not achieve levels of college completion on a par with non-Hispanic whites.

The debilitating effects of membership exclusion on the children of immigrants are clearly apparent in reduced levels of educational attainment among the children of unauthorized immigrants, even when positive countervailing forces come into play. However, when we examine the graph in figure 5.5 for males with authorized backgrounds, we see that notable education increases from the second to the third generations do not emerge, even for those men whose grandparents were all born in Mexico. In other words, higher levels of schooling among grandsons are only minimally larger than those for second-generation males with authorized backgrounds. So while membership exclusion helps explain differences in levels of human capital acquisition between the authorized- and unauthorized-background children of immigrants, that only small gains in schooling occur from the second to the third generation for males with authorized backgrounds suggests a need to consider other theoretical explanations to account for this lack of substantial mobility. To assess whether working-class delay ideas are relevant here, we turn to analyses of income.

Generational Income Patterns

At one level, income might seem to be an indicator of economic (and thus structural) integration that mostly reflects education, telling us little on its own that is different from what we have already learned. However, it is also a factor that can vary independently of education, thus providing additional information. Such independent variation may occur for multiple reasons. For example, income may be especially likely to reflect the strength of motivation to achieve in the United States, thus fluctuating more than schooling does simply through effort (that is, it could be relatively higher among those coming from families most selected by immigration to work hard, something especially likely among the unauthorized, all else being equal). The working-class delay hypothesis expects higher income among the third generation than the second, and it expects this more for men than women because of men's stronger obligation to support their families. To the degree that such dynamics come into play, the rate of income returns to education should be lower for men than for women. In fact this is the case. In our examinations, we start by looking at simple generational patterns in income, we then move to assessing the effects of unauthorized background, looking at how controlling for other variables affects the generational patterns. Finally, we examine how education affects the pattern and magnitude of generational and gender differences in income.

Males

What do the generation patterns for unadjusted income indicate about support for the membership-exclusion and the family-ethnic-density hypotheses, especially for males? Males in the 1.5 generation make $28,650 on average, an income level only slightly exceeded in the 2.0 generation ($29,550), a gain of 3 percent (table 5.3). It then rises even more slightly (to $29,700) in the 2.5 generation, or about 0.5 percent, before jumping to $47,370 in the 3.0 generation, a boost of 59.4 percent. Note that this latter group is the one with four Mexican-born grandparents. In the 3.5 generation (those with two Mexican-born and two U.S.-born grandparents), the average income level is $36,300, or 22.2 percent higher than in the 2.5 generation. Thus for men who are the children of immigrants, income differences are scant between the 1.5 to the 2.5 generations, but then escalate appreciably in the third-generation groups, particularly for those whose grandparents were all born in Mexico. For males, the pattern of results is thus compatible with the expectations of both the membership-exclusion and the family-ethnic-density hypotheses. These patterns are, respectively, that a large gain occurs between the second and the third generation (because the hindrances associated with unauthorized parental status no longer apply) and that within both generations, those with more family ties to the immigrant generation will show additional increases, with this motivation-related jump tending to occur less strongly for males in the second generation because of the continuation of strong imperatives to work to meet family needs instead of continuing in school to obtain more education.

If we look at the descriptive data in table 5.3, we obtain additional insight into the meaning of these income differences. For one thing, we note that the income differences across generations are likely to be somewhat (but not much) affected by age differences. The 3.0 and 3.5 generations are slightly older than the group of second-generation children of immigrants, so this can account for only a small part of the former's tendencies to have higher incomes. The third-generation categories also exhibit slightly higher education levels than do the second-generation ones. But the main thing that stands out between the children of immigrants and the grandchildren of immigrants are the latter's higher percentages of persons working full time, which among those males with four grandparents born in Mexico reaches a nearly universal level, 96.0 percent. This unusually high level is consistent with the expectation that this group of males in particular will evince an unusually strong work tendency as predicted by the family-ethnic-density hypothesis. Males in the 3.5 generation are also more likely to work full time (81 percent) than are second-generation groups, but not nearly to the same degree as the 96 percent of 3.0 generation men who do. So it is notable that the third-generation groups of men are making considerably more money than second-generation men, and doing so in part by dint of extra work. We return to this later in the chapter.

Females

For women, the income difference between the 1.5 and the 2.0 generation is modest (average income declines from $23,400 to less than $21,000, a drop of 10.4 percent) (table 5.3). In the 2.5 generation, the average climbs back past $22,800. This occurs for those with only one Mexican-born parent, a result that is not in conformity with the family-ethnic-density motivational hypothesis. However, in the 3.0 generation, which is the group with four Mexican-born grandparents, the annual income rises to $35,600, a jump of $14,650 from the 2.0 generation, or nearly 70 percent. Among both third-generation women and men then, the grandchildren of immigrants with only Mexican-born grandparents do exceptionally well insofar as income attainment is concerned, showing patterns consistent with the expectations of both the membership-exclusion background and family-ethnic-density-motivation theoretical expectations. Among women, however, those with two U.S.-born grandparents (the 3.5 generation) drop back to an annual income level of $29,550, one that is only about 30 percent greater than that of the 2.5 generation. Unlike the case of men, the additional descriptive data for women (table 5.3) do not reveal much in the way of interesting patterns. For example, the proportion of women working in the various generation groups does not vary much at all.

As with education, average income of males and females is thus especially high among those with Mexican-born parents or grandparents. We suggest the reason is that those with higher incomes show stronger ties to the family's experience of labor migration as indicated by both parents being Mexican migrants or all four grandparents being Mexican migrants. This pattern is consistent with the family-ethnic-density and selective-acculturation expectation that immigrants in general, and Mexican immigrants in particular (especially unauthorized migrants), are selected for motivation and optimism (the very act of migrating requires both), and that this motivation will be even stronger among those with more U.S.-born parents or U.S.-born grandparents. The one exception to this pattern in the case of income involves second-generation (2.0) women, for whom having two Mexican-born parents seems not to translate into disproportionate earnings attainment. Because women's schooling in Mexico has traditionally fallen considerably below that of males, especially relative to the greater gender equality prevalent in the United States, Mexican American females have more to gain from migration and schooling than do males. Perhaps the second-generation women with Mexican-born parents have risen so much relative to their origins that they feel they have already achieved a great deal.

Three-Generational Patterns for Those with Unauthorized Backgrounds   In general, we would expect the cross-generational pattern of differences in income to be similar to those for education. However, that the relative income increases for males between the second and the third generation are so much larger than those for schooling suggest that there are important sources of structural integration occurring for males independently of education. Without controlling for other variables, we see that second-generation males do not exhibit higher income levels than the 1.5-generation, with neither the 2.0 nor the 2.5 generation showing any significant income difference compared with the 1.5 generation (table 5.5, model 1). Yet income is substantially higher in the third generation categories, especially among those men with four Mexican-born grandparents (the 3.0 generation), whose income is 72 percent above that of 1.5-generation men.[18] This provides evidence of sharply higher earnings between second- and third-generation men.

How does unauthorized background affect male income? Second-generation men from families with unauthorized backgrounds earn about 10 percent less than the 1.5-generation males (table 5.5, model 2). The income differences for second generation men compared with the 1.5 generation men when unauthorized background and work variables are controlled (in model 4) are still notable, unlike those for education level, which shows little significant difference when unauthorized background is controlled. There, the higher male schooling levels in the second generation were mostly explained by the effects of parental unauthorized background. Here, however, the second generation differences in male income (at least for the 2.0 generation) emerge after controlling unauthorized background status and work variables, indicating that male earnings are in part a function of other factors than schooling and membership-exclusion dynamics. Interestingly, this pattern does not hold for women, for whom differences in *both* education and income persist after controlling for unauthorized status. Because second-generation males are also less likely to work full-time and more likely to be enrolled in school than

Table 5.5   OLS Coefficients from Models of Annual Income (Natural Log), Regressed on Immigrant Generation, Migration-Status Background, and Control Variables, Mexican American Men, Aged Twenty to Forty, Los Angeles, 2004

	Model 1		Model 2		Model 3		Model 4		Model 5		Model 6	
	B	SE	B	SE	B	SE	B	SE	B	SE	B	SE
Generation 1.5												
Generation 2.0	0.035	0.109			0.033	0.115	0.261**	0.099	-0.009	0.113	0.223*	0.098
Generation 2.5	0.112	0.143			0.110	0.149	0.155	0.126	0.065	0.145	0.120	0.124
Generation 3.0	0.717***	0.221			0.714**	0.226	0.371+	0.194	0.637**	0.221	0.308	0.190
Generation 3.5	0.400*	0.195			0.397*	0.201	0.326*	0.171	0.337+	0.196	0.279+	0.167
Unauthorized background			-0.100	0.135	-0.009	0.143	-0.019	0.122	0.144	0.143	0.106	0.122
Age							0.057***	0.007			0.052***	0.007
Enrolled in school							-0.034	0.090			-0.116	0.090
Not working (ref.)												
Works full time							0.828***	0.104			0.806***	0.101
Works part time							0.234+	0.139			0.183	0.136
Years of education									0.103***	0.021	0.088***	0.019
Constant	9.849	0.085	9.958***	0.049	9.852***	0.097	7.589***	0.223	8.504***	0.292	6.633***	0.298
R-squared	0.031		0.001		0.034		0.309		0.077		0.341	

Source: Data from Immigration and Intergenerational Mobility in Metropolitan Los Angeles (see Bean, Leach et al. 2011).
Note: The 1.5 generation is the reference category.
***$p < .001$; **$p < .01$; *$p < .05$; +$p < .10$

1.5-generation males, we see that when we take this into account, their incomes exceed that of 1.5-generation men (model 4). Because the third-generation groups are more likely to work full-time and less likely to be in school than the second-generation males, some of the earnings advantage for the third-generation categories over the second diminishes but does not disappear (model 4). When we control for respondent's education (model 6), this pattern does not change. Nor does it change when we add parents' education to the model (result not shown for reasons of space but available from the authors).

The theoretical considerations introduced in previous chapters suggest that the negative effects of unauthorized background are more likely to be evident for males than for females because the strong work expectations arising from the experience of Mexican labor migration fall disproportionately on them, with the consequence that statistical controls for such backgrounds reduce or eliminate socioeconomic differences between second- and third-generation categories. This is what we have just seen for males. For women, however, this does not happen. After the introduction of controls for unauthorized background, as well as controls for working full time and not being enrolled in school (table 5.6, models 3 and 4), higher incomes for third-generation females persist, particularly for those with four Mexican-born grandparents. Thus coming from an unauthorized background does not result in conditions that exert as much downward force on second-generation women's attainment as men's. Moreover, women with four Mexican-born grandparents, as the selective acculturation-related family-ethnic-density hypothesis would expect, exhibit especially large incomes relative to the reference category (that is, they show annual earnings that are 47 percent higher than the 1.5 generation after all statistical controls are included in the model). And controlling for respondent's own and parents' education does not change this pattern.

The different results for men and women thus tend to support the membership-exclusion ideas advanced in previous chapters about the effects of unauthorized parental background. These emphasize that migration- and family-related cultural-repertoire pressures impinge on males and females to behave in ways that help them cope with vulnerable and precarious family positions resulting from unauthorized background and very low socioeconomic status. For males this often means finding work at all costs, including frequently making the sacrifice of giving up the pursuit of more education for immediate work to bring in money for the family. We see evidence of this in the substantially lower socioeconomic attainments of males with unauthorized backgrounds, a pattern that is stronger than it is for females, as expected. Also, evidence in support of theoretical ideas about selective acculturation emerges more for females in their greater tendencies to exhibit unusually high socioeconomic attainments (education and income) when they come from

Table 5.6   OLS Coefficients from Models of Annual Income (Natural Log), Regressed on Immigrant Generation, Migration-Status Background, and Control Variables, Mexican American Women, Aged Twenty to Forty, Los Angeles, 2004

Variable	Model 1 B	Model 1 SE	Model 2 B	Model 2 SE	Model 3 B	Model 3 SE	Model 4 B	Model 4 SE	Model 5 B	Model 5 SE	Model 6 B	Model 6 SE
Generation 1.5												
Generation 2.0	0.201+	0.115			0.182	0.116	0.274**	0.101	0.028	0.111	0.149	0.097
Generation 2.5	0.406**	0.145			0.369*	0.148	0.302*	0.127	0.346*	0.140	0.289*	0.120
Generation 3.0	0.792**	0.280			0.755**	0.281	0.635**	0.242	0.568*	0.266	0.467*	0.229
Generation 3.5	0.326	0.215			0.289	0.217	0.253	0.186	0.200	0.205	0.178	0.176
Unauthorized background			-0.311+	0.162	-0.190	0.166	-0.159	0.143	0.095	0.161	0.069	0.139
Age							0.063***	0.007			0.059***	0.007
Enrolled in school							-0.083	0.093			-0.172+	0.089
Not working												
Works full-time							0.629***	0.097			0.522***	0.093
Works part-time							0.195	0.128			0.105	0.122
Years of education									0.142***	0.02	0.122***	0.018
Constant	9.506***	0.089	9.742***	0.051	9.542***	0.095	7.349***	0.242	7.702***	0.273	5.999***	0.300
R-squared	0.031		0.009		0.037		0.301		0.148		0.378	

Source: Data from Immigration and Intergenerational Mobility in Metropolitan Los Angeles (see Bean, Leach et al. 2011).
Note: The 1.5 generation is the reference category.
***$p < .001$; **$p < .01$; *$p < .05$; +$p < .10$

backgrounds with high family ethnic density (either both parents born in Mexico or all grandparents born in Mexico). In other words, women, as expected, reveal patterns with their having a stronger penchant to strive to compensate for the migration sacrifices of previous generations.

However, evidence also emerges that seems to support only working-class-delay ideas, namely, higher income but not education gains for third-generation men compared with second-generation men. This is true even though our analyses use a third-only generation measure of education that is not biased downward because of selective attrition. But more striking, in contrast, is that the income gains for males in the third generation are quite large relative to education gains. Although their years of schooling rise by only about 4 percent (making for an average schooling gain of less than half a year), the income increase is almost 40 percent. For 3.0 generation men (those with all Mexican-born grandparents), the rise is almost $18,000 per person, a difference of 62 percent over the second generation. Clearly, third-generation men are finding ways to make more money while acquiring little in the way of more schooling compared with the second generation. To check if this might result from their having shifted to different occupations, we decomposed the income gain into that part owing to occupational change versus that part that does not come from such shifts. We found that only about 10 percent of the income gain could be attributed to differences in occupations for third-generation men compared with second-generation men (results available from authors upon request). This means that most of the income increase for males in the third generation occurs even though they are doing similar kinds of work as second-generation men.

The importance of this for economic integration is that male Mexican Americans, most of whom are working class, are able to find blue-collar employment that is considerably more gainful in the third generation than is similar work is in the second generation. This parallels recent research showing that large proportions of Mexican immigrants, especially males, are able to locate and take advantage of work opportunities that pay more even when occupationally similar to their previous jobs.[19] This same opportunistic tendency is evident here for third-generation males, suggesting that because income mobility can still be achieved without more schooling, this may contribute to the absence of greater schooling gains in the third generation for Mexican American males. This is precisely the kind of possibility implied by working-class-delay notions. We return in the final chapter to a discussion of what this might mean for overall conclusions about Mexican American integration.

Education and Other Effects on Income

At this point, we address three further questions. The first concerns whether the income differences we have observed are a function of other variables, and, if this is the case, to what extent do these work in directions consistent with the idea that those with more Mexican-born parents and grandparents are more motivated to work hard. The second concerns whether generational and ethnic differences in income (the gap between the third generation and non-Hispanic whites) are mostly explained by generational differences in education, as has been repeatedly found in previous research.[20] This is important because the lack of such differences would imply an absence of pay discrimination in the labor market. The third concerns whether the remaining generational income differences after education is controlled (that is, the deficit or increment in income unexplained by education and controls) follow the generational pattern predicted by the membership-exclusion hypothesis of narrowing income differences between the second- and third-generation categories.

Regarding the first, we conduct analyses regressing the natural log of annual income on education, controlling successively for age, being enrolled in school, and working full time. Controlling for age removes any differences in income across generations and between the Mexican American third-generation and non-Hispanic whites owing to birth-cohort differences. The controls for being in school and working full time not only adjust for pay differences in these factors, they tell us whether such tendencies, both of which may be interpreted as reflecting high motivation, help to explain generational differences. As is evident in the results without controls (model 1 in table 5.7), the males in the 1.5, 2.0, and 2.5 generations show incomes 32 to 43 percent below those of whites, whereas those in the 3.0 generation (those with four Mexican-born grandparents) are 29 percent above average white incomes, with the 3.5 generation showing a level 3 percent below whites. For the 3.0 generation males, controlling for being enrolled in school shaves 3 percentage points off the income advantage (results from models not shown). In other words, a higher proportion of the 3.0 generation males are working instead of going to school. Similarly, working full time reduces the advantage by 23 percentage points. In short, most of the 3.0 generation income advantage derives from, respectively, working at a younger age (not being in school) and working longer hours, variables that reflect either a motivational tendency to work more or a working-class tendency to work earlier (that is, to work rather than go to college). These together account for almost all of the higher income level in the 3.0 generation (comparing models 1 and 3 results in table 5.7).

Adjusting for the effects of unauthorized background shrinks only slightly the tendency for the male children of immigrants (the second-generation categories) to show income levels below those of the third-generation males (model 2), indicating that a substantial part of income integration occurs independently of education. Controlling for age and work differences as well (as in model 3), however, reduces substantially

Table 5.7 OLS Coefficients from Models of Annual Income (Natural Log), Regressed on Ethnoracial and Generation Group, Migration-Status Background, and Control Variables, Mexican American Men, Aged Twenty to Forty, Los Angeles, 2004

	Model 1	Model 2	Model 3	Model 4	Model 5	Model 6
Non-Hispanic White						
1.5 Generation Mexican	−0.427***	−0.424**	−0.357**	−0.226+	−0.269*	−0.237*
2.0 Generation Mexican	−0.392***	−0.391***	−0.095	−0.273**	−0.281**	−0.017
2.5 Generation Mexican	−0.315*	−0.314*	−0.207+	−0.203	−0.207	−0.123
3.0 Generation Mexican	0.290	0.290	0.019	0.360+	0.363+	0.080
3.5 Generation Mexican	−0.027	−0.027	−0.025	0.061	0.064	0.048
Unauthorized background		−0.009	−0.020		0.154	0.109
Age			0.057***			0.051***
Enrolled in school			−0.005			−0.086
Not working (ref.)						
Working full time			0.728***			0.696***
Working part time			0.014			−0.035
Years of education				0.107***	0.110***	0.090***
Constant	10.277***	10.277***	8.039***	8.736***	8.683***	6.966***
R-squared	0.044	0.044	0.304	0.097	0.098	0.338

Source: Data from Immigration and Intergenerational Mobility in Metropolitan Los Angeles (see Bean, Leach et al. 2011).

Note: Non-Hispanic whites are the reference category.

***$p < .001$; **$p < .01$; *$p < .05$; +$p < .10$.

the income differences among the Mexican American male generational categories and the difference between these and non-Hispanic whites. And, most significant of all for present purposes, when we control for all factors, including education, the income differences between every Mexican American generational category and whites but one disappears altogether (model 6). The exception is the 1.5 generation, which consists of the one group born in Mexico. Their average income falls 24 percent below that of whites even after the introduction of all controls.

For women, the 2.5, 3.0, and 3.5 generations show zero-order incomes above those of non-Hispanic whites, the first being about 15 percent higher, the second about 53 percent higher, and the third about 7 percent higher (table 5.8, model 1). Only the second of these differences is statistically significant, but our sample sizes are small. Controlling for working full time has a different effect for women and men. Adjusting for working full time, staying in school, and age only slightly reduce the advantage for those third-generation females with Mexican-born grandparents, diminishing the advantage by only 5 percentage points.

In the case of the second question, we see that controlling for education affects the income differences for both men and women relative to whites, and in the case of women it actually moves income above the level of whites. In other words, the generational categories generally show lower levels of Mexican American schooling than whites. However, giving both Mexican Americans and non-Hispanic whites statistically the same schooling levels, as would be the case when we introduce controls, causes the income differences relative to whites in the later generation groups actually to increase above those of whites. Stated in substantive terms, both males and females with four grandparents born in Mexico display higher incomes than non-Hispanic whites, and this persists in the case of women even after the introduction of work and education controls. For men, the positive advantage remains when education is controlled but becomes statistically insignificant when degree of work is controlled (see table 5.5). In other words, Mexican American males work more than whites. But when they have the same schooling levels as non-Hispanic whites, the income advantage persists. We return to this finding in just a moment. For now, we note that, when all variables are controlled (including education) (tables 5.5 and 5.6, model 6), the income advantage for both of the female third-generation groups persists, reaching 54 percent higher for women with four Mexican-born grandparents.

These results show somewhat better labor-market outcomes for Mexican males than those estimated by the 2006 National Research Council study on Hispanics.[21] That study used much larger national samples, although it could rely only on a third-plus-generation measure rather than the third-only-generation measure that we employ here, and it could not separate those third-generation persons with four Mexican-born grandparents from

Table 5.8 OLS Coefficients from Models of Annual Income (Natural Log), Regressed on Ethnoracial and Generation Group, Migration-Status Background, and Control Variables, Mexican American Women, Aged Twenty to Forty, Los Angeles, 2004

	Model 1	Model 2	Model 3	Model 4	Model 5	Model 6
Non-Hispanic White						
1.5 Generation Mexican	-0.259*	-0.222+	-0.152	0.029	0.022	0.033
2.0 Generation Mexican	-0.058	-0.040	0.089	0.080	0.077	0.177+
2.5 Generation Mexican	0.147	0.147	0.152	0.371**	0.373**	0.328**
3.0 Generation Mexican	0.533+	0.533+	0.482+	0.622*	0.623*	0.541*
3.5 Generation Mexican	0.067	0.067	0.092	0.237	0.238	0.220
Unauthorized background		-0.190	-0.153		0.045	0.021
Age			0.049***			0.045***
Enrolled in school			-0.101			-0.165*
Not working (ref.)						
Working full-time			0.762***			0.680***
Working part-time			0.176*			0.095
Years of education				0.117***	0.117***	0.093***
Constant	9.764***	9.764***	7.842***	8.017***	8.003***	6.669***
R-squared	0.023	0.025	0.264	0.098	0.098	0.307

Source: Data from Immigration and Intergenerational Mobility in Metropolitan Los Angeles (see Bean, Leach et al. 2011).
Note: Non-Hispanic whites are the reference category.
***$p < .001$; **$p < .01$; *$p < .05$; +$p < .10$.

those with fewer such grandparents. That study reported an estimate of an income deficit net of education and other factors for the third-plus-generation males of 13.1 percent, whereas the estimate here shows an advantage of about 6 percent (taking a weighted average for the 3.0- and 3.5-generation male coefficients from table 5.6). Estimates based on third-plus samples, however, would be expected to show less favorable results from an integration standpoint because they would be more affected by the negative effects of selective attrition as well as other factors whose effects we analyze in appendix C.

The results here for women also indicate better labor-market positions than those indicated in the National Research Council study. Again, this is not unexpected because of the selective attrition that was in the data and because a much higher proportion of the national sample would consist of persons with Texas backgrounds, a state of origin that is historically associated with substantially limited Mexican American socioeconomic attainment.[22] More interesting for the moment is that the results for both males and females from model 5 in tables 5.5 and 5.6 indicate that controlling only for education, the remaining generational differences in income, as with education, show a pattern generally consistent with the membership-integration hypothesis. That is, they are more favorable for the grandchildren of immigrants and less so for the children of immigrants. Thus a generational pattern of discontinuity emerges, with the third generation showing a steeper upward gain over the second generation than the latter does over the 1.5 generation.

And finally, turning to the third question, the present results indicate that once education and working differences are controlled (tables 5.7 and 5.8, model 6), either minimal differences in income between the third-generation groups and non-Hispanic whites remain (in the male case) or Mexican Americans actually show an advantage (in the female case). These results thus imply, like those of the National Research Council study, that labor-market discrimination in pay does not appear substantially to influence Mexican American income attainment.

Conclusions

This chapter has delved into the patterns of difference in education and income across immigrant generations to assess the membership-integration and other integration hypotheses. For Mexican Americans, the schooling of third-generation females shows notable improvements over that of second-generation women. The same is true for males coming from unauthorized backgrounds. However, this is not the pattern for males with authorized backgrounds, suggesting that Mexican American third-generation men remain disproportionately represented in working-class and lower-middle-class jobs. More positively, however, having two Mexican-born parents is associated with decidedly higher educational attainment. This same effect emerges among the grandchildren of immigrants, where those with four Mexican-born grandparents far out-perform those with only two. This accords with the ethnic-density, migration-related motivational hypothesis, which is akin in many respects to selective-acculturation hypotheses.[23] However, despite this, Mexican American men who come from authorized backgrounds, although they start at higher schooling levels in earlier generations than their unauthorized counterparts, show only minimal increases in schooling across generations.

In regard to income, we find support for males for the membership-exclusion expectation of a discontinuity in income between the children of Mexican immigrants (the 2.0 and 2.5 generations) and the grandchildren of immigrants (the 3.0 and 3.5 generations). This pattern is expected because the initial unauthorized status of so many Mexican immigrants often necessitates that sons work instead of attending school, thus lowering later-generation income. For this same reason, the hypothesis also expects the discontinuous pattern to be more characteristic of boys than girls. In general, we find that larger differences for unauthorized males emerge between the two main generational groups than within them. The biggest jump in attainment occurs after the second generation. In the case of income, this pattern is also mediated by differences in working full time and starting to work at earlier ages, variables that also explain income differences between Mexican American generational categories and whites. And females actually make more money than do their white counterparts, even after the introduction of controls.

When we look at education and income for males within the two major generation groupings, we find that education accounts for most of the differences in income between the male generational groups and non-Hispanic whites, consistent with results that have emerged in countless prior studies. This suggests that those Mexican Americans who can attain high levels of education may not face significant pay discrimination in the labor market. But it leaves unanswered the question of what keeps so many Mexican American males, including those from unauthorized backgrounds, from attaining higher levels of education than they do, and why higher levels of education are not attained until the third generation, though even then still falling below non-Hispanic white schooling levels. The membership-exclusion hypothesis in combination with the working-class-delay theoretical perspective explains much of this gap. The former specifies that unauthorized status in the first generation carries substantial negative consequences for education into the second generation and even into the third. The latter expects working-class Mexican American males to eschew increasingly costly investments in higher education when they can make sizable income gains without obtaining much more schooling. Both of these together are likely to contribute to limiting male education advancement in the third generation.

═ Chapter 6 ═

Spatial Integration

Since the last chapter shows rising incomes across generations for Mexican Americans in greater Los Angeles, it stands to reason that later generations also can afford to live in a greater variety of neighborhoods and may become more spatially integrated with the overall population. But does this happen? This chapter examines Mexican American spatial integration, or how the residential neighborhoods of Mexican Americans change across generations, and shows how neighborhood attainment relates to education and income as well as to parental disadvantages in legal status and language. We document that the locational attainment of third-generation Mexican Americans in Los Angeles improves significantly from the second generation. We also emphasize that metropolitan-wide population trends may mask the individual-level mobility of the third generation, and we examine how this has happened in Los Angeles. The chapter also suggests the importance of affordability for spatial integration, in that moving to more suburban or exurban areas with less expensive housing enables some of the members of earlier generations to jump-start spatial mobility.

Neighborhoods matter because they provide amenities and safety on one hand and access to social networks and a sense of belonging on the other. Even as commerce and communication become more global, the character of neighborhoods endures,[1] and a mobile population sorts itself according to the location and characteristics it desires and can afford.[2] Neighborhoods contribute to a sense of collective identity among residents. Sampson writes that "neighborhoods are still salient in the contemporary city: they are markers for one's station in life and are frequently invoked for this purpose. This does not mean neighborhoods are homogenous, only that they gain their identity through an ongoing commentary between themselves and outsiders, a collective version of the 'looking-glass self.'"[3] Neighborhoods also matter for socioeconomic outcomes, although the degree to which this is true is debated.[4] The immigration literature on neighborhood effects has often examined social disorganization, as indicated by studies focusing on oppositional culture and poor

119

schooling or health outcomes,[5] although in recent years the literature has also noted the benefits of middle-class ethnic concentrations.[6]

The Spatial Structure
of Greater Los Angeles

Greater Los Angeles offers geographic opportunity through a sprawling spatial and organizational structure that takes in five counties. As a city so big that its interconnecting freeways in places widen to sixteen lanes, L.A. juxtaposes multiple kinds of land use.[7] The distinction between urban and suburban is less obvious than in older cities of the East and Midwest. Los Angeles's traditional employment center is less its central business district, which is relatively small, than a vast nineteen-mile arc extending from Santa Monica to East L.A.[8] In addition, the metropolitan area features subcenters of large office parks and retail centers, so that jobs are decentralized. For example, the central part of Orange County contains an enormous business district in Irvine, which has been called both an "edge city" and a postsuburban development.[9]

The region's sprawl has fueled enormous population growth, with the metro area emerging first as a major manufacturing and entertainment center and then as a global city, always in need of low-skilled labor and ultimately drawing in millions of less-skilled Mexicans as well as members of other groups. Large-scale immigration began in the 1970s and increased in the 1980s, with the Mexican-origin population in metropolitan Los Angeles more than doubling between 1980 and 2000. Thanks to this heavy immigration as well as native out-migration, native Mexican Americans from Los Angeles live now in areas that are more heavily Latino than the neighborhoods in which they grew up. Edward Telles and Vilma Ortiz conclude that this new neighborhood context "could be interpreted as dis-assimilation."[10] Other observers refer to the phenomenon as the "Latinization" of Los Angeles, such that the clear spatial boundaries of Mexican neighborhoods that emerged after World War II have now blurred, with communities becoming connected more by social networks than by proximity.[11] The distinction is important, because *Latinization* implies a structural change that affects the entire population of the city, while *dis-assimilation* implies a negative outcome for the immigrant group.

Ultimately, however, immigration outstripped the ability of the economy in Los Angeles County to absorb the newcomers. The decline in the early 1990s of aerospace and defense-related manufacturing, which cost many natives their jobs, also led many immigrants to move on to other areas or bypass Los Angeles in the first place—a move abetted by state and local enforcement of policies on industries and housing.[12] However, some of the migrants did not go far—just one county to the east. This makes metropolitan Los Angeles a particularly appropriate site for examination of spatial integration, because its vast scale encompasses both an old immigrant gateway in Los Angeles County and to a lesser extent Orange and Ventura counties, as well as areas of new suburban and exurban settlement in neighboring Riverside and San Bernardino counties, collectively known as the Inland Empire.

Because metropolitan Los Angeles is bounded on the north by mountains, on the west by the Pacific Ocean, and on the south by master-planned communities, mountains, and Camp Pendleton, its areas of the greatest recent population growth have been eastward. Although Riverside and San Bernardino counties extend from Los Angeles and Orange counties through the Mojave Desert all the way to the state border, their population growth has been especially concentrated in their western ends, within commuting distance of Los Angeles and Orange County. From 1980 to 2010, the total population of Riverside County grew by 230.2 percent, and San Bernardino County by 127.4 percent.[13] The Latino flow into these counties was especially pronounced, so that by 2010, more than 40 percent of their residents were of Mexican origin (surpassing the 35.8 percent in Los Angeles County).

Figure 6.1 shows the concentration of the population identifying as Mexican in 2000 across census tracts in the five-county area. The areas of densest Mexican-origin population remain East Los Angeles and east of that in the San Gabriel Valley, as well as in the San Fernando Valley and in northern Orange County, near Santa Ana and Anaheim. Near coastal Ventura County, the city of Oxnard has a large Mexican-origin population, as do more rural areas inland. Lesser concentrations also appear across the Inland Empire, particularly in the city of San Bernardino and in Corona in western Riverside County. Segregation levels vary considerably within the region, too. Despite the growth in the proportion of Latinos in the Inland Empire, their segregation levels there have remained moderate. According to the index of dissimilarity, the segregation of Hispanics from non-Hispanic whites in the Inland Empire stood at 42.4 in 2010, almost the same as it was in 2000, meaning that 42.4 percent of one group would have to move for it to be randomly distributed with the other group. That level ranked 118th among metropolitan areas in the country. By contrast, the Los Angeles–Long Beach statistical area had the fourth highest ranking of segregation of Hispanics from non-Hispanic whites in the country in 2010.[14] Research on African American migration to the Inland Empire also has found that race matters less for residential attainment there than in Los Angeles County.[15]

Theoretical Considerations and Background

Where immigrants and their descendants live can matter in ways that relate to but still differ from other types of incorporation. As chapter 2 notes, both the relevant scholarly literature and our analyses suggest

Figure 6.1   Concentration of Mexican-Origin Population in 2000
in the Five-County Area of Metropolitan Los Angeles
(percentage)

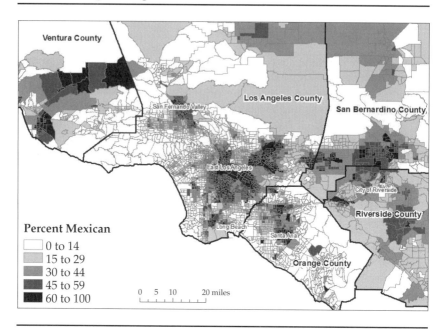

Source: Adapted from U.S. Bureau of the Census 2000a.

that spatial integration often occurs independently of economic integration. The theory connecting social, economic, and spatial dimensions of integration dates to the ecological principles of the Chicago School, particularly the observation by Robert Park that spatial relations tend to mirror social relations.[16] Originally formulated to describe the dispersion of early-twentieth-century immigrants from the ethnic enclaves in which they initially settled, the concept refers broadly to the residential convergence of racial-ethnic groups in general but particularly to the ability of minorities, often immigrant groups, to access the neighborhoods of the majority population.[17] As members of an immigrant group acculturate in customs and language and find better jobs, they start to seek better neighborhoods and housing amenities generally associated with higher-status natives. Greater contact with the native born creates opportunities for social and economic inclusion, particularly for children, whose playmates and schoolmates often live in the same neighborhood.[18] Thus the traditional conception of spatial integration holds that it works roughly in tandem with sociocultural and economic dimensions of integration and may be an intermediate step in the overall process of integration. It both reflects and reinforces socioeconomic status and may coincide with growth in primary structural ties that may hasten many other dimensions of incorporation.[19] Still, ethnic ties persist even in integrated and high-status neighborhoods, so it is important to distinguish social mixing from mere proximity.[20]

However, studies of both old and new immigrant groups to North America have questioned how closely residence relates to culture and socioeconomic status.[21] Among highly educated immigrant groups to the United States, such as Chinese, Koreans, and to a lesser extent Filipinos, some new arrivals settle in ethnic enclaves and some do not.[22] James Allen and Eugene Turner have refined the concept of spatial assimilation to include distance from the immigrant concentration and an expectation that when family immigration takes place over many years, some new immigrants will not settle in enclaves because they are coming to the United States to join relatives who have already moved out.[23] The relatively recent formation of suburban middle-class enclaves also suggests that spatial incorporation may take place somewhat apart from economic incorporation.[24]

Spatial assimilation is thus appropriately considered a distinct dimension of immigrant incorporation, for several theoretical and methodological reasons. First, spatial assimilation takes a long time. For European immigrant groups coming to the United States in the nineteenth and early twentieth centuries, the process of residential dispersion proceeded across decades if not generations and, generally, linearly.[25] Second, spatial assimilation depends more on life-course factors than other types of integration. People tend to move when they are young or when they marry and have children; then they tend to stay put in middle age.[26] Spatial mobility for any given generation may end at an age when incomes continue to rise. Third, immigrants may not be able to translate the same level of income to the same level of housing as the native born do. As newcomers, immigrants may know little about the housing market and may face discrimination, so that their housing choices are constrained and the cost of housing is higher for them.[27] Poor and working-class immigrant groups may face additional claims on their income and time from extended family, so they may be unable to translate income gains into better neighborhoods.[28] The availability of housing and the degree to which an affluent native majority occupies it may keep spatial mobility separate from other dimensions of incorporation.[29] In particular, a large supply of new housing can ease integration.[30] Finally, immigrants may prefer at least moderate coethnic concentration, especially if the neighborhood has many coethnic institutions and social networks and possibly a middle-class presence.[31]

The degree of preference for coethnics appears to vary in Los Angeles. Hispanics and Asians with poor English skills prefer coethnic neighborhoods, and other Hispanics and Asians lean more toward neighborhoods integrated with whites than to neighborhoods integrated with blacks.[32] All this variation can lead to distinctive patterns of spatial assimilation. In Los Angeles, for example, Mexicans appear to be following a traditional spatial-assimilation path, sometimes within the first generation.[33] Some of this assimilation may result from group mixing at work, since work spaces in Los Angeles are more integrated than residential neighborhoods.[34] Spatial assimilation of the Mexican American population in L.A. with whites also appears strong by the third generation.[35] By contrast, Chinese immigrants quickly buy homes in high-status areas, often suburban, without socially adapting, and Koreans tend to be more urban but not residentially concentrated.[36]

Varying preferences raise the question of whether white middle-class suburbia should be considered the mainstream criterion for achieving spatial assimilation. Some evidence suggests the emergence of panethnic spatial assimilation.[37] In cities with high immigration, such as Los Angeles, immigrant groups may tend first to stratify by socioeconomic status rather than simply leave behind their expanding coethnic population.[38]

Beyond Los Angeles, empirical studies of residential settlement patterns of Hispanics in general and Mexican Americans in particular have produced mixed results. Some show results consistent with classic spatial-assimilation theory.[39] Nevertheless, in most cities, the segregation level of Hispanics has been rising, and they still face discrimination in the housing market.[40] Mexicans are less likely than blacks to leave high-poverty neighborhoods.[41] Other research finds continuing segregation, residential inequality, or panethnic settlement.[42] More specifically, nativity, low socioeconomic status, and high levels of ethnic concentration help to sustain separation of the Hispanic population from non-Hispanic whites,[43] although large nearby concentrations of immigrants can also slow the out-migration of the native born, presumably by reducing their choices of places to move.[44] In particular, longitudinal research appears much less clear-cut about spatial assimilation,[45] particularly in areas with heavy immigration, because newcomers arrive faster than old-timers acculturate and integrate.

Yet even as early as the 1960s, the entrance of Hispanics into non-Hispanic white neighborhoods did not necessarily precipitate an ethnic turnover in the neighborhood,[46] suggesting that many whites accepted Mexicans as neighbors. Indeed, a study by Camille Charles shows that 45 percent of whites in Los Angeles County indicated that they were comfortable moving into a neighborhood that was half Hispanic.[47] Moreover, a study examining fifty years of census data at the neighborhood level in Southern California found that immigrant inflows did not lower property values or increase unemployment.[48]

Although the growth of the Latino population in the Los Angeles area has been widespread, the change in the proportion Latino was not evenly distributed throughout the region. Segregation levels from non-Hispanic whites were high, and the Los Angeles–Long Beach area has been described as "hypersegregated."[49] Two countervailing patterns appear to have been occurring. In keeping with historical patterns of immigrant settlement in general, many new Mexican immigrants settled in barrios, and crowding there rose substantially, with unauthorized Latinos burdened with high housing costs than their legal counterparts.[50] Allen and Turner estimate that by the year 2000, 61.4 percent of Los Angeles's Mexican-origin population was living in census tracts with coethnic concentrations of at least 40 percent.[51] At the same time, the availability of service jobs in L.A.'s edge cities proved a magnet for the suburban settlement of Hispanics, so that immigrants to Los Angeles became more likely to settle in peripheral areas than immigrants to cities like New York.[52] More particularly, between 1990 and 2000 in Los Angeles County, the greatest areas of Latino succession to whites centered on the San Fernando Valley, the southeastern suburbs of Los Angeles, and the central San Gabriel Valley to Pomona, while the greatest succession to black areas occurred in South Los Angeles and its surrounding areas. Areas with the least Hispanic succession were the white enclaves on the Westside (for example, Hollywood Hills and Malibu) and the East Side areas that were already overwhelmingly Hispanic but were becoming even more densely populated.[53] And, as noted earlier, the Inland Empire drew residents from the whole metropolitan area.

Empirical Patterns of Spatial Integration

Using the census tract as an approximation of neighborhood and geocoding with tract-level data from Summary File 3 of the 1980, 1990, and 2000 censuses, data from the Immigration and Intergenerational Mobility in Metropolitan Los Angeles survey permit analyses of locational attainment across immigrant generations as well as within the same family. We geocoded current addresses for 1,328 of the Mexican-origin respondents and childhood addresses for 984. Childhood addresses were collected only for those respondents who grew up in greater Los Angeles, thus eliminating data for the entire first generation, who, by definition, migrated as adults. To determine childhood address, respondents were asked for the cross-streets nearest to where they had lived the longest between the ages of six and eighteen. This strategy acknowledges that even though immigrants (and by extension, their children) tend to be more mobile than the native born, the majority have found fairly stable housing by the age of forty.[54] For earlier census data, we relied on census tracts normalized to their boundaries in 2000. For measurements of

Figure 6.2   Dispersion of Childhood and Current Residence of the
Mexican-Origin Population, by Generation, Metropolitan
Los Angeles, 2004

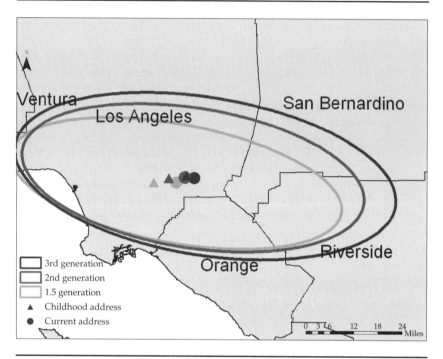

Source: Adapted from Immigration and Intergenerational Mobility in Metropolitan
Los Angeles (see Bean, Leach et al. 2011) and Census CD (2002).

childhood neighborhood context, we used linear interpolation between
decennial censuses to estimate the tract-level characteristics for the neighborhoods in which respondents lived at the age of twelve. Determination
of neighborhood-level mobility from childhood to adulthood is possible
only for those respondents who grew up in Los Angeles, but they account
for the majority of sample: 90.0 percent of the 1.5 generation, 92.2 percent
of the second generation, and 86.3 percent of the third generation.

Figure 6.2 shows the general eastward and northward drift of the
Mexican American population across generations. The dispersion ellipse
shows the shift from the childhood neighborhoods (triangles) to adult
neighborhoods (circles). The distance moved is greatest for the 1.5 generation, who are most likely to have grown up in barrios. Each successive generation moves farther away from the ethnic clusters, increasing
the size of the ellipse even as the average distance moved declines. The
shape and rotation of the ellipse remain the same, reflecting a continuity

of eastward-looking residential choices across generations. For example, in the 1.5 generation, 20.9 percent of respondents live inland, in San Bernardino or Riverside counties. That rises to 25.6 percent in the second generation and 31.6 percent in the third generation.

As dependent variables, we use three indicators of neighborhood mobility and integration: the education level of the neighborhood, measured at the level of both high school and college completion; the percentage of the neighborhood below the poverty level; and the percentage of the neighborhood that is not Mexican. We chose poverty level rather than median household income because of the relative youth of our respondents, many of whom are just beginning their careers. We also chose non-Mexican as the measure of ethnic integration because in greater Los Angeles, no majority group exists, though research has shown similar results for measurements of integration among non-Mexicans and non-Hispanic whites.[55] We additionally examine home ownership among the respondents as a marker of socioeconomic advancement that is tied to location.

Although earlier chapters distinguish more finely between generations, this chapter uses the designation of the second generation to refer to anyone with either one or two foreign-born parents and the third generation to refer to anyone with one to four foreign-born grandparents. Here we focus on assessing where Mexican Americans move to and how living in different parts of the metropolitan area can affect integration. Our sample size does not let us do that and also consider the generational homogeneity of parents and grandparents. Nor do we theoretically examine gender, since moving so often occurs as part of a household, not just at the individual level.

Generational Differences in Mobility

Table 6.1 shows the zero-order change in the measures of integration from the 1.5 to the second to the third generations. In every case, the most substantial residential mobility occurs between the second and third generations. Some mobility appears between the 1.5 and second generations, but only in the case of leaving behind neighborhood-level poverty is it statistically significant. Indeed, of all three measures, the one for neighborhood-level poverty shows the most mobility for the Mexican American respondents. It is the only measure on which the third generation outstrips the metropolitan average. The third generation respondents on average live in neighborhoods where 15.3 percent of the population is below the poverty line, a figure less than the overall poverty rate of 15.6 percent for metropolitan Los Angeles in 2000. On this indicator, the pattern seems indicative of classic assimilation.

The patterns for achieving residence among educated neighbors do not follow the classic straight line, however. The second generation lives

Table 6.1   Neighborhood-Level Integration and Educational Attainment, by Generation and Area of Residence, for Mexican American Respondents and for Metropolitan Los Angeles (percentage)

Characteristic	Area	Generation			Total for Metro Los Angeles
		1.5	2	3	
Mean percentage below poverty line	Five-county total	21.9	19.1*	15.3**	15.6
	L.A., Orange, Ventura	23.3	19.3*	14.6**	15.8
	Inland Empire	16.6	18.4	16.8	15.0
Mean percentage high school diploma or more	Five-county total	55.1	59.7	69.9**	73.0
	L.A., Orange, Ventura	51.9	57.6	69.7**	72.6
	Inland Empire	66.9	66.0	70.3	74.6
Mean percentage bachelor's degree or more	Five-county total	11.8	13.5	18.2**	24.4
	L.A., Orange, Ventura	11.4	13.7	20.6**	26.3
	Inland Empire	13.0	12.7	12.9	16.3
Mean percentage non-Mexican	Five-county total	51.7	53.3	65.1**	69.7
	L.A., Orange, Ventura	49.7	52.1	66.3**	69.8
	Inland Empire	59.3	56.9	62.5	69.4

Source: Data from Immigration and Intergenerational Mobility in Metropolitan Los Angeles (see Bean, Leach et al. 2011) and U.S. Bureau of the Census (2000a, 2000b).
*Significantly different from the 1.5 generation at the .05 level.
**Significantly different from the 2nd generation at the .05 level.

in neighborhoods with only slightly higher levels of education than the 1.5. Only in the third generation does neighborhood education level rise substantially, and even then, it is more than 25 percent below the metro-wide average for the proportion of neighbors who hold college degrees. These two socioeconomic indicators, combined, suggest that the neighborhood choices of Mexican Americans mirror the tendencies shown in the previous chapter for the third generation to be able to attain higher levels of income without concomitant gains in education, a pattern we suggest is consistent with working-class assimilation.

As for the ethnoracial composition of neighborhoods, by the third generation the average Mexican American respondent lives in a neighborhood that is nearly 65 percent non-Mexican, that is, a neighborhood where Mexican Americans are outnumbered nearly 2 to 1 by other groups. In the U.S. context, this represents a surprising level of ethnoracial integration, only 5 percentage points off the average expected if the third generation were randomly distributed among the rest of the Angeleno population. That previous research has found that the Hispanic population as a whole in Los Angeles is "hypersegregated" from non-Hispanic whites makes the findings for the third generation that much more astonishing.[56] Here the finding seems to show unqualified mobility. At first glance, these results appear at odds with the findings of Telles and Ortiz, who conclude that Mexican American adults in Los Angeles and San Antonio are living with more coethnics than they did as children.[57] But both findings can be correct. The enormous immigration of Mexicans into Los Angeles in the late twentieth century established a greater Mexican presence throughout most parts of the city but particularly in areas that were already largely Latino. At the same time, people who grew up in those neighborhoods have often moved out.

Analyzing Individual and Structural Components of Change

Table 6.2 examines the neighborhood change among those respondents who grew up in Los Angeles. From childhood to adulthood, each generation of Mexican Americans has experienced a loss of integration, as more Mexicans or Mexican Americans moved into their neighborhoods and the percentage of non-Mexicans decreased. This trend is part of the Latinization of Los Angeles. As the first line of panel A shows, the total decline in integration was steepest for the 1.5 generation, at 6.4 percentage points, and smallest for the third generation, at 4.1 percentage points. This is measured as the change in neighborhood integration (as measured by percentage of the population that is not of Mexican background) from the time the respondents were twelve years old until their adulthood. For any given respondents, the change depends both on what census tracts

Table 6.2 Structural and Mobility Change in Neighborhood Ethnicity and Education Level since Respondent's Youth, by Generation and Part of Metropolitan Los Angeles

	Generation		
Variable	1.5	2	3
Change in level of neighborhood integration (percentage of non-Mexicans) since age twelve			
A. Total percentage-point change	-6.4	-4.5	-4.1
Los Angeles, Orange, and Ventura counties	-8.0	-4.2	-2.5
Riverside and San Bernardino counties	-0.2	-5.3	-8.2
B. Percentage-point change owing to inflows of persons of Mexican origin into childhood neighborhood	-9.2	-8.5	-10.6
Los Angeles, Orange, and Ventura counties	-9.1	-7.5	-9.9
Riverside and San Bernardino counties	-9.7	-11.9	-12.2
C. Percentage-point change owing to moving to new neighborhood	2.8	4.0	6.5
Los Angeles, Orange, and Ventura counties	1.1	3.2	7.4
Riverside and San Bernardino counties	9.0	6.9	4.1
Change in neighborhood percentage of high school graduates since age twelve			
D. Total percentage-point change	2.9	4.3	4.9
Los Angeles, Orange, and Ventura counties	1.2	3.8	5.7
Riverside and San Bernardino counties	9.6	6.3	2.7
E. Percentage-point change owing to influx of less educated people into childhood neighborhood	-2.2	-0.7	-0.2
Los Angeles, Orange, and Ventura counties	-2.3	-0.5	-0.1
Riverside and San Bernardino counties	-1.5	-1.3	-0.6
F. Percentage-point change in level of high school graduates owing to moving	5.1	5.0	5.1
Los Angeles, Orange, and Ventura counties	3.5	4.2	5.8
Riverside and San Bernardino counties	11.2	7.6	3.3

Source: Data from Immigration and Intergenerational Mobility in Metropolitan Los Angeles (see Bean, Leach et al. 2011) and Census CD (2002).

they lived in and how many years had elapsed since they were twelve. The interpolation of the census data builds in the control for their age.

The neighborhood-level change can be decomposed into its two component parts, the structural part, caused by an influx of other people of Mexican background moving into the childhood neighborhood, and the individual part, caused by moving from the childhood neighborhood to the current residence. The first line of panel B shows the total structural change, which was high for all generations as many Mexican immigrants moved in. The percentage-point drop in integration caused by this influx ranged from 9.2 percentage points for the 1.5 generation to 8.5 percentage points for the second generation to 10.6 percentage points for the third. However, offsetting part of this change was the greater integration attained by individuals moving out of the neighborhood, as shown in the top line of panel C. The gains from integration range from 2.8 percentage points for the 1.5 generation to 6.5 percentage points for the third generation. Thus despite the structural change throughout Los Angeles, respondents in all generations are moving toward more ethnically integrated areas. These average gains are all the more remarkable because many of the younger respondents are still living with their parents in their childhood neighborhoods; the proportion still at home ranges from 10.8 percent in the 1.5 generation to 22.2 percent in the second generation to 18.0 percent in the third generation.

Integration varies for the generations according to the part of the metro area where they live, as the second and third lines of panel C show. In the more traditional coastal settlement areas of Los Angeles, Orange, and Ventura counties, moving leads to the greatest increases in integration among the third generation—more than twice the percentage-point gain of the second generation. This finding is entirely consonant with findings in earlier chapters about the delay in achieving full membership. Residents of the Inland Empire are the exception. In the two counties with the fastest growth rates and most affordable housing, the 1.5 generation gets the biggest boost in integration from moving. Moving brings a 9.0 percentage-point boost in integration for the 1.5 generation, yet only a 4.1 percentage-point boost for the third generation. This shift is consistent with the result in table 6.1, where the level of overall integration with non-Mexicans changes little from the 1.5 to the third generations. In the Inland Empire, ethnoracial integration takes place much earlier in the overall integration process than in the coastal counties of Los Angeles, Orange, and Ventura.

But the human capital of the two sets of counties varies considerably, as table 6.1 shows, and this difference accrues over generations. While the overall level of high school completion in the Inland Empire was close to the state average of 76.8 percent for adults in 2000, the proportion of the area's overall population with a bachelor's degree or more fell far below the state average. Only 16.3 percent of the total population in the Inland Empire had a bachelor's degree in 2000, compared with 26.3 percent for Los Angeles, Orange, and Ventura counties and 26.6 percent for all of California. Thus across generations, Mexican Americans remaining in the Inland Empire tend to live amid relatively fewer college graduates, whereas the third generation in L.A., Orange, and Ventura counties lives in more-educated neighborhoods than earlier generations.

While the top panels of table 6.2 show that massive coethnic inflows overshadow the effects of moving within the area to more residentially integrated areas, the bottom three panels tell a different story. Unlike the measure for ethnoracial integration, the change in the neighborhood percentage of high school graduates rose between the respondents' youth and the time of their interviews. As a measure of a basic threshold level of human capital, it is an important indicator of employment potential and likely neighborhood stability. The overall change in the neighborhood percentage of high school graduates rises for all generations from childhood to adulthood, although the gains are bigger for the second and third generations than for the 1.5 generation, as the first line in panel D shows. The difference in the change across generations was slight but consistent: 2.9 percentage points for the 1.5 generation, 4.3 percentage points for the second, and 4.9 percentage points for the third generation. For the L.A. metropolitan area as a whole, the proportion of adults with a high school diploma dropped by 1.1 percentage points from 1980 to 2000, so the respondents were in fact bucking a negative trend. That structural trend shows up in the first line of panel E, which shows the change in education levels in childhood census tracts from the time respondents were twelve until 2000. The greatest percentage-point drop in education occurred most heavily in the neighborhoods of the 1.5 generation.

In all generations, mobility to new neighborhoods resulted in an average 5 percentage-point gain in the neighborhood level of high school completion, as shown in the first line of panel F. But the similarity of the overall gains masks some large differences within the metropolitan region. In Los Angeles, Orange, and Ventura counties, the gains rose across generations, so that the mobility of the 1.5 generation led to a 3.5 percentage-point gain in neighborhood-level high school completion rates, as shown in the second line of panel F. The second generation showed a gain of 0.7 percentage points more, and the third generation more than doubled that gain, suggesting again that the third generation accrued greater gains in socioeconomic mobility than the generations before. This was not the case in the Inland Empire, as shown in the last line of panel F. There, the 1.5 generation got a substantial 11.2 percentage-point boost in neighborhood education levels by moving, and successive generations got less. The differences here again suggest that residential integration proceeds at different rates for Mexican Americans depending on where they live within the metropolitan area. The 1.5 generation is attaining neighborhoods with more high school graduates by moving to the Inland Empire. By the third generation, however, a move within the coastal counties also leads to neighborhoods with higher levels of high school completion.

Assessing the Effects of Unauthorized Background

The question remains whether the persistent unauthorized status of parents, especially mothers, is related to the overall status of the neighborhoods in which their children live, in a manner consistent with membership exclusion. To test this, we regress neighborhood poverty, education level, and coethnic composition on a variety of characteristics, including generation, legal status, and other indicators of family disadvantage and the respondents' socioeconomic and demographic characteristics. The indicators for neighborhood poverty and bachelor's degree attainment have slightly skewed distributions, and we ran regressions with them transformed into natural logarithms. But because the results were so similar to those with untransformed variables, we present the untransformed variables for ease of interpretation.

The indicators of family disadvantage are whether the respondent sends remittances to family members and whether both parents speak poor English. We expect these to tap different dimensions of disadvantage. Respondents cannot send remittances unless they have disposable income, but that means they are not spending that income on themselves and thus potentially attenuating the expected link between household income and neighborhood characteristics. Questions about remittances were asked only of the 1.5 and second generations. In our sample, nearly 63 percent of those whose mothers remained unauthorized reported sending remittances. Only 27 percent of those with legal or citizen mothers did so. The inability of parents to speak English might mean that respondents could be obligated to help their parents navigate U.S. institutions that operate primarily in English; such an obligation might keep children from moving far. Almost 60 percent of the 1.5 generation and 35 percent of the second generation report that their parents speak poor English. Counterintuitively, when mothers had remained unauthorized, the parents spoke significantly better English than when the mothers were legal or citizens. Achieved characteristics include whether respondents still live with their parents, in which case the neighborhood characteristics would correspond with the preferences and earnings of the parents, who are one generation back and later in the life course. We further control for whether the respondent is married and has children. We also control for household income, educational attainment, and the presence of some type of wealth, in the form of stocks, bonds, or a retirement plan.

Table 6.3 shows the relationship between unauthorized status and neighborhood poverty. While model 1 confirms the significant difference between the 1.5 and later generations, even when controlling for age and gender, model 2 shows that parental unauthorized status accounts for nearly a full percentage point of the difference between the 1.5 and third generations. Persistently unauthorized mothers are associated with a rise of 2.7 percentage points in neighborhood poverty. The other forms of disadvantage, introduced in model 3, have substantial effects on the neighborhood poverty rate apart from unauthorized status. Accounting

Table 6.3   OLS Coefficients of Models of Neighborhood Poverty Rate Regressed on Generation, Family Disadvantage, and Respondent Characteristics, Mexican American Adults, Aged Twenty to Forty, Metropolitan Los Angeles, 2004

Characteristic	Model 1	Model 2	Model 3	Model 4
Generation				
1.5 (reference)				
2	−3.041***	−2.431***	−1.004	−0.035
3	−6.342***	−5.555***	−2.474**	−1.383
Ascribed characteristics				
Age	−0.193***	−0.186***	−0.159***	−.033
Female	0.307	0.406	0.401	0.473
Family disadvantage				
Unauthorized background		2.731***	3.230***	0.512
Respondent sends remittances			1.825***	2.155***
Parents speak poor English			3.218***	2.710***
Achieved characteristics				
Living with parents				−0.757
Married				−2.384***
Has children				−0.034
Household income (000s)				−0.054***
Finished high school or vocational school				−3.916***
At least some college				−4.263***
Has stocks, bonds, or retirement plan				−1.961**
Constant	27.308***	26.271***	22.371***	27.214***
R-squared	0.053	.059	0.081	0.177
N	1,056	1,056	1,056	1,056

Source: Data from Immigration and Intergenerational Mobility in Metropolitan Los Angeles (see Bean, Leach et al. 2011) and U.S. Bureau of the Census (2000b).
*$p < .10$, **$p < .05$, ***$p < .01$, one-tailed test.

for them attenuates the difference in the neighborhood poverty rate experienced by the 1.5 and third generations to less than 2.5 percentage points. The introduction of marital status and respondents' socioeconomic status in model 4 nearly halves the remaining difference between the 1.5 and third generations. As expected, income and education are strongly related to the neighborhood poverty level. The influence of parental unauthorized status on neighborhood poverty thus appears to be almost completely mediated through children's socioeconomic attainment. However, the effects of sending remittances and parental language ability remain strong, suggesting that membership exclusion is not the only way that parents affect the level of neighborhood poverty experienced by Mexican Americans.

Mothers' persistent unauthorized status thus affects the kind of neighborhoods their children can attain, but the influence appears to run through the children's income and education and to be stronger at the more basic thresholds of socioeconomic attainment. In particular, mothers' status appears to have a stronger connection to the neighborhood level of high school completion than to the neighborhood level of college completion. As table 6.4 shows in models 2 and 3, having an unauthorized mother is associated with roughly a 4 percentage-point difference in high school graduates in respondent's neighborhood, but this falls sharply in model 4, when respondents' characteristics are added. Paying remittances and having parents who speak poor English also are associated with living in less educated neighborhoods, and these change little from model 3 to model 4. When the dependent variable is the level of high school graduation, membership exclusion seems to matter substantially for the kind of neighborhood the 1.5 and second generations can attain. The findings are similar for neighborhood education at the level of bachelor's degree or higher. Unauthorized mothers are associated with more than a 2 percentage-point drop in the neighborhood levels of college completion, and again, this effect is mediated through respondents' education and income. Even accounting for income, education, and other personal characteristics, the third generation is able to attain neighborhoods with significantly more people who have finished college than the 1.5 generation.

Table 6.5 examines the level of integration with greater proportions of non-Mexicans. And while "non-Mexicans" can refer to people from any other ethnic or racial background, a majority are non-Hispanic white. The change from the second to third generations in model 1 is so pronounced—nearly a 13 percentage-point increase in non-Mexican neighbors—that family disadvantage and socioeconomic attainment can account for only half of it. Unauthorized background is not significantly associated with residence in neighborhoods with large Mexican populations, although a notable tendency in that direction emerges. Other forms of disadvantage are significantly associated with residence in less integrated

Table 6.4 OLS Regression of Neighborhood Education Level on Generation, Family Disadvantage, and Respondent Characteristics, Mexican American Adults, Aged Twenty to Forty, Metropolitan Los Angeles, 2004

Characteristic	High School Diploma				Bachelor's Degree			
	Model 1	Model 2	Model 3	Model 4	Model 1	Model 2	Model 3	Model 4
Generation								
1.5 (reference)								
2	5.203***	4.412***	2.060	0.641	2.020***	1.535**	0.807	0.039
3	14.037***	13.016***	7.850***	5.926***	5.964***	5.338***	3.714***	2.543**
Ascribed characteristics								
Age	0.524***	0.516***	0.476***	0.189*	0.281***	0.276***	0.265***	0.111*
Female	−0.970	−1.099	−1.102	−0.964	−0.752	−0.831	−0.835	−0.519
Family disadvantage								
Unauthorized background		−3.546**	−4.062**	−0.512		−2.173**	−2.242**	−0.474
Respondent sends remittances			−3.869***	−4.521***			−1.453**	−1.839**
Parents speak poor English			−4.809***	−3.779***			−1.342**	−0.671
Achieved characteristics								
Living with parents				−3.705**				−2.974***
Married				2.299*				0.794
Has children				−1.529				−1.995**
Household income (000s)				0.091***				0.054***
Finished high school or vocational school				5.698***				3.076***
At least some college				6.402***				3.412***
Stocks, bonds, or retirement plan				2.373**				0.179
Constant	40.576***	41.922***	48.298***	46.563***	4.085**	4.910***	6.867***	7.667***
R-squared	0.087	0.090	0.107	0.179	0.061	0.050	0.071	0.147
N	1,056	1,056	1,056	1,056	1,056	1,056	1,056	1,056

Source: Data from Immigration and Intergenerational Mobility in Metropolitan Los Angeles (see Bean, Leach et al. 2011) and U.S. Bureau of the Census (2000b).
*p < .10, **p < .05, ***p < .01, one-tailed test.

Table 6.5   OLS Regression Coefficients of Percentage Non-Mexican in Neighborhood on Generation, Family Disadvantage, and Respondent Characteristics, Mexican American Adults, Aged Twenty to Forty, Metropolitan Los Angeles, 2004

Characteristic	Model 1	Model 2	Model 3	Model 4
Generation				
1.5 (reference)				
2	2.180	1.474	−0.262	−1.236
3	12.781***	11.870***	7.967***	6.318***
Ascribed characteristics				
Age	0.468***	0.460***	0.435***	0.180
Female	−1.563	−1.678	−1.691	−1.084
Family disadvantage				
Unauthorized background		−3.162	−3.234	−1.176
Respondent sends remittances			−3.728**	−4.319***
Parents speak poor English			−3.053*	−1.925
Achieved characteristics				
Living with parents				−6.649***
Married				−0.382
Has children				−3.750**
Household income (000s)				0.073***
Finished high school or vocational school				2.138
At least some college				4.138**
Has stocks, bonds, or retirement plan				0.719
Constant	39.032***	40.233***	44.889***	49.639***
R-squared	0.062	.064	0.073	0.118
N	1,056	1,056	1,056	1,056

Source: Data from Immigration and Intergenerational Mobility in Metropolitan Los Angeles (see Bean, Leach et al. 2011) and U.S. Bureau of the Census (2000b). *$p < .10$, **$p < .05$, ***$p < .01$, one-tailed test.

neighborhoods. Even when respondents' education and income are accounted for, model 4 shows the persistent effects of sending remittances on living in more-Mexican areas. Of course, it is not possible to determine the mechanism at work here. Remittances reduce the available income for moving, but sending them also signals the persistence of coethnic ties and perhaps some preference for coethnic neighborhoods. However, because sending remittances is also associated with living in neighborhoods with greater poverty, evidence suggests the importance of the economic role.

The Role of Home Ownership

One further indicator of mobility deserves discussion. This is the likelihood of home ownership, long considered a benchmark of the American dream. In this sample, where the mean age is 28.5, determining home ownership patterns is at best a preliminary exercise. In the 1.5, second, and third generations, 28.3 percent are homeowners, with little variation by generation. Among their parents, however, nearly 60 percent are homeowners, ranging from 41.7 percent of the parents of the 1.5 generation to 78.3 percent of the parents of the third generation. For this model, we add parental home ownership as a control, because it could capture family resources or an unmeasured aspiration to own property. We also drop the cases of respondents who are still living with their parents. Table 6.6 shows the odds of home ownership among the respondents. Unsurprisingly, in model 1, age rather than immigrant generation proves to be the overwhelming predictor of home owning. Model 2, however, shows that having mothers who remained unauthorized nearly halves the likelihood of home ownership, at least at these respondents' ages. Model 3 adds other forms of family disadvantage, as well as parents' home ownership. Sending remittances has no effect on home ownership, nor does parents' English ability. But parents' home ownership is a strong factor and appears as one path through which unauthorized status works: families in which mothers remain unauthorized are far more likely than other parents to be renters. A generation later, the children of homeowners are twice as likely to own their homes as those whose parents rent. That legacy, which appears in model 3, does not disappear when the respondents' own characteristics are accounted for in model 4.

This discussion leaves unanswered one big question: Where does a young population whose family background is working class (or lower working class) purchase houses in an expensive metro area? In 2004, when the survey was taken, the median home sales price in Los Angeles County was $446,380, and it was at least $150,000 more than that in Orange and Ventura counties. However, in the Inland Empire, the median home sales price was less than $300,000.[58] Table 6.7 shows the mean home ownership rates by generation, residence, and place of origin. Among the 1.5 generation who grew up in the coastal counties and moved to the Inland Empire, fully 80 percent were homeowners. By comparison, among the 1.5 generation who grew up in the coastal counties and stayed there, only 26 percent were homeowners. However, in the Inland Empire, home ownership rates declined over the generations, suggesting that the earlier generations moving there are motivated by the prospect of home ownership. As table 6.1 shows, for the 1.5 and second generations, their new neighborhoods in the Inland Empire are also relatively more ethnoracially

Table 6.6 Odds Ratios of Home Ownership, by Generation, Family Disadvantage, Respondent Characteristics, and Region of Residence, Mexican American Adults, Aged Twenty to Forty, Metropolitan Los Angeles, 2004

Characteristic	Model 1	Model 2	Model 3	Model 4	Model 5	Model 6
Generation						
1.5	1.173	1.399	1.454	1.763	1.544	1.305
2	1.146	1.205	1.167	1.209	1.082	1.096
3 (reference)						
Ascribed characteristics						
Age	1.144***	1.141***	1.139***	1.103***	1.104***	1.106***
Female	0.993	0.966	0.993	0.981	1.026	1.023
Family disadvantage/advantage						
Unauthorized background		0.546***	0.729	0.951	0.954**	0.931
Respondent sends remittances			1.032	0.911	0.978	1.001
Parents speak poor English			1.203	1.290	1.366	1.390
Parents own home			2.021***	1.448*	1.418*	1.391*
Achieved characteristics						
Married				2.247***	2.115***	2.204***
Has children				1.800***	1.811***	1.783***
Household income (000s)				1.016***	1.016***	1.016***
Finished high school or vocational school				1.047	1.105	1.175
At least some college				1.361	1.413	1.453
Has stocks, bonds, or retirement plan				1.583*	1.616*	1.685**
Residence						
Moved to Inland Empire					3.545***	1.335
Moved to Inland Empire * 1.5 generation						9.652**
Moved to Inland Empire * 2.0 generation						1.293
Constant	−4.712***	−4.619***	−5.127***	−6.317***	−6.432***	0.034***
−2 log likelihood	968.584	961.541	943.953	835.082	817.408	807.659
N	786	786	786	786	786	786

Source: Data from Immigration and Intergenerational Mobility in Metropolitan Los Angeles (see Bean, Leach et al. 2011).

$*p < .10, **p < .05, ***p < .01$, one-tailed test.

Table 6.7 Homeownership Rates, Mexican American Adults, Aged Twenty to Forty, by Generation, Residence, and Place of Origin, Metropolitan Los Angeles, 2004

	Owns Home in L.A./Orange/Ventura Counties, Grew Up in						Owns Home in Inland Empire, Grew Up in					
Generation	L.A., Orange, or Ventura County	N	Inland Empire	N	Outside metro L.A.	N	Inland Empire	N	L.A., Orange, or Ventura County	N	Outside metro L.A.	N
1.5	26.1	207	0.0	2	22.7	22	39.3	28	80.0	25	42.9	7
2	22.9	380	0.0	6	28.0	25	18.0	78	48.9	45	52.6	19
3	35.0	120	25.0	4	19.0	21	23.5	51	50.0	8	37.5	8

Source: Data from Immigration and Intergenerational Mobility in Metropolitan Los Angeles (see Bean, Leach et al. 2011).

integrated and more educated than the ones they left. By contrast, home ownership among respondents in the coastal counties rises across generations more slowly, in a pattern of classic mobility. Model 5 of table 6.6 shows that moving to the Inland Empire is associated with a tripling of the odds of home ownership. But when moving is interacted with generation, as in model 6, the results show that the association of home ownership with the Inland Empire is a phenomenon primarily found among the 1.5 generation.

Conclusions

Not until the third generation does the integration and human-capital level of the neighborhoods in which Mexican Americans live approach the average levels of the metropolitan area as a whole. The break between the second and third generations is significant and dramatic. In ethnic integration, the change between the 1.5 and second generations is minuscule, but it is followed by an 11.2 percentage-point change between the second and third generations in the neighborhood percentage of non-Mexicans. The education gains are equally noteworthy: a 10.6 percentage-point gain in the percentage of neighbors who have completed high school. While the level of neighborhood college graduates is lower, it still rises more than 50 percent between the 1.5 and third generations. If the trajectory between the second and third generations is an indicator, it bodes well for sustained incorporation, because the children of the third generation are growing up in neighborhoods with more human capital than those in which their parents grew up.

An important exception to the delay in spatial assimilation is movement to the Inland Empire. The Mexican Americans there attain much higher neighborhood levels of education and integration in the 1.5 generation. Those moving to the Inland Empire are buying houses and finding integrated neighborhoods. But the advantages of the Inland Empire fade by the third generation. At that point, the residential opportunities in Los Angeles, Orange, and Ventura counties appear to be stronger, and the overall locational attainment for Mexican Americans better. This finding represents an additional nuance in traditional locational-attainment theory, which has long examined the desirability of suburbs versus urban areas.[59] In the Inland Empire, the relative affordability of housing and the racial and ethnic integration come at a price, in terms of additional smog, summer heat, and especially traffic. In counts of commuter flows, the Inland Empire tops the nation's worst "mega commutes" of at least ninety minutes and fifty miles to work.[60] Nor can these data show how any of these early-generation homeowners fared in the Great Recession, which struck the Inland Empire particularly hard, as Inland Empire neighborhoods with concentrations of African Americans and Latinos were targeted by subprime lenders.[61]

All of these changes tend to go less noticed because of the vastness of immigration to Los Angeles from both Latin America and Asia. With 5 million more people of Mexican origin, many of them low skilled, arriving in the city over the course of two decades, most neighborhoods became more Mexican. The overall education level declined. These trends overwhelmed the much quieter and slower process of Mexican American residential mobility, particularly given that advancement took two generations to show up as substantial. The overall story appears to be one of ethno-racial and socioeconomic integration requiring three generations within a metropolis that has become much more diverse in only one generation. Membership exclusion has further delayed this already slow process of residential integration. That effect is consistent. Regardless of respondents' own education and income, the long-term unauthorized status of their mothers is associated with their staying in neighborhoods that are more coethnic, poorer, and less educated, by 3 to 4 four percentage points in each case. While respondents' own characteristics ultimately mediate these delays, they are nonetheless substantial.

= Chapter 7 =

The Mosaic of
Sociocultural Integration

Not surprisingly, the sociocultural aspects of integration have been particularly important in sociological studies of assimilation. The social and cultural challenges facing America's early-twentieth-century immigrants and their descendants received predominant attention in sociology's canonical assimilation studies.[1] Moreover, the unidimensionality predominant in assimilation perspectives has resulted in sociologists sometimes seeming scarcely to recognize that nonsocial factors might also be involved in integration, although they often genuflect in the direction of more material matters by mentioning that structural (or socioeconomic) along with sociocultural incorporation are the twin pillars of immigrant integration.[2] In an important refinement, the recent extension of the classical assimilation theoretical perspective by Richard Alba and Victor Nee has highlighted the essential role played by social institutions in fostering successful structural incorporation,[3] thus giving explicit emphasis to the fact that labor-market outcomes are embedded in organizational forms that constitute the social underpinnings of economic life.[4] Clearly, a full-fledged examination of Mexican American integration would not be complete without attention to how sociocultural aspects of incorporation vary across three generations.

We consider two issues. The first concerns what the pattern of empirical associations among sociocultural indicators reveals about the extent to which assimilation-based or pluralist-based theoretical approaches appear more salient for understanding this dimension of integration. This is the question of how aspects of sociocultural integration relate to one another and to other dimensions of integration in general. Theoretical and empirical assessments of the dimensionality of incorporation suggest that sociocultural indicators, unlike those in other domains, do not appreciably bundle together into a notably distinct dimension to the degree that indicators in other areas do. Thus education, income, and homeownership, in the economic area, and neighborhood ethnic composition and neighborhood income, in the spatial integration area, tend to be highly correlated with one another. This relative lack of association among aspects of socioculturality reflects, we argue, societal trends toward a sociocultural world increasingly compatible with the tenets of postindustrial-individualistic theoretical perspectives on integration. These tenets predict that sociocultural profiles will vary across both groups and individuals, a different view from that of multicultural perspectives, which emphasize the existence (and coexistence) of variegated group-based sociocultural realms.[5] In multicultural approaches, scholars tend to characterize groups as differing in their embrace of value orientations, customs, and practices, while individual differences within groups are less acknowledged and emphasized.

Such approaches implicitly lean toward assuming sociocultural unidimensionality within groups, if not between groups. It is not that such ideas preclude the possibility of empirically examining multiple aspects of sociocultural integration separately, but rather that they tend to assume that within groups, these do not vary independently of one another. The postindustrial-individualistic perspective, by contrast, envisions aspects of socioculturality as tending toward independence both between groups and within groups. In a world with literally hundreds of television channels, multiple modes of fashion and dress, and seemingly countless preferences for alternative lifestyles, the mainstreams of national origin or minority groups, just as with those of majority groups, may consist more of multiple separate rivulets, each with its own nature and flow, than a single predominant stream. This trend can be overstated, of course, although it does seem likely that today's sociocultural reality falls somewhere between the idealized homogeneity we have painted for the multicultural perspective and the idiosyncratic one for the postindustrial-individualistic approach. Whatever the case, individualism appears today to grow ever more prominent even as group affiliations and conformity continue to matter, although perhaps less strongly than before.[6]

The significance of this point lies in what it implies about the scope of the dimensionality of integration. As noted in earlier chapters, and as we emphasize again here, it is likely that more than one theoretical approach will characterize a given group's integration experience. One of the reasons is that groups increasingly appear to have multiple experiences, at least in the complex and highly differentiated societies in which most migrants settle. Their experiences are thus multidimensional, and different dynamics may characterize different dimensions. Multicultural approaches partially allow for such differences, but in our view do not go far enough to take into account the tendencies toward individualism in most of today's receiving countries. The postindustrial-individualistic approach by definition accommodates individualism, although perhaps at the price of overstating the case. Here we classify membership exclusion as closer to the postindustrial-individualistic category than not, in part because of its expectation that an even steeper upward gradient of generational mobility will characterize sociocultural aspects of incorporation more than structural ones. Saying this does not imply a de-emphasis of sociocultural integration but rather puts forward the idea that the various sociocultural facets of integration, even though many vary as a function of exposure, occur relatively independently and must be examined one at a time. Accordingly, it would follow that "integration" with respect to these facets may vary (that is, that integration may occur statistically for some aspects and not others, without this variation signifying an overall lack of incorporation). This unbundling represents a departure from how sociologists have long tended to view the sociocultural side of incorporation.

These separate elements together may thus make up a mosaic of sociocultural integration. This was suggested earlier by the results of principal components analyses of multiple measures of sociocultural integration showing that such indicators do not appear to be strongly related to one another or to the other major dimensions of integration (see appendix B). Thus a second-generation Mexican immigrant today may well report that ethnicity is "quite important" while indicating at the same time a Protestant religious affiliation, even as another second-generation person reports just the opposite. Similarly, knowing that one person is a Protestant or that another places considerable importance on ethnic identity is likely to tell us little concerning whether these persons exhibit irregular or frequent patterns of church attendance. We thus analyze separately how each of several sociocultural aspects of incorporation vary across three generations. We would note here that evidence of some statistical convergence between immigrants and natives can occur without those individuals who converge on one facet necessarily converging on another. In other words, considerable individual heterogeneity may increasingly characterize the sociocultural profiles of both immigrants and natives. Because of this individual heterogeneity, we do not expect or theorize substantial gender differences in sociocultural integration across generations.

The second issue is this: Does having an unauthorized migrant background forestall sociocultural integration? Stated differently, do those coming from unauthorized backgrounds show less sociocultural integration than those coming from legal backgrounds? Again, we examine patterns across generations, focusing on sociocultural differences both among Mexican Americans by generation and between third-generation Mexican Americans and non-Hispanic whites. We eschew the latter comparison in the case of those sociocultural markers that do not apply to non-Hispanic whites (for example, it makes little sense to compare Mexican Americans and whites with respect to such indicators as the importance of Mexican ethnicity). We examine nine indicators, selected for parsimony and prima facie importance. These are (stated in a direction reflecting more statistical integration across generations): prefers speaking only English at home; "does not speak Spanish very well;" "infrequently watches Spanish-language TV;" reports a non-Catholic religious identification; hardly ever attends church; "says Mexican identity is not important;" holds a favorable view of marrying outside the ethnic group; is married to an Anglo; and reports few children ever born. This selection does not exhaust the sociocultural indicators available in the IIMMLA data. It does, however, encompass much of the breadth involved in the large sociocultural domain. In any case, our analyses of additional sociocultural indicators not shown here yield similar generational patterns to the ones we report below.

Based on a membership exclusion theoretical perspective, what would we hypothesize? In general, we suggest that it depends. For those sociocultural indicators like English proficiency that are mostly a function of exposure, we would anticipate a pattern of steady increase across generations and perhaps convergence with non-Hispanic whites. For those indicators that are likely to depend more on interethnic structural contact, such as becoming non-Catholic, not attending church very often, or thinking ethnicity is not important, we would expect a more discontinuous pattern involving notably greater integration in the third generation than in the second, and perhaps convergence with non-Hispanic whites. In other words, we do not expect lack of first-generation membership to independently slow down sociocultural integration beyond the retarding effects of structural disadvantage.

Linguistic Integration

We begin our three-generational assessment by devoting special attention to linguistic integration. Language is important if for no other reason than it constitutes a prerequisite for other kinds of incorporation, especially in a world in which English functions as the lingua franca for much of global commerce. In this sense language could just as easily be deemed an indicator of structural incorporation. In any case, analyzing linguistic incorporation is particularly revealing because, unlike many other aspects of sociocultural incorporation, it varies substantially as a function of exposure, or as a result of the length of time newcomers have spent in the host society. Linguists the world over have long noted that new arrivals in foreign areas come to speak the local languages the longer they reside there, regardless of motivation.[7] That is, when newcomers come into contact with persons speaking the receiving area's language, which of course they almost always do, they learn the receiving country language even when they are not self-consciously trying to learn it. This ability implies that proficiency and usage of the host language are likely to some extent to follow a classic assimilation pattern across generations rather than a stunted or discontinuous pattern of integration.

However, a different logic may apply to the retention of heritage language. The reason is that language preservation varies more as a function of motivation than exposure. Although motivation is not irrelevant to learning the language of the receiving country, since actively trying to learn a new language often speeds the process, motivation appears likely to be especially salient for avoiding heritage-language loss. In looking at language integration, it is thus instructive to examine both language acquisition and heritage-language preservation, not just one or the other. The former is more likely to exhibit generational patterns that follow the predictions of classic assimilation (for example, a pattern of regular upward progression across generations in the percentage of persons preferring to speak English at home), whereas the latter is more likely suited to capture blocked or discontinuous incorporation (for example, a discontinuous pattern in which a sharp upward "catch-up" progression occurs). For purposes of carrying out analyses to assess this, we define adult Mexican American generations as follows: the 1.0 generation of immigrants are those who arrived as adults at the age of fifteen or older; the 1.5 generation are those who arrived in the United States before the age of fifteen; the 2.0 generation are those born in the United States of two Mexican-born parents; the 2.5 generation are those born in the United States of one Mexican-born parent and one U.S.-born parent; the 3.0 generation are those with three or four Mexican-born grandparents; and the 3.5 generation are those with only one or two Mexican-born grandparents.

Information from the IIMMLA data is available for both preferring to speak English at home and for degree of Spanish-speaking proficiency.[8] We first examine generational differences in preferring to speak only English at home. In the 1.0 generation, not surprisingly, only 2 percent of the respondents indicate they prefer to speak only English at home (see table 7.1). In the 1.5 generation, this figure jumps to 39 percent, a substantial increase. In the 2.0 generation, the percentage preferring only English language usage rises further, moving to 57 percent, before climbing again in the 2.5 generation to 80 percent. In the later generations, preferring to speak only English at home becomes almost universal, characterizing 95 percent of the 3.0 generation and 99 percent of the 3.5 generation. Thus, within the confines of the home, where one might expect a preference for only English to be least likely, preference for English usage approaches near totality, even among those whose immediate-family ties to Mexico include three or four grandparents born in Mexico. Moreover, in keeping with the idea that host-country language acquisition is likely to be affected mostly by length of temporal exposure, the pattern of change across generations shows monotonic increases, as would be expected by the classic assimilation hypothesis.

Focusing on language preservation, however, or the retention of proficiency in the Spanish mother tongue, may better reveal dynamics related

Table 7.1 Means and Standard Deviations of Sociocultural Indicators, Mexican American Adults and Non-Hispanic Whites, Aged Twenty to Forty, by Generation and Gender, Los Angeles, 2004

	1.0		1.5		2.0		2.5		3.0		3.5		Non-Hispanic White	
	Mean	SD	Mean	SD	Mean	SD	Mean	SD	Mean	SD	Mean	SD	Mean	SD
Prefers English at home	0.02	0.13	0.39	0.49	0.57	0.50	0.80	0.40	0.95	0.23	0.99	0.12	0.99	0.25
Speaks Spanish very well	0.98	0.13	0.61	0.50	0.56	0.50	0.35	0.48	0.13	0.34	0.03	0.17	0.00	0.05
Watches Spanish TV less than weekly	0.11	0.32	0.24	0.43	0.37	0.48	0.55	0.50	0.79	0.41	0.93	0.26	0.80	0.40
Ethnicity not important	0.08	0.27	0.13	0.34	0.16	0.37	0.15	0.35	0.32	0.47	0.26	0.44	0.33	0.47
Non-Catholic	0.14	0.35	0.28	0.45	0.35	0.48	0.39	0.49	0.39	0.50	0.57	0.50	0.82	0.38
Attends religious services twice a year or less	0.18	0.39	0.18	0.39	0.22	0.41	0.25	0.44	0.32	0.47	0.34	0.48	—	—
Ethnicity of marriage partner not important	0.71	0.45	0.81	0.40	0.82	0.39	0.83	0.38	0.84	0.37	0.93	0.26	0.92	0.28
Has non-Hispanic white spouse[a]	0.02	0.15	0.08	0.27	0.10	0.30	0.20	0.40	0.23	0.43	0.42	0.50	0.75	0.43
Number of children ever born[b]	2.27	1.35	1.67	1.35	1.29	1.40	1.71	1.45	1.92	1.75	1.14	1.14	0.84	1.14
N	125		308		456		171		38		68		402	

Source: Data from Immigration and Intergenerational Mobility in Metropolitan Los Angeles (see Bean, Leach et al. 2011).
[a]Restricted to persons who are married or partnered; sample sizes by generation are: 94 (1.0), 176 (1.5), 199 (2.0), 85 (2.5), 26 (3.0) & 33 (3.5).
[b]Restricted to women; sample sizes by generation are: 54 (1.0), 155 (1.5), 230 (2.0), 85 (2.5), 13 (3.0), 35 (3.5).

to nonassimilation forces. Here we use the indicator speaking Spanish "very well," a measure that is important because lack of fluency in the heritage language implies lack of literacy and the beginnings of the eventual demise of the language altogether. Looking first at immigrants, we see that in the first (1.0) generation, 98 percent of the respondents report they speak Spanish "very well," nearly the mirror image of the 2 percent who reported a preference for "speaking only English at home." This drops to 61 percent in the 1.5 generation, and then again to 56 percent in the 2.0 generation. While one might be tempted to view this slight drop as reflecting a lack of assimilation, it probably merely reflects the fact that for 2.0 generation persons, whose parents are both Mexican born, the extended family on both sides are likely to speak Spanish. Thus, Spanish retention is double the proportion of Spanish speakers among the 2.5 generation, in which the percentage reporting they "speak Spanish very well" falls to 35 percent among those with only one Mexican-born parent. The percentage speaking Spanish well plunges in the 3.0 and 3.5 generations, dropping to 13 percent in the former case and to a mere 3 percent in the latter. This sharp drop-off is compatible with the observation that heritage-language indicators may more readily capture other sources of influence on linguistic change than host-country language indicators.

It is also instructive to compare Mexican Americans with white European Americans to see if the former show a notably stronger tendency to retain their own heritage language. White Europeans might be expected to discard heritage languages relatively quickly because they presumably more easily become structurally integrated in the United States and have less access to heritage-language media. Here we examine preference for speaking the mother tongue at home for both groups. In the case of this measure, if persons cease to prefer speaking their heritage language at home, they probably prefer not to speak it anywhere else as well, making this measure a particularly telling indicator of language loss. Among Mexican Americans, 98 percent of the first generation prefer Spanish at home. In the 1.5 generation, 61 percent prefer Spanish at home (whereas only 13 percent of white Europeans report such a preference) (see figure 7.1). In the 2.0 generation, this figure is 43 percent for Mexican Americans, whereas among White Europeans it is 11 percent. The 2.5 generation falls to 20 percent for Mexican Americans and 2 percent for White Europeans. The percent preferring mother tongue then declines to 5 percent in the 3.0 generation for Mexican Americans, and then to 1 percent in the 3.5 generation, while the counterpart figures for White Europeans are vanishingly small. Thus, by the third generation there is scarcely any survival of mother tongue preference among either Mexican Americans or white Europeans.

Researchers using the IIMMLA data and working on linguistic topics have also fruitfully applied the techniques of life-table analysis to

Figure 7.1   Fluency in Mother Tongue, Mexican Americans and White Europeans, by Generation

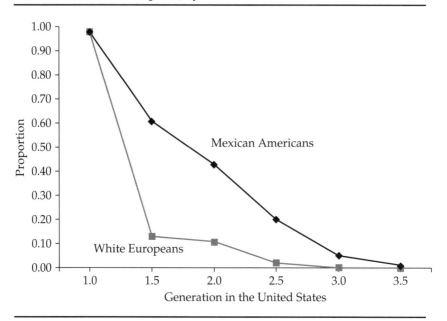

Source: Data from Immigration and Intergenerational Mobility in Metropolitan Los Angeles (see Bean, Leach et al. 2011).

calculate linguistic survival probabilities and language "life expectancies" that "give the average number of generations a foreign language can be expected to survive within the cultural and linguistic milieu of contemporary Southern California."[9] The conversion of such probabilities to life expectancies enables the statement of results in terms of the average number of generations a language can be expected to "live" (that is, survive). For Mexican Americans, this yields a figure of about three generations on average for continuing to speak Spanish "very well," as opposed to two generations on average for continuing to prefer speaking mother tongue at home (figure 7.2). The low levels of retention of Spanish proficiency and household usage thus imply that heritage language preservation for later-generation Mexican Americans is minimal in the United States. And in the case of preferring to speak only English at home, a classic assimilation pattern of steady increase from the 1.5 to the later generations occurs. As previously noted, this undoubtedly results in large measure from the dynamics of exposure, which clearly are strong enough to override other kinds of influence that might be pushing or pulling linguistic incorporation in other directions.

Figure 7.2   Average Life Expectancy of Native Language of Mexican-Origin and White European-Origin Americans, by Generation

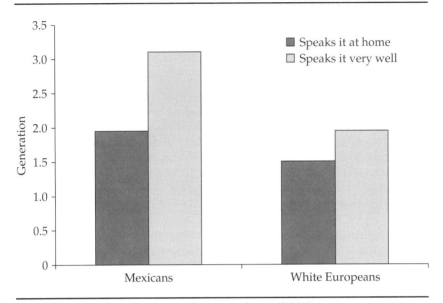

Source: Adapted from Rumbaut, Massey, and Bean (2006).

Of course, agency is not altogether absent from the process of English acquisition in the case of Mexican Americans. Mexican first- and second-generation immigrants are more likely than those from any other country to show low levels of English proficiency on average (in large part because until recently, most have had little exposure to English in Mexico, either on the street or in school, compared with immigrants from other countries, although this has been changing rapidly).[10] For these and other reasons, Mexican immigrants start at the very bottom of the occupational structure in the United States. Because of beginning at such low points, they also have the most to gain from integration, which implies they may be motivated to try especially hard to acquire English. If this were the case, it should be reflected in their patterns of English usage. For example, Mexican immigrants should be relatively more likely to speak only English under circumstances that seem likely to foster upward mobility, even though in general Mexican immigrants have low levels of education. In fact, Mexican Americans who are not at the very bottom of the education distribution and who have young children (whose presence we might reasonably expect to motivate English usage at home), are more likely than those with little education and no children to use only English at home (by a difference of 10 percentage points).[11] In short, English-only usage is more likely among Mexican immigrants under conditions where it might enhance upward mobility, suggesting that agency in addition to mere exposure contributes to Mexican American linguistic integration.

Generational Differences in Other Sociocultural Indicators

We next examine the other sociocultural factors from our selected set of indicators. Because little reason exists to our knowledge to think these vary primarily as a product of exposure (that is, with length of time in the country), we expect them to be much more likely to reflect the influence of forces associated with structural blockage if these are operating to limit incorporation. We again use the more detailed generational breakdown running through the 3.5 generation. We do not use the four-plus generation because it gives unreliable results for the same reasons that three-plus measures do, as discussed in previous chapters. That is, this group is more subject to selective attrition than the group consisting of persons with some Mexican-born grandparents. As a consequence, even were we to include results for this group, we would need to remain aware that values for such persons need to be interpreted with caution because they are biased downward insofar as their reflection of integration is concerned.

Watching Spanish TV

Further evidence of linguistic assimilation emerges from a measure of the frequency with which Mexican Americans watch Spanish-language television (see table 7.1). Almost nine in ten members of the 1.0 generation say they watch Spanish television at least once a week. This drops to three in four by the 1.5 generation, and then again to about three in five by the 2.0 generation. It drops further for the 2.5 generation to about one in two, cascading to one in five in the 3.0 generation and then collapsing almost entirely in the 3.5 generation, when scarcely one in twelve of those Mexican Americans with only one or two Mexican-born grandparents watches Spanish-language TV more than once a week. Although a pattern of discontinuity appears to emerge between the second and third generations, this fails to hold up to tests of statistical significance.

Importance of Ethnic Identity

The next indicator we examine is based on a question asking, "How important is ethnic identity to you?" We look at those who responded "not very important" as exhibiting higher overall sociocultural incorporation than those responding that ethnic identity mattered to them. For this indicator, the results for the first generation indicate that 92 percent say their ethnic identity is "important" to them (table 7.1). Turning to the other generational groups, we see that in the 1.5 generation, 87 percent say their ethnic identity is "important" to them, a nearly identical level of response to that of the 2.0 and 2.5 generations, of whom 84 percent and 85 percent indicate it is "important." By the third generation, however, ethnicity begins to lose its grip, as nearly one-third say it is not important, and more than one-fourth of the 3.5 generation feel that way. Comparing the early-generation groups with the third-generation groups, some evidence emerges for a discontinuity in the importance of ethnicity. But overall, ethnicity retains its salience.

Religious Affiliation

Most Mexicans are Catholics, at least nominally.[12] Thus a large majority (86 percent) of the 1.0 generation members of the Los Angeles study sample report being Catholic (stated the other way, around 14 percent report something else, that is, either Protestant, some other religious affiliation, or no religious affiliation). But in the 1.5 generation, the inroads of the more diverse American religious landscape begin to become evident, with 28 percent indicating some non-Catholic affiliation. This rises modestly to 35 percent in the 2.0 generation and then escalates slightly more in the 2.5 generation (to 39 percent) before stalling in the 3.0 generation (at 39 percent) and then jumping to 57 percent in the 3.5 generation. Even with this notable increase, the percentage remains appreciably below that for the non-Hispanic white group in Los Angeles, which shows a non-Catholic affiliation of 82 percent. The relative low value in the 3.0 generation (for those with three or four Mexican-born grandparents) reflects that family ethnic-density may foster the retention of Catholicism. For those parents in the 3.5 generation, however, with grandparents who were born in the United States, familiarity with the broader American experience is greater, resulting in greater non-Catholicism.

Church Attendance

Moving to an explicitly behavioral facet of religious integration, frequency of church attendance, we see that only about one in five Mexican immigrants, along with a similar number of Mexican Americans who are the children of immigrants (that is, the 1.5, 2.0, and 2.5 generations) attend church each year only once or not at all. Stated differently, about four in five members of these generations attend church twice or more per year. In the 3.0 and the 3.5 generations, the number hardly attending at all rises to about one-third, reaching a proportion equivalent to that shown by non-Hispanic whites in the metropolitan area. Thus in the case of this measure of sociocultural orientation, third-generation Mexican Americans behave in ways very much the same as majority whites.

Ethnic Preference for Marriage Partner and Anglo Intermarriage

Attitudes toward marriage and actual behavioral patterns in regard to establishing marital relationships also constitute important elements of sociocultural incorporation. When we look at the percentage of first-generation immigrants who say they do not have a preference for their marriage partner belonging to their ethnic group, we find that 71 percent respond that they have no such preference. This rises to 81 percent in the 1.5 generation, and then remains at about this same level (roughly four in five saying they have no preference) through the 3.0 generation. In the 3.5 generation the percentage climbs to 93 percent, the same level of lack of in-group preference shown by non-Hispanic whites (table 7.1). The difference in this measure between the members of those generational groups consisting of the children of immigrants and those consisting of the grandchildren of immigrants is not large and does not suggest a notable jump in the third-generation groups.

Turning our attention next to actual behavior as revealed by differences in patterns of intermarriage with Anglos (we use this indicator because the vast majority of Mexican American interethnic marriages are with non-Hispanic whites),[13] we find a near total absence of intermarriage among those in the immigrant generation. This creeps upward to 8 percent in the 1.5 generation and 10 percent in the 2.0 generation. It rises to around 20 percent in the 2.5 and 3.0 generations and then climbs to 42 percent in the 3.5 generation. Although the latter is a sizable increase, in the case of this indicator, similar relative increases occur also at earlier generational points. Thus interethnic intermarriage with Anglos shows a pattern of steady intergenerational increase as predicted by the classical assimilation hypothesis. One reason perhaps is that intermarriage, like learning the host-country language, is a function of both exposure and cultural change (which may operate through motivation). Across generations, relatively more Mexican Americans either work with or live closer to non-Hispanic whites, or both, leading to more interpersonal contact and thus more intermarriage.

Number of Children

The last sociocultural indicator we examine is fertility, or the number of children Mexican Americans have. Although fertility has been dropping steadily in Mexico for several decades, the families of Mexican immigrants are larger than those of non-Hispanic whites. And the family sizes of later-generation immigrants also appear to remain larger than those of Anglos, although this conclusion is often reached on the basis of data that does not separate out immigrants, thus biasing the measures upward.

When we turn to the IIMMLA data, we see that the 1.0 generation women report having 2.3 children on average, and the 1.5 generation women in Los Angeles report 1.7 children. This declines to 1.3 in the 2.0 generation, before ticking upwards to 1.7 in the 2.5 generation. In the 3.0 generation, women's fertility is 1.9 children per family and 1.1 children in the 3.5 generation. A similar pattern characterizes men (not shown here). These figures, however, are affected by other variables, including age and education, so the pattern would likely change when these are taken into account.

Controlling for the Influence of Other Factors

On balance, the above results suggest that the single indicators of sociocultural integration follow for the most part a pattern of gradual steady increase in integration. This is especially clear for certain indicators (speaking Spanish very well, intermarriage to a non-Hispanic white, and, to a lesser extent, infrequency of watching Spanish TV), measures that one would expect to vary positively with amount of exposure. Thus their tendency to conform to the expectations of an assimilation hypothesis probably results from the influence of such factors. An obvious question concerns whether this overall pattern holds up when other variables are controlled. We address this by examining how adjusting for age, gender, and education differences affect the pattern. The first two of these provide a check on whether the small but evident differences in age and gender composition across the generation groups matter for the sociocultural factors enough to influence the patterns observed. We also adjust for education to see if this important source of structural difference affects the patterns of differences.

Controlling for education seems to contradict the mosaic conceptualization of sociocultural integration, the idea that the elements of sociocultural integration are not very strongly related to one another or to other incorporation dimensions. If education is an important part of structural incorporation, then controlling for it would seem to violate the idea that integration involves multiple relatively independent dimensions. In fact, if controlling for education substantially affects the patterns already observed in the data for the sociocultural indicators, it would undermine somewhat the postindustrial-individualistic interpretation that sociocultural incorporation consists of separate heterogeneous facets.

We present descriptive statistics for the entire sample in table 7.2. It is particularly important to note that the intercorrelations among the sociocultural indicators are generally small. Of the thirty-six correlations in the table, only four exceed 0.15, and all of these involve correlations between pairs of indicators, at least one of which is a measure that varies appreciably with exposure (either one of the language measures or the intermarriage

Table 7.2 Intercorrelations for Sociocultural Indicators, Mexican American Adults, Aged Twenty to Forty, Los Angeles, 2004

Indicator	Means	A	B	C	D	E	F	G	H	I
A	Prefers English at home	0.60	1.000								
B	Speaks Spanish very well	0.46	-0.158	1.000							
C	Watches Spanish TV less than weekly	0.41	0.421	-0.227	1.000						
D	Non-Catholic	0.35	0.134	-0.013	0.140	1.000					
E	Attends religious services twice a year or less	0.22	0.072	-0.082	0.060	-0.023	1.000				
F	Ethnicity not important	0.16	0.092	-0.096	0.123	0.081	0.051	1.000			
G	Ethnicity of marriage partner not important	0.82	0.057	-0.062	0.044	0.075	0.048	0.094	1.000		
H	Has non-Hispanic white spouse[a]	0.07	0.192	-0.035	0.160	0.073	0.028	0.036	0.065	1.000	
I	Number of children ever born[b]	1.14	-0.030	0.058	-0.057	-0.093	-0.116	-0.013	-0.041	0.042	1.000

Source: Data from Immigration and Intergenerational Mobility in Metropolitan Los Angeles (see Bean, Leach et al. 2011).
[a]Restricted to persons who are married or partnered; sample sizes by generation are: 94 (1.0), 176 (1.5), 199 (2.0), 85 (2.5), 26 (3.0) & 33 (3.5).
[b]Restricted to women; sample sizes by generation are: 54 (1.0), 155 (1.5), 230 (2.0), 85 (2.5), 13 (3.0), 35 (3.5).

measure). Overall, the relationships are not strong and thus do not call into question the idea that elements of sociocultural incorporation appear to occur relatively independently of one another. Checking this same idea with respect to education, table 7.3 presents the results of ordinary least squares (OLS) regressions of each of the sociocultural indicators on dummy variables for generation and variables for age, gender, unauthorized background, and education (the results from using logistic regression for these analyses were substantively similar, but we present the OLS results for simplicity's sake). The patterns observed in the descriptive data are generally repeated here. That is, the tendency for the generation groups to show steady (although sometimes small) increases is not much affected by adjusting for these sources of difference across generation groups. We thus conclude that the results to this point support the idea that sociocultural integration involves multiple relatively independent facets that tend to reflect increasing integration across generational categories.

We also ran these regressions including unauthorized background as a control. In the previous chapters examining dimensions of structural integration, we found that unauthorized background exerted a notably depressing effect on most measures of structural incorporation (income sometimes constituting an interesting exception), whether those consisted of indicators of education or spatial assimilation. In many instances, controlling for unauthorized background in examinations of generational differences also muted or smoothed out the magnitude of differences between the children of immigrants and the grandchildren of immigrants. In other words, the pattern of integration across generations observed without controls was somewhat eliminated by adjusting for unauthorized background status. Although the theoretical considerations of membership exclusion do not imply that this same result would emerge for sociocultural integration, we nonetheless also ran similar kinds of models for the indicators examined here. Having grown up with an unauthorized parental background only occasionally affects the sociocultural measures and clearly does not make much difference for the pattern of generational differences observed. Thus, as we have already noted, most of these sociocultural indicators show a somewhat steady change across the generational categories in the direction of convergence with the majority group. We do not call this assimilation because the sociocultural indicators do not positively correlate very strongly with one another, something we contend is implied by an assimilation theoretical perspective.

Conclusions

In the case of sociocultural measures, we find that notable increases occur across generational categories, especially in those indicators that might most be expected to vary as a function of exposure. Thus preferring to

Table 7.3 OLS Regression Coefficients from Models of Sociocultural Incorporation Indicators Regressed on Immigrant Generation, Migration-Status Background, and Control Variables, Mexican-Origin Adults, Aged Twenty to Forty, Los Angeles, 2004

	A	B	C	D	E	F	G	H	I
1.5 Gen (reference)	—	—	—	—	—	—	—	—	—
2.0 Gen	0.143***	-0.001	0.113**	0.040	0.043	0.043	-0.002	-0.005	0.109
2.5 Gen	0.350***	-0.226***	0.296***	0.101*	0.088*	0.020	0.020	0.043+	0.175
3.0 Gen	0.462***	-0.465***	0.519***	0.113	0.164*	0.181**	0.035	0.082+	0.507
3.5 Gen	0.525***	-0.555***	0.667***	0.281***	0.178**	0.138**	0.115	0.144***	-0.294
Unauthorized background	-0.147**	-0.203**	0.016	-0.028	0.065	0.021	-0.003	-0.014	0.076
Age	0.007*	0.001	0.001	-0.007**	-0.003	0.004+	-0.003	0.005***	0.108***
Education	0.022***	0.020*	0.017**	0.011	-0.001	0.001	0.006	0.009*	-0.174***
Number of siblings	—	—	—	—	—	—	—	—	0.030+
Constant	-0.039	0.274*	-0.014	0.362**	0.277*	0.008	0.822***	-0.194**	0.484
R-Squared	0.173	0.125	0.150	0.033	0.016	0.018	0.010	0.054	0.300

Source: Data from Immigration and Intergenerational Mobility in Metropolitan Los Angeles (see Bean, Leach et al. 2011).
Note: A: Prefers English at home; B: speaks Spanish very well; C: watches Spanish TV infrequently; D: non-Catholic; E: infrequent religious attendance; F: ethnic identity not important; G: not important to marry same race/ethnicity; H: non-Hispanic white spouse; I: number of children ever born.
*** $p < .001$; ** $p < .01$; * $p < .05$; + $p < .10$.

speak English at home becomes nearly universal by the third generation. But interestingly, as expected by a postindustrial-individualistic theoretical perspective, which emphasizes a societal trend toward heterogeneity, fluidity, and differentiation of sociocultural life in today's advanced economies, the sociocultural measures used here, other than those of language and intermarriage, do not correlate very highly with one another across individuals. We thus think it makes little sense to speak of an assimilation model as characterizing the cross-generational patterns. Earlier we noted that research has shown that more exclusionary countries tend to exhibit more unidimensional integration patterns, implying stronger tendencies toward sociocultural conformity. The results presented here show considerable sociocultural differentiation (little correlation across facets among individuals), implying that Los Angeles and the United States depart appreciably from such a pattern. The sociocultural differentiation we observe here thus seems most comfortably joined with a membership-exclusion, postindustrial-individualistic view of integration, which together emphasize structural integration under conditions of full societal membership with individual sociocultural integration occurring as well. Both of these patterns appear largely complete by the third generation.

== Chapter 8 ==

Mexican Migration and Integration: Trends, Explanations, and Implications for U.S. Policy

Our multigenerational and multidimensional empirical assessment of the nature and extent of Mexican American integration is now nearly complete. Among the tasks that remain are synthesizing our findings, evaluating how well the theoretical perspectives explicated in chapter 2 fit the experience of Mexican Americans, and articulating what the implications of the findings are for both U.S. immigration and immigrant policy. The latter is particularly important at this point in time. Before we can pursue that objective, it is necessary to address another question. How important is Mexican immigration for the U.S. economy? To what extent has Mexican immigration over the past twenty-five years or so constituted an essential element of the U.S. workforce? If the migration of less-skilled workers to the country stopped today, would we be better off or worse off? These are difficult questions to answer, but their resolution affects whether reforming U.S. immigration and immigrant policy is an urgent matter. Answering these questions depends on knowing how many Mexican migrants have come to the country at different points in time, why they came, and what factors have affected the size and nature of these flows. It also depends on understanding demographic changes that influenced the size and structure of the U.S.-born workforce over the last half century.

These are the objectives of this chapter. To the extent that the United States truly needs the labor of unauthorized migrants, strong reasons would exist for the country to foster the advancement and integration of migrants, including legalizing their status. This would make sense if for no other reason than workforce preservation. Despite heated popular debate about whether migrants are taking jobs from the native born, research on the labor-market implications of unauthorized migration for less-skilled natives finds little in the way of effects, although some evidence indicates negative repercussions for earlier-arriving less-skilled migrants.[1] The latter could result from migrants using their social networks to find work in destinations already popular with other Mexican migrants. But the virtual absence of labor-market effects on natives implies that the United States genuinely relies on unauthorized Mexican migrants to do difficult manual work and that the employment of such migrants entails need, not just convenience or exploitation.

To shed light on the above issues, we organize the rest of this chapter into four parts. First, we examine trends in the kinds and size of Mexican migration to the United States. We document growth since 1970 both in the flow of Mexican migrants and in the size of the stock of unauthorized Mexican-born migrants, noting how U.S. policies from the 1960s opened doors for Mexican migration in general and contributed to a renewal of unauthorized migration in particular. We also chart the acceleration of unauthorized Mexican migration beginning around 1990. Second, because policy changes better explain why unauthorized migration begins than why it grows, we look to theories of migration to see how well these account for the rapid rises in unauthorized Mexican migration occurring over the past twenty-five years (except during the Great Recession). Third, because standard theories of migration appear to explain only some of the growth in such migration, we suggest that a significant part of the rise stems from demographic changes that have reduced the U.S.-born less-skilled working-age population. Fourth, we suggest what these trends mean for the importance of the integration of Mexican immigrants and their descendants and thus for immigration and immigrant policy.

Mexican Migration and U.S. Immigration Policies

Since about 1970, the number of new entrants to the United States each year has risen nearly tenfold, from 5 million to about 49 million in 2010.[2] Most of these new arrivals are not immigrants but students, tourists, business people, exchange visitors, and temporary workers. To a considerable extent, the expansion reflects broad international trends involving flows of people and money as more national economies have joined the global marketplace.[3] For example, since 1970, the share of the U.S. economy deriving from international trade increased from 12 to 31 percent.[4] Greatly improved communication technologies and less expensive forms of transportation have rapidly boosted the potential and actual supply of both visitors and immigrants.[5] In the United States, Mexicans dominate the flows of immigrants overall and have shown disproportionate increases among both nonimmigrants (that is, nonpermanent foreign-born residents) and unauthorized immigrants (the latter consisting of both border crossers and visas overstays). Altogether, the Mexican portion of total foreign-born in-flows over the past decade (legal permanent residents, unauthorized entrants, and nonimmigrants) has risen from about 13 percent in 2000 to almost 28 percent in 2010.[6]

Trends in Mexican Legal and Unauthorized Migration

The absolute number of legal immigrants from Mexico also remains high, as can be seen in the flow numbers shown in figure 8.1, top panel. The bottom panel compares the stock of unauthorized immigrants from Mexico with those from the second-largest sending country, El Salvador. Although the annual number of Mexican legal permanent residents has leveled off in recent years, Mexico still dominates the flows. In 2000 the number of Mexicans entering legally was about four times as great as that from the second-largest sending country, the Philippines. By 2010, although Mexican immigration had decreased, it was still about twice as high as that year's second-leading country, China. Also, the size of the unauthorized immigrant net in-flow to the United States from Mexico dwarfs to an even greater degree the volume from any other single source country (as can be inferred from differences in the cumulative stock numbers across time periods shown in figure 8.1, bottom panel). Nearly three in every five unauthorized immigrants in the country today come from Mexico, a fraction about the same as in earlier decades.[7] Moreover, the increasing flow of Mexican nonimmigrants during this period has risen to levels higher than those from any other country (figure 8.2), increasing the likelihood that the number of Mexicans who overstay temporary visas has risen both absolutely and relatively.[8]

Trends in Temporary Worker Visas

The number of temporary Mexican workers coming to the United States with legal visas has also climbed. These workers are not readily discernible in statistics on total legal nonimmigrant admissions, which consist overwhelmingly of students and tourists. But a breakdown of the history of nonimmigrant admissions by type, shown in figure 8.3, demonstrates that temporary worker entrances had begun to increase noticeably by the mid-1990s. One factor fueling this was the U.S. high-tech economic boom, during which tens of thousands of high-skilled temporary technology workers (H1B visas) arrived, especially from India and China. At the same time, however, the U.S. also admitted ever larger numbers of less-skilled Mexican seasonal agricultural workers with H2A visas and nonagricultural workers with H2B visas.[9] These latter categories of

Figure 8.1   Legal Permanent Residency and Unauthorized Migration from Mexico and from Countries of Next Largest Migration, 1981 to 2010

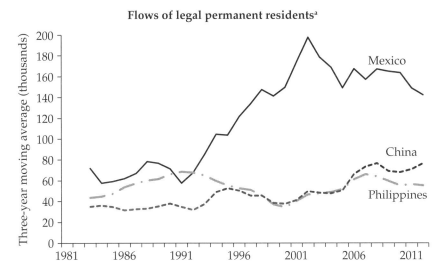

Flows of legal permanent residents[a]

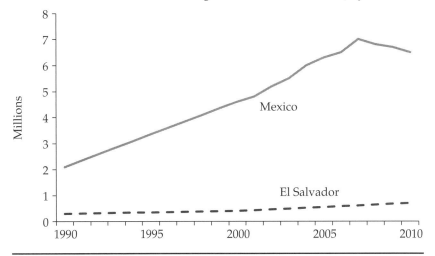

Stock of unauthorized migrants in the United States, by decade[b]

Sources: Hoefer, Rytina, and Baker (2011); Passel and Cohn (2011); Passel, Van Hook, and Bean (2004); U.S. Department of Homeland Security (2003, 2009, 2012); U.S. Immigration and Naturalization Service (1987, 1994, 1999). Adapted from figure 1 in Bean, Bachmeier, Brown, Van Hook, and Leach 2014.
[a]Excludes persons legalized under the provisions of the 1986 Immigration Control and Reform Act (IRCA).
[b]Annual estimates are shown for Mexicans between 2000 and 2010.

Figure 8.2   Nonimmigrant Admissions to the United States from Japan, Mexico, and the United Kingdom and from China-Korea-India, 1993 to 2009

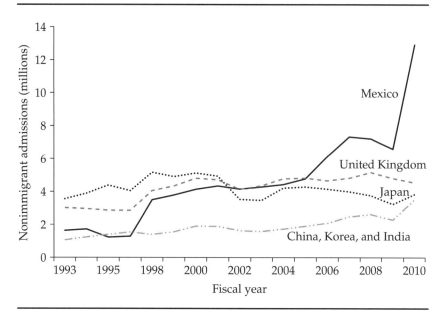

Source: U.S. Department of Homeland Security, Office of Immigration Statistics. Adapted from figure 2 in Bean, Bachmeier, Brown, Van Hook, and Leach (2014). *Note:* I-94 only.

Figure 8.3   Temporary Mexican Worker Admissions to the United States, by Visa Type, 1986 to 2011

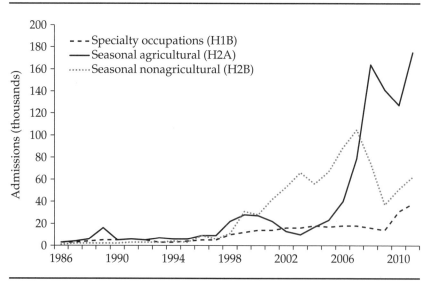

Source: U.S. Department of Homeland Security, Office of Immigration Statistics. Adapted from figure 3 in Bean, Bachmeier, Brown, Van Hook, and Leach (2014).

temporary Mexican workers reached levels in 2011 that were about ten times their 1970 levels. In sum, except for the slowdowns from 2009 to 2011 stemming from the Great Recession, migrant flows over the past forty years to the United States (especially those involving either unauthorized or temporary entrants and temporary workers) are sharply distinctive in two ways: one is their steady rise, especially since the early 1990s, and the other is their overwhelming Mexican character. No other country contributes so much to the presence of less-skilled labor migrants in the United States.

The Bracero Program and the Onset of Unauthorized Mexican Migration

Although legal and unauthorized migrants have come to the United States from many countries, why have Mexican flows, particularly Mexican unauthorized flows, predominated so heavily? What accounts for the persistently high levels of growth in numbers of Mexican unauthorized migrants, particularly since in the 1990s, even though unauthorized Mexicans often encountered hostility from a vocal minority of natives? To answer these questions, we begin in an earlier era, when changes in U.S. policy unintentionally opened the door for unauthorized Mexican migration. Under a series of agreements with Mexico that came to be known as the Bracero Program, the United States relied on Mexican contract labor from 1942 to 1964. Tens of thousands of agricultural and other manual workers entered the United States annually.[10] After Congress ended the program, the most viable option for many agricultural employers was to continue to hire Mexicans, but the Mexicans, especially circulatory labor migrants, generally now had to enter the country illegally, since they could no longer come as contract laborers.[11] The chances of getting a temporary work visa fell even further in 1976, when Congress expressly limited the number of such legal entrants to the extremely low number of 20,000 persons per year.[12] As a result, unauthorized migration began to emerge.[13]

The 1965 Immigration Reforms

In 1965, a year after the Bracero Program was terminated, Congress passed the Hart-Celler Act, which reformed immigration law by abolishing national-origins quotas. This legislation further set the stage for unauthorized Mexican immigration, although those who pushed for the legislation's passage did not intend for it to increase Mexican migration in any way.[14] Indeed, the opposite was true. The main thrust of the reforms was to privilege a policy of family reunification. But as part of a political compromise, the law retained many restrictionist features of the earlier McCarran-Walter Act of 1952 and added new ones.[15] Essentially, the agreement broke a stalemate between conservatives and liberals within both parties from that earlier time. Restrictionists acceded to front-door modifications (that is, changes in the criteria for legal immigration) in exchange for ostensibly tightened side-door migration (that is, a ceiling on Western Hemispheric entrants).[16]

Hart-Celler imposed caps on legal entrants, initially 170,000 for the Eastern and 120,000 for the Western Hemispheres, as well as a per-country limit of 20,000 visas for the Eastern Hemisphere. The House and Senate Judiciary Committees supported both caps on grounds of fairness (a cap for only one hemisphere seemed unfair) and out of fear of unregulated spillover from rapid nonwhite population growth in Latin America.[17] These provisions offered little possibility of providing less-skilled legal labor or replacing the Braceros.

The law's provisions for family reunification eventually permitted gradual growth in legal Mexican migration.[18] Legal Mexican migration had averaged only about 30,000 per year during the 1950s, but after 1965, legal permanent residents could more easily bring in immediate family members. In addition, employers used Hart-Celler provisions to sponsor workers previously covered as Braceros. These "sponsored" workers were allowed to become legal permanent residents and bring immediate family members to join them. But because the new ceiling on legal visas was too low to accommodate all the Mexican entrants seeking to reunite with their families, this also fostered unauthorized migration. Moreover, the demand for agricultural and factory workers grew substantially in part because of the rapid expansion of California irrigation and manufacturing in Los Angeles.[19] Not surprisingly, during the 1970s, the bulk of unauthorized entrants, almost all Mexican, settled in California.[20]

Accounting for Growth in Unauthorized Migration

Although the 1965 reforms and the end of the Bracero Program created an opening for Mexican migration, they do not fully explain why the number of unauthorized entrants has increased so much. While the 1965 changes allowed modest increases in legal immigration through its family reunification provisions,[21] what factors explain the substantial unauthorized increases? To help answer this question, it is useful to review theories about the causes of international migration and to assess their relevance for accounting for the changes. In evaluating their explanatory power, we rely on the results of previous empirical research, the ability of certain theories to explain unauthorized Mexican migration better than others,[22] and the tendency for certain types of flows to occur at different times than others, especially recently.[23]

Broadly speaking, explanations of migration, including those of unauthorized migration, may be loosely classified as falling into either of two categories, so-called push or pull theories. Within each of these, theories may be further distinguished as emphasizing either structural or individual forces as drivers of migration. One of the arguments this book makes is that ultimately it often takes at least one push and one pull factor to spur migration, and often more than two such factors. In other words, at least one characteristic of the place of origin and of the migrant before migration and some characteristic of the place of destination or of the migrant after migrating are necessary for an adequate explanation. In particular, the destination must offer either a better life than the one at origin or at least the prospect of a better life. Otherwise, potential movers may have reasons to migrate but nowhere to go.

Neoclassical Economic Theories

Neoclassical economists envision migration as stemming from macro-level imbalances between countries (or areas) in the supply of and demand for labor and the resultant wage differences these disequilibria generate.[24] At the micro-level, this perspective assumes rational calculations on the part of individuals concerning the benefits (usually assumed to be economic) of a move relative to its costs.[25] Migration thus represents an investment strategy for individuals to maximize their returns to labor power relative to the costs of migrating that may be incurred during the migration process or after settlement. For instance, Karl Eschbach, Jacqueline Hagan, and Stanley Bailey assess the deterrent effect of U.S.-Mexico border enforcement in terms of the ultimate cost: the risk of death while crossing.[26] Migrants also consider expected costs of living after they settle at their destination. Living costs include rents, food, and clothing, and, especially in the United States, the cost of automobile transportation.[27]

Research examining the influence of multiple variables on the likelihood that Mexicans undertake migration has consistently reported that indicators reflecting the possibility of income gains relate positively to movement, although these studies also tend to find that other factors explain more variation in flows than do simple wage differences alone.[28] Filiz Garip's pathbreaking analysis of various kinds of migration notes that "income maximizers" predominate among this type of mover.[29] Such persons tend mostly to be rural male household heads involved in agriculture with little education and few ties to other U.S. migrants. Garip's analyses of Mexican Migration Project data stretching over nearly forty years show the highest prevalence of this kind of migration during the early to mid 1970s.

New Economic Theories of Migration

Other theorists amend microeconomic theories by devoting emphasis to the intersection of labor market considerations with family and household needs in affecting migration decisions and by incorporating into the

theory the importance of minimizing risk along with that of maximizing earnings.[30] This perspective predicts that indicators like social rank,
relative income, and potential for social mobility will influence migration.
For example, Edward Taylor et al. emphasize that not only lower average
wages but also greater social and economic inequality in Mexico stimu-
late migration to the United States.[31] Similarly, others argue that urbaniza-
tion generates emigration because of greater relative social inequality and
atomization (that is, fragmentation of families) in Mexico's largest cities.[32]

Among the factors generating such inequalities are market failures
(for example, external conditions that lead to the unavailability of investment capital or land), which often impede social and economic mobility
in sending countries. Households in such places respond by sending one
or more members to foreign labor markets to generate income and capital that can be used to minimize short- and long-term risk in the sending country in which the primary households are located.[33] Remittances
from these migrants are then consumed or reinvested in household production, agriculture, or new small businesses.[34] Even migrants who are
settled permanently in the United States may send money to aging parents in Mexico.[35] Also, migrants who are married and bring their wives
to the United States and then have U.S.-born children tend to become
permanent settlers.[36] Risk minimization can also be a significant force in
these households, especially when the husband who is working is unauthorized. Maintaining continuity of employment is thus an important
risk-minimization strategy in such households.

Because new household economic theories emphasize household organizational factors operating in response to external social and economic
conditions, they help to explain the unusually high levels of employment
at low-wage levels among Mexican unauthorized migrant households.
This contrasts with neo-classical theory, which essentially implies that
migrants may endure nonemployment while they seek higher wages.
Using the theoretical concept of "socially expected durations," Roberts
explicates how labor market conditions in both sending and receiving
countries influence not only migrants' expected returns to their labor but
the length of their time horizons as well as their tolerance for spells of
non-employment.[37] Although neo-classical theory may provide an explanation for potential migrants' initial motivations to consider moving, new
economic theories explain more adequately the importance of employment, its continuity, and the settlement dynamics of Mexican labor flows.

Migrants of this type generally are somewhat more prosperous than
income maximizers. The typical migrant is likely to own property, land,
or a business, to be the son of the household head, and to have a primary school education.[38] However, because the representative migrant
comes from a household with assets that are at risk, migration occurs
for the purpose of diversifying income sources to guard against the

hazards resulting from economic volatility in Mexico. Empirical studies thus tend to show a connection between the likelihood of migrating and the circumstances associated with this kind of migration orientation.[39] Such migrants have been termed "risk diversifiers,"[40] and they were most prevalent in migration flows occurring from the late 1970s through the mid-1980s.

Network/Social Capital Theory

Network theory seeks to explain, at the micro level, how connections among actors influence migration decisions, often by linking individual immigrants with their family members and with jobs, both before and after arrival.[41] While labor markets in sending and receiving countries create push and pull factors stimulating migration, migration may continue after these push and pull factors have diminished.[42] When large numbers of people have moved from one particular location to another, a process of "cumulative causation" may ensue, whereby multiple ties to communities of origin facilitate ongoing and at times increasing migration.[43] The exchange of information and the formation of relationships of trust are the building blocks of migration networks. Migrants sometimes do not even know about the availability of jobs or the relative price of labor between their home country and their desired destination. Rather, they usually possess information about a particular job, and this information signals an opportunity in the destination labor market.[44] Migrants also rely on informal trust relationships to minimize the risks associated with moving to a foreign land.[45] These networks, in the form of contacts with friends, families, and employers, provide an important means through which immigrants gain and accumulate social capital that minimizes risk.

Empirical studies of network-based migration have found strong relationships between network indicators and the tendency to undertake unauthorized migration.[46] Garip finds that such migrants are highly likely to have family ties to other migrants, to be connected to U.S. residents, and to live in communities with a high prevalence of migration. She describes the typical network migrant as "the unemployed daughter of the household head . . . whose father or husband . . . is a current or prior migrant to the US."[47] Such migrants were especially prevalent from the late 1980s until the mid-1990s, when many Mexican spouses migrated to join husbands who had obtained legal permanent resident status under the provisions of the 1986 Immigration Reform and Control Act.

Labor-Market-Segmentation Theory

In contrast to economic approaches, labor-market-segmentation theories emphasize how structural social-stratification factors affect migration. Dual-labor-market theory envisions firms and their employees as stratified into primary and secondary sectors. The primary sector meets "basic demand" in the economy and consists of larger, better-established firms that provide capital-intensive, better-paying jobs. The secondary sector, by contrast, meets fluctuating or seasonal demand and relies primarily on lower-paid, labor-intensive jobs.[48] While human-capital theorists argue that investments in education provide increasing returns for workers, segmentation theorists emphasize that barriers among segments and the nature of secondary-sector employment limit upward mobility and returns to human capital. Such conditions often dissuade native-born workers from taking secondary-sector jobs, especially when they are temporary or seasonal. Immigrants, however, are often willing to fill such jobs, especially if they expect to stay in the receiving country only a short time.[49] This is also likely to be the case if they are unauthorized, even if they want to stay in the United States because they have U.S.-born children. Labor-market segmentation implies that competition between immigrants and native-born workers is minimal because natives (being mostly located in the primary sector) do not want to do the jobs immigrants do.

The strength of the labor-market segmentation perspective is that it locates the propensity for international migration in demand factors.[50] That is, it envisions migration as occurring because potential workers are needed. Its weakness is that it conceptualizes this demand as resulting from the importance of maintaining structural divisions in advanced societies, not from the need for labor per se. It hypothesizes that very low-end workers are recruited partly to perpetuate the structure rather than to fill job openings that may have expanded owing to economic growth or other factors. Segmentation is difficult to measure and thus to assess in research. In their comprehensive study of factors affecting migration flows, Douglas Massey and Kristin Espinosa use employment growth as the main indicator of labor-market segmentation, taking it as a reflection of rising demand for labor.[51] They find that it relates positively (but not strongly) to temporal variation in the tendency to undertake unauthorized migration, leading to the conclusion that other factors are more important in influencing movement. It is also worth noting that some of this observed employment growth effect could also derive from population growth, which itself can generate increases in labor demand.

World Systems and Globalization Theories

World systems analysts emphasize the influence on migration of the structural character of relationships among countries, and among regions and cities within countries. Core cities such as New York, Los Angeles, and London exercise influence over the system through financial, labor, and commodity chains linking them to markets across the world.[52] These links not only move labor-intensive production "offshore" to low-cost countries and regions of the world, they also concentrate capital in and attract migrants to core cities. New York, Los Angeles, and London have great numbers of immigrants from countries all over the world, but especially from those countries with the strongest specific financial and production links to these cities.[53] The evolution of the global economy has not only stimulated international migration, it has also generated linkages between individual sending and receiving nations.[54] For example, Mexico contains large numbers of U.S. multinational manufacturing plants and sends the most migrants to the United States.[55] Migration to the United Kingdom has been dominated by former colonies in India and the Caribbean, while migration to France has occurred mainly from Algeria and Morocco.[56] The predictions of world systems and globalization theories, in contrast to those of other perspectives, are useful in explaining why migrants from certain countries fill certain jobs in global cities, although empirical research has not found that the push-related structural factors implied by world-systems theory indicators (like growth in direct foreign investment) bear much relationship to changes in Mexican migration flows.[57]

Economic Restructuring Theories

In recent years, economic restructuring in Mexico has also been emphasized as a factor influencing migration, especially for Mexicans located in urban areas.[58] During the late 1960s through the 1980s, large numbers of Mexicans migrated to the major cities of Mexico, especially Mexico City, Guadalajara, and Monterrey. When Mexico began to phase out import-substitution (an emphasis on heavy industry development for the Mexican market) as a development strategy and to invest in newer, more efficient production technologies, the ensuing restructuring left many urban Mexicans without jobs.[59] This created an impetus for migration to the United States. In a related vein, it is noteworthy that political scientists have often lamented that many theories about international migration have failed to incorporate the role of the state in spurring or curtailing migration.[60] These concerns certainly apply to the Mexican case, especially in the wake of the 1993 North American Free Trade Agreement and the Mexican peso crisis of 1994 to 1995. Both of these fostered restructuring in Mexico and coincided with the rise in unauthorized migration to the United States, although some of this kind of restructuring was in rural areas.[61]

Garip's analysis of Mexican Migration Project data from 1970 through 2000 identifies a fourth type of migrant emerging from urban restructuring. The representative migrant in this case, whom she labels an urban migrant, is the son of a household head with some secondary education from an urban area.[62] Not owning risky assets such as a business or land

and without other international migrants in his family, he reflects a new kind of migrant, one prevalent in the late 1990s and undoubtedly well up into the new century (although the data she examines end in 2000). Different in individual characteristics from the other types of migrants, and motivated to move by the disappearance of urban-industry jobs in Mexico, this type of mover is also likely to be especially affected by the availability of work in the United States.

Summary

The theoretical perspectives presented here are complementary rather than competitive alternatives. That is, the kinds of forces they emphasize could hypothetically operate all at once in the case of a given migrant. The neo-classical-economic and the new-economics approaches provide bases for predicting that poor Mexicans are likely to seek to migrate to the United States. The new-economics perspective, however, better explains why few migrants are drawn from the very lowest ranks of Mexican society, in that it shows how households and persons with some resources are more likely to be able to afford the costs of migration. Moreover, it draws attention to the importance of risk minimization as an important element in migration decisions. Even as those migrants who move for other reasons confront substantial elements of risk (for example, deportation), this perspective suggests the likely significance of risk minimization at destination, so that finding and maintaining employment may be more important to Mexican migrants than individually maximizing their wages. This is also reflected in the importance of networks in Mexican migration. Relying on family and friends for work opportunities better minimizes the risk of nonemployment than relying on one's own initiative.[63] Such reliance is undoubtedly especially important for unauthorized migrants.[64]

The segmented-labor-market and world-systems perspectives have received less empirical support in research studies than the other perspectives. The same may be true of the economic-restructuring perspective, the dynamics of which have been thoroughly outlined by Rubén Hernández-León but not quantitatively assessed relative to other perspectives.[65] This perspective points especially to urban dwellers who appear motivated to move because of job losses in Mexico. Losing a job in Mexico, however, although providing a reason to migrate, is not likely to result in moving without there also being strong prospects of finding employment in the United States. The same applies to the motivations noted in the other perspectives, all of which emphasize the influence of individual and Mexican community characteristics as affecting the propensity to consider migration. But these factors operating alone would seem inadequate to explain the especially large increases in unauthorized migration from the 1990s up until 2006, when construction started to decline in the United States, unless some parallel pull factors were at work. Notably, the period up through the Great Recession was a time of above-average job growth in the United States, suggesting that job availability for less-skilled immigrants accounted for some of the migration. But this availability was not unusually strong because of economic growth alone. Such growth, although robust, was not unusually high. Rather, something else added to its effects, namely that the numbers of younger less-skilled U.S.-born persons available to do such work started to decline during this period. This demographic change and its sources are what we next explore.

Recent U.S. Demographic Changes and Job Availability

Annual U.S. population growth since 1980 has rarely edged past 1 percent, even allowing for the inclusion of both unauthorized and legal immigration. Since 1990, population growth has fallen below this level, noticeably so since 2000. Economic growth over the overall period, however, has been substantially higher. Until the recent recession, the annual percentage change in gross domestic product averaged more than 3 percent annually.[66] Even including periods of recession, each decade since 1970 has averaged job growth at or well above the levels needed to absorb population growth. For example, during the 1970s, economic growth generated more than 1.9 million new jobs per year, about 50 percent more than the number required to absorb both the baby boomers, then coming of age, and the new immigrants.[67] During the 1980s, job growth was almost as high, about 1.8 million new jobs per year, and during the 1990s, higher still, averaging more than 2.1 million jobs per year.[68] From 2000 until 2008, the economy would have needed to add 1.3 million new jobs each year to keep up with population expansion, but it surpassed that threshold by more than half-a-million per year.[69] Of course, some of the jobs are part time, particularly during recessions. The share of part-time employment peaked in 1983 at 20.3 percent, higher even than in the Great Recession.[70]

Thus during most years since 1990, job expansion has outstripped the levels needed to keep up with population growth, even though that population growth includes legal and unauthorized immigration. And even if levels of unauthorized migration were in fact somewhat higher than those factored into estimates of population growth,[71] many jobs were available for less-skilled Mexican migrants. Was this because unauthorized migrants were taking jobs away from natives? Most evidence suggests that less-skilled immigrants are not competing with comparable natives. Why not? Because even as demand for less-skilled workers remained high, the size of the native-born workforce with that skill level was beginning to decline.

Education Upgrading

Changes in education constitute one important reason for the depletion of the U.S. supply of less-skilled natives. The upgrading that began early in the twentieth century with the high school completion movement continued after World War II with the expansion of public higher education.[72] Notwithstanding debates about why the rate of increase in college attendance slowed in the 1990s and the early years of this century, only to rise recently, the fraction of the population with exposure to postsecondary schooling has steeply risen for most of the last six decades.[73] Adults with more than a high school education now make up nearly 60 percent of the population twenty-five and over, up from 5.3 percent in 1950.[74]

The number of native-born adult Americans without a high school diploma has fallen in both relative and absolute terms. In 1950, more than 87 percent of U.S. adults (80 million) had never finished high school. By 2010, only 12.9 percent (25.7 million) failed to graduate. In short, by 2010, there were 68 percent fewer persons in the country than in 1950 without a high school diploma or its equivalent.[75] Strikingly, this figure is for the entire adult population, which includes the substantial number of poorly educated immigrants who have come here over the past three decades.

Declining Native Fertility and Cohort Change

After the baby boom ended in 1964, U.S. fertility rates sharply declined. As measured by the total fertility rate, or the average number of children a woman would be expected to have if her childbearing followed the fertility pattern shown during that year, fertility rates by the mid-1970s had dropped by about half, dipping below 2.1, the point at which population replacement occurs. Afterward, they inched up, hovering for years at a rate of around 2.0 to 2.1 children per woman[76] before dipping again during the recent recession to 1.7 births per woman, a level about 20 percent below replacement level.[77] The results have been startling. Between 2000 and 2010, the population of children under the age of ten declined in seventeen states, in some cases in the Northeast by more than 10 percent.

Such a fertility decline directly affects the number of workers twenty-five years later.[78] From about 1970 until 1990, as the baby boom generation reached adulthood, the numbers of less-skilled natives aged twenty-five to forty-four (with high school diplomas or less) grew appreciably, despite education upgrading (figure 8.4). The expansion of the economy more than absorbed the increase. But in 1990, the earliest baby boomers reached the age of forty-five, and the numbers of people in that age cohort started to shrink and has continued to do so since then. There are fewer people under the age of forty-five to take the lower-skill jobs the expanding economy was generating, especially physically demanding manual work.

Figure 8.4   Trends in the Education Background of the Less-Skilled U.S. Workforce, Aged Twenty-five to Forty-four, by Gender and Nativity, 1970 to 2010

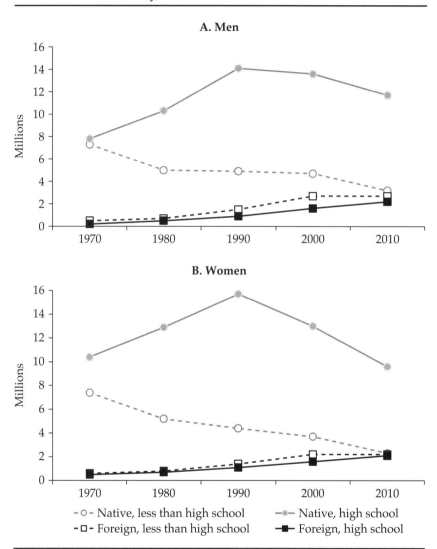

A. Men

B. Women

- ○ - Native, less than high school   ── Native, high school
- □ - Foreign, less than high school   ──■── Foreign, high school

Source: Adapted from Bean, Leach et al. (2011); Decennial U.S. Census Public-Use Micro-Data for 1970 to 2000 and 2010 American Community Survey Data, Ruggles et al. (2010).

As the cohort aged twenty-five to forty-four years ages, it provides insight into what the U.S. workforce might look like in the future. As baby boomers retire, these younger workers will step in to replace them. Younger Americans are also most likely to compete with less-skilled immigrants for jobs in physically intense fields such as farm labor or construction. Between 1990 and 2010, the population of younger, U.S.-born residents at all skill levels shrank by roughly 1 percent. This loss of potential workers was especially notable in the less-skilled end of the spectrum: The younger, less-skilled, U.S.-born population eroded at almost double the overall rate, dropping by almost 2 percent.[79]

Thus for a quarter of a century (about 1965 through 1990), the "extra" increment of baby boomers entering the labor market has been subsiding. Now the country's fertility rate remains below replacement level. By 2010, the boomers were between forty-six and sixty-four, and the labor market started to contract as they began to retire. Their retirement seems likely to help immigrants by opening up jobs and creating opportunities for upward mobility.[80] Furthermore, retiring boomers may sell their homes, creating vacancies that may foster spatial assimilation.[81] These are looming changes. However, the shrinkage in the younger native-born population (those aged twenty-five to forty-four), especially the less-skilled U.S.-born group, has already occurred. As further aging occurs, the forty-five to sixty-four-year-old group will also shrink until about 2030.

An important question is whether this decline in the pool of younger native workers since 1990 has coincided with a shrinkage in less-skilled work. If we looked only at manufacturing, the answer would be a qualified yes. From 1970 until today, the share of manufacturing jobs in the economy dropped from more than one in four to approximately one in eight. The drop-off in the share of manufacturing jobs held by persons with a high school diploma or less has been similarly precipitous (also falling from approximately one in four in 1970 to approximately one in eight today).[82] Interestingly, over this same time, the overall number of manufacturing jobs remained approximately 21 million. But because of population and job growth, a relatively smaller share of less-skilled persons today work in manufacturing employment than in the past. Also, many of today's manufacturing jobs require at least some college.[83] Thus the relative demand for less-skilled workers in manufacturing has declined.

During this same period, however, the share of the less-skilled workforce in service jobs has grown considerably.[84] Since 1990, the overall number of jobs held by less-skilled males (of any age or nativity or ethnic-racial background) has held steady at roughly 45.7 million, or approximately 45 percent of the male workforce.[85] Thus despite a decline in the workforce share of less-skilled manufacturing workers, the share of less-skilled workers in general is as large today as it was more than twenty years ago because of growth in the share of less-skilled service workers.[86]

Shortfalls in Native Workers Relative to Growth in Immigration

How large is the decline in the number of less-skilled natives, and how does it compare with the number of similar immigrants? We start by focusing on males aged twenty-five to forty-four who did not finish high school. This group might potentially compete the most with less-skilled immigrants, including less-skilled Mexican migrants. In 1970 few working-age immigrant males without diplomas were in the country; by 2010 their numbers had grown to about 2.7 million (figure 8.4), many of whom had arrived after 1990. The comparable native population, however, lost about 4 million potential workers over this period. Thus the native male workforce of this age range and skill level shrank considerably more than the immigrant workforce expanded. Note that we are talking about all immigrants with less than a high school education. The differences would be even more dramatic if we focused only on Mexican immigrants. A similar pattern characterizes the change for women.

Figures 8.5 and 8.6 show further evidence in the gains or losses in the size of this less-skilled age group, by gender and by nativity. Among both males and females lacking high school diplomas, a drop occurred in the number of native persons who might be candidates to hold less-skilled jobs every decade, especially from 1970 to 1980 and from 2000 to 2010. For both genders, this deficit does not emerge until 1990, primarily because large numbers of baby boomers were coming of working age during the 1970s and 1980s. But once that demographic tidal wave subsided, the numbers of natives holding only high school diplomas also declined. Again, the shrinkages substantially exceeded the growth in the numbers of comparable foreign-born males and females. Overall, the cumulative decline from 1990 until 2010 of those with only a high school diploma or less adds up to more than 4 million men and 8.2 million women. By contrast, the increase in the number of comparable foreign-born persons is less, about 3.8 million males and about 2.5 million females.

These figures illustrate workforce shifts for younger potential less-skilled workers (those aged twenty-five to forty-four), the age group most likely to be able to do the arduous work required in most less-skilled jobs. In sum, the less-skilled working age population of the United States changed considerably during the period 1990 to 2010, with the baby boomers starting the period under the age of forty-five and ending the period being over the age of forty-five. This, along with the education upgrading that was also occurring, resulted in a sizable decline by 2010 in younger U.S.-born potential workers.

Figure 8.5   Change in the Number of Males in the Less-Skilled U.S. Workforce, Aged Twenty-five to Forty-four, by Nativity, Education Background, and Decade, 1970 to 2010

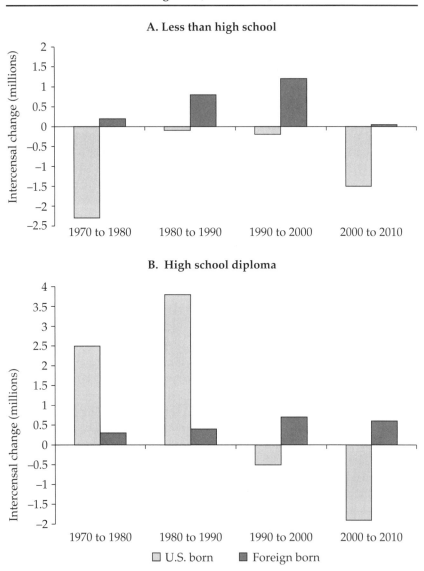

A. Less than high school

B. High school diploma

Source: Decennial U.S. Census Public-Use Micro-Data for 1970 to 2000 and 2010 American Community Survey Data, Ruggles et al. (2010).

Figure 8.6   Change in the Number of Females in the Less-Skilled U.S.
Workforce, Aged Twenty-five to Forty-four, by Nativity,
Education Background, and Decade, 1970 to 2010

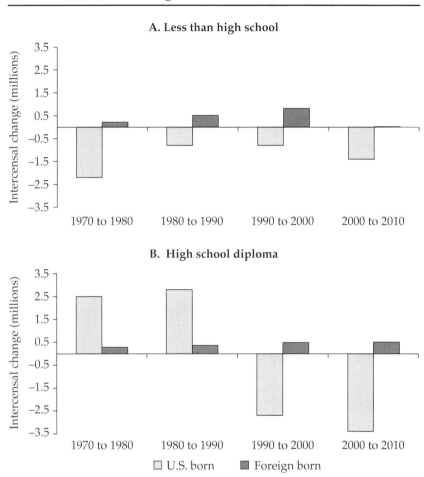

A. Less than high school

B. High school diploma

□ U.S. born   ■ Foreign born

Source: Decennial U.S. Census Public-Use Micro-Data for 1970 to 2000 and 2010 American Community Survey Data, Ruggles et al. (2010).

Note: While the broad preference categories that existed under the McCarran-Walter Act privileged highly skilled immigrants, the Hart-Celler Act emphasized family reunification criteria as the fundamental bases for immigrant entry. Four of the top five preference categories gave priority to the reunification of families and amounted to nearly three-fourths of the slots (Zollberg 2006). In addition, the law added parents of adult U.S. citizens to the list of immigrants not subject to numerical limitations (Keely 1971). But family-based entries had now to occur within the framework of overall limits. Notably, the new Western Hemisphere cap of 120,000 was less than the average annual migration then occurring from the region. A ceiling of 120,000 visas per year was placed on the total number of legal immigration admissions, which included legal migrants from Mexico.

It is also useful to look more closely at specific estimates of the size of the effects of rising education and fertility trends—"population change"—on these two age groups from 1990 to 2010.[87] About 12.7 million more individuals in the broader working-age population (aged twenty-five to sixty-four) had gone to college by 2010 and moved out of the "less-skilled" category. At the same time, however, the effect of some baby boomers still moving into the working-age population caused some overall population growth, resulting in 5.4 million individuals being added to the working-age population compared with generations before. Together, this resulted in a decline of 7.3 million people (12.7 million minus 5.4 million) in the potential less-skilled workforce. Among only those in the younger cohort (twenty-five to forty-four), the dynamics of education and population change led to a particularly notable shrinkage of less-skilled workers. While more than 5.2 million individuals were lost from this group owing to rising levels of education, a smaller overall population by 2010 removed almost 7.1 million more. Together, these two factors totaled 12.3 million fewer U.S.-born, less-skilled, younger individuals whom employers could potentially hire by 2010.[88] Note also that, because baby boomers who were forty-five to sixty-four in 2010 will move out of the working-age population altogether by 2030, this number represents a lower-bound figure for how many fewer U.S.-born less-skilled persons there will be in the country at that time. A small portion of this deficit may be offset by slightly larger birth cohorts coming of working age by then, but not much, in part because these cohorts are not very much larger than their predecessors and in part because they are likely to receive relatively more education. In sum, by 2030, the United States will have a much smaller U.S.-born, less-skilled working-age population than it does today.

Hence, cohort change from the aging of baby boomers, education upgrading, and lower fertility in the native-born population have led to large declines in the pool of younger U.S.-born persons with high school diplomas or less, the group of natives most likely to fill arduous, less-skilled jobs. These same dynamics will lead to an even bigger decline by 2030. In an economy that is expanding, as was the U.S. economy during the 1990s and much of the new century, this drop in the less-skilled working-age population left a workforce void. Immigrants, mostly from Mexico, filled this gap. This helps to explain the persistence of unauthorized Mexican migration and its growth over the period 1990 to 2010 and the likely need for its continuation. Mexican immigrant workers have increasingly filled jobs because of a shortage of native-born workers. Increasingly, most of these immigrant workers are unauthorized because needed workers have few ways to enter the country legally under today's immigration policies.

Conclusions

There is a logic to Mexican migration to the United States. Through the Bracero Program, which ran from 1942 to 1964, the United States encouraged temporary circular migration, and growers came to depend on it. When the country ended the program, it did not provide a replacement policy adequate to handle the demand for migrant laborers.[89] The migrants still came, but without legal authorization. Over time, the United States further tightened laws allowing these migrants to come legally or to become legal after coming. Yet demand for such laborers has continued to grow. As more natives began to go to college, the availability of natives for seasonal and other less-skilled jobs diminished. This trend was exacerbated over time by the sharp drop in the fertility rate from the baby-boom levels of the 1950s and early 1960s. All these factors converged to lead to a climb in unauthorized migration. Moreover, the increasing availability of steady work for less-skilled migrants in the United States meant that many stayed in the country, brought spouses or married, and began having families. Where once they may have seen themselves as sojourners, they became settlers, even those without papers.[90] These trends may resume under a strong economy. But, the decline in the Mexican total fertility rate to about 2.3 (just over replacement level) means that in years to come, fewer young Mexicans may seek to migrate.[91] And education levels in Mexico continue to rise.[92] On the other hand, rising anxiety about crime and security in Mexico and Central America imply that Mexican and Central American migrants may continue to come to the United States to fill the less-skilled jobs that U.S. natives are increasingly unavailable to do.

The facilitation of migration through social networks and cumulative causation appears insufficient by itself to explain the magnitude of the increases in flows of unauthorized immigrants and their spread throughout the country since 1990.[93] Unless information is also conveyed through such networks about job availabilities in the United States, the motivation to migrate may not be matched by a tangible reason to do so. That numerous research studies have shown that less-skilled Mexican immigrants during the 1990s and afterward were not dislodging natives from such jobs implies that this might indeed have been the case.[94] The research conducted by Garip shows also that network migrants predominated in the late 1980s and early 1990s, not the late 1990s and early years of this century, when urban migrants predominated and when different kinds of communications were likely to have been reaching Mexicans about the growing availability of less-skilled jobs.[95] Moreover, if conditions in Mexico were changing so as to slow migration, annual flows of Mexicans should have gradually subsided over the past twenty years or so as birth rates in Mexico dropped, as the Mexican economy added more jobs, and as education improved enough to qualify more Mexicans for many of these new jobs.[96] However, this has not occurred (except during the Great Recession). Rather, the flows of Mexicans of all kinds have increased.[97]

Neither do other arguments appear to account for all the growth in Mexican flows. One is that increases in border enforcement, starting with those legislatively mandated by the 1986 Immigration Reform and Control Act, have made it so difficult for immigrants to come that they have increasingly decided, after arriving, to stay instead of returning to Mexico.[98] This line of reasoning contends that unauthorized migrants have more and more tended to become permanent settlers rather than circular sojourners, thus accounting for growth in the stock of unauthorized Mexicans living in the country. Although this dynamic has undoubtedly occurred, the timing of the increases suggests other factors have operated as well. The rise in permanent settlements began before the immigration law was passed in 1986 and especially well before the border enforcement buildup that started in the 1990s.[99] In addition, most migrants had been accumulating social and economic reasons not to return to their places of origin for years, the main one being that villages and small towns in Mexico, as in the United States, were becoming less economically viable places. This is reflected in the slow pace of return migration of urban migrants in Mexico, who face no enforcement constraints but still are not returning to the small towns and villages whence they came.[100] Moreover, as noted above, urban migrants in Mexico (those who had moved from rural areas to cities within Mexico) started to come to the United States during the 1990s as economic restructuring expanded in Mexico rather than returning to rural areas within Mexico. Changes in U.S. enforcement policies thus seem unlikely to explain fully the acceleration of flows of unauthorized migrants from the 1990s to the present.

Understanding how changes in U.S. demographic factors have influenced the kind and volume of Mexican migration to the United States over the past four decades, however, is important. A majority of these migrants are unauthorized, and among them, migration overwhelmingly occurs to find work.[101] Although other countries also send labor migrants to the United States, Mexicans are more likely than other immigrant groups to seek (and find) jobs.[102] One of the central themes of this book is that the nature and experience of this labor migration give rise to migrant cultural frames and repertoires that distinctively influence how immigrants and their children behave in regard to family, labor market, and schooling after they arrive in the United States. That is, Mexican migrants' unusually strong reliance on and penchant for work generate high levels of participation in the workforce, even as their low levels of education channel them into arduous low-wage positions necessitating such long hours and multiple jobs that it is hard for them to afford both the time and money to educate their children.[103]

At the same time, both the social and public policy contexts affecting migrants' lives after they arrive have changed.[104] U.S. immigration and immigrant policies have substantially shifted such that unauthorized Mexican labor migrants are not only less warmly welcomed than before but also more frequently viewed as inappropriately here. Increasingly a relatively small but disproportionately influential native minority, often invoking the specter of terrorism to justify expensive public expenditures on "border control," has come to define labor migrants primarily as lawbreakers rather than as workers who do jobs natives do not want or are not available to do.[105] Moreover, as a result of both the 1996 welfare reform and antiterrorism acts, unauthorized Mexican workers and many of their family members have become less eligible for social services and made more subject to deportation, in some cases even after they have become legal permanent residents.[106] Mexican labor migrants and their families in the United States are ever more needed and officially unwelcome, circumstances that simultaneously impede and paradoxically work in other ways to facilitate their integration. But most of all, their integration, as we have shown in previous chapters, depends on whether they are able to legalize their migration status. We next suggest what we think this means for both immigration and immigrant policy.

= Chapter 9 =

Conclusions and Policy Implications: Integration and Addressing Workforce and Inequality Dilemmas

Now it is time to weave together into conclusions and policy recommendations the separate strands of inquiry we have addressed in the preceding chapters. Each is important; discarding any would leave a void. Several are conceptual or theoretical in nature. For example, we lay out a number of theoretical perspectives providing expectations about empirical patterns for multigenerational and multidimensional integration in the early twenty-first century. Because none of these fully accounts for Mexican American incorporation, we also articulate and name a membership-exclusion perspective on integration. Although not entirely new in many respects, this approach explicitly emphasizes the importance of societal membership for integration. Most especially, it stresses the debilitating and limiting but potentially temporary nature of exclusion from membership. Such a perspective has arguably not received the attention it deserves in the United States, where the American experience with slavery has often seemed to compel scholarly obsession with black-white intergroup relations,[1] leading to tendencies to perceive (indeed, one might suggest misperceive) the experiences of other groups as similar to those of African Americans.[2] We also assess the role that gender plays in Mexican American integration, specifying and taking note of the important ways in which integration patterns differ for Mexican American men and women.

Other strands have been more empirical or methodological. Thus we estimate for the first time the degree to which unauthorized Mexican migration (as a crucial, concrete example of the lack of membership) leads to conditions that limit schooling gains more for male than female children of immigrants, including those who are U.S.-born. Conversely, we also observe greater gains for daughters in the second generation from the legalization of their parents, particularly their mothers. We also map out theoretically and gauge empirically the implications of unauthorized migration, not just for second-generation schooling but also for third-generation schooling and for other dimensions of integration through the third generation. In these analyses, we adopt research methods that cover a wide enough span of the Mexican American experience (that is, integration through three generations) so as not to limit our assessment of the longer-term process. We look at third-only generations so comparisons are not distorted by selective attrition, as in third-plus-generation data, and we systematically seek not to omit important aspects of integration that deserve separate attention. We thus lay the groundwork for conclusions about which combinations of theoretical perspectives are most apt for explaining the full nature and extent of male and female Mexican American integration. Now, taking today's demographic and economic inequality realities into consideration, we outline what we think all of this means for immigrant integration in general, Mexican American integration in particular, and U.S. immigration and immigrant policies. We organize this in four major sections: empirical results, theoretical significance for immigrant integration, changing demographic and inequality contexts, and policy implications and recommendations.

Empirical Results

Analyses of many indicators of integration in Los Angeles reveal three major components of integration—economic, spatial, and linguistic. No single sociocultural dimension emerges from the many indicators, suggesting that sociocultural distinctiveness prevails across and within individuals. Stated differently, knowing something about one trait—religion, religiosity, ethnic identification, tendency to see ethnicity as important, family life, or fertility behavior—is of little help in predicting anything about the others, or even anything about the main dimensions of incorporation—those of economic, spatial, or linguistic integration. Variation in the sociocultural aspects of integration appears to be substantially idiosyncratic rather than group specific, as models of individualistic-pluralism would expect. The finding of such a pattern suggests that variation in aspects of sociocultural integration is less influenced by the structural blockages deriving from membership exclusion than by sheer exposure to the destination society and the length of time spent in a new environment. We thus find that the tendency to remain affiliated with the Catholic Church, which we view as one particular sociocultural indicator, is something that declines across generations, with the percentage non-Catholic increasing substantially by the third generation, but it is not something that correlates much with other indicators.

In education, income, and neighborhood attainment—the critical structural dimensions—our analyses show that the unauthorized status of Mexican immigrants to the United States holds back and limits their offspring's integration. Both men and women whose mothers entered and stayed unauthorized start their U.S. experiences from severely disadvantaged positions. By the third generation, nearly all respondents display notable gains, but not ones large enough for the legacy effect of unauthorized grandparents to have disappeared. Because women with unauthorized backgrounds now start their U.S. experiences from the lowest point of all (and because they most likely also did so two generations ago), the gains of third-generation women surveyed by the Immigration and Intergenerational Mobility in Metropolitan Los Angeles study are especially notable. Overall, then, the picture is one of considerable improvement from the 1.5 to the 2.0 generation and beyond, but one nonetheless where the improvement across generations of those with legal parents consistently surpasses that of respondents with unauthorized parents. Among this latter group, some of whom are U.S.-born, many began their journeys as children trying to cope with the disadvantages of their parents' status. Their first hurdle involved simply locating the road to mobility, not to mention learning how to navigate its bumpy and hazardous twists and turns. Nonetheless, if their parents (especially their mothers) were able to legalize, they achieved considerable headway; those whose mothers could not legalize do not progress nearly so much. Legalization and birthright citizenship thus clearly matter a great deal and enable many children of immigrants to take advantage of new opportunities to realize their dreams.

Our findings also reveal other causes for concern. The research results show that the educational attainments of third-generation males, even those without the drag of unauthorized status in their backgrounds, surpass those of the second generation only modestly, reaching an average of 13.4 years of schooling. This indicates that many of them did not even start college, let alone obtain a bachelor's degree (in fact, 86.9 percent finished high school and 20.6 percent finished college). Even though their ancestral families have been in the country at least three-quarters of a century, most have only a high-school diploma or its equivalent, and most are employed in working-class jobs, thus continuing to lag behind non-Hispanic white males. Evidence of this emerges despite the fact that we examine data for third-only generation males, not the downwardly biased information that would come from data on third-plus-generation males. Thus, at least for this group, integration along the education dimension appears to have slowed. In this respect, our findings echo those of Edward Telles and Vilma Ortiz, who observe a similar leveling off of schooling attainment in later Mexican American generations.[3]

Yet we also find that third-only-generation men show income gains, and women do remarkably well overall. Among women, those with

authorized backgrounds reach an average level of 14.3 years of schooling by the 3.0 generation, an attainment level only slightly less than that
of non-Hispanic whites. Moreover, Mexican American women report
income levels considerably above those of similar non-Hispanic whites.
Third-generation Mexican American women in Los Angeles from authorized backgrounds thus measure up well when compared with their white
counterparts. Interestingly, much of this comes about among women with
four Mexican-born grandparents, the high-ethnic-density background
that seems most likely to encourage the greatest achievement by emphasizing the importance of working hard and doing well in school to compensate for the sacrifices made by immigrant grandparents. Men from
high-ethnic-density backgrounds also show higher levels of attainment,
but ones that are statistically insignificant.

Moreover, for Mexican American men the usual linkage between
education and income involves a notable twist between the second and
third generations. Although education gains from the second to the third
generation remain low, the annual incomes of third-generation men are
appreciably higher than those of the second generation, staying on a par
with those of non-Hispanic whites even after differences in schooling
are controlled. Moreover, having an unauthorized background does not
curtail earnings among second-generation men, although it does their
schooling. Thus for third-generation males, neither education nor the legacy of an unauthorized background bears much relationship to income—
a result we suggest reflects the influence of working-class opportunities
in their lives. Further support for this comes from the fact that the higher
incomes of younger third-generation Mexican American males (compared with whites before other factors are controlled) result mostly from
their greater tendency to work full time and their smaller likelihood of
enrolling in college. Although this finding suggests male mobility in the
third generation, that kind of mobility carries a high price, for two reasons that are related to societal inequality. First, the returns to U.S. college
completion have been rising for several decades, and second, the greatest
relative benefits from having a bachelor's degree accrue to those least
likely to have gone to college.[4] The immediate working-class opportunities that we see these third-generation men pursue are seized in large part
because they cannot pay for higher education opportunities that would
benefit them even more in the long run.

Theoretical Significance of Immigrant Integration

Although the various theoretical approaches outlined in chapter 2 often
imply similar outcomes, they envision different forces as drivers. Hence
we argue it is important to consider a new perspective, one we term

membership exclusion. We emphasize this approach not because scholars have neglected the hardships faced by marginal newcomers in society (indeed, they have not) but rather because the provision of societal membership is both a necessary and sufficient condition for undertaking other kinds of structural incorporation. That is, marginality may begin to dissipate once membership is extended, at least more so than in the case of factors such as race, which tends to be more deeply embedded in culture and institutions and thus whose effects are more enduring. In using the concept of membership exclusion, we mean by the "membership" side of this label that legal status, the initial aspect of political incorporation, is crucial for sociostructural incorporation. By the "exclusion" side, we mean the structural lack of access that is caused by denial of legal and social citizenship but also the potential removal of this barrier when membership and structural inclusion are granted.

Herbert J. Gans has memorably described assimilation as a "bumpy line," not a straight one.[5] For Mexican Americans, the road to integration has indeed been bumpy. In the Mexican American case, integration is not reached by just one uneven road but rather many. Charting these routes involves ascertaining whether the Mexican American experience reflects a more assimilation-based or a more pluralist-based pathway. Even though unauthorized status hinders key aspects of integration, we also find that it does not matter much for many aspects of sociocultural integration. Moreover, the components of sociocultural integration examined here are relatively distinct from one another. That is, they do not necessarily occur in tandem. This finding bears out the increasing relevance for immigrant integration of pluralist theoretical perspectives, especially the one we call postindustrial-individualistic integration, because of its emphasis on individual as well as group differences in socioculturality. Thus we tend to speak of postindustrial-individualistic integration rather than assimilation when referring to patterns of steady increase in structural integration across generations. While some might prefer the label *assimilation* when describing these, we adopt the term *integration*, adding the modifier postindustrial-individualistic, because sociocultural trends seem, in part, to be moving in the direction of more individual pluralism, and even more pluralism and change within individuals over time. Despite our choice of labels, we recognize that today's sociocultural reality probably falls somewhere between assimilation-based relative homogeneity and pluralist-based individual idiosyncrasy and fluidity.

The severe negative effects of unauthorized status observed here also testify to the relevance of the membership-exclusion theoretical approach. While a rapidly growing literature documents the individual struggles of unauthorized students in obtaining an education,[6] much less emphasis has been placed on the economic, psychological, and legal mechanisms by which the unauthorized status of parents creates conditions that dampen educational attainment among their children, including their citizen children.[7] What do we know from the results presented here about such mechanisms? We know that unauthorized parents are forced to lead highly constrained lives,[8] facing limitations that are particularly hard to escape or compensate for when one speaks English poorly. Unauthorized immigrants thus necessarily must keep a low profile.[9] They constantly fear detection and deportation. Many cannot get driver's licenses (although this has eased somewhat recently), thus necessitating endless worry when driving to work or elsewhere that an accident will expose them to authorities and the risk of deportation. The need for caution and furtiveness inevitably causes stress and fosters social isolation and often physical separation of parents. Social isolation especially affects women, in part because they are often more embedded in a traditional culture that makes them more dependent on men, a vulnerability that can become exacerbated when they also face workplace isolation.[10] It is thus little surprise that we find that mother's unauthorized status relates more negatively to children's attainment than does father's status.

At the same time, because most of the unauthorized are impoverished labor migrants with little education or English, they must take poorly paying jobs, often multiple jobs in a limited range of occupational sectors, with nighttime or irregular hours. Lack of education and English ability limits parents' ability to deal with schooling issues, and long and irregular work hours limit their available time. The family's low income level reinforces a family- and household-based social-insurance orientation to the labor market.[11] That is, given their migration and survival exigencies, it is more important, especially for men, to obtain work than to spend time finding the best-paying work.[12] In short, the family chooses to minimize its risk of unemployment rather than to pursue individual wage gains, which may be meager in any case. This means that for unauthorized parents, their "reservation wage," the level of pay at which they are willing to accept a job, is likely to be much lower than for legal Mexican immigrants or native-born Mexican Americans. This helps explain the fact that lack of legal status rather than differences in education mostly explains the lower wages and slower wage growth for unauthorized Mexican immigrants compared with legal Mexican immigrants.[13]

This low reservation wage also makes it important to maximize the number of earners in the family. Adolescents are often encouraged to work as soon as they can, unless they show promise of being exceptionally good students, in which case they are encouraged to concentrate on their studies.[14] This kind of dual encouragement produces a greater tendency toward role specialization among the male children of Mexican immigrants, especially among boys, on whom the work imperative falls the most. Compared with African Americans and whites, Mexican-origin immigrant and second-generation males are more likely to be working when they are not enrolled in school and also more likely not to be working when they are enrolled in school. Boys who migrated to the United States when they were twelve to seventeen years old (the 1.25 generation) are more than ten times as likely to be working when not enrolled versus when enrolled, whereas whites or blacks show ratios about two times as likely. Working and providing income for the family are overwhelmingly important among Mexican immigrants and their children. Our finding that unauthorized parental status is related to less educational attainment among second-generation males compared with females is consistent with this reality.

Finally, the poverty of unauthorized migrants is likely also to exert its own effects. We have already mentioned how being poor may engender social isolation and strong family norms about working. The Mexican children of immigrants are more likely than non-Hispanic whites to grow up in neighborhoods marked by poverty, female-headed households, and unemployment[15] and more likely to attend lower-quality schools.[16] Thus, not surprisingly, we find substantial negative effects on the educational attainments of both sons and daughters. Daughters, however, are more able than sons to take advantage of parents' legalization to bolster their education. Women's education gains are not unique to Mexican Americans: Women in all American demographic groups are now outpacing men in college attendance and completion.[17] We cannot say with certainty to what degree mechanisms associated with maternal social isolation, migration- and family-related cultural repertoires, or debilitating poverty account for the patterns of poor education outcomes we observe here. The low educational attainment in the second generation on the part of the children of unauthorized parents may result from any or all of these. Parsing out the effects of the various mechanisms more exactly is an important task for further research.

The patterns observed in the previous chapters also demonstrate why information about the third generation fleshes out our understanding of the Mexican American integration experience. Two generations offer insufficient basis for discerning the integration outcomes emerging in the third generation and the different outcomes by gender. Several of the theoretical approaches would expect subpar levels of structural attainment in the second generation. But these approaches do not offer the same reasons for why such poor outcomes occur. Racialization, ethnic disadvantage, and segmented assimilation, for example, envision stunted mobility resulting from lasting prejudice and discrimination that prevent the children of immigrants from attaining what they seek and are capable of. With the possible exception of ethnic disadvantage, these perspectives also see these barriers as leading to scarring that is more permanent and relatively immutable. By contrast, membership exclusion conceptualizes legalization as constituting a major turning point in the life course. Once it is navigated, the hindrances of unauthorized status are likely to diminish. In accordance with this perspective but not the other three just mentioned, we find in this research that second-generation Mexican Americans whose mothers entered as unauthorized migrants but were subsequently able to legalize show schooling levels at least as high as those of their counterparts whose parents were legal when they arrived (including those who also naturalized or married a U.S.-born partner).

Despite the benefits of such legalization turnarounds for women, full education integration does not occur in the third generation for males. Most significant, this is true even for those without unauthorized backgrounds. Why does their education lag when other structural incorporation dimensions such as income seem to reflect more integration? We suggest the theoretical perception of working-class-delay applies here, for several reasons. For one, it fits the fact that this pattern occurs more for males than females. Men are more integrated into a strong working-class culture in the 1.5 and 2.0 generations. The pressure on them to work long hours for their families starts even before the occurrence of migration. This can continue even into the third generation, especially when young men can make considerably more money than second-generation males without much increasing their schooling. Here we see third-generation male incomes as much as 60 percent higher than those of the second generation, even though their average schooling levels rise only a little. The availability of working-class opportunities to make more money thus seems likely to reinforce the tendency to pursue employment in the short run rather than making the much longer term investment in attending and graduating from college. Of course, the ever-higher price of college also impedes Mexican Americans' education attainment, as recent research has shown.[18] Most of the members of the Los Angeles study sample came of age during the 1980s and 1990s, when going to college was less expensive than now but still costly. And even those third-generation males whose incomes may be similar to those of whites came from families with more children on average than white families, meaning that parental financial support had to stretch further. Progress in education is particularly difficult to attain when it depends on multiple children attending college.[19]

In this study, we have examined men and women separately. That is, those we interviewed were not married or living with one another, so we have not focused on the integration of the family or household unit, although we have in places relied on theories about families and households in developing expectations for how the integration experiences of males and females might look similar and how they might appear different. It is tempting at this point to conclude that the overall integration situation of Mexican Americans seems somewhat favorable on account of a fairly positive integration experience for women. That is, although suffering substantial educational penalties as a result of unauthorized backgrounds, Mexican American women reveal notable upward movement across generations and rises into the third generation. At that point, their incomes, adjusted for education, even surpass those of non-Hispanic white women. They are thus making substantial contributions to their own and their families' financial support, thereby playing a crucial role in family structural integration. However, it must be remembered that when Mexican American women have reached educational and pay parity with non-Hispanic whites, women start their careers making at best 90 percent of what men do, and often end up making even less.[20] In other words, without full gender equity, successful female Mexican American integration, although significant and contributory, is still not enough for full Mexican American family integration, especially in an era of persisting economic inequality and middle-class income stagnation.

In sum, several different theoretical perspectives help explain Mexican American integration, and different combinations fit the situations of males and females. For males, a hybrid combination consisting of postindustrial-individualistic, membership exclusion, and working-class delays best applies to their case. For women, a hybrid combination of postindustrial-individualistic, membership-exclusion and ethnic-advantage (or selective-acculturation) perspectives best applies. We have noted why we think the postindustrial-individualistic approach is the most apt perspective, namely, because, for both males and females, multiple sociocultural aspects of integration across generations show patterns of idiosyncratic group and individual variation. The sociocultural indicators, along with English proficiency, follow a pattern of steady (although modest) group convergence across generations with non-Hispanic whites, but instances of convergence across individuals do not correlate much with one another. We prefer not to call this assimilation because the structural indicators do not show a similar such pattern. The membership-exclusion tag better applies to both men and women because both end up disadvantaged as a result of their parents' unauthorized status (when that entry status is not followed by legalization), and conversely both are helped by legalization, although women more so. Working-class delay applies for men because the forces of membership exclusion, which encourage men in particular to follow pathways that minimize risks to the family, necessitate that they prioritize work over schooling. This is all the more likely when opportunities for better-paying working-class jobs are plentiful. For women, strong achievement and hard work appear to be boosted by high ethnic density, motivating them especially to succeed to compensate for the sacrifices of the immigrant generation.

Changing Demographic
and Inequality Contexts

Because prognosticators of social and economic trends often misconstrue today's world as different from that of the past, we return with trepidation to some of the issues raised earlier about the importance of changing context for integration. Two societal characteristics in particular seem different now compared with thirty years ago: the demographic structure and behavior of U.S. society and its economic inequality. Demographically, the nation has been experiencing three trends relevant to immigration: declining fertility, rising education, and the aging of the baby boomers out of the working-age population.[21] These have all contributed to shrinking the size of the available U.S.-born less-skilled working-age population for the past twenty-five years. As the fertility of U.S.-born women has slipped below the replacement level, as more males and more females have attended and graduated from college, and as more baby boomers have retired, the number of U.S.-born men and women who have no more than a high school education and are available to do less-skilled work has diminished and will further shrink. But the size of the economy (despite the Great Recession) has not shrunk, nor has the relative number of jobs that have been filled by workers with high school education or less. Despite the contraction of the less-skilled manufacturing sector, growth in the less-skilled service sector has more than compensated. These trends have squeezed employers, and immigrants, most of them Mexican unauthorized immigrants, have filled the void.

Consider, for example, just the trend involving the baby boomers, those in the extraordinarily large birth cohorts from 1946 to 1964. In 1990 the oldest baby boomers (those born in 1946) were forty-four, and in 2010, they were sixty-four. In other words, in 1990, the baby boomers were starting to become too old to do hard, tedious manual labor, and by 2010, they were starting to retire. From 1990 until 2010, about 12.3 million U.S.-born men and women with high school degrees or less turned forty-four, and from 2010 until 2030, nearly this same number can be expected to retire. Not all of these people are in the workforce, of course, but about three-fifths are. That represents a lot of jobs to be filled—or risk leaving empty. Occupational projections suggest almost all of these involve essential services, so they involve things that need doing. Over the past twenty-five years, the loss of U.S.-born less-skilled people from onerous manual jobs or from the workforce altogether created a large vacuum that was filled by immigrants. In short, starting around 1990 and increasing ever since, there has been more and more less-skilled work to do in the United States with fewer and fewer U.S.-born persons available to do it. Interestingly, over this same time (from 1990 until 2010), the number of less-skilled natives leaving the working-age population surpassed the number of immigrants with high school degrees or less, including unauthorized Mexican immigrants, moving to the United States.[22] Over the next fifteen years, this trend will only continue.[23]

This constitutes a new demographic reality, one some analysts have termed a "third demographic transition," meaning that declining low "first-world" fertility requires filling workforce needs with immigrants from developing or middle-income countries.[24] The work that unauthorized Mexican immigrants have been doing in the United States, and will continue doing, is likely to be more and more essential. This is a departure from the past, when such immigrants seemed to do jobs natives did not want to do, or take jobs in places where natives did not live. The implication then was that natives might have been able to do this work under different circumstances. But for the past twenty to twenty-five years, the implication appears to be closer to the idea of a third demographic transition, namely, that now enough workers to do all of the less-skilled work that needs doing are just not here.

Regardless, research indicates labor-market competition between less-skilled immigrants and natives is minimal. Sensationalistic headlines from anti-immigrant organizations trumpeting such allegations as "Immigrants fill 90 percent of new less-skilled jobs over the past year!" miss the point. Implicit in these has been the suggestion that immigrant employment was taking place at the expense of natives. But what these accounts have omitted is that at least an equivalent *reduction* in the availability of less-skilled natives to do the jobs has also occurred. To be sure, analysts often note that new less-skilled immigrants do compete with earlier arriving less-skilled immigrants, driving down the wages of both groups. And as considerable other evidence also shows, the earnings of all Americans in at least the bottom half of the income distribution has declined in real terms over this period.[25] In other words, if new less-skilled immigrants are making less money than 25 years ago, it is not necessarily from increased labor market competition, but rather from broader inequality that is affecting all of the working class and much of the middle class as well. So the new context facing United States immigration and immigrant policy is one involving an ever greater need for less-skilled workers who are paid less and less, not because of labor market competition, but because of an economy and social and economic policies that have widened income inequality.

Policy Implications and Recommendations

What then are the implications for public policy of the above research findings, theoretical conclusions, and contextual considerations? The answer depends in part on the number of unauthorized Mexican immigrants in the country and on how many children they have. Clearly, the more migrants and the more numerous their children, the deeper and more urgent the integration challenge will be. From about 1970 through passage of the Immigration Reform and Control Act in 1986 and nearly up to the onset of the Great Recession in 2008, unauthorized migration from Mexico steadily increased, especially during the boom years of the late 1990s. Recent estimates indicate about 6.1 million unauthorized Mexicans lived in the United States in 2012.[26] Their children, some born in Mexico but most in this country, number about 3.85 million.[27] In terms of sheer numbers, the challenge to integration is considerable. Moreover, these numbers may undercount the Mexican unauthorized population because they often are missed in official government surveys.[28] Recent research suggests that coverage error for the Mexican-born population in the U.S. Census and other government surveys has probably been higher than previously thought, particularly during periods of prosperity, when immigrant flows are highest.

Unauthorized entry status and the subsequent lack of opportunities for Mexican immigrants to legalize matter strongly for the success of their children and grandchildren. At present, unauthorized migrants have few pathways to legalization and a long wait when a pathway becomes available. Over the past two decades, the waiting time for Mexican applicants to obtain legal permanent residence through the family reunification provisions has gone from two years to five years and can go up to nearly seventeen years for some categories.[29] Without immigration reform, a greater proportion of the unauthorized population will remain unauthorized longer than their predecessors who came during the 1960s and 1970s. Unless the United States provides pathways to legalization and avoids difficult or punitive requirements (including long wait times, large fines for having been unauthorized, sizable fees for legalizing, and prohibitively high thresholds in general that discourage applications), the size of the unauthorized group will remain high. These immigrants are not heading home so long as they can find work in the United States, owing to the relatively small number of natives to do less-skilled work. Meanwhile, their U.S.-born children will continue to suffer from their parents' unauthorized status. The unauthorized status of mothers net of other factors appears to reduce children's schooling by about a one-and-a-quarter years, all else being equal. The children of legal Mexican immigrants averaged a bit over thirteen years of schooling, so a reduction of one-and-a-quarter years marks the difference between attending some college and not finishing high school. Without a high school diploma, Americans earn about $500,000 less over their lifetimes and die about seven years earlier than those with some college.[30] The lingering disadvantage to the third generation would presumably be less, but nonetheless notable.

Our findings thus indicate the crucial role that opportunities for legalization play in the success or failure of Mexican Americans and other immigrant groups. The disadvantages of remaining unauthorized are evident. But legal status alone exerts its own positive force on second-generation education. The conclusion that pathways to legalization will help overcome the risk of an underclass of Mexican Americans is unavoidable. Since most children of unauthorized immigrants are born in the United States, our analysis also suggests that legislation providing the possibility of entry into full societal membership for their parents helps not only the immigrants themselves but also their children and their children's children. Evidence shows that those unauthorized entrants who do legalize overcome many of the disadvantages confronting them, as do their children. Because parents' socioeconomic status has such sizable effects on children's education,[31] the benefits of legal membership in the immigrant generation carry over to later generations as well, as we have shown (albeit in understated terms because of quite conservative estimates).

The results from this research also carry implications for immigration policy. Immigration policy refers to laws and practices about which and how many persons can come, whereas immigrant policy refers to laws and practices affecting those already here. The United States should legalize those already here because it needs the workforce contributions of unauthorized Mexican immigrants. Legalizing people with longstanding histories of workforce contributions in effect recognizes the importance of such inputs and views them as qualifications for societal participation. Moreover, legalizations help those who make these contributions build better lives and become citizens. In addition, the United States needs a new immigration policy for less-skilled workers. As already noted, at the national level, the size of the less-skilled U.S.-born workforce (those with high school diplomas or less) has shrunk appreciably over the past twenty-five years. And because of the looming retirement of baby boomers, this shrinkage is becoming even larger.

Why is this reduction happening and why is it going to get worse? Four reasons are important: U.S. population growth has fallen disproportionately below economic growth in recent decades, meaning that the demand for workers has often exceeded the levels that normal U.S.-born population growth and legal immigration can provide; gains in college education among the U.S.-born have reduced the number of less-skilled persons; the fertility rate among the U.S.-born is below replacement level, lowering the relative numbers of younger U.S.-born persons; and the aging of the baby boomers means they contribute less and less to the pool of potential less-skilled native workers. As a result, the number of younger less-skilled natives in the country has declined by more than 7 million persons since 1990, and the overall number will continue to drop for the foreseeable future. How many fewer? The unavailability of U.S.-born less-skilled workers over the past twenty-five years is arguably the main reason so many more unauthorized migrants have come to the

United States. But despite this pull, the number of less-skilled unauthorized immigrants coming to the country over the past couple of decades actually is less than the U.S.-born decline. And, by 2020, the number of less-skilled natives will drop by 12.3 million more. If immigrants have been partly filling this void, they will need to do so even more going forward.

What do such trends mean for U.S. immigration policy reform? They clearly imply that Congress eventually must provide for more legal low-skilled migrants. For more than thirty years, population growth in the United States has not exceeded 1 percent per year, even including estimates of both authorized and unauthorized migration. And except during recessions, job growth has usually outstripped the levels required to keep up with population growth. Even in less-skilled economic sectors, the share of overall jobs has generally held steady, because the loss of manufacturing jobs has been offset by growth in service jobs. Can the United States make do with a substantially smaller less-skilled workforce, one that includes fewer immigrants? These numbers suggest not. Some claim that higher pay levels will attract more workers to the kinds of jobs less-skilled immigrants have been filling. But this overlooks the fact that many less-skilled immigrants, especially before the Great Recession, were already being paid above the minimum wage, often substantially so. The demographic changes causing the declines in the numbers of natives who might potentially fill less-skilled jobs are sizable and only now beginning to exert their full force. Their effects are not likely to be compensated for easily by other adjustments in the economy if less-skilled immigration were to disappear. Some able-bodied natives who are not working or working part time might be pulled back into the full-time workforce, but they would not cover the overall population decline.

As the U.S. economy approaches full employment, shortages of less-skilled workers already have developed, just as they did in the strong economy in the late 1990s.[32] If immigration policy fails to provide enough slots for less-skilled workers, either labor shortages will check new growth in U.S. businesses while others fold or move out of the country or unauthorized migration may continue. In the early years of the recovery, from 2009 to 2012, the overall number of unauthorized migrants in the U.S. labor force held steady at 8.1 million, or 5.1 percent of the overall labor force, though the proportion of new Mexican unauthorized entrants declined even as the proportion from Central America increased.[33] But a growing economy is already spurring growth in construction, one of the chief employers of unauthorized workers. In short, unauthorized migration is likely to continue regardless of the level of enforcement at the U.S.-Mexico border, because so many alternative channels to land crossings exist for obtaining entry.[34]

It would thus be preferable to include provisions in immigration reform that allow for more legal migration for less-skilled workers, as legislation passed by the Senate in 2013 did, and then seek to forestall illegal entries through other means, including employment verification systems and bilateral emigration-control mechanisms. Given current low levels of population growth, it now takes about a hundred thousand new jobs a month to keep up with population growth. Although the economy is often viewed as still not back to full strength as of early 2015, job growth has far exceeded that level for more than two years. If future legislation on immigration sets a low cap on the levels of legal less-skilled immigration, two consequences are possible: the insufficiency of visas for legal workers will contribute to labor shortages and cause hardship and disruptions in sectors like agriculture and many service businesses, or substantial unauthorized migration will continue, resulting in even larger informal and underground economies and enabling widespread exploitation of workers by employers. If the immigrants cannot legalize, their families' chances of joining the middle class will be dismal. Legislation that allows for enough low-skilled legal immigrant workers would not only boost the integration prospects of these workers and their families, it would also be good for the economy and for the country.

Such legislation is also important if the country is going to keep inequality from increasing. If below-replacement-level fertility and rising education levels in the United States and other more advanced countries spur a need for less-skilled work, people from less developed countries will find their way to the jobs (often with the help of exploitative smugglers). Lower fertility and more job availability in Mexico may curtail Mexican migration, although political crises in Mexico suggest previously untapped sources of migration are likely to emerge.[35] But if the labor migrants do not come from Mexico, they will come from elsewhere. Without opportunity to legalize, some of these low-skilled immigrant workers will remain exploited and the mobility of most of their children stymied. Because such new workers are usually nonwhite, their presence at the bottom of the socioeconomic ladder tends to harden the link between socioeconomic and ethnoracial disadvantage. The research results here suggest that Mexican immigrants, who have done much of the country's less-skilled work the past few decades, have generally not been prevented, because of their ethnoracial status, from moving from the very bottom of the job hierarchy into better working-class jobs. But our research also suggests that it will be harder for them to move appreciably further unless more of them can graduate from college and unless the country can remedy middle-class income stagnation. These same prohibitive college costs also burden other members of the working class and middle class, whether immigrant or not, whether white or nonwhite, and income stagnation afflicts all. The challenge the country faces in seeking to achieve further integration for Mexican Americans is the same as the mobility challenge it faces in seeking to reduce inequality for all Americans.

═ Appendix A ═

Immigration and Intergenerational Mobility in Metropolitan Los Angeles Study

The main data source we use comes from a survey called Immigration and Intergenerational Mobility in Metropolitan Los Angeles (IIMMLA). Other supplementary data sets are also relied on at certain points, including the Survey of Income and Program Participation (SIPP), the Current Population Survey (CPS), the U.S. Census and American Community Survey (ACS), and various historical decennial census microfiles. These are described when they are used.

Conducted by telephone in 2004, IIMMLA targeted random samples of 1.5- and second-generation adults aged twenty to forty in the five counties of the greater metropolitan area (Los Angeles, Orange, Riverside, San Bernardino, and Ventura counties). Immigrants were defined as 1.5 generation if they came to the United States before the age of fifteen, and as second-generation if they were born in the United States but had at least one foreign-born parent. The survey also included samples of third-plus generation non-Hispanic whites, African Americans, and people of Mexican origin. To be included in these samples as third-generation persons, respondents would have been native born with native-born parents but at least one immigrant grandparent. The fourth-plus generation was native born, with native-born parents and grandparents. A supplemental survey included 125 first-generation Mexican immigrants who arrived in the United States from age fifteen to forty.

The total sample size was 4,780 respondents, of whom roughly eight hundred were third-plus-generation non-Hispanic whites and African Americans, and four hundred were third-plus-generation Mexican Americans. The targeted sample size for the 1.5 and second-generation Mexican Americans was eight hundred. The remaining 1.5- and second-generation respondents were divided among Chinese, Filipinos, Koreans, Vietnamese, separately; Salvadorans and Guatemalans taken together; and a residual group of immigrants from other national origins. Each of these samples consisted of four hundred respondents.

A multiframe sampling procedure called for random-digit dialing of house-holds in proportion to the population, except for telephone prefixes found in areas with very high concentrations of non-Hispanic whites. Once the quotas for whites, blacks, and those of Mexican origin were filled using random-digit dialing and the incidence rates for finding other groups became too low, the survey switched to sampling derived from more targeted geographic and race-ethnic frames. These included random-digit dialing of households in areas with high-density Asian populations and random sampling of telephone numbers derived from listings of Chinese, Korean, Vietnamese, and Filipino surnames. In all, 1,833 interviews were obtained from these augmented samples.

The overall cooperation rate among potential respondents was 76.2 percent for the screening survey and 82.1 percent for the main survey questionnaire, which, when multiplied, yield an overall cooperation rate of 63 percent. This represents the ratio of completed interviews to all eligible units ever contacted. The response rate, a broader measure that is defined as the ratio of completed interviews to the total number of eligible reporting units, is harder to measure, because a substantial proportion of telephone numbers that repeatedly yield no answer are unusable residential numbers. Estimates of the gross response rate run about 28 percent, not taking into account unusable numbers. To get these results, 263,783 distinct telephone numbers were dialed at least once.[1]

The survey was designed to take about thirty minutes. More than 90 percent of respondents chose to answer the questions in English, although a Spanish-language version was available. Questions included employment status and history; education; neighborhood of residence; community and civic participation and engagement; interest in politics and political self-identification; religious preference; nativity and place of residence during the respondent's youth; marital status and household composition; where applicable, a spouse's racial-ethnic background, nativity, citizenship, education background and status; the number of siblings and their education; and nativity, citizenship, educational attainment, employment history, and English-language fluency of their parents.[2]

═ Appendix B ═

Principal Components Analyses of Structural and Sociocultural Indicators

mpirical analyses can reveal how multidimensional the structure of integration is in postindustrial countries. How many key independent dimensions of integration are there, what defines them, and to what degree are these various dimensions associated with one another? This appendix addresses these questions. By independent, we mean relatively uncorrelated with one another. Without independence, the various indicators would simply reflect the results of a single unidimensional integration process. To gauge the number of independent dimensions of incorporation, we conduct a series of principal components analyses of a number of empirical indicators of incorporation obtained from questions asked in the survey on Immigration and Intergenerational Mobility in Metropolitan Los Angeles (IIMMLA) (see appendix A). The analyses here focus on the 1.5- and second-generation Mexican respondents ($N = 935$) weighted to their share of the overall L.A. metro population aged twenty to forty.

We report the total set of indicators across the four conceptual dimensions of immigrant incorporation that constitute the starting point for the analyses in appendix table B.1. These data include items on educational attainment, employer-provided health insurance, and personal income (as indicators of economic incorporation); items on attitudes toward racial-ethnic exogamy, mother-tongue proficiency, home-language preference, ethnic media consumption, and frequency of religious attendance (as indicators of linguistic-cultural assimilation); two indicators characterizing respondents' neighborhoods on the basis of tract-level data from the 2000 U.S. census, one measuring its ethnoracial composition and the other its socioeconomic status (as indicators of spatial incorporation); and three political measures: a scale measuring the extent to which respondents favor federal intervention to ensure that citizens have a good standard of living, a scale of political engagement (registering to vote, contacting government officials, participating in political meetings, and engaging in protests), and whether an individual voted in the last election (as indicators of political incorporation). Appendix table B.2 reports the means and standard deviations of all indicators used in the analyses.

Appendix Table B.1   Indicators of Incorporation among Second-Generation Mexican American Adults, Aged Twenty to Forty, Los Angeles, 2004

Dimension	Indicator	Operational Definition
Economic	Education	Years of completed schooling
	Health insurance	Has job-related health insurance (dummy coded)
	Income	Natural log of annual individual income
Cultural or linguistic	Ethnicity unimportant	Does not place importance in maintaining ethnic group (dummy coded)
	Language loss	Does not speak parents' native language well (dummy coded)
	Speaks English at home	Prefers to speak English at home (dummy coded)
	Low ethnic-media usage	Does not partake of ethnic-specific media on a weekly basis (dummy coded)
	Nonreligious	Attends services fewer than two times annually (dummy coded)
Spatial	Ethnoracial composition of neighborhood	Percent U.S. born, non-Latino white in census tract, 2000
	Socioeconomic status of neighborhood	Median household income of census tract, 2000
Political	Pro–government intervention	Scale (low = unfavorable toward federal interventions, high = favorable)
	Political engagement	Scale (low = low engagement, high = high engagement)
	Voting	Voted in recent election (dummy coded)

Source: Data from Immigration and Intergenerational Mobility in Metropolitan Los Angeles (see Bean, Leach et al. 2011).

We use a statistical technique called principal components analysis to assess the multidimensionality of the incorporation structure within Los Angeles. This approach helps to reveal both the number of dimensions of incorporation and the extent to which these dimensions take on similar or different structures in accordance with the ideas introduced earlier. It shows which indicators constitute a particular dimension and how tightly they bundle together in doing so. Of course, no absolute criterion exists for determining whether a structure is unidimensional or multidimensional. The answers yielded by our approach depend as much on theoretical as empirical considerations. To some extent, of course, the results also depend on the inputs to the analyses. However, and most important, any uni-dimensionality that does emerge among a given set of indicators does not depend on the particular inputs. That is, although we start with indicators in four broad integration domains, this does not preclude most or all of the indicators bundling together on a single principal component. We are especially interested in the extent to which indicators do not bundle together. As expected, Los Angeles reveals a multidimensional structure, with three separate multi-indicator incorporation

Appendix Table B.2 **Means and Standard Deviations for Indicators of Incorporation among Second-Generation Mexican Americans, Aged Twenty to Forty, Los Angeles, 2004**

	Los Angeles ($N = 935$)	
	Mean	SD
Economic		
Education	13.7	2.4
Health insurance	0.53	0.50
Income	8.2	3.8
Language-Culture		
Ethnicity unimportant	0.83	0.38
Language loss	0.33	0.47
English at home	0.69	0.43
No ethnic media	0.52	0.50
Nonreligious	0.36	0.48
Spatial		
Non-Hispanic whites in neighborhood	0.27	0.21
Median household income in tract	43,975	16,985
Political		
Pro–government intervention	4.4	1.2
Political engagement	0.0	1.0
Voted	0.38	0.48

Source: Data from Immigration and Intergenerational Mobility in Metropolitan Los Angeles (see Bean, Leach et al. 2011).
Note: See table B.1 for variable definitions.

components emerging (economic-political, spatial, and linguistic) (see appendix table B.3).

To ascertain whether a component (or dimension) was meaningful, we require that it show an eigenvalue greater than 1.10 (implying that the amount of variation explained by its components exceeds chance by 10 percent or more) and that this occur "above the elbow" of a scree plot of eigenvalues for all components.[3] Because we have relatively few indicators and many are not continuous, we did not employ confirmatory factor analyses to assess the structure of the components. The first principal component extracted always (by definition) explains the most variance and invariably involves the greatest number of indicators.[4] Moreover, the more variance the first component explains, the more the component reflects consolidation toward a unidimensional general pattern, which in the present case would reflect unidimensional integration. It is notable that this does not happen in the analyses, with the first component not markedly overwhelming the other two notable components that emerge.

It is worth noting that political and economic aspects of incorporation bundle closely together in the first component. This implies that the aspects of political incorporation examined here vary as a function of economic incorporation. In

204   Appendix B

Appendix Table B.3   **Varimax-Rotated Factor Loadings from Principal Components Analysis of Indicators of Incorporation of Second-Generation Mexican Americans, Los Angeles, 2004**

| | Dimensions | | |
	Economic	Linguistic	Spatial
Education	**0.537**	0.037	0.348
Health insurance	**0.576**	−0.009	0.016
Income	**0.515**	0.057	−0.100
Ethnicity important	−0.073	0.218	0.053
Language loss	−0.001	**−0.732**	−0.110
English at home	0.119	**0.741**	0.026
Low ethnic media use	0.016	**−0.722**	−0.052
Nonreligious	−0.099	0.085	−0.099
Non-Hispanic whites in tract	0.076	0.051	**0.847**
Median household income of tract	−0.017	0.062	**0.860**
Pro–government intervention	−0.280	0.123	0.094
Political engagement	**0.629**	0.026	0.040
Voted	**0.653**	0.096	0.031

Source: Data from Immigration and Intergenerational Mobility in Metropolitan Los Angeles (see Bean, Leach et al. 2011).
Note: Loadings greater than or equal to |.400| in bold.

other words, the higher the socioeconomic status of the respondent, the more politically involved that person is. It is also worth highlighting that no multi-indicator sociocultural dimension emerges, with the exception of one largely defined by linguistic indicators. This does not mean that sociocultural facets of incorporation are unimportant, only that indicators such as ethnic group importance, religious behavior, and language usage do not bundle or covary strongly with one another. The language component reflects the tendency of immigrants everywhere to learn the host-country language, irrespective of their other characteristics, especially when that language is English.[5] But the sociocultural aspects of incorporation do not hang together among themselves to the same degree as do the aspects of the other major dimensions. This confirms our expectation that we can less readily predict one facet of sociocultural incorporation from another, a result in keeping with postindustrial-individualistic theoretical perspective on integration, which views sociocultural phenomena as having become more independent, "optional," and situationally fluid in recent decades.

We have focused exclusively on the degree to which indicators of incorporation take on a multidimensional structure, but we have not addressed the degree to which the three dimensions are related to one another. The dimensional structure reported in table B.3 is based on an orthogonal factor rotation solution, which means, by definition, the three incorporation dimensions are perfectly independent of one another (that is, their intercorrelation is zero). Such independence between factors is not assumed, however, when the factor rotation is done using a so-called oblique solution, which allows for the incorporation dimensions to be correlated with one another. Theoretical perspectives viewing incorporation as multidimensional would be supported by results showing that the various incorporation dimensions are only weakly related to one another when independence is not imposed on the structure. Using an oblique, as opposed to orthogonal, rotation does not yield meaningful changes to the incorporation structure reported here. Moreover, consistent with notions that incorporation is multidimensional, the various (obliquely rotated) dimensions are weakly correlated with one another. For instance, the correlation between the economic-political and sociocultural dimensions is 0.134, and that between the sociocultural and spatial dimensions is −0.207, suggesting that sociocultural integration is only weakly correlated with economic-political and spatial integration. Economic-political and spatial have a correlation of only −0.057.

= Appendix C =

Demographic Simulation of the Extent of Education Bias Owing to Various Sources of Sample Attrition

We have repeatedly emphasized the necessity of examining processes and outcomes across three generations to assess adequately the extent of immigrant-group integration. This is particularly the case for Mexican Americans, for whom unauthorized migration adversely affects even the U.S.-born children of the immigrant generation, thus hindering mobility in the second generation and potentially holding back the third generation (the grandchildren of the immigrants). Unfortunately, the outcomes for the third generation have been hard to address because little satisfactory information exists on them in large, nationally representative data sets. Although datasets like the Current Population Survey (CPS) provide information on the birthplace of parents, every generation from the third on has U.S.-born parents. As a result, it is not possible to distinguish the grandchildren of immigrants from the great-great-great-grandchildren of immigrants in survey data. Moreover, evidence exists that these subcategories are subject to measurement error, particularly selective attrition out of the groups by education. That is, the more highly educated members of the group are more likely to intermarry and stop identifying themselves as Mexican American, or their children are less likely to do so. The significant question remaining is the extent of this and other similarly biasing effects.

One way to assess attrition is to take a past Mexican American population and project it forward based on what we know about various demographic factors that have actually affected the structure of the group over time (for example, its fertility, mortality, levels of education, and migration across regions and states). This projection can then be compared to today's actual population structure. If these two are close, researchers might conclude that the earlier population constitutes a good baseline comparison. Then they can repeat the process holding the various demographic factors constant one at a time (or specifying their value), while allowing the others to vary in the way that they actually did. For example, we can assume there is no attrition across time and recalculate what today's population would look like under the circumstance that all else varied but that there was no attrition. The difference between this result and the baseline projection one would give us a lower-bound estimate of how much attrition has contributed to today's population structure (that is, how much difference attrition makes for schooling structure). In broad outline, this is what we do in following paragraphs. We do this estimating the effects of attrition, state of residence, fertility differences by region and state, and changing amounts of immigration. The rest of this Appendix discusses these procedures and the results they yield.

Historical-Regional Factors

The grandparents (and great-grandparents, etc.) of today's third-plus generation of Mexican Americans grew up in the United States, but at a time when relatively few people finished high school, segregation was legal, and civil rights programs had yet to be adopted. As noted in Chapter 3, before 1960, a majority of the Mexican-origin population lived in Texas, where the development of compulsory schooling lagged behind almost all other states and where school completion rates were especially low for the Mexican-origin population in particular. Thus, in 1970, middle-aged Texas-born Mexican-origin women averaged only half a year more of schooling than Mexican-immigrant women of the similar ages. This means the third-plus generation in Texas today is the product of a much more disadvantaged educational background than the one faced by Mexican immigrants and their children today in Texas. It also means that the third-plus generation in Texas today, because of its more adverse legacy, will in all likelihood not show nearly as high schooling levels as third-plus generation Mexican Americans in states such as California. But even in California, schooling levels may be influenced by Texas. For example, as we noted, 15 percent of the later-generation Mexican Americans living in California in 1970 were born in Texas, and that proportion may have grown during the 1970s. Thus, the lower educational attainment seen among later-generation Mexican Americans throughout the country may have roots in the Mexican-origin population's concentration in Texas in the first half of the twentieth century.

Ethnic Attrition

A second legacy-related process that may bias educational attainment of later-generation Mexican Americans is that of ethnic attrition.[6] Over time, persons with Mexican ancestry may no longer identify as having Mexican origin or ethnicity in surveys and censuses. While the exact rate of such attrition is largely unknown, research by Brian Duncan and Stephen Trejo strongly implies that it is substantial and, crucially, positively related to educational attainment.[7] The selectivity of ethnic attrition will bias the observed educational attainments of later-generation Mexican-origin persons downward. However, any third-plus generation results for the IIMMLA sample may be less biased by ethnic attrition, because with the IIMMLA data one can include both persons who subjectively identify as Mexican origin as well as those who may not identify themselves as being Mexican American, but report that one or more of their grandparents was born in Mexico or that they have relatives with Mexican ancestry.

Projecting the Educational Profile of Third-Plus Generation Mexican Americans

To approximate empirically the degree to which historical legacy effects and ethnic attrition have affected the observed educational attainments of the Mexican American third-plus generation, we present in appendix table C.1 results from demographic projections calculated under sets of alternative assumptions. The first objective is to estimate the educational attainment profile of Mexican-origin women aged twenty-five to forty in 2010, using as our starting point the female Mexican-origin population observed in microdata from the 1940 census.[8] The 1940 population is thus survived forward using inputs for levels of mortality, fertility (with the assumed rate varying with educational attainment), ethnic attrition, immigration from Mexico, and state of residence. We systematically vary these inputs one at a time to gauge their effects on generational differences in

Appendix Table C.1   Prevalence of Education Beyond High School, Mexican-Origin Women, Aged Twenty-five to Forty, by Generation, United States, 2010 (percentage)

	Generation			3rd-Plus Deficit or Surplus	Exceeds or Falls Below Baseline
	1st	2nd	3rd-Plus		
1. Observed (2010 CPS)	23.0	53.0	50.0	−3.0	—
2. Baseline percentages	23.6	53.4	50.2	−3.2	−0.2
3. If everyone lived in Texas	23.6	53.0	47.7	−5.3	−2.1
4. If everyone lived in California	23.5	53.7	55.7	2.0	5.2
5. If there were no ethnic attrition	23.6	53.8	55.6	1.8	5.0
6. If there were no fertility gradient	23.6	54.6	51.6	−3.0	0.2
7. If there were constant immigration	23.3	52.7	51.6	−1.1	2.1
8. If there were no change in immigrant educational attainment	1.0	50.6	50.2	−0.4	2.8
9. If (4), (5), (6), (7), and (8) above	1.0	51.2	65.4	14.2	17.6

Source: March 2010 Current Population Survey; Bachmeier and Van Hook 2013.
Note: The observed results are based on the authors' analyses of the March 2010 Current Population Survey. The estimated results are based on projections of the Mexican-born population in the United States from 1940 to 2010 under varying assumptions about the effects of state of residence, ethnic attrition, the educational gradient in fertility, the level of Mexican immigration, and the level and educational attainment of Mexican immigrants (Bachmeier and Van Hook 2013).

educational attainment in 2010. We provide a more detailed description of the inputs and method later in this appendix.

Technical Details for Simulation Projections   We simulate the percentage who attained more than a high school diploma in 2010 among Mexican-origin women aged twenty-five to forty by generational status. Each simulation brings forward the U.S. Mexican-origin female population from 1940 to 2010 using an elaboration of the cohort-component method.[9] The standard cohort component method uses age-specific probabilities of mortality, fertility rates, and net migration to project populations forward in time. We elaborate on this approach by breaking down the results by educational attainment, immigrant generation, and state of residence and by accounting for ethnic attrition, intergenerational mobility in education, and variations in mobility by state of residence. To simplify the simulations, we restrict the projections to females living in Texas or California, and we assume there is no interstate migration. Across multiple simulations, we sequentially modify various inputs one at a time (for example, the level of ethnic attrition or the percentage living in California) to estimate the unique effects of these factors on generational differences in educational attainment in 2010.

Baseline Simulation (1940)   The starting population for the baseline simulation is the Mexican-origin female population enumerated in the 1940 census by five-year age groups, educational attainment, and generational status. Educational attainment is a categorization of less than high school, high school diploma, or more than high school. Generational status is based on place of birth and parent's place of birth, with the first generation defined as those born in Mexico, the second generation as U.S.-born persons with at least one foreign-born parent, and the third-plus generation as U.S.-born persons with at least one U.S.-born parent. All census data, including data from 1940, are obtained from the IPUMS website.[10] The baseline simulation is the projected 2010 population that results from bringing the 1940 population forward allowing all of these factors to change as they actually do in the data from 1940 to 2010.

Survivors   The number of survivors is estimated for each five-year projection period by multiplying the population in each five-year age group by its corresponding five-year survival ratio. Survival ratios are obtained from female life tables from 1945 to 2005 for the United States from the Human Mortality Database.[11] We select life tables from the midpoint of each decade for each projection period (for example, we use the 1945 life table for the 1940 to 1949 projection periods).

Fertility   We estimate fertility as the average number of children ever born among Mexican-origin women aged forty-five to sixty-four by educational attainment and nativity (foreign born versus U.S. born), based on the 1940 to 1990 censuses and 2010 American Community Survey, and interpolate the estimates for 2000 because the 2000 census did not collect data on children ever born.[12] We convert the number of children ever born to age-specific female fertility rates by distributing the number of births according to a standard Mexican American fertility schedule obtained from the National Center for Health Statistics and dividing by two (to obtain fertility rates for female births only). Some of the simulations assume there is no education gradient in fertility. For these simulations, we apply the average female fertility across all education categories.

Net Immigration   Net immigration is estimated using the residual method. At the end of each decade, we estimate net migration by subtracting the expected Mexican-born female population if no migration had occurred during the decade from the enumerated population. The expected population is the population at the beginning of the decade minus the estimated number of deaths. We distribute the number of net immigrants by age, educational attainment, and state according to the distributions observed among the foreign born in the censuses for each decade. Some simulations assume that immigration did not change over time, or that the educational attainment of immigrants has not changed since 1940. For these simulations, we apply respectively a constant immigration level across all decades (the average from 1940 to 2010), and we distribute immigrants according to the 1940 education distribution for all decades.

Education-Mobility Tables   We distribute all births into educational-attainment categories (signifying the child's eventual attainment) by applying probabilities obtained from intergenerational education-mobility tables. A mobility table is a cross-tabulation of parent's educational attainment by the child's. For example, contemporary data sources suggest that among Mexican American women whose mothers have less than a high school education, 17.8 percent attain less than a high school diploma, 27.1 percent complete high school, and 56.4 percent go beyond high school. In our simulations, we therefore distribute births of women with less than a high school diploma according to the same proportions. In Texas in the pre-civil-rights era (before 1960), there are several reasons to think that mobility was very low among Hispanics (even lower than among African Americans at the time).[13] Therefore, for Texas before 1960, we use a mobility table that averages mobility observed for African American women at the time and no mobility.[14] For all other states and time periods, we use the average of two mobility tables obtained for U.S.-born Mexican Americans for the post-civil-rights era. One is generated from IIMMLA data (discussed in this volume) and the second is generated from data collected by the Mexican American Study Project.[15] The mobility pattern from these two sources is so similar that we use the average of the two.

Ethnic Attrition   Not all daughters of Mexican-origin mothers grow up to identify as Mexican, a phenomenon referred to as ethnic attrition. Ethnic attrition increases across generations and educational attainment.[16] We estimate ethnic attrition as the average of two sets of estimates. First, we estimate attrition from the March Current Population Surveys for 2008 to 2011 as the percentage of persons who do not identify as Mexican-origin among those who were born in Mexico or who have at least one parent who was born in Mexico. Second, we estimate attrition from the 1979 cohort of National Longitudinal Survey of Youth (NLSY79). At the first interview, the NLSY asked respondents (then aged fourteen to twenty-one) to list up to six different ethnic identities, and those who listed more than one were asked which ethnicity they identified with most. We ascribe attrition to respondents who do not indicate Mexican as their only or preferred ethnicity among those who list Mexican as any of their ethnicities. Ethnic attrition rates are higher when based on the NLSY survey responses than the CPS. We suspect this stems from the fact that the NLSY respondents were younger than the CPS respondents; as adolescents, they were in a life-course stage during which identities are more fluid. The difference may also stem from different definitions of ethnic attrition; the CPS population at risk is restricted to those with objective indicators of Mexican ancestry, while the NLSY measure is more subjective because it includes anyone who identifies as Mexican. Because a case could be made for both the CPS and the NLSY measure, we opt to use the average of the two in the simulations. This is a conservative assumption about attrition because it makes no allowance for attrition beyond the second generation in the case of the CPS data, whereas the NLSY study may capture more later-generation attrition. Averaging the two thus results for this reason alone in a conservative lower-bound estimate.

Simulation Results

The simulations focus on those Mexican-origin women who completed levels of education beyond high school, and we assume that the Mexican-origin population lived in either California and Texas. The first row of appendix table C.1 reports the percentages observed among such women, aged twenty-five to forty, in the 2010 March Current Population Survey, by immigrant generation. Twenty-three percent of Mexican immigrant women had more than a high school education, a figure that climbs to 53 percent in the second generation. Evidence of the deficit, often termed a decline between the third-plus and the second generation, that has been observed in previous research also appears in these data for third-and-later-generation women, 50 percent of whom complete education beyond high school, a difference of 3 percentage points relative to second-generation women.

Row 2 of the table presents the results from what we call the baseline simulation, which demonstrates that the inputs used in the backward projection are sufficient to bring forth seventy years later an intergenerational education profile of the Mexican-origin population that almost exactly matches the one actually observed in the 2010 CPS. In the third row of the table, we assume that the entire Mexican-origin population in 1940 faced the particularly limited access to educational opportunities characteristic of pre-civil-rights Texas. Under this assumption, an even smaller percentage of third-plus-generation women, 47.8, would have proceeded beyond high school, and as a consequence, the deficit between the second and the third-plus generations would have been substantially greater (−5.3 as opposed to −3.2 percentage points). Conversely, the simulation in the fourth row indicates that no third-plus-generation decline would exist today if the entire Mexican-origin population in 1940 had resided in California, where education policies influenced by the progressive movement were much more effective in ameliorating Mexicans' relative inequality in educational opportunity. Under this scenario, the third-plus generation would make modest improvements over the second with respect to educational attainment beyond high school, increasing from 53.7 to 55.7 percent.

The fifth row of appendix table C.1 indicates that the observed third-plus-generation decline can also be explained by ethnic attrition. If there were no attrition from the Mexican-origin population observed in 1940, 55.6 percent of the third-plus generation would have progressed beyond high school in 2010 compared with 53.8 percent of the second generation, a similarly modest inter-generational gain to the one observed in row 4.

The fertility gradient (that is, the association between educational attainment and fertility) accounts for very little of the observed third-plus-generation deficit (row 6). If the fertility rate were the same for women of all education levels, the percentage of women projected to have more than a high school education in 2010 would increase slightly among both second- and third-plus-generation women, which results in roughly the same magnitude of intergenerational deficit observed in the baseline simulation.

In row 7 we estimate the educational attainment of Mexican-origin women assuming a constant rate of immigration between 1940 and 2010. This would have resulted in a slight decrease in the proportion proceeding beyond high school in the second generation (from 53.4 in baseline to 52.7 in row 7) and a slight increase in the percentage doing so in the third-plus generation (from 50.2 at baseline to 51.6 in row 7). As a result, the degree of third-plus-generation deficit would be reduced by more than half, from −3.0 in the baseline to −1.1. And in row 8, we assume that there was no increase in the educational attainment of immigrants arriving from Mexico between 1940 and 2010. This of course has no impact on the estimated third-plus generation because no one in this group would have descended from immigrants arriving from Mexico after 1940. This adjustment reduces the percentage advancing beyond high school in the second generation by 2.8 percentage points, from 53.4 percent at baseline to 50.6 percent in row 8, and thus all but erases the estimated deficit from the second to the third-plus generation (taking it to −0.4 percentage points).

Finally, in row 9 we include all of the assumptions made individually in rows 4 through 8 and estimate a female Mexican-origin population raised entirely in California, absent any ethnic attrition, and with no fertility gradient, who experienced a constant flow of immigration from Mexico with no education upgrading among immigrants. Adopting all of these assumptions together dramatically improves the educational attainment of the estimated third-plus generation, as the percentage who attained more than a high school diploma increases from just 50.2 at baseline to 65.4 percent in the final row. Thus, had all of these conditions obtained, instead of a third-plus-generation deficit of 3.2 percentage points, we would have observed an improvement from the second to the third-plus generation of 14.2 percentage points.

In sum, results from the simulation exercise reported in appendix table C.1 provide substantial empirical support for the notion that third-plus-generation educational attainment among Mexican Americans is appreciably affected by a pre-civil-rights-era historical legacy in Texas, by demographic change, and by ethnic attrition processes that unfold as more highly educated members of the population intermarry and their offspring no longer report Mexican ancestry in survey data. Today's second generation from Mexico comes of age within an education system that, while still imperfect, offers considerably more educational opportunity than what was available to the grandparents of the third- and later-generation Mexican Americans concentrated largely in Texas well before the civil rights era. Moreover, the educational attainment of the second generation is practically unaffected by ethnic attrition, as nearly all members of the second generation identify as Mexican. Because the education profile of the third-plus generation is pulled down by its pre-civil-rights-era Texas legacy, by demographic change, and by selective ethnic attrition, we urge caution when interpreting research results from studies based on cross-sectional survey data that appear to show educational "delay" or "decline" between the second and third-plus generation.[17]

= Appendix D =

Description of Methodology for and Results of the Latent Class Analyses of Couple Migration-Status Trajectories

R ather than impose an arbitrary scoring scale for entry and other statuses on mothers and fathers separately, or on the couple, we instead allow actual empirical clusters (combinations) of mother and father status trajectories to emerge from the data among the parents of the respondents. This is achieved by applying latent class analyses to the accrual of increments of early political-entry incorporation conceptualized in terms of the six key steps of the entry process as noted in appendix table D.1. Conducting such analyses tells us what combinations of mixed-status trajectories cluster together, helping us assess relationships between such clusters and educational outcomes among offspring.

We use a maximum-likelihood latent class model to sort the IIMMLA respondents into classes based on similarities among their parents' steps in making transitions from entry to citizenship. To determine these transitions, respondents were asked a series of questions about each parent's nativity and about each parent's migration status, both for when their parents entered the United States and at the time of the interview. If the parent was born in the United States or was foreign born but had never lived in the United States or if the parents' status was unknown to the respondent (or the respondent refused to answer questions), further questions about the parents' status ceased. Such parents were classified into one of three groups: native born, never lived in the United States, or status unknown.

For each parent who did not fall into one of these groups, we ascertained their entry and interview statuses using a four-step sequence. First, we inferred a parent's legal status at the time of the interview indirectly by a process of elimination. If the parent was foreign born and had lived in the United States for more than five years, we asked if the parent had become a U.S. citizen or had acquired legal permanent residence. All those remaining were tentatively classified as unauthorized.

Second, following a similar process of elimination, we determined an initial entry status for each parent and classified them into one of six possible categories: legal permanent resident (LPR), refugee, work-student–travel visa,

Appendix Table D.1   Indicators of Early Political-Entry Incorporation Associated with Various Step-to-Citizenship Trajectories

| | Step-to-Citizenship Transitions | | | | | |
| | (1) | (2) | (3) | (4) | (5) | (6) |
Trajectory	Migrated to U.S. or Not[a]	Entered Legally or Not	Became an LPR[b] or Not	Naturalized Eventually or Not	Naturalized Quickly or Not	U.S. Born
Status unknown or never migrated to U.S.	0	0	0	0	0	0
Unauthorized (or unknown) to unauthorized	1	0	0	0	0	0
Unauthorized (or unknown) to legal permanent resident	1	0	1	0	0	0
Authorized to legal permanent resident	1	1	1	0	0	0
Unauthorized (or unknown) to naturalized	1	0	1	1	0,1	0
Authorized to naturalized	1	1	1	1	0,1	0
U.S. born	1	1	1	1	1	1

Source: Data from Immigration and Intergenerational Mobility in Metropolitan Los Angeles (see Bean, Leach et al. 2011).
[a] Also status unknown.
[b] LPR = legal permanent resident.

border-crossing card, unauthorized (when volunteered by the respondent), or other. The "other" category consists of parents for whom the respondent refused to provide information about or did not know their status on entering the country.

Third, we classified each parent into one of three final entry statuses using a combination of the initial six-category entry status, their status at interview, and other background information. Four of the initial entry-status groups were straightforward. We labeled parents who entered as legal permanent residents or as refugees as authorized. We grouped parents in the unauthorized or other categories together as unauthorized-unknown. The statuses of parents who entered with a temporary visa or a border-crossing card were more complicated. If parents did not change their status and become legal permanent residents (in other words, their interview status from the first step is unauthorized), then we assume the parent acquired a visa or border card as a means to enter the country and stay but with no way to regularize their legal status in the long term. We grouped such parents into the unauthorized category. If a parent said he or she entered with a temporary visa or border card and subsequently became a legal permanent resident or citizen, we then considered their highest education attained and the amount of time that they had been in the United States to infer their entry status. We categorized parents who had not completed high school and had been in the country for more than five years at the time of the interview as unauthorized entrants (that is, likely to be low-skill labor migrants who entered unauthorized or with a short-term visa but became legal permanent residents under the 1986 amnesty). Those with higher educational attainment or more time in the country most likely entered the country with the means to become legal permanent residents, given enough time, so we categorized their entry status as authorized.

Fourth, we then reassessed the interview statuses of certain parents to rectify a mistake that had occurred in the interview process and to determine whether a parent remained in the country without authorization or overstayed his or her visa. A mistake in the interview process occurred when respondents were not asked about a parent's status at interview if the parent had not been in the country for at least five years. In such cases, we inferred the interview status to be LPR if a parent had entered the country as an LPR. We grouped all other such cases as unauthorized-unknown. We also found inconsistencies in some respondents' answers. Several respondents stated that their parents had entered the country as LPRs but did not indicate that they were LPRs at the time of the interview. Giving the benefit of the doubt, we labeled such parents' current status as LPR. And if respondents stated that their parent had entered as a refugee but was not an LPR at interview (this mostly occurred among Mexicans, who cannot have entered the country as refugees), we inferred their interview status to be unauthorized. We relabeled the interview status of the other parents with an initial entry status of unauthorized to unauthorized. See the following list.

Step 1: Initial current status
Naturalized
Legal permanent resident
Other

Step 2: Initial entry status
  Legal permanent resident
  Refugee
  Border-crossing card
  Unauthorized
  Other

Step 3: Final entry status
  Authorized
  Unauthorized

Step 4: Final current status
  Naturalized
  Legal permanent resident
  Unauthorized

Note: Entry and interview not applicable if native born, parent information is unknown (or refused), or parent never lived in the United States.

The latent class analyses were then applied to the transitions. The analyses involve using a variant of finite-mixture models, which have often been used to identify groups with distinctive patterns of behaviors.[18]

In this case, the classes consist of groups of immigrant parents with similar combinations of steps toward naturalization. Although the actual size and pattern of such classes are not directly observed, the latent class analyses enable the inference of such clusterings from similarities in the data.[19] They provide a basis for estimating the proportion of cases in each class and the probabilities of membership in a class stemming from different patterns of transitions in migration status. Because a higher proportion of Mexican immigrant parents at any point are still making the transition from temporary to permanent immigrant, and because U.S. immigration policy is so complicated that it encourages multiple legal entry strategies,[20] Mexicans would be expected to show numerous, parental mixed-status classes.

We also use the results of the latent class analyses to examine how various parental mixed-status groups (for example, latent classes) relate to children's educational attainment. We do this by gauging the extent to which children's schooling varies by parents' class group, controlling for antecedent factors affecting parent's class membership. In other words, we examine education differences among the children of immigrants as affected by their parents' mixed-status group, controlling for observed background factors that may affect class membership. This is accomplished by conducting a two-step analysis. First, we estimate the latent class models and then classify parents and their children into parental mixed-status classes based on the results. Second, we estimate the degree to which antecedent characteristics affect the sorting of parents into these mixed-status classes using multinomial regression models.

In keeping with Mexicans' frequent status as temporary migrants and their initial unauthorized entry, we expect the latent class analyses to indicate that they are characterized by several parental mixed-status latent classes. After applying standard statistical criteria for determining the number of latent classes,[21] seven

Appendix Figure D.1   Latent Class Analysis Modeling Framework

Source: Data from Immigration and Intergenerational Mobility in Metropolitan Los Angeles (see Bean, Leach et al. 2011).

clusters emerge. To determine the number of classes, we applied the usual statistical criteria (AIC, BIC, adjusted BIC, and entropy), using relative rather than absolute thresholds for assessing improvements in fit combined with criteria of substantive coherence. We sought an entropy value (measure of distinctiveness of classes) of at least 0.95 and a relative improvement in fit of at least 1.0 percent.[22] On the basis of these and the substantive criteria discussed later in this appendix, we chose a seven-class model.

Substantively, we prefer the seven-class model over the six-class model because, for respondents with both a mother and father who were legal at interview, the seven-class model distinguishes parents who had entered the country without authorization from parents who entered as authorized. We stopped at seven classes because the eight-class model separates respondents with a native-born or early-naturalizing mother from those with early-naturalizing fathers and those with late-naturalizing or legal but not naturalizing fathers, distinctions that made little substantive sense.

The analyses show variegated patterns of probabilities of belonging to a given class for Mexican mothers and fathers (appendix table D.1). These classes are described in the text in chapter 5. Those parents who either had entered and remained unauthorized or whose status was unknown constituted the last class. A comparison of both parents' and children's characteristics for these two kinds of parents indicated that those classed as status unknown showed virtually identical values on these variables as those in the class consisting of parents who were unauthorized at entry and unauthorized at interview. Given that our major research objective is to ascertain if the mixed-status groups among immigrant parents independently relate to the education level attained by their children, we first classify the respondents according to their parents' mixed-status class (assigning them to the class to which the results of the latent class analyses indicate they have the highest probability of belonging),[23] and then we estimate a multinomial logistic-regression model that regresses class membership on mother and father antecedent variables. The overall modeling framework that serves as a guide for the estimations is shown in appendix figure D.1. We were unable, however, to estimate all of the pieces of this model simultaneously because linear dependency between membership in the mixed-status classes and parental antecedent variables forestalls statistical estimation. As a result, we estimated relationships among variables in different parts of the framework separately. Although estimating the complete model simultaneously would increase the efficiency of the estimates, this was not possible given the size and complexity of the model. In particular, the larger model encountered difficulties in which empty cells for some of the measures in smaller classes introduced complete linear dependence that precluded estimation in certain instances. Our approach of estimating the pieces of the model separately introduces no bias, and the diminished efficiency is of minimal concern given the large overall size of our sample.

= Appendix E =

Procedures Followed to Calculate Average Years of Schooling Completed for Third-Generation Categories of Authorized- and Unauthorized-Background Mexican Americans

The third-only generation respondents in the IIMMLA Survey are persons whose parents (but not grandparents) were born in the United States. None of these respondents was queried about their parents' migration status because neither they nor their parents were migrants. Also, information on the migration status of respondents' grandparents was not collected in the survey. Thus we do not have individual-level data about the migration status of the grandparents of third-only-generation respondents, meaning we cannot identify which particular third-only-generation individuals came from families with unauthorized backgrounds in the sense that we apply that term here (that is, as persons whose grandmothers entered the country illegally and later still had not legalized). We can, however, estimate in the aggregate what the education levels of the third-only-generation respondents would be if all of those unauthorized grandparents had legalized (a group we call the authorized-background case) or if all of those coming were unauthorized migrants who never legalized (a group we call the unauthorized-background case).

To calculate an expected mean level of schooling for the authorized case, we assume that the same proportion of third-only-generation persons in the IIMMLA survey have unauthorized-grandparent backgrounds as do the second-generation respondents, which is 12.3 percent for women and 15.3 percent for men. Then we assume the gender-specific age-adjusted schooling penalty for the children of immigrant mothers who entered illegally but then legalized gets passed on from the second generation (which consists of those incurring the penalty) to the third generation in accordance with the rate of intergenerational transmission of mothers' and fathers' education to the schooling of the members of the third generation. The transmission rate we use is the average of the coefficients for mother's and father's education from the gender-specific regressions of third-generation offspring's education on parents' schooling variables, using the IIMMLA data. The averages of these coefficients for males are 0.290 for father's schooling + 0.104 for mother's = 0.394/2 = 0.197 and for females 0.175 for father's schooling + 0.190 for mother's = 0.367/2 = 0.183. In short, we assume that about 20 percent of the gender-specific legalization premium realized in the second generation is transmitted to the third generation. This is a conservative assumption that probably understates the actual degree of transmission.

Among males, 15.3 percent of the second-generation respondents had unauthorized mothers, so 15.3 percent would have been penalized an average of 1.54 years of schooling (see table 5.2). Multiplying this penalty by the average transmission rate for males (1.54 ∗ 0.197 = 0.303) gives 0.303 years of schooling not transmitted to the next generation, if everyone were subjected to this penalty. However, we assume only 15.3 percent of the third-generation male respondents are subject to the penalty. On average then, the average number of years of schooling that the observed value in the data for third-only males will be too low by is (0.153 ∗ 0.303 = 0.046 years). This is the number we use to adjust upward the level of observed schooling for third-only-generation males for the authorized case. Applying these same assumptions to females yields a parallel adjustment of 0.052 years of schooling.

In the unauthorized case, we assume that all of the third-generation males would have been subject to grandparents who were unauthorized (this means an additional 84.7 percent of grandparents in the IIMMLA data; 15.3 percent already show unauthorized backgrounds). Under this condition, the observed male education value would be too high by (.847 ∗ 0.303) = 0.257 years. This is the number of years we subtract from the observed years of schooling for males to obtain a value for the unauthorized case. A parallel calculation was done for females. Based on these assumptions, we then calculate new values for the education of the 3.0 and 3.5 generations, assuming in the authorized case no unauthorized-background legacy effects, and in the unauthorized case universal unauthorized-background legacy effects.

= Notes =

Chapter 1

1. Bean and Stevens 2003; Borjas and Tienda 1987; Jasso 2014.
2. Bean, Bachmeier, and Brown 2014; Massey 2013; Smith 2013.
3. U.S. Department of Homeland Security 2014.
4. Passel, Cohn, and Rohan 2014.
5. Ruggles et al. 2010.
6. Agius Vallejo 2012; Alba 2006; Alba, Jiménez, and Marrow 2013.
7. Lichter 2013; López and Stanton-Salazar 2001; Telles and Ortiz 2008.
8. For example, see Bean and Tienda 1987; Bean and Stevens 2003; Tienda and Mitchell 2006. Studies that focus only on immigrants, or only on the children of immigrants (the second generation) and their parents, or even on Mexican Americans in general without disaggregating by generation, tend to produce findings about integration outcomes that are diluted by the exceptionally low socioeconomic status of the immigrant generation and (sometimes by low outcomes in the second generation as well) compared with those of later-born Mexican Americans. On the other hand, researchers who focus only on the U.S. born but omit the Mexican born necessarily obtain findings that are skewed toward favorable integration outcomes. Despite the long insistence of critics that it is necessary both to analyze three generations of information about Mexican Americans and to disaggregate such results by generation, practices to the contrary persist, sometimes because data on generations are not available.
9. For example, Alba and Nee 2003.
10. For example, see Telles and Ortiz 2008.
11. For example, see almost all of the chapters in Hochschild et al. 2013.
12. Bean and Brown 2015.
13. For an exception, see Sisk 2013.
14. Hout 2015.
15. Foner and Fredrickson 2004; Lee and Bean 2010; Perez and Hirschman 2009.
16. Waters and Kasinitz 2013.
17. Lee and Bean 2010.

18. Hochschild et al. 2013; Hochschild and Mollenkopf 2009; Joppke 2010; Zolberg 1999.
19. Papademetriou 2006.
20. Alba and Silberman 2002; Freeman 1979.
21. Alexander 2012; Fredrickson 1988; Morgan 1975; Woodward 2001.
22. Solinger 1999.
23. Bauer et al. 2005.
24. Daniel Sokatch and David Myers, "Israel's Dilemma: Who Can Be an Israeli?," *Los Angeles Times*, January 14, 2014.
25. Foley 2004; Lee 2002; Lieberson 1980; Montejano 1987; Perdue and Green 2007; Rumbaut 2006.
26. Nee and Holbrow 2013.
27. Gonzales 2011; Nee and Holbrow 2013; Yoshikawa 2011.
28. Bean, Brown, and Castillo 2015.
29. Bean, Vernez, and Keely 1989.
30. Massey 2013; Tienda and Sánchez 2013; Waters and Kasinitz 2013.
31. Bean, Leach et al. 2011; Gonzales, Suárez-Orozco, and Dedios-Sanguineti 2013; Nee and Holbrow 2013; Yoshikawa 2011.
32. For example, see Boyd 1989; Foner 1999; Glick 2010; Massey et al. 1987; Stark 1991b.
33. Bean, Berg, and Van Hook 1996; Rossi 1980; Wilkerson 2010; Van Hook and Glick 2007.
34. Dreby 2012; Landale, Oropesa, and Noah 2014.
35. Van Hook and Bean 2009.
36. Bachmeier and Bean 2011.
37. Ibid.; Segura 1994; Tafoya-Estrada 2008; Zhou and Bankston 1998.
38. Brown 2007.
39. Alba and Islam 2009; Bean et al. 2013; Duncan and Trejo 2011a, 2011b, 2011c.
40. This claim may hold even for the pioneering longitudinal study of Mexican Americans undertaken by Telles and Ortiz (2008). While they assiduously tracked the descendants of the Mexican American Study Project of the 1960s, the original study was based on respondents with Spanish surnames and may have missed some of the Mexican-origin population, particularly out-married women.
41. See Bean, Leach et al. 2011; Rumbaut et al. 2004. For a description of the IIMMLA study, see appendix A.
42. Kasinitz et al. 2008.
43. Grebler, Moore, and Guzmán 1970.
44. Bean and Stevens 2003.
45. Ruggles et al. 2010.
46. González Baker 1997.
47. Abu-Lughod 1999.
48. Bachmeier 2013a; Grebler, Moore, and Guzmán 1970.
49. Romo 1983.
50. Park, Myers, and Jiménez 2014.
51. Frey and Liaw 1999.
52. For example, Alba, Jiménez, and Marrow 2013; Telles and Ortiz 2008.
53. For example, see Nee and Holbrow 2013.

Chapter 2

1. Alba and Nee 2003; Brown and Bean 2006; Gordon 1964.
2. Alba and Nee 2003.
3. Bean and Stevens 2003.
4. Clemens and Sandefur 2014; Kasinitz et al. 2008; Lee and Bean 2010; Waters 2010.
5. Alba, Reitz, and Simon 2012; Aleinikoff and Weil 2006; Jachimowicz and O'Neil 2006.
6. Alba and Foner 2015.
7. Fischer and Hout 2006; Inglehart and Welzel 2005; Logan 2014.
8. Lipset 1990.
9. Eaton 1952; White 2002.
10. Glazer and Moynihan 1963; Jaynes and Williams 1989.
11. Gans 1992.
12. Bean et al. 2012.
13. Gans 1992.
14. For example, see Merton 1957; Portes 1999; Ritzer 2011, 1–3.
15. Alba and Nee 2003.
16. Kivisto and Faist 2010.
17. Park and Burgess 1969, 735.
18. Warner and Srole 1945.
19. Gordon 1964.
20. Alba and Nee 2003.
21. Alba and Foner 2014.
22. Glazer and Moynihan 1963.
23. Sanders and Nee 1987.
24. Portes 1999; Portes and Zhou 1993; Zhou and Bankston 1998.
25. Jiménez and Horowitz 2013; Lareau 2011.
26. Domínguez 2011; Nee and Holbrow 2013; Zhou 2009.
27. Lee and Zhou 2013.
28. Domínguez 2011.
29. Fiske and Markus 2012; Lamont 2000.
30. Bean, Leach et al. 2011; Nee and Holbrow 2013.
31. Abrego 2014; Dreby 2010; Hondagneu-Sotelo 1994.
32. Glazer and Moynihan 1963; Portes and Rumbaut 2001; Portes and Zhou 1993.
33. Waters and Kasinitz 2013.
34. Merle Franke, personal communication to authors 2012.
35. Lee and Bean 2010.
36. Alba 1990; Waters 1990.
37. Massey 2013; Telles and Ortiz 2008.
38. For example, see Perez and Hirschman 2009.
39. Lee and Bean 2010.
40. Gans 1992.
41. Hirschman, Kasinitz, and DeWind 1999; Portes and Rumbaut 2001.
42. Portes and Zhou 1993.
43. Portes, Fernández-Kelly, and Haller 2005.

44. Alba, Jiménez, and Marrow 2013; Bean and Stevens 2003; Kasinitz et al. 2008; Smith 2014.
45. Bean and Stevens 2003; Brown and Bean 2006; Perlmann and Waldinger 1997; Waldinger, Lim, and Cort 2007.
46. Terriquez 2014.
47. Brown and Bean 2006.
48. Leach and Bean 2008.
49. Terriquez 2014. See also Congressional Budget Office 2011; Esping-Andersen 2007; Stiglitz 2012.
50. Hagan, Hernández-León, and Demonsant 2015.
51. Waldinger, Lim, and Cort 2007.
52. For an exception, see Bean et al. 2012.
53. Papademetriou 2006.
54. Fix 2007.
55. Fokkema and de Haas 2011; Kymlicka 1995; Montserrat and Rex 2010.
56. Vertovec and Wessendorf 2010.
57. Bean et al. 2012.
58. Brubaker 2004.
59. Fischer and Hout 2006; Inglehart and Welzel 2005.
60. Fiske 2013; Swencionis and Fiske 2013.
61. Lesthaeghe 2010; van de Kaa 2001.
62. Inglehart 1997.
63. Ritzer 2011.
64. Kymlicka 1995; Parekh 2006; Soysal 1994.
65. Modood 2007; Reitz et al. 2009; Wright and Bloemraad 2012.
66. For example, Telles and Ortiz 2008.
67. Ibid., 264 (emphasis added).
68. Hondagneu-Sotelo 1994; Waldinger 2013.
69. Hochschild and Mollenkopf 2009.
70. Marshall 1950.
71. Joppke 2010.
72. Brubaker 1992.
73. Koopmans et al. 2005.
74. See Nee and Holbrow 2013.
75. Ngai 2004.
76. Chácon 2012; Golash-Boza and Hondagneu-Sotelo 2013.
77. Brettell and Nibbs 2011; Chávez 2008.
78. Bosniak 2006.
79. Massey and Pren 2012a.
80. Marrow 2011; Massey and Sánchez R. 2010; Yoshikawa 2011.
81. Chauvin and Garcés-Mascareñas 2012; Marrow 2011.
82. Motomura 2014.
83. Coutin 2003; Menjívar 2000.
84. Motomura 2014.
85. Chauvin and Garcés-Mascareñas 2012.
86. Chacón 2012; Motomura 2014.
87. Foner and Lucassen 2012; Mize and Peña Delgado 2012.
88. Massey et al. 1987.
89. See Massey 2013; Massey and Pren 2012a.

90. Menjívar 2006; Mize and Peña Delgado 2012.
91. Motomura 2006.
92. Fischer and Hout 2006; Inglehart and Welzel 2005; Luhmann 1998.
93. Bean et al. 2012; Waters 1990.
94. Hirschman 2001, 318.
95. Bean and Stevens 2003; Jiménez 2010; Kasinitz et al. 2008; Telles and Ortiz 2008.
96. Alba and Nee 2003.
97. Fokkema and de Haas 2011; Kymlicka 1995; Montserrat and Rex 2010.
98. Modood 2007; Reitz et al. 2009; Wright and Bloemraad 2012.
99. Kymlicka 1995; Parekh 2006; Soysal 1994.
100. Bean and Stevens 2003; Waters 1990.
101. Massey 1985.
102. Logan, Zhang, and Alba 2002; Murdie and Ghosh 2010.
103. Logan, Zhang, and Alba 2002.
104. Ramakrishnan 2013.
105. Hochschild and Mollenkopf 2009.
106. Other aspects of political integration encompass everything from the mere presence of international migrants within a polity to their participation in voting (Andersen and Cohen 2005; Hero and Wolbrecht 2005; Hochschild and Mollenkopf 2009; Ramakrishnan and Bloemraad 2008). A common research focus often involves gauging active involvement in electoral politics and coalitions (Bloemraad, Korteweg, and Yurdakul 2008; Browning, Marshall, and Tabb 1984; Jones-Correa 2005). Also, the nature and form of immigrant political engagement in destination countries can clearly change over time, across the life course, and across generations (Haller and Landolt 2005; Hollifield 2004; Portes, Escobar, and Arana 2008). Political incorporation thus may often connect ambiguously with other dimensions and facets of incorporation. Both economically successful and economically marginal immigrant groups may see political mobilization as important to their futures—or not. And political engagement is sometimes cause and sometimes effect of trends in other dimensions in the incorporation process (Bloemraad, Korteweg, and Yurdakul 2008; Bean, Leach et al. 2011).
107. Entzinger 2000; Hammar 1985; Koopmans et al. 2005; Meuleman 2009; Mitchell and Russell 1996; Penninx et al. 2004; Rex 1997; Soysal 1994.
108. Bean et al. 2012. Inclusionary tendencies are also likely to be more characteristic of global cities and other very large metropolitan areas, which tend to exhibit more differentiated structures and more opportunities for immigrants, of both formal and informal varieties (Kloosterman, Van Der Leun, and Rath 1999; Portes and Sassen-Koob 1987; Sassen 1991, 2000). Such cities also tend to attract greater numbers (absolutely and relatively) of both high- and less-skilled immigrants (Price and Benton-Short 2008). In contrast to inclusionary places with their more differentiated opportunity structures and diverse pathways of mobility, noninclusionary places are characterized by more consolidated structures (Simmel 1923). That is, they are likely to show fewer independent dimensions of differentiation with their structures allowing fewer separate paths to opportunity and mobility (Blau 1977, 1994; Blau and Schwartz 1984).

109. Hansen 2008.
110. Goodman 2010; Herzog-Punzenberger 2003. One reason immigrant groups are more likely to fare well in multidimensional inclusionary places is that separate groups can more readily find and take advantage of the particular activities and niches most suited to their strengths. Similarly, a given group might fare differently in different places. By contrast, in exclusionary places all immigrant groups might be expected to fare poorly, and a given group to fare equally poorly across cities. Gary Freeman (2004) observes that Austria, Germany, and Switzerland have often displayed immigrant-restrictive (or exclusive) orientations in almost all domains (state, market, and culture) of integration, with generosity only in welfare, and that only because the state initially expected such support to be temporary. By contrast, the domains of integration for more inclusive places involve different kinds of support for immigrants (that is, more inclusionary places show different ways of being favorable toward immigrants).
111. Bean et al. 2012.
112. Joppke 2005, 32.
113. Waldinger 2013, 354.
114. Glazer 1993.
115. Portes and Rumbaut 2001; Portes and Zhou 1993.
116. Lee and Bean 2010; Portes and Vickstrom 2011.
117. Portes and Rumbaut 2001.
118. Massey 1999, 2014.

Chapter 3

1. Alba and Nee 2003; Bean and Stevens 2003; Grebler, Moore, and Guzmán 1970; Jiménez 2010; Telles and Ortiz 2008. Edward Telles and Vilma Ortiz (2008) note that three generations should be sufficient for integration in a normative sense. That is, if full integration were to take longer than three generations, this alone would raise questions, at least from a public policy point of view, about why integration was such a drawn-out process. From the standpoint of newcomers, if integration is that slow, then perhaps it is not appropriate to view it as integration. However, this perspective marks a departure from classic assimilation theorists, especially Lloyd Warner and Leo Srole (1945), who saw three generations as the minimum for full integration.

2. Immigration researchers sometimes base conclusions about immigrant integration on information only on immigrants, for example, see Borjas 1985; Chiswick 1978; Gubernskaya, Bean, and Van Hook 2013. However, this does not assess a group's full integration experience but rather focuses only on what happens in the first generation, a topic of importance in its own right but one that cannot gauge the entirety of the process, except, of course, in the unlikely event that complete integration takes place in one generation. Although second-generation studies involve persons whose formative and adult years are spent in the host society, they are often similarly incomplete.

3. Portes and Rumbaut 2001; Kasinitz et al. 2008. Portes and Rumbaut also examine Mexican second-generation youth, as we elaborate later in this chapter. Mexicans are not one of the new immigrant groups but rather a

group with a long history of migration and one that needs more than two generations of study.

4. Telles and Ortiz 2008; Bachmeier et al. 2014.
5. Blumberg 1991; Hondagneu-Sotelo 1994.
6. That similar outcomes seem to be assumed by these theoretical perspectives is testified to by the fact that none of the recent major three-generation assessments of Mexican American integration examine men and women separately or present theoretical hypotheses about possible gender differences. Jiménez 2010; Terriquez 2014; Telles and Ortiz 2008.
7. Alba and Islam 2009; Duncan and Trejo 2011a, 2011b, 2011c.
8. Brown 2007.
9. Grebler, Moore, and Guzmán 1970; Telles and Ortiz 2008.
10. Alba, Jiménez, and Marrow 2013.
11. Jiménez 2010.
12. Ibid., 259.
13. Alba et al. 2011.
14. Kao, Vaquera, and Goyette 2013.
15. Adams, Coltrane, and Parke 2007; Coltrane and Adams 2008; Gándara 1982; Gil and Vazquez 1996.
16. Menjivar 2002, Yoshikawa 2011.
17. Lamont 1992, 2000. Cultural repertoires thus involve what sociologists call constitutive aspects of culture, or culture that is integral to all things social in that "the diverse meanings and beliefs that individuals and groups adopt to interpret their life experiences . . . are in turn consequential in their social lives" (Binder et al. 2008, 10). Relatively enduring cultural repertoires and scripts may emerge out of previous collective experiences and influence subsequent individual and group behaviors (Lamont 2000; Sewell 1992; Swidler 1986; Wuthnow 1987). Such collective experiences may include the immigration experience itself, as Max Weber noted in defining "ethnic groups" as those that "entertain a subjective belief in their common descent because of similarities of physical type or of customs, or both, or *because of memories of . . . migration*" (1968, 389, emphasis added).
18. Swidler 2000.
19. Kao and Tienda 1995.
20. Hsin and Xie 2014, 8419.
21. Massey and Denton 1987; Portes and Bach 1985.
22. Bean and Stevens 2003; Chávez 2007; Dohan 2003; Fix and Passel 1994; Sánchez 1993.
23. Stark 1991b; Hernández-León 2008.
24. Kandel and Massey 2002.
25. Massey et al. 1998; Stark 1991a; Stark and Taylor 1989.
26. Bachmeier and Bean 2011; Kandel and Massey 2002; Ovink 2014.
27. Waldinger 2001; Waldinger and Lichter 2003. Research evidence also suggests that Mexican migrant cultural repertoires support a strong drive among women to seek employment, even though their aggregate levels of employment fall below those for men (Bean et al. 2012). This evidence comes from studies of the behavior of Mexican immigrant women in regard to welfare receipt and work. Using data from the Survey of Income and Program

Participation (SIPP), Van Hook and Bean (2009) found that although Mexican women were more likely than white women to receive welfare, this resulted from their being poorer—that is, once controls for socioeconomic status were introduced, Mexican women were actually less likely to receive welfare than other white women. More significantly, among those who were receiving welfare, Mexican women were more likely to leave welfare to work than were white women and were more likely to do so after a shorter period of time. And most significant of all, this tendency to leave welfare for work sooner was most pronounced among Mexican women living in states paying higher welfare benefits compared with those living in states paying lower benefits, suggesting that welfare for these women was used more as a form of support to survive unemployment spells than as an incentive not to work. In short, even among Mexican immigrant women, the patterns of welfare receipt support the idea that a strong tendency to work to provide for family (a social insurance cultural repertoire) overrides other possible motives for welfare utilization.

28. Iceland 2013; Martin 2009.
29. Fiske and Markus 2012.
30. Stephens, Fryberg, and Markus 2012, 88.
31. Ibid.
32. Haller et al. 2011; Telles and Ortiz 2008.
33. Mayer 2009.
34. Sampson and Laub 2005.
35. Dreby 2010; Feliciano and Rumbaut 2005; Hondagneu-Sotelo 1994; Smith 2006; Vasquez 2014.
36. Bean, Berg, and Van Hook 1996.
37. Glick and Van Hook 2002.
38. Kandel and Kao 2001.
39. Fuligni and Pedersen 2002; Suárez-Orozco and Suárez-Orozco 1995.
40. Bachmeier and Bean 2011.
41. Tafoya-Estrada 2004; Smith 2002.
42. Dumka et al. 2009; Segura 1994; Tafoya-Estrada 2004; Zhou and Bankston 1998, 2001.
43. Bachmeier and Bean 2011.
44. Bean, Bachmeier, and Brown 2014.
45. DiPrete and Buchmann 2013, 2014.
46. Sidanius 1999.
47. Dreby 2010; Fuligni 1998; Fuligni and Pedersen 2002; Greenfield et al. 2003; Hardaway and Fuligni 2006; Roche, Ghazarian, and Fernandez-Esquer 2012.
48. Agius Vallejo 2012; Sánchez 1993.
49. Interestingly, this possibility runs counter to the usual expectation that having a parent or grandparents born in the United States is a key family factor in fostering integration. Our family ethnic density hypothesis implies that in the Mexican case common immigration background will be the stronger factor. In fact, the possibility that family nativity heterogeneity may foster greater integration is enshrined in the way immigration researchers often "decimal-code" generational combinations. For example, the second generation is often defined as persons with at least one foreign-born parent, with further distinctions sometimes being drawn between those with two foreign-born parents

often designated as the 2.0 generation, and those with one foreign-born parent often coded as the 2.5 generation (Rumbaut 2004). The assumption, altogether reasonable, is that a child of immigrants with one U.S.-born parent is more "proximate" in myriad ways to American society and thus closer to the third generation than one without any U.S.-born parents. But this logic concentrates on the importance of the number of U.S.-born parents, not the importance of the number of Mexican-born parents or grandparents.

50. DiPrete and McManus 2000; Mayer 2009.
51. Allison, Long, and Krauze 1982; DiPrete and Eirich 2006.
52. Jiménez and FitzGerald 2007.
53. Ibid.
54. Alba and Nee 2003.
55. Jiménez and FitzGerald 2007.
56. For example, see Bachmeier and Bean 2011; Portes and Rumbaut 2001.
57. Jiménez and FitzGerald 2007, 342.
58. Taeuber and Taeuber 1967.
59. Telles and Ortiz 2008.
60. This definition is conceptual, not operational, so when working with actual data we have to take into account those who are the children of one first-generation parent and one second-generation parent, and so on, an issue we return to below.
61. Jiménez 2010; Lesthaeghe and Neidert 2006, 2009.
62. Smith 2003, 2005; Telles and Ortiz 2008.
63. Farley and Alba 2002; Grogger and Trejo 2002; McKeever and Klineberg 1999; Reed et al. 2005; Zsembik and Llanes 1996.
64. Bean et al. 1994; Keller and Tillman 2007; Wojtkiewicz and Donato 1995.
65. Boyd 2002; Chiswick and DebBurman 2003; Glick and White 2004; Kao and Tienda 1995; Ramakrishnan 2004.
66. Alba et al. 2011.
67. Duncan and Trejo 2011a, 2011c.
68. Alba and Islam 2009.
69. Bean and Stevens 2003; Duncan and Trejo 2011a, 2011b, 2011c; Mittelbach and Moore 1968; Rosenfeld 2002.
70. Alba 2006.
71. Richardson 1980.
72. Montejano 1987.
73. Mare and Chang 2006.
74. Black 1997; Montejano 1987.
75. Sánchez 1993.
76. Bachmeier 2013b.

Chapter 4

1. Bean and Stevens 2003.
2. Fix 2007.
3. Hout 2012.
4. Duncan, Hotz, and Trejo 2006.
5. Crosnoe 2006.

6. For a detailed explication of the approach, see Van Hook et al. 2015.
7. Yoshikawa 2011; Abrego and Gonzales 2010; Brabeck and Xu 2010; Potochnick and Perreira 2010; Ortega et al. 2009.
8. Massey and Gentsch 2014; Donato et al. 2008; Donato, Aguilera, and Wakabayashi 2005.
9. Bachmeier, Van Hook, and Bean 2014; Clark and King 2008.
10. Kossondji and Cobb-Clark 2002.
11. Borjas and Tienda 1993.
12. Rivera-Batiz 1999.
13. Massey 1987.
14. Donato and Massey 1993; Massey, Durand, and Malone 2002; Massey and Gelatt 2010; Massey and Gentsch 2011, 2014.
15. Donato and Massey 1993.
16. Massey and Gentsch 2014.
17. Hall, Greenman, and Farkas 2010.
18. Borjas and Tienda 1993; Kossondji and Cobb-Clark 2002; Rivera-Batiz 1999.
19. Donato and Massey 1993; Massey and Gentsch 2014; Hall, Greenman, and Farkas 2010.
20. Hall, Greenman, and Farkas 2010.
21. Massey et al. 1987; Durand, Massey, and Zenteno 2001.
22. Durand, Massey, and Capoferro 2005; Leach and Bean 2008.
23. Massey, Rugh, and Pren 2010.
24. Cerruti and Massey 2004.
25. Martin 2009.
26. Massey, Durand, and Malone 2002.
27. Hall, Greenman, and Farkas 2010.
28. Van Hook et al. 2015.
29. Batalova et al. 2014; Van Hook et al. 2015.
30. Oropesa and Landale 2009.
31. While educational attainment in Mexico cannot possibly be endogenous to migrants' legal status in the United States, that does not mean that the two are unrelated to one another. For example, if unauthorized migrants are more likely to originate in less developed areas in Mexico where there are fewer education opportunities, then the association between educational attainment and earnings among 1.0 generation immigrants will in part be related to factors that cannot be measured in our data. Nevertheless, these unmeasured variables will most likely be captured in educational attainment, resulting in greater certainty that net legal status differences in earnings among 1.0 generation immigrants derive from legal status per se. By contrast, in theory the association between legal status, educational attainment, and earnings is more complex among members of the 1.5 generation, whose school continuation decisions are likely to be determined, at least in part, by their legal status. Bean, Leach et al. 2011; Gonzales 2011; Terriquez 2014. Thus net earnings differences among members of the unauthorized 1.5 generation, relative to their legally resident or naturalized counterparts, probably derive from legal status effects on education. In later chapters, we analyze data from three generations to help determine which theoretical perspectives best portray the integration experience of Mexican Americans.

32. Gonzales and Chavez 2012; Dreby 2012; Gonzalez 2011; Suárez-Orozco et al. 2011; Yoshikawa 2011.
33. Passel and Cohn 2011.
34. King et al. 2010; Passel and Cohn 2011.
35. Passel and Cohn 2009.
36. Hochschild and Mollenkopf 2009.
37. Bean et al. 2012; Nee and Holbrow 2013.
38. Cornelius 1992; Portes and Bach 1985; Massey, Durand, and Malone 2002.
39. Roberts 1995.
40. Menjívar 2006; Roberts, Frank, and Lozano-Ascencio 1999.
41. Chávez 1988.
42. Curiel 2004; Glick 2010; Hondagneu-Sotelo 1994.
43. Bean and Stevens 2003; Brown 2007; Nee and Holbrow 2013.
44. Sisk 2013.
45. Bean et al. 2012; Rumbaut et al. 2004.
46. Council on Foreign Relations 2009.
47. Bean, Leach et al. 2011.
48. Chávez 1988; Massey et al. 1987.
49. Bean, Leach et al. 2011.
50. Included in this category are a small number of parents whose children did not respond to the questions about migration status at time of entry and interview. Because their profiles of characteristics were virtually identical by gender with those of unauthorized entrants who remained unauthorized, we included them in that category.
51. While the term *second-generation* typically refers to persons born in the United States with at least one immigrant parent, the IIMMLA sample also includes immigrants who arrived in the United States as children before the age of fifteen. Very few of these respondents were themselves unauthorized; they were not numerous enough to affect the research results.
52. None of the education levels of those whose parents fell in these five classes containing mothers who were legal from the start or who became legal are statistically different from one another.
53. Menjivar 2000.
54. Yoshikawa 2011.
55. Vasquez 2011; Hondagneu-Sotelo 1994.

Chapter 5

1. Binder and Woodruff 2002; Marteleto, Gelber, and Hubert 2012.
2. For example, looking at males in the 1.5 generation (those coming to the country before the age of fifteen), the average number of years of schooling completed is 12.4 years (see figure 5.1). This is 2.8 years more than Mexican males who arrived after the age of fourteen, reflecting a structural difference between the Mexican and U.S. school systems. In the United States, enrollment in school is required until the age of sixteen, and at no cost, while in Mexico universal free public education has still not been fully adopted (Escobar Latapí et al. 2013). Thus, in Mexico, in 2000 (four years before the year of the IIMMLA survey), the average years of schooling completed among males was 7.5 years, whereas in the United States it was 13.2, a "structural" deficit of

5.7 years (Barro and Lee 2013). Subtracting this from the years of schooling for 1.5 generation males gives 6.7 years. That is, except for this structural advantage of attending school in the United States, 1.5 generation males would actually fall below the educational attainment of males living in Mexico. Turning to women, we find much the same pattern, only in more pronounced form, at least compared with men. For example, in the 1.5 generation, Mexican-origin women complete an average of 12.2 years of schooling, a level less than a year different from women in Mexico when adjusted for the structural difference in the school systems. After an adjustment for this, the level would be 6.0 years, below that of women in Mexico in 2004. This is again not surprising since more highly educated persons from Mexico would be less likely to migrate.

3. In those analyses in which we distinguish the 3.0 and the 3.5 generations, we exclude the 3.25 generation (those with three Mexican-born grandparents), because fewer than ten cases fall into this category. We also exclude the 3.75 generation (those with only one Mexican-born grandparent and three U.S.-born grandparents) because this group scarcely qualifies as having a substantial degree of Mexican-family ethnic density.

4. See DiPrete and Buchmann 2014.

5. Hout 2012; Morgan and Gelbgiser 2014.

6. See Carnavale, Rose and Cheah 2011 for a fuller explanation of the range of earnings potential by education level, race, and gender.

7. On the first generation, see Hagan, Hernández-León, and Demonsant 2015; on the second, Perlmann and Waldinger 1997; Waldinger, Lim, and Cort 2007.

8. Everett et al. 2011; Buchmann and DiPrete 2006.

9. Bloome 2014; Mare 2011.

10. Frisbie 1975; Glick and Van Hook 1998; Portes 1974.

11. Portes 1974.

12. Motomura 2014; *Plyler v. Doe* 1982.

13. Boyd 1989; Donato et al. 2006; Gabaccia 1995; Hondagneu-Sotelo 1994; Pessar 1999.

14. Hagan 1998; Pessar 1999; Parrado and Flippen 2005.

15. Buchmann, DiPrete, and McDaniel 2008; Legewie and DiPrete 2012.

16. The numbers presented in figure 5.3 are based on OLS regression models (coefficients and standard errors available upon request). We regressed years of schooling on immigrant generation, which we score 1 to 5 for each of the generational groups spanning the 1.5 to the 3.5 generations. This variable is entered into the model as a linear term. We also include a dummy-coded variable indicating whether or not the respondent grew up with an unauthorized mother who never regularized her status, and we interact this indicator with the linear generation term. Because members of the 2.0 and 3.0 generations have especially high levels of education, we also include an indicator on which they are coded 1 and their "0.5" generation counterparts are all coded 0, in order to smooth out the lines presented in figure 5.3. Finally, the model also controls for age. The models were estimated separately among men and women using Stata, version 13. The years of schooling numbers presented in figure 5.3 are average predicted values for each generation and legal status background combination, holding other variables constant at their mean.

17. The third-only generation respondents in the IIMMLA survey all have parents born in the United States. None of these parents were queried about

their migration status because they were not migrants. Also, information on the migration status of grandparents was not collected in the survey. Thus we do not have individual-level data about the migration status of the grandparents of the third-only generation respondents, meaning we cannot identify which third-only generation individuals have unauthorized backgrounds in the sense that we apply that concept here. We can, however, estimate in the aggregate what the education levels of the third-only respondents would be were none of them to have unauthorized backgrounds among their grandparents. We do that here by assuming the third-only generation persons have unauthorized backgrounds in the same proportion as second-generation respondents, namely about 25 percent, and by assuming that the gender-specific penalty for such background remains the same in the third generation as in the second generation. Based on these assumptions, we then calculate new values for the education of the 3.0 and 3.5 generations, assuming, in effect, no unauthorized-background legacy effects. These values are then used for the third-generation persons for purposes of obtaining the graphed lines shown in figure 5.3 for those of "authorized backgrounds." For purposes of obtaining the graphed lines in figure 5.3 for those of "unauthorized backgrounds," the observed (that is, unadjusted) education values are used because these capture the penalizing effects of such background.

18. We refer to the estimated log earnings differentials as if they represented percentage earnings differences. Strictly speaking, however, log differentials closely approximate percentage differences only when the log differentials are on the order of 0.25 or less in absolute value. For larger differentials, the implied percentage difference can be calculated as $ec - 1$, where c is the log differential and e is Euler's number (that is, the base of natural logarithms).

19. Hagan, Hernández-León, and Demonsant 2015.

20. For example, see Duncan, Hotz, and Trejo 2006.

21. Duncan, Hotz, and Trejo 2006.

22. Bachmeier 2013b; Grebler, Moore, and Guzmán 1970; Montejano 1987.

23. That is, extra motivation to achieve in school may come from having more and stronger Mexican-born parental and grandparental ties, not fewer, thus providing more opportunities for reinforcement of cultural repertoires emphasizing the importance of working hard to achieve the purposes of parental or grandparental migration sacrifices. In other words, such ties foster stronger achievement motivation from its inception through the process of settlement in the country, providing more channels of communication about the significance of that experience, and its sacrifices, thus reinforcing the idea that working hard to make a better life in a new country is worth the effort.

Chapter 6

1. Sampson 2012.

2. Tiebout 1956.

3. Sampson 2012, 54.

4. Dietz 2002; Furstenberg and Hughes 1997; Harding et al. 2010; Kroneberg 2008; Pong and Hao 2007; Sampson, Morenoff, and Gannon-Rowley 2002; Tienda 1991.

5. Osypuk et al. 2009; Pong and Hao 2007; Portes and Zhou 1993.
6. Logan, Zhang, and Alba 2002; Li 2009.
7. Dear 2002.
8. Giuliano and Small 1991.
9. Garreau 1988; Kling, Olin, and Poster 1991.
10. Telles and Ortiz 2008, 167–68.
11. Rocco 1996; Sánchez 1993.
12. Leach and Bean 2008; Light 2006; Wright, Ellis, and Reibel 1997.
13. Forstall 1995; U.S. Bureau of the Census 2000a, 2010.
14. US2010 2013.
15. Pfeiffer 2012.
16. Park 1926.
17. Alba and Nee 2003; Iceland 2009; Massey 1985; Rosenbaum and Friedman 2007.
18. Sampson, Morenoff, and Earls 1999.
19. Alba and Nee 2003, 29; Massey 1985; Massey and Denton 1987; Vang 2012.
20. Briggs 2007; Britton 2011; Brown 2006; Peach 2005; Schnell and Harpaz 2005.
21. Guest and Weed 1976; Kantrowitz 1973; Logan, Zhang, and Alba 2002; Murdie and Ghosh 2010; Vang 2012.
22. Logan et al. 2002; Zelinsky and Lee 1998.
23. Allen and Turner 1996.
24. Logan, Zhang, and Alba 2002.
25. Guest and Weed 1976; Jonassen 1949; Lieberson 1963; White and Glick 1999.
26. Courgeau 1985; Kulu and Milewski 2007; Michielin and Mulder 2008; Rabe and Taylor 2009.
27. Charles 2006; Humphreys and Whitelaw 1979; see Clark 1989 for a summary of debate on this issue.
28. Agius Vallejo and Lee 2009; Brown 2007; de Haas 2006; Maloutas 2004; Mansoor and Quillin 2006.
29. Bolt, Özüekren, and Phillips 2010; Huff 1986.
30. Farley and Frey 1994; Sharp and Iceland 2013; South and Crowder 1997.
31. Breton 1964; Gans 1982; Li 2009; Zhou 2011.
32. Charles 2006; Nguyen 2004.
33. White and Glick 2009; Wright, Ellis, and Parks 2005; Yu and Myers 2007.
34. Ellis, Wright, and Parks 2004.
35. Brown 2007.
36. Yu and Myers 2007.
37. Kim and White 2010.
38. Wright, Ellis, and Parks 2005.
39. Alba and Nee 2003; Iceland and Wilkes 2006; Massey and Mullan 1984.
40. Logan, Stults, and Farley 2004; Ross and Turner 2005; Yinger 1995.
41. South, Crowder, and Chavez 2005a.
42. Allen 2002; Flippen 2004; Kim and White 2010; Krivo and Kaufman 2004; Telles and Ortiz 2008.
43. Alba et al. 2014; Denton and Massey 1991; Hwang and Murdock 1998; Massey 1979; Massey and Denton 1991; South, Crowder, and Chavez 2005b.
44. Crowder, Hall, and Tolnay 2011.
45. Alba, Logan, and Stults 2000.
46. Massey and Mullan 1984.

47. Charles 2000.
48. Hipp and Boessen 2012.
49. Massey and Denton 1989; Wilkes and Iceland 2004, 29.
50. Clark, Deurloo, and Dieleman 2000; McConnell 2013; Myers and Lee 1996; Solari and Mare 2012.
51. Allen and Turner 2006.
52. Beveridge and Weber 2003; Marcelli 2004.
53. Reibel and Regelson 2007.
54. Bonvalet, Carpenter, and White 1995.
55. Brown 2007.
56. Wilkes and Iceland 2004.
57. Telles and Ortiz 2008.
58. Los Angeles Almanac 2014.
59. For example, Alba and Logan 1993; Friedman and Rosenbaum 2007; Logan, Zhang, and Alba 2002.
60. Rapino and Fields 2013.
61. Mayer and Pence 2008; Rugh and Massey 2010.

Chapter 7

1. Gordon 1964; Park and Burgess 1921; Thomas and Znaniecki 1927; Warner and Srole 1945.
2. Bean and Stevens 2003; Waters 1990.
3. Alba and Nee 2003.
4. Dobbin 2004.
5. Brubaker 2004.
6. Marsden 2012; Taylor 2014.
7. King 1997.
8. Rumbaut, Massey, and Bean 2006.
9. Ibid., 457.
10. Noam and Brown 2013.
11. Ibid.
12. FitzGerald 2009.
13. Duncan and Trejo 2007.

Chapter 8

1. Bean, Bachmeier et al. 2011; Holzer 2011.
2. Passel, Cohn, and Gonzalez Barrera 2012; U.S. Department of Homeland Security 2011.
3. Massey and Taylor 2004.
4. U.S. Department of Commerce 2012.
5. Castles and Miller 2009; Czaika and de Haas 2014; Friedman 2005; Hutton and Giddens 2000; Massey and Taylor 2004.
6. Bean, Bachmeier, Brown et al. 2014.
7. Passel, Cohn, and Gonzalez-Barrera 2012.
8. Bachmeier et al. 2011.

9. Massey 2013.
10. Calavita 1992; Woodrow-Lafield 2014.
11. Martin 2004; Massey 2013.
12. Cerruti and Massey 2004; Fragomen and Del Rey 1979.
13. Massey and Pren 2012b; Zolberg 2006.
14. Bean and Stevens 2003; Martin 2011; Massey and Pren 2012a.
15. Martin 2011.
16. Zolberg 2006. While the broad preference categories that had existed under the McCarran-Walter Act had privileged highly skilled immigrants, the Hart-Celler Act emphasized family reunification criteria as the fundamental bases for immigrant entry. Four of the top five preference categories gave priority to the reunification of families and amounted to nearly three-fourths of the slots (Zolberg 2006). In addition, the law added parents of adult U.S. citizens to the list of immigrants not subject to numerical limitations (Keely 1971). But family-based entries had now to occur within the framework of overall limits. Notably, the new Western Hemisphere cap of 120,000 was less than the average annual migration then occurring from the region. A ceiling of 120,000 visas per year was placed on the total number of legal immigration admissions, which included legal migrants from Mexico.
17. Charles Bartlett, "House Balky on Immigration Issue," *Los Angeles Times,* August 24, 1965, A5; United Press International, "Johnson Stays Silent on Hemisphere Immigrants," *Los Angeles Times,* September 13, 1965, 14; Zolberg 2006.
18. Keely 1971; Ueda 1998.
19. Vernez 1993.
20. Bean, Vernez, and Keely 1989; Passel and Woodrow 1984.
21. Martin 2011.
22. Massey 2014.
23. Garip 2012.
24. Harris and Todaro 1970.
25. Todaro and Maruszko 1987.
26. Eschbach, Hagan, and Bailey 1999.
27. Grasmuck and Pessar 1991; Hagan 1994; Hondagneu-Sotelo 1994.
28. Bean, Edmonston, and Passel 1990; Massey and Espinosa 1997.
29. Garip 2012, 409.
30. For example, Stark 1991a, 1991b; Taylor et al. 1997.
31. Taylor et al. 1997.
32. Roberts and Escobar Latapi 1997; but see Fussell and Massey 2004 for an alternative argument.
33. Massey 1999; Massey et al. 1998.
34. Lozano-Ascencio 1993; Taylor et al. 1997.
35. Brown 2007; Soehl and Waldinger 2012.
36. Chávez 1988; Massey et al. 1987.
37. Roberts 1995, p. 44.
38. Garip 2012.
39. Massey and Espinosa 1997.
40. Garip 2012, 409.
41. Bankston 2014.
42. Bachmeier 2013a; Light 2006; Massey et al. 1987; Reichert 1981.

43. Massey et al. 1993; Massey et al. 1998, 45.
44. Sassen 1995.
45. Granovetter 1985, 1995; Granovetter and Swedberg 1992.
46. Massey and Espinosa 1997.
47. Garip 2012, 409.
48. Averitt 1968; Massey et al. 1998; Piore 1979; Tolbert, Horan, and Beck 1980.
49. Piore 1979.
50. Ibid.; Massey and Espinosa 1997.
51. Massey and Espinosa 1997.
52. Furtado 1964; Wallerstein 1983.
53. Sassen 1988, 1991; Waldinger 1996.
54. Massey and Taylor 2004.
55. Yang 1995.
56. Castles and Miller 1998.
57. Massey and Espinosa 1997.
58. Hernández-León 2008.
59. Escobar Latapí, Bean, and Weintraub 1999; Weintraub 2010.
60. Hollifield 2000; Zolberg 1999.
61. Martin 2004.
62. Garip 2012.
63. Massey and Taylor 2004.
64. Bachmeier and Bean 2011.
65. Hernández-León 2008.
66. U.S. Department of Commerce 2010a, 2010b.
67. Bean and Stevens 2003.
68. U.S. Bureau of Labor Statistics 2011.
69. Bean et al. 2012; Federal Reserve Bank of Atlanta 2012; U.S. Bureau of Labor Statistics 2012.
70. Valletta and Bengali 2013.
71. Van Hook et al. 2014.
72. Goldin and Katz 2008.
73. For an overview, see Duncan and Murnane 2011.
74. Current Population Survey 2010; Minnesota Population Center 2011.
75. Ibid.
76. U.S. Department of Health and Human Services 2010.
77. Bean et al. 2012.
78. Myers 2013.
79. Bean, Bachmeier, and Brown 2014.
80. Alba 2009.
81. Myers 2007.
82. Bean et al. 2012.
83. Creticos and Sohnen 2013.
84. Freeman 2007.
85. Bean, Bachmeier, and Brown 2014.
86. Blank 2009.
87. Bean, Bachmeier, and Brown 2014.
88. Ibid.
89. Massey 2013.

 90. Chávez 1988.
 91. U.S. Bureau of the Census 2013.
 92. National Research Council 2011.
 93. Massey 1999.
 94. For reviews, see Bean, Bachmeier, and Brown 2013; Bean, Lowell, and Taylor 1988; Card and Lewis 2007; Holzer 2011; Ottaviano, Peri, and Wright 2013.
 95. Garip 2012.
 96. See, for example, Hanson and McIntosh 2010; National Research Council 2011.
 97. Also see Massey 2013.
 98. Massey, Durand, and Malone 2002; Massey and Pren 2012a.
 99. Bean and Lowell 2007; Bean, Vernez, and Keely 1989.
100. Villarreal and Hamilton 2012.
101. See, for example, see Portes and Bach 1985; Portes and Rumbaut 2006.
102. Bean et al. 2014; Bean, Bachmeier et al. 2011; Hernández-León 2008; Telles, Sawyer, and Rivera-Salgado 2011.
103. Bachmeier and Bean 2011; Dohan 2003; Kandel and Massey 2002.
104. Gonzales and Chavez 2012; Jones-Correa and de Graauw 2013.
105. Douglas and Sáenz 2013; Ngai 2004.
106. Fix 2010; Massey and Pren 2012a, 2012b.

Chapter 9

 1. Bean and Bell-Rose 1999.
 2. Lee and Bean 2004.
 3. Telles and Ortiz 2008.
 4. Brand and Xie 2010; Card 1999; Goldin and Katz 2008.
 5. Gans 1992.
 6. Abrego 2006; Gonzales 2011; Pérez 2012.
 7. Suárez-Orozco et al. 2011.
 8. Chávez 1988.
 9. García 2014.
10. Hondagneu-Sotelo 2001; Menjívar 2000.
11. Bachmeier and Bean 2011; Van Hook and Bean 2009.
12. Orrenius and Zavodny 2015.
13. Hall, Greenman, and Farkas 2010.
14. Bachmeier and Bean 2011.
15. Tran, Brown, and Schneider 2012.
16. Crosnoe 2005.
17. Bailey and Dynarski 2011; DiPrete and Buchmann 2014.
18. Morgan and Gelbgiser 2014.
19. Bean, Swicegood, and Berg 2000.
20. Goldin 2014.
21. For example, Bean et al. 2012; and Bean, Bachmeier, and Brown 2014.
22. Bean et al. 2012.
23. Alba 2009.
24. Coleman 2006.
25. Stiglitz 2012.
26. Passel, Cohn, and Gonzalez-Barrera 2013.

27. Passel, Cohn, and Gonzalez-Barrera 2012.
28. Van Hook et al. 2014.
29. Bachmeier et al. 2011; Johnson and Trujillo 2011; U.S. Department of State 2011.
30. Julian and Kominski 2011; Meara, Richards, and Cutler 2008.
31. Fischer and Hout 2006.
32. Freeman 2007; Dean Starkman, "Construction Jobs Up in Most Metro Areas," *Los Angeles Times*, December 31, 2014, B3; Neil Irwin, "Where Have All the Truckers Gone?," *New York Times*, August 8, 2014, BU6.
33. Passel, Cohn, and Rohan 2014.
34. Bean and Lowell 2005.
35. Guillermoprieto 2015.

Appendices

1. Field Research Corporation 2004.
2. For more information on the data set, see Bean, Leach et al. 2011; Brown 2007; Rumbaut et al. 2004.
3. See Brown 2006.
4. Brown 2006.
5. Esser 2006; Rumbaut, Massey, and Bean 2006.
6. Alba and Islam 2009; Duncan and Trejo 2011a, 2011b, 2011c.
7. Duncan and Trejo 2011a, 2011b, 2011c.
8. Ruggles et al. 2010.
9. Rowland 2008.
10. Ruggles et al. 2010.
11. Human Mortality Database 2013.
12. Ruggles et al. 2010
13. Bachmeier 2013b.
14. Mare 1997.
15. Telles and Ortiz 2008.
16. Duncan and Trejo 2011a, 2011b, 2011c.
17. Alba 2006; Alba, Jimenez, and Marrow 2013.
18. Clogg 1995; Muthén 2001b.
19. Muthén 2001a; Wagmiller et al. 2006.
20. Council on Foreign Relations 2009.
21. For example, see Muthén 2002; Wagmiller et al. 2006.
22. Raftery 1995.
23. McCutcheon 1996; Muthén and Muthén 2000.

═ References ═

Abrego, Leisy J. 2006. "'I Can't Go to College Because I Don't Have Papers': Incorporation Patterns of Latino Undocumented Youth." *Latino Studies* 4(3): 212–31.

———. 2014. *Sacrificing Families: Navigating Laws, Labor, and Love Across Borders.* Stanford, Calif.: Stanford University Press.

Abrego, Leisy J., and Roberto G. Gonzales. 2010. "Blocked Paths, Uncertain Futures: The Postsecondary Education and Labor Market Prospects of Undocumented Youth." *Journal of Education for Students Placed at Risk* 15(1): 144–57.

Abu-Lughod, Janet. 1999. *New York, Chicago, Los Angeles: America's Global Cities.* Minneapolis: University of Minnesota Press.

Adams, Michele, Scott Coltrane, and Ross D. Parke. 2007. "Cross-ethnic Applicability of the Gender-Based Attitudes Towards Marriage and Child Rearing Scales." *Sex Roles* 56(5–6): 325–39.

Agius Vallejo, Jody. 2012. *Barrios to Burbs: The Making of the Mexican American Middle Class.* Stanford, Calif.: Stanford University Press.

Agius Vallejo, Jody, and Jennifer Lee. 2009. "Brown Picket Fences: The Immigrant Narrative and 'Giving Back' among the Mexican Middle-Class." *Ethnicities* 9(1): 5–31.

Alba, Richard D. 1990. *Ethnic Identity: The Transformation of White America.* New Haven, Conn.: Yale University Press.

———. 2006. "Mexican Americans and the American Dream." *Perspectives on Politics* 4(2): 289–96.

———. 2009. *Blurring the Color Line: The New Chance for a More Integrated America.* Cambridge, Mass.: Harvard University Press.

Alba, Richard, Dalia Abdel-Hady, Tariqul Islam, and Karen Marotz. 2011. "Downward Assimilation and Mexican Americans: An Examination of Intergenerational Advance and Stagnation in Educational Attainment." In *The Next Generation: Immigrant Youth in a Comparative Perspective,* edited by R. Alba and M. C. Waters. New York: New York University Press.

Alba, Richard, Glenn Deane, Nancy A. Denton, Ilir Disha, Brian McKenzie, and Jeffrey Napierala. 2014. "The Role of Immigrant Enclaves for Latino Residential Inequalities." *Journal of Ethnic and Migration Studies* 40(1): 1–20.

Alba, Richard, and Nancy Foner. 2014. "Comparing Immigrant Integration in North America and Western Europe: How Much Do the Grand Narratives Tell Us?" *International Migration Review* 48(Fall): 263–91.

————. 2015. *Strangers No More: Immigration and the Challenges of Integration in North America and Western Europe.* Princeton, N.J.: Princeton University Press.

Alba, Richard, and Tariqul Islam. 2009. "The Case of the Disappearing Mexican Americans: An Ethnic-Identity Mystery." *Population Research and Policy Review* 28(2): 109–21.

Alba, Richard, Tomás R. Jiménez, and Helen B. Marrow. 2013. "Mexican Americans as a Paradigm for Contemporary Intra-Group Heterogeneity." *Ethnic and Racial Studies* 37(3): 446–66.

Alba, Richard D., and John R. Logan. 1993. "Minority Proximity to Whites in Suburbs: An Individual-Level Analysis of Segregation." *American Journal of Sociology* 98(6): 1388–427.

Alba, Richard D., John R. Logan, and Brian J. Stults. 2000. "The Changing Neighborhood Contexts of the Immigrant Metropolis." *Social Forces* 79(2): 587–621.

Alba, Richard D., and Victor Nee. 2003. *Remaking the American Mainstream: Assimilation and the New Immigration.* Cambridge, Mass.: Harvard University Press.

Alba, Richard, Jeffrey G. Reitz, and Patrick Simon. 2012. "National Conceptions of Assimilation, Integration, and Cohesion." In *The Changing Face of World Cities: Young Adult Children of Immigrants in Europe and the United States,* edited by M. Crul and J. Mollenkopf. New York: Russell Sage Foundation Press.

Alba, Richard, and Roxane Silberman. 2002. "Decolonization Immigrations and the Social Origins of the Second Generation: The Case of North Africans in France." *International Migration Review* 36(4): 1169–93.

Aleinikoff, T. Alexander, and Patrick Weil. 2006. "Building Successful Urban Policy in the New Era of Migration." In *Europe and Its Immigrants in the 21st Century: A New Deal or a Continuing Dialogue of the Deaf?* edited by Demetrios G. Papademetriou. Washington: Migration Policy Institute.

Alexander, Michelle. 2012. *The New Jim Crow: Mass Incarceration in the Age of Colorblindness.* Rev. ed. New York: The New Press.

Allen, James P. 2002. "The Tortilla-Mercedes Divide in Los Angeles." *Political Geography* 21(5): 701–09.

Allen, James P., and Eugene Turner. 1996. "Spatial Patterns of Immigrant Assimilation." *Professional Geographer* 48(2): 140–55.

————. 2006. "Ethnic Residential Concentrations in United States Metropolitan Areas." *Geographical Review* 95(2): 267–85.

Allison, Paul D., J. Scott Long, and T. K. Krauze. 1982. "Cumulative Advantage and Inequality in Science." *American Sociological Review* 47(5): 615–25.

Andersen, Kristi, and Elizabeth F. Cohen. 2005. "Political Institutions and Incorporation of Immigrants." In *The Politics of Democratic Inclusion,* edited by C. Wolbrecht and R. E. Hero. Philadelphia, Pa.: Temple University Press.

Averitt, Robert T. 1968. *The Dual Economy: The Dynamics of American Industry Structure.* New York: W. W. Norton.

Bachmeier, James D. 2013a. "Cumulative Causation, Co-Ethnic Settlement Maturity, and Mexican Migration to U.S. Metropolitan Areas, 1995–2000." *Social Forces* 91(4): 1293–317.

————. 2013b. "Third Generation 'Decline' in Mexican-American Educational Assimilation: The Role of Temporal Geographic Legacy Effects." Paper presented at the annual meeting of the American Sociological Association, New York, August 9.

Bachmeier, James D., and Frank D. Bean. 2011. "Comparative Patterns of Schooling and Work among Adolescents: Implications for Mexican Immigrant Incorporation." *Social Science Research* 40(6): 1579–95.

Bachmeier, James D., Zoya Gubernskaya, Jennifer Van Hook, and Frank D. Bean. 2011. "Non-Immigrant Overstay among Mexican Nationals Admitted to the United States: 1990–2010." Paper presented at the annual conference of the Western Economics Association, San Diego, Calif., July 2.

Bachmeier, James D., and Jennifer Van Hook. 2013. "The Historical and Demographic Origins of Third-Generation Delay in Mexican-American Educational Assimilation: Lessons from Population Projections." Paper presented at the Fall 2013 Colloquium Series, Population Studies, Center, University of Pennsylvania, Philadelphia, November 25.

Bachmeier, James D., Jennifer Van Hook, and Frank D. Bean. 2013. "Legal Status and Immigrant Health: Are Unauthorized Migrants More Susceptible to 'Negative' Health Assimilation?" Paper presented at the annual Population Association of America Conference, New Orleans, La. (April 11–13).

———. 2014. "Can We Measure Immigrants' Legal Status? Lessons from Two U.S. Surveys." *International Migration Review* 48(2): 538–66.

Bailey, Martha J., and Susan M. Dynarski. 2011. "Inequality in Postsecondary Education." In *Whither Opportunity? Rising Inequality, Schools, and Children's Life Chances,* edited by G. J. Duncan and R. J. Murnane. New York: Russell Sage Foundation.

Bankston, Carl L., III. 2014. *Immigrant Networks and Social Capital.* Cambridge, U.K.: Polity Press.

Barro, Robert J., and Jong-Wha Lee. 2013. "A New Data Set of Educational Attainment in the World, 1950–2010." *Journal of Development Economics* 104(1): 184–98.

Batalova, Jeanne, Sarah Hooker, Randy Capps, and James D. Bachmeier. 2014. *DACA at the Two-Year Mark: A National and State Profile of Youth Eligible and Applying for Deferred Action.* Washington, D.C.: Migration Policy Institute.

Bauer, Thomas, Barbara Dietz, Klaus F. Zimmermann, and Eric Zwintz. 2005. "German Migration: Development, Assimilation, and Labour Market Effects." In *European Migration: What Do We Know?* edited by K. F. Zimmermann. New York: Oxford University Press.

Bean, Frank D., James D. Bachmeier, and Susan K. Brown. 2014. *A Crucial Piece of the Puzzle: Demographic Change and Why Immigrants Are Needed to Fill America's Less-Skilled Labor Gap.* Research report prepared for the Partnership for a New American Economy, New York.

Bean, Frank D., James D. Bachmeier, Susan K. Brown, and Rosaura Tafoya-Estrada. 2011. "Immigration and Labor Market Dynamics." *Just Neighbors? Research on African American and Latino Relations in the United States,* edited by E. Telles, M. Q. Sawyer, and G. Rivera-Salgado. New York: Russell Sage Foundation.

Bean, Frank D., James D. Bachmeier, Susan K. Brown, Jennifer Van Hook, and Mark A. Leach. 2014. "Unauthorized Mexican Migration and the Socioeconomic Integration of Mexican Americans." In *Diversity and Disparities: America Enters a New Century,* edited by J. R. Logan. New York: Russell Sage Foundation.

Bean, Frank D., and Stephanie Bell-Rose. 1999. *Immigration and Opportunity: Race, Ethnicity, and Employment in the United States*. New York: Russell Sage Foundation.

Bean, Frank D., Ruth R. Berg, and Jennifer V. W. Van Hook. 1996. "Socioeconomic and Cultural Incorporation and Marital Disruption among Mexican Americans." *Social Forces* 75(20): 593–617.

Bean, Frank D., and Susan K. Brown. 2015. "Demographic Analyses of Immigration." In *Migration Theory: Talking Across Disciplines*, edited by Caroline B. Brettell and James F. Hollifield. 3rd ed. New York: Routledge.

Bean, Frank D., Susan K. Brown, James D. Bachmeier, Zoya Gubernskaya, and Christopher D. Smith. 2012. "Luxury, Necessity, and Anachronistic Workers: Does the United States Need Unskilled Immigrant Labor?" *American Behavioral Scientist* 56(8): 1008–28.

Bean, Frank D., Susan K. Brown, and Esther Castillo. 2015. "An Unexpected Legacy: The Positive Consequences of LBJ's Immigration-Policy Reforms." In *LBJ's Neglected Legacy: How Lyndon Johnson Reshaped Domestic Policy and Government*, edited by N. J. Glickman, L. E. Lynn, and R. H. Wilson. Austin, Tex.: University of Texas Press.

Bean, Frank D., Susan K. Brown, Mark A. Leach, James D. Bachmeier, and Rosaura Tafoya-Estrada. 2013. "The Implications of Unauthorized Migration for the Educational Incorporation of Mexican-Americans." In *Regarding Educación: Mexican-American Schooling in the 21st Century*, edited by Adam Sawyer and Bryant Jensen. New York: The Teachers College Press.

Bean, Frank D., Jorge Chapa, Ruth R. Berg, and Kathryn A. Sowards. 1994. "Educational and Sociodemographic Incorporation Among Hispanic Immigrants to the United States." In *Immigration and Ethnicity: The Integration of America's Newest Immigrants*, edited by B. Edmonston and J. S. Passel. Washington, D.C.: Urban Institute Press.

Bean, Frank D., Barry Edmonston, and Jeffrey S. Passel. 1990. *Undocumented Migration to the United States: IRCA and the Experience of the 1980s*. Santa Monica, Calif.: RAND Corporation.

Bean, Frank D., Mark Leach, Susan K. Brown, James D. Bachmeier, and John Hipp. 2011. "The Educational Legacy of Unauthorized Migration: Comparisons Across U.S. Immigrant Groups in How Parents' Status Affects Their Offspring." *International Migration Review* 45(2): 348–85.

Bean, Frank D., Jennifer Lee, and James D. Bachmeier. 2013. "Immigration and the Color Line at the Beginning of the 21st Century." *Daedalus* 142(3): 123–40.

Bean, Frank D., and B. Lindsay Lowell. 2005. "NAFTA and Mexican Migration to the United States." In *NAFTA'S Impact on North America: The First Decade*, edited by S. Weintraub. Washington, D.C.: Center for Strategic and International Studies.

———. 2007. "Unauthorized Migration." In *The New Americans: A Guide to Immigration Since 1965*, edited by M. Waters and R. Ueda. Cambridge, Mass.: Harvard University Press.

Bean, Frank D., B. Lindsay Lowell, and L. Taylor. 1988. "Undocumented Mexican Immigrants and the Earnings of Other Workers in the United States." *Demography* 25(1): 35–52.

Bean, Frank D., and Gillian Stevens. 2003. *America's Newcomers: Immigrant Incorporation and the Dynamics of Diversity*. New York: Russell Sage Foundation.

Bean, Frank D., C. Gray Swicegood, and Ruth Berg. 2000. "Mexican-Origin Fertility: New Patterns and Interpretations." *Social Science Quarterly* 81(1): 404–20.

Bean, Frank D., and Marta Tienda. 1987. *The Hispanic Population of the United States.* New York: Russell Sage Foundation.

Bean, Frank D., Georges Vernez, and Charles B. Keely. 1989. *Opening and Closing the Doors: Evaluating Immigration Reform and Control.* Santa Monica, Calif.: RAND Corporation.

Beveridge, Andrew A., and Susan Weber. 2003. "Race and Class in the Developing New York and Los Angeles Metropolises." In *New York and Los Angeles: Politics, Society, and Culture, A Comparative View,* edited by David Halle. Chicago, Ill.: University of Chicago Press.

Binder, Amy, Mary Blair-Loy, John Evans, Kwai Ng, and Michael Schudson. 2008. "The Diversity of Culture." Introduction to *The Annals of the American Academy of Political and Social Science* 619(September): 6–14.

Binder, Melissa, and Christopher Woodruff. 2002. "Inequality and Inter-generational Mobility in Schooling: The Case of Mexico." *Economic Development and Cultural Change* 50(2): 249–67.

Black, Mary S. 1997. "Schoolhouse in the Field: How Agrarian Cultural Values Shaped Texas Schools for Mexican Children, 1910–1930." *Interchange* 28(1): 15–30.

Blank, Rebecca M. 2009. "Economic Change and the Structure of Opportunity for Less-Skilled Workers." In *Changing Poverty, Changing Policies,* edited by M. Cancian and S. Danziger. New York: Russell Sage Foundation.

Blau, Peter M. 1977. *Inequality and Heterogeneity.* New York: Free Press.

———. 1994. *Structural Contexts of Opportunities.* Chicago, Ill.: University of Chicago Press.

Blau, Peter M., and Joseph E. Schwartz. 1984. *Crosscutting Social Circles: Testing a Macrostructural Theory of Intergroup Relations.* Orlando, Fla.: Academic Press.

Bloemraad, Irene, Anna Korteweg, and Gökçe Yurdakul. 2008. "Citizenship and Immigration: Multiculturalism, Assimilation, and Challenges to the Nation-State." *Annual Review of Sociology* 34: 153–79.

Bloome, Deirdre. 2014. "Racial Inequality Trends and the Intergenerational Persistence of Income and Family Structure." *American Sociological Review* 79(6): 1196–225.

Blumberg, Rae Lesser. 1991. "The 'Triple Overlap' of Gender Stratification, Economy, and Family." Introduction to *Gender, Family, and Economy: The Triple Overlap,* edited by R. L. Blumberg. Newbury Park, Calif.: Sage Publications.

Bolt, Gideon, A. Sule Özüekren, and Deborah Phillips. 2010. "Linking Integration and Residential Segregation." *Journal of Ethnic and Migration Studies* 36(2): 169–86.

Bonvalet, Catherine, Juliet Carpenter, and Paul White. 1995. "The Residential Mobility of Ethnic Minorities: A Longitudinal Analysis." *Urban Studies* 32(1): 87–103.

Borjas, George J. 1985. "Assimilation, Changes in Cohort Quality, and the Earnings of Immigrants." *Journal of Labor Economics* 3(4): 463–89.

Borjas, George J., and Marta Tienda. 1987. "The Economic Consequences of Immigration." *Science* 235(4789): 645–51.

———. 1993. "The Employment and Wages of Legalized Immigrants." *International Migration Review* 27(4): 712–47.

Bosniak, Linda S. 2006. *The Citizen and the Alien: Dilemmas of Contemporary Membership*. Princeton, N.J.: Princeton University Press.

Boyd, Monica. 1989. "Family and Personal Networks in International Migration: Recent Developments and New Agendas." *International Migration Review* 23(3): 638–70.

———. 2002. "Educational Attainments of Immigrant Offspring: Success or Segmented Assimilation?" *International Migration Review* 36(4): 1037–60.

Brabeck, Kalina, and Qingwen Xu. 2010. "The Impact of Detention and Deportation on Latino Immigrant Children and Families: A Quantitative Exploration." *Hispanic Journal of Behavioral Sciences* 32(3): 341–61.

Brand, Jennie E., and Yu Xie. 2010. "Who Benefits Most from College?" *American Sociological Review* 75(2): 273–302.

Breton, Raymond. 1964. "Institutional Completeness of Ethnic Communities and the Personal Relations of Immigrants." *American Journal of Sociology* 70(2): 193–205.

Brettell, Caroline B., and Faith G. Nibbs. 2011. "Immigrant Suburban Settlement and the 'Threat' to Middle Class Status and Identity: The Case of Farmers Branch, Texas." *International Migration* 49(1): 1–30.

Briggs, Xavier de Souza. 2007. "Some of My Best Friends Are. . . : Interracial Friendships, Class, and Segregation in America." *City and Community* 6(4): 263–90.

Britton, Marcus L. 2011. "Close Together but Worlds Apart? Residential Integration and Interethnic Friendship in Houston." *City and Community* 10(2): 182–204.

Brown, Susan K. 2006. "Structural Assimilation Revisited: Mexican-Origin Nativity and Cross-Ethnic Primary Ties." *Social Forces* 85(1): 75–92.

———. 2007. "Delayed Spatial Assimilation: Multi-Generational Incorporation of the Mexican-Origin Population in Los Angeles." *City and Community* 6(3): 193–209.

Brown, Susan K., and Frank D. Bean. 2006. *Assimilation Models Old and New: Explaining a Long-Term Process*. Washington, D.C.: Migration Policy Institute.

Browning, Rufus P., Dale Rogers Marshall, and David H. Tabb. 1984. *Protest Is Not Enough: The Struggle of Blacks and Hispanics for Equality in Urban Politics*. Berkeley, Calif.: University of California Press.

Brubaker, Rogers. 1992. *Citizenship and Nationhood in France and Germany*. Cambridge, Mass.: Harvard University Press.

———. 2004. *Ethnicity Without Groups*. Cambridge, Mass.: Harvard University Press.

Buchmann, Claudia, and Thomas A. DiPrete. 2006. "The Growing Female Advantage in College Completion: The Role of Family Background and Academic Achievement." *American Sociological Review* 71(4): 515–41.

Buchmann, Claudia, Thomas A. DiPrete, and Anne McDaniel. 2008. "Gender Inequalities in Education." *Annual Review of Sociology* 34: 319–37.

Calavita, Kitty. 1992. *Inside the State: The Bracero Program, Immigration, and the I.N.S.* New York: Routledge.

Card, David. 1999. "The Causal Effect of Education on Earnings." In *The Handbook of Labor Economics*, edited by Orley Ashenfelter and David Card. Vol. 3. New York: Elsevier.

Card, David, and Ethan G. Lewis. 2007. "The Diffusion of Mexican Immigrants During the 1990s: Explanations and Impacts." In *Mexican Immigration to the United States*, edited by G. J. Borjas. Chicago, Ill.: University of Chicago Press.

Carnavale, Anthony P., Stephen J. Rose, and Ban Cheah. 2011. *The College Payoff: Education, Occupations, Lifetime Earnings.* Washington, D.C.: Georgetown University Center on Education and the Workforce. Accessed September 27, 2014. http://hdl.handle.net/10822/559300.

Castles, Stephen, and Mark J. Miller. 1998. *The Age of Migration: International Population Movements in the Modern World.* 2nd ed. New York: Guilford Press.

———. 2009. *The Age of Migration: International Population Movements in the Modern World.* 4th ed., rev. and exp. New York: Guildford Press.

Census CD. 2002. *Summary File, Long Form, 1980–2000.* East Brunswick, N.J.: GeoLytics.

Cerrutti, Marcela, and Douglas S. Massey. 2004. "Trends in Mexican Migration to the United States, 1965–1995." In *Crossing the Border: Research from the Mexican Migration Project,* edited by J. Duran and D. S. Massey. New York: Russell Sage Foundation.

Chacón, Jennifer M. 2012. "Overcriminalizing Immigration." *Journal of Criminal Law and Criminology* 102(3): 2013–91.

Charles, Camille Zubrinsky. 2000. "Residential Segregation in Los Angeles." In *Prismatic Metropolis: Inequality in Los Angeles,* edited by Lawrence D. Bobo, Melvin L. Oliver, James H. Johnson Jr., and Abel Valenzuela Jr. New York: Russell Sage Foundation.

———. 2006. *Won't You Be My Neighbor? Race, Class, and Residence in Los Angeles.* New York: Russell Sage Foundation.

Chauvin, Sébastien, and Blanca Garcés-Mascareñas. 2012. "Beyond Informal Citizenship: The New Moral Economy of Migrant Illegality." *International Political Sociology* 6(3): 241–59.

Chávez, Christina. 2007. *Five Generations of a Mexican American Family in Los Angeles.* Lanham, Md.: Rowman and Littlefield.

Chávez, Leo. 1988. "Settlers and Sojourners: The Case of Mexicans in the United States." *Human Organization* 47(2): 95–108.

———. 2008. *The Latino Threat: Constructing Immigrants, Citizens, and the Nation.* Stanford, Calif.: Stanford University Press.

Chiswick, Barry R. 1978. "The Effect of Americanization on the Earnings of Foreign-Born Men." *Journal of Political Economy* 86(5): 897–921.

Chiswick, Barry R., and Noyna DebBurman. 2003. "Educational Attainment: Analysis by Immigrant Generation." Discussion Paper 731. Bonn, Ger.: Institute for the Study of Labor.

Clark, Rebecca L., and Rosalind Berkowitz King. 2008. "Social and Economic Aspects of Immigration." *Annals of the New York Academy of Sciences* 1136(1): 289–97.

Clark, W. A. V. 1989. "Residential Segregation in American Cities: Common Ground and Differences in Interpretation." *Population Research and Policy Review* 8(2): 193–97.

Clark, William A. V., Marinus C. Deurloo, and Frans M. Dieleman. 2000. "Housing Consumption and Residential Crowding in U.S. Housing Markets." *Journal of Urban Affairs* 22(1): 49–63.

Clemens, Michael, and Justin Sandefur. 2014. "Let the People Go: The Problem with Strict Migration Limits." *Foreign Affairs* 93(1): 152–59. Review of *Exodus: How Migration Is Changing Our World,* by Paul Collier (2013).

Clogg, Clifford C. 1995. "Latent Class Models." In *Handbook of Statistical Modeling for the Social and Behavioral Sciences,* edited by Gerhard Arminger, Clifford C. Clogg, and Michael E. Sobel. New York: Plenum Press.

Coleman, David. 2006. "Immigration and Ethnic Change in Low-Fertility Countries: A Third Demographic Transition." *Population and Development Review* 32(3): 401–46.

Coltrane, Scott, and Michele Adams. 2008. *Gender and Families.* 2nd ed. Lanham, Md.: Rowman and Littlefield.

Congressional Budget Office. 2011. "Trends in the Distribution of Household Income Between 1979–2007." Washington, D.C.: Government Printing Office.

Cornelius, Wayne A. 1992. "From Sojourners to Settlers: The Changing Profile of Mexican Immigration to the United States." In *U.S.-Mexico Relations: Labor Market Interdependence,* edited by Jorge A. Bustamante, Clark W. Reynolds, and Raúl A. H. Ojeda. Palo Alto, Calif.: Stanford University Press.

Council on Foreign Relations. 2009. *U.S. Immigration Policy.* New York: Council on Foreign Relations.

Courgeau, Daniel. 1985. "Interaction Between Spatial Mobility, Family, and Career Life-Cycle: A French Survey." *European Sociological Review* 1(2): 139–62.

Coutin, Susan Bibler. 2003. "Borderlands, Illegality, and the Spaces of Non-existence." In *Globalization under Construction: Governmentality, Law, and Identity,* edited by Richard Perry and Bill Maurer. Minneapolis: University of Minnesota Press.

Creticos, Peter A., and Eleanor Sohnen. 2013. *Manufacturing in the United States, Mexico, and Central America: Implications for Competitiveness and Migration.* Washington, D.C.: Migration Policy Institute.

Crosnoe, Robert. 2005. "Double Disadvantage or Signs of Resilience? The Elementary School Contexts of Children from Mexican Immigrant Families." *American Educational Research Journal* 42(2): 269–303.

———. 2006. *Mexican Roots, American Schools: Helping Mexican Immigrant Children Succeed.* Stanford, Calif.: Stanford University Press.

Crowder, Kyle, Matthew Hall, and Stewart E. Tolnay. 2011. "Neighborhood Immigration and Native Out-Migration." *American Sociological Review* 76(1): 25–47.

Curiel, Enrique Martínez. 2004. "The Green Card as a Matrimonial Strategy: Self-Interest in the Choice of Marital Partners." *Crossing the Border: Research from the Mexican Migration Project,* edited by Jorge Durand and Douglas S. Massey. New York: Russell Sage Foundation.

Current Population Survey. 2010. *Annual Social and Economic (ASEC) Supplement* [machine-readable data file]. Conducted by the Bureau of the Census for the Bureau of Labor Statistics. Washington, D.C.: U.S. Census Bureau (producer and distributor).

Czaika, Mathias, and Hein de Haas. 2014. "The Globalization of Migration: Has the World Become More Migratory?" *International Migration Review* 48(2): 283–323.

Dear, Michael. 2002. "Los Angeles and the Chicago School: Invitation to a Debate." *City and Community* 1(1): 5–32.

de Haas, Hein. 2006. "Cherishing the Goose with the Golden Eggs: Trends in Migrant Remittances from Europe to Morocco, 1970–2004." *International Migration Review* 40(3): 603–34.

Denton, Nancy A., and Douglas S. Massey. 1991. "Patterns of Neighborhood Transition in a Multiethnic World: U.S. Metropolitan Areas, 1970–1980." *Demography* 28(1): 41–63.

Dietz, Robert D. 2002. "The Estimation of Neighborhood Effects in the Social Sciences: An Interdisciplinary Approach." *Social Science Research* 31(4): 539–75.

DiPrete, Thomas A., and Claudia Buchmann. 2013. *The Rise of Women: The Growing Gender Gap in Education and What It Means for American Schools.* New York: Russell Sage Foundation.

———. 2014. "Gender Disparities in Educational Attainment in the New Century: Trends, Causes, and Consequences." *Diversity and Disparities: America Enters a New Century,* edited by John R. Logan. New York: Russell Sage Foundation.

DiPrete, Thomas A., and Gregory M. Eirich. 2006. "Cumulative Advantage as a Mechanism for Inequality: A Review of Theoretical and Empirical Developments." *Annual Review of Sociology* 32: 271–97.

DiPrete, Thomas A., and Patricia A. McManus. 2000. "Family Change, Employment Transitions, and the Welfare State: Household Income Dynamics in the United States and Germany." *American Sociological Review* 65(3): 343–70.

Dobbin, Frank. 2004. "The Sociological View of the Economy." In *The New Economic Sociology: A Reader,* edited by F. Dobbin. Princeton, N.J.: Princeton University Press.

Dohan, Daniel. 2003. *The Price of Poverty: Money, Work, and Culture in the Mexican American Barrio.* Berkeley: University of California Press.

Domínguez, Silvia. 2011. *Getting Ahead: Social Mobility, Public Housing, and Immigrant Networks.* New York: New York University Press.

Donato, Katharine M., Michael B. Aguilera, and Chizuko Wakabayashi. 2005. "Immigration Policy and Employment Conditions of U.S. Immigrants from Mexico, Nicaragua, and the Dominican Republic." *International Migration* 43(5): 5–29.

Donato, Katharine M., Donna R. Gabaccia, Jennifer Holdaway, and Martin Manalansan IV. 2006. "A Glass Half Full? Gender in Migration Studies." *International Migration Review* 40(1): 3–26.

Donato, Katharine M., and Douglas S. Massey. 1993. "Effects of the Immigration Reform and Control Act on the Wages of Mexican Migrants." *Social Science Quarterly* 74(3): 523–41.

Donato, Katharine M., Chizuko Wakabayashi, Shirin Hakimzadeh, and Amada Armenta. 2008. "Shifts in the Employment Conditions of Mexican Migrant Men and Women: The Effect of U.S. Immigration Policy." *Work and Occupations* 35(4): 462–95.

Douglas, Karen M., and Rogelio Sáenz. 2013. "The Criminalization of Immigrants and the Immigration-Industrial Complex." *Daedalus* 142(3): 199–227.

Dreby, Joanna. 2010. *Divided by Borders: Mexican Migrants and Their Children.* Berkeley: University of California Press.

———. 2012. "The Burden of Deportation on Children in Mexican Immigrant Families." *Journal of Marriage and the Family* 74(4): 829–45.

Dumka, Larry E., Nancy A. Gonzales, Darya Bonds, and Roger E. Millsap. 2009. "Academic Success of Mexican Origin Adolescent Boys and Girls: The Role of Mothers' and Fathers' Parenting and Cultural Orientation." *Sex Roles* 60(7–8): 588–99.

Duncan, Brian, V. Joseph Hotz, and Stephen J. Trejo. 2006. "Hispanics in the U.S. Labor Market." In *Hispanics and the Future of America*, edited by Marta Tienda and Faith Mitchell. Washington, D.C.: National Academies Press.

Duncan, Brian, and Stephen J. Trejo. 2007. "Ethnic Identification, Intermarriage, and Unmeasured Progress by Mexican Americans." In *Mexican Immigration to the United States*, edited by George J. Borjas. Chicago: The University of Chicago Press.

———. 2011a. "Intermarriage and the Intergenerational Transmission of Ethnic Identity and Human Capital for Mexican Americans." *Journal of Labor Economics* 29(2): 195–227.

———. 2011b. "Tracking Intergenerational Progress for Immigrant Groups: The Problem of Ethnic Attrition." *American Economic Review: Papers and Proceedings* 101(3): 603–08.

———. 2011c. "Who Remains Mexican? Selective Ethnic Attrition and the Intergenerational Progress of Mexican Americans." In *Latinos and the Economy: Integration and Impact in Schools, Labor Markets, and Beyond*, edited by David L. Leal and Stephen J. Trejo. New York: Springer.

Duncan, Greg J., and Richard J. Murnane, eds. 2011. *Whither Opportunity? Rising Inequality, Schools, and Children's Life Chances*. New York: Russell Sage Foundation.

Durand, Jorge, Douglas S. Massey, and Chiara Capoferro. 2005. "The New Geography of Mexican Immigration." In *New Destinations: Mexican Immigration in the United States*, edited by Victor Zúñiga and Rubén Hernández-León. New York: Russell Sage Foundation.

Durand, Jorge, Douglas S. Massey, and Rene M. Zenteno. 2001. "Mexican Immigration to the United States: Continuities and Changes." *Latin American Research Review* 36(1): 107–27.

Eaton, Joseph W. 1952. "Controlled Acculturation: A Survival Technique of the Hutterites." *American Sociological Review* 17(3): 331–40.

Ellis, Mark, Richard Wright, and Virginia Parks. 2004. "Work Together, Live Apart? Geographies of Racial and Ethnic Segregation at Home and at Work." *Annals of the Association of American Geographers* 94(3): 620–37.

Entzinger, Han. 2000. "The Dynamics of Integration Policies: A Multidimensional Model." In *Challenging Immigration and Ethnic Relations Politics: Comparative European Perspectives*, edited by Ruud Koopmans and Paul Statham. Oxford, U.K.: Oxford University Press.

Eschbach, Karl, Jacqueline Hagan, and Stanley Bailey. 1999. "Death at the Border." *International Migration Review* 33(2): 430–54.

Escobar Latapí, Augustín, Frank D. Bean, and Sidney Weintraub. 1999. "The Dynamics of Mexican Emigration." In *Emigration Dynamics in Developing Countries*. edited by Reginald Appleyard. Vol. 3, *Mexico, Central America and the Caribbean*. Aldershot, England: Ashgate.

Escobar Latapí, Augustín, Susan F. Martin, B. Lindsay Lowell, and Rafael Fernández de Castro. 2013. "Estudio Binacional Sobre Migrantes Mexicanos en Estados Unidos y en México: Las Implicaciones de la Emigración Cero de México a Estados Unidos." *Foreign Affairs: Latinoamerica* 13(3): 12–17.

Esping-Andersen, Gøsta. 2007. "Sociological Explanations of Changing Income Distributions." *American Behavioral Scientist* 50(5): 639–58.

Everett, Bethany G., Richard G. Rogers, Robert A. Hummer, and Patrick M. Krueger. 2011. "Trends in Educational Attainment by Race/Ethnicity, Nativity, and Sex in the United States, 1989–2005." *Ethnic and Racial Studies* 34(9): 1543–66.

Farley, Reynolds, and Richard Alba. 2002. "The New Second Generation in the United States." *International Migration Review* 36(3): 669–701.

Farley, Reynolds, and William H. Frey. 1994. "Changes in the Segregation of Whites from Blacks During the 1980s: Small Steps Toward a More Integrated Society." *American Sociological Review* 59(1): 23–45.

Federal Reserve Bank of Atlanta. 2012. "Jobs Calculator." Center for Human Capital Studies. Accessed December 31, 2012. http://www.frbatlanta.org/chcs/calculator/index.cfm.

Feliciano, Cynthia, and Rubén G. Rumbaut. 2005. "Gendered Paths: Educational and Occupational Expectations and Outcomes among Adult Children of Immigrants." *Ethnic and Racial Studies* 28(6): 1087–118. doi:10.1080/01419870500224406.

Fischer, Claude S., and Michael Hout. 2006. *Century of Difference: How America Changed in the Last One Hundred Years.* New York: Russell Sage Foundation.

Fiske, Susan T. 2013. *Social Beings.* 4th ed. New York: Wiley.

Fiske, Susan T., and Hazel Rose Markus. 2012. "Facing Social Class: How Societal Rank Influences Interaction." New York: Russell Sage Foundation.

FitzGerald, David. 2009. *A Nation of Emigrants: How Mexico Manages Its Migration.* Berkeley: University of California Press.

Fix, Michael. 2007. "Securing the Future: U.S. Immigrant Integration Policy." Washington, D.C.: Migration Policy Institute.

Fix, Michael, and Jeffrey S. Passel. 1994. *Immigration and Immigrants: Setting the Record Straight.* Washington, D.C.: The Urban Institute Press.

Flippen, Chenoa. 2004. "Unequal Returns to Housing Investments? A Study of Real Housing Appreciation among Black, White, and Hispanic Households." *Social Forces* 82(4): 1523–51.

Fokkema, Tineke, and Hein de Haas. 2011. "Pre- and Post-Migration Determinants of Socio-Cultural Integration of African Immigrants in Italy and Spain." *International Migration.* Accessed May 4, 2015. doi:10.1111/j.1468-2435.2011.00687.x.

Foley, Neil. 2004. "Straddling the Color Line: The Legal Construction of Hispanic Identity in Texas." In *Not Just Black and White: Historical and Contemporary Perspectives on Immigration, Race, and Ethnicity in the United States* edited by Nancy Foner and George M. Fredrickson. New York: Russell Sage Foundation.

Foner, Nancy. 1999. "The Immigrant Family: Cultural Legacies and Cultural Changes." In *The Handbook of International Migration: The American Experience,* edited by C. Hirschman, P. Kasinitz, and J. DeWind. New York: Russell Sage Foundation.

Foner, Nancy, and George M. Fredrickson. 2004. "Not Just Black and White: Historical and Contemporary Perspectives on Immigration, Race, and Ethnicity in the United States." New York: Russell Sage Foundation.

Foner, Nancy, and Leo Lucassen. 2012. "Legacies of the Past." In *The Changing Face of World Cities: Young Adult Children of Immigrants in Europe and the United States,* edited by Maurice Crul and John Mollenkopf. New York: Russell Sage Foundation Press.

Forstall, Richard. 1995. California Population of Counties by Decennial Census: 1900 to 1990. Accessed September 4, 2013. http://www.census.gov/population/cencounts/ca190090.txt.

Fragomen, Austin T., Jr., and Alfred J. Del Rey Jr. 1979. "The Immigration Selection System: A Proposal for Reform." *San Diego Law Review* 17: 1–36.

Fredrickson, George M. 1988. *The Arrogance of Race: Historical Perspectives on Slavery, Racism, and Social Inequality.* Middletown, Conn.: Wesleyan University Press.

Freeman, Gary P. 1979. *Immigrant Labor and Racial Conflict in Industrial Societies: The French and British Experience, 1945–1975.* Princeton, N.J.: Princeton University Press.

———. 2004. "Immigrant Incorporation in Western Democracies." *International Migration Review* 38(3): 945–69.

Freeman, Richard B. 2007. *America Works: Critical Thoughts on the Exceptional U.S. Labor Market.* New York: Russell Sage Foundation.

Frey, William H., and Kao-Lee Liaw. 1999. "Internal Migration of Foreign-Born Latinos and Asians: Are They Assimilating Geographically?" In *Migration and Restructuring in the United States: A Geographic Perspective,* edited by Kavita Pandit and Suzanne D. Withers. Lanham, Md.: Rowman and Littlefield Publishers.

Friedman, Benjamin M. 2005. *The Moral Consequences of Economic Growth.* New York: Knopf.

Friedman, Samantha, and Emily Rosenbaum. 2007. "Does Suburban Residence Mean Better Neighborhood Conditions for All Households? Assessing the Influence of Nativity Status and Race/Ethnicity." *Social Science Research* 36(1): 1–27.

Frisbie, W. Parker. 1975. "Illegal Migration from Mexico to the United States: A Longitudinal Analysis." *International Migration Review* 9(1): 3–13.

Fuligni, Andrew J. 1998. "Authority, Autonomy, and Parent-Adolescent Conflict and Cohesion: A Study of Adolescents from Mexican, Chinese, Filipino, and European Backgrounds." *Developmental Psychology* 34(4): 782–92.

Fuligni, Andrew J., and Sara Pedersen. 2002. "Family Obligation and the Transition to Young Adulthood." *Developmental Psychology* 38(5): 856–68.

Furstenberg, Frank F., Jr., and Mary Elizabeth Hughes. 1997. "The Influence of Neighborhoods on Children's Development: A Theoretical Perspective and a Research Agenda." In *Indicators of Children's Well-being,* edited by Robert M. Hauser, Brett V. Brown, and William R. Prosser. New York: Russell Sage Foundation.

Furtado, Celso. 1964. *Development and Underdevelopment.* Translated by R. W. de Aguiar and E. C. Drysdale. Berkeley: University of California.

Fussell, Elizabeth, and Douglas S. Massey. 2004. "The Limits to Cumulative Causation: International Migration from Mexican Urban Areas." *Demography* 41(1): 151–71.

Gabaccia, Donna R. 1995. *From the Other Side: Women, Gender, and Immigrant Life in the U.S., 1820–1990.* Bloomington: Indiana University Press.

Gándara, Patricia. 1982. "Passing Through the Eye of the Needle: High-Achieving Chicanas." *Hispanic Journal of Behavioral Sciences* 4(2): 167–79.

Gans, Herbert J. 1982. *The Urban Villagers: Group and Class in the Life of Italian-Americans.* Rev. ed. New York: The Free Press.

———. 1992. "Comment: Ethnic Invention and Acculturation: A Bumpy-Line Approach." *Journal of American Ethnic History* 11(1): 42–52.

García, Angela S. 2014. "Hidden in Plain Sight: How Unauthorized Migrants Strategically Assimilate in Restrictive Localities." *Journal of Ethnic and Migration Studies* 40(12): 1895–914.

Garip, Filiz. 2012. "Discovering Diverse Mechanisms of Migration: The Mexico-U.S. Stream 1970–2000." *Population and Development Review* 38(3): 393–433.

Garreau, Joel. 1988. *Edge City: Life on the New Frontier.* New York: Anchor Books.

Gil, Rosa Maria, and Carmen Inoa Vazquez. 1996. *The Maria Paradox: How Latinas Can Merge Old World Traditions with New World Self-Esteem.* New York: G. P. Putnam's Sons.

Giuliano, Genevieve, and Kenneth A. Small. 1991. "Subcenters in the Los Angeles Region." *Regional Science and Urban Economics* 21(2): 163–82.

Glazer, Nathan. 1993. "Is Assimilation Dead?" *Annals of the American Academy of Political and Social Science* 530(Fall): 122–36.

Glazer, Nathan, and Daniel P. Moynihan. 1963. *Beyond the Melting Pot: The Negroes, Puerto Ricans, Jews, Italians, and Irish of New York City.* Cambridge, Mass.: MIT Press.

Glick, Jennifer E. 2010. "Connecting Complex Processes: A Decade of Research on Immigrant Families." *Journal of Marriage and the Family* 72(3): 498–515.

Glick, Jennifer E., and Jennifer Van Hook. 1998. "The Mexican-Origin Population of the United States in the Twentieth Century." In *Migration Between Mexico & the United States: Binational Study, Research Reports, and Background Materials.* Vol. 2. Mexico City and Washington, D.C.: Mexican Ministry of Foreign Affairs and U.S. Commission on Immigration Reform.

———. 2002. "Parents' Coresidence with Adult Children: Can Immigration Explain Racial and Ethnic Variation?" *Journal of Marriage and the Family* 64(1): 240–53.

Glick, Jennifer E., and Michael J. White. 2004. "Post-secondary School Participation of Immigrant and Native Youth: The Role of Familial Resources and Educational Expectations." *Social Science Research* 33(2): 272–99.

Golash-Boza, Tanya Maria, and Pierrette Hondagneu-Sotelo. 2013. "Latino Immigrant Men and the Deportation Crisis: A Gendered Racial Removal Program." *Latino Studies* 11(3): 271–92.

Goldin, Claudia. 2014. "A Grand Gender Convergence: Its Last Chapter." *American Economic Review* 104(4): 1091–119.

Goldin, Claudia, and Lawrence F. Katz. 2008. *The Race Between Education and Technology.* Cambridge, Mass.: Belknap Press of Harvard University Press.

Gonzales, Roberto G. 2011. "Learning to Be Illegal: Undocumented Youth and Shifting Legal Contexts in the Transition to Adulthood." *American Sociological Review* 76(4): 602–19.

Gonzales, Roberto G., and Leo R. Chavez. 2012. "Awakening to a Nightmare: Abjectivity and Illegality in the Lives of Undocumented 1.5 Generation Latino Immigrants in the United States." *Current Anthropology* 53(3): 255–81.

Gonzales, Roberto G., Carola Suárez-Orozco, and Maria Cecilia Dedios-Sanguineti. 2013. "No Place to Belong: Concepts of Mental Health among Undocumented Immigrant Youth in the United States." *American Behavioral Scientist* 57(8): 1174–99.

González Baker, Susan. 1997. "The 'Amnesty' Aftermath: Current Policy Issues Stemming from the Legalization Programs of the 1986 Immigration Reform and Control Act." *International Migration Review* 31(1): 5–27.

Goodman, Sara Wallace. 2010. "Integration Requirements for Integration's Sake? Identifying, Categorising, and Comparing Civic Integration Policies." *Journal of Ethnic and Migration Studies* 36(5): 753–72.

Gordon, Milton M. 1964. *Assimilation in American Life: The Role of Race, Religion, and National Origins.* New York: Oxford University Press.

Granovetter, Mark. 1985. "Economic Action and Social Structure: The Problem of Embeddedness." *American Journal of Sociology* 91(3): 481–510.

———. 1995. "The Economic Sociology of Firms and Entrepreneurs." In *The Economic Sociology of Immigration,* edited by Alejandro Portes. New York: Russell Sage Foundation.

Granovetter, Mark S., and Richard Swedberg. 1992. *The Sociology of Economic Life.* Boulder, Colo.: Westview Press.

Grasmuck, Sherri, and Patricia R. Pessar. 1991. *Between Two Islands: Dominican International Migration.* Berkeley, Calif.: University of California.

Grebler, Leo, Joan Moore, and Ralph C. Guzmán. 1970. *The Mexican-American People: The Nation's Second Largest Minority.* New York: Free Press.

Greenfield, Patricia M., Ashley Maynard, and Carla Childs. 2003. "Historical Change, Cultural Learning, and Cognitive Representation in Zinacantec Maya Children." *Cognitive Development* 18(4): 455–87.

Grogger, Jeffrey, and Stephen J. Trejo. 2002. *Falling Behind or Moving Up? The Intergenerational Progress of Mexican Americans.* San Francisco, Calif.: Public Policy Institute of California.

Gubernskaya, Zoya, Frank D. Bean, and Jennifer Van Hook. 2013. "(Un)healthy Citizens: Relationships Between Naturalization and Activity Limitations among Older Immigrants." *Journal of Health and Social Behavior* 54(4): 427–43.

Guest, Avery M., and James A. Weed. 1976. "Ethnic Residential Segregation: Patterns of Change." *American Journal of Sociology* 81(5): 1088–111.

Guillermoprieto, Alma. 2015. "Mexico: The Murder of the Young." *The New York Review of Books,* January 8.

Hagan, Jacqueline Maria. 1994. *Deciding to Be Legal: A Maya Community in Houston.* Philadelphia, Pa.: Temple University.

———. 1998. "Social Networks, Gender, and Immigrant Incorporation: Resources and Constraints." *American Sociological Review* 63(1): 55–68.

Hagan, Jacqueline Maria, Rubén Hernández-León, and Jean Luc Demonsant. 2015. *Skills of the "Unskilled": Work and Mobility among Mexican Migrants.* Berkeley, Calif.: University of California Press.

Hall, Matthew, Emily Greenman, and George Farkas. 2010. "Legal Status and Wage Disparities for Mexican Immigrants." *Social Forces* 89(2): 491–514.

Haller, William, and Patricia Landolt. 2005. "The Transnational Dimensions of Identity Formation: Adult Children of Immigrants in Miami." *Ethnic and Racial Studies* 28(2): 1182–214.

Haller, William J., Alejandro Portes, and Scott Lynch. 2011. "Dreams Fulfilled, Dreams Shattered: Determinants of Segmented Assimilation in the Immigrant Second Generation." *Social Forces* 89(3): 733–62.

Hammar, Tomas. 1985. "European Immigration Policy: A Comparative Study." Cambridge, U.K.: Cambridge University Press.

Hansen, Randall A. 2008. *A New Citizenship Bargain for the Age of Mobility? Citizenship Requirements in Europe and North America.* Washington, D.C.: Migration Policy Institute.

Hanson, Gordon H., and Craig McIntosh. 2010. "The Great Mexican Emigration." *Review of Economics and Statistics* 92(4): 798–810.

Hardaway, Christina, and Andrew J. Fuligni. 2006. "Dimensions of Family Connectedness among Adolescents with Mexican, Chinese, and European Backgrounds." *Developmental Psychology* 42(6): 1246–58.

Harding, David J., Lisa Gennetian, Christopher Winship, Lisa Sanbonmatsu, and Jeffrey Kling. 2010. "Unpacking Neighborhood Influences on Education Outcomes: Setting the Stage for Future Research." In *Whither Opportunity? Rising Inequality, Schools, and Children's Life Chances*, edited by Greg Duncan and Richard Murnane. New York: Russell Sage Foundation.

Harris, John R., and Michael P. Todaro. 1970. "Migration, Unemployment, & Development: A Two-Sector Analysis." *American Economic Review* 60(1): 126–42.

Hernández-León, Rubén. 2008. *Metropolitan Migrants: The Migration of Urban Mexicans to the United States.* Berkeley: University of California Press.

Hero, R. E., and Christina Wolbrecht. 2005. Introduction to *The Politics of Democratic Inclusion,* edited by C. Wolbrecht and R. E. Hero. Philadelphia, Pa.: Temple University Press.

Herzog-Punzenberger, Barbara. 2003. "Ethnic Segmentation in School and Labor: 40-Year Legacy of Austrian Guestworker Policy." *International Migration Review* 37(4): 1120–44.

Hipp, John R., and Adam Boessen. 2012. "Immigrants and Social Distance: Examining the Social Consequences of Immigration for Southern California Neighborhoods over Fifty Years." *Annals of the American Academy of Political and Social Science* 641(May): 192–219.

Hirschman, Charles. 2001. "The Educational Enrollment of Immigrant Youth: A Test of the Segmented-Assimilation Hypothesis." *Demography* 38(3): 317–36.

Hirschman, Charles, Philip Kasinitz, and Josh DeWind, eds. 1999. *The Handbook of International Migration: The American Experience.* New York: Russell Sage Foundation.

Hochschild, Jennifer, Jacqueline Chattopadhyay, Claudine Gay, and Michael Jones-Correa. 2013. *Outsiders No More? Models of Immigrant Political Incorporation.* New York: Oxford University Press.

Hochschild, Jennifer, and John Mollenkopf. 2009. *Bringing Outsiders In: Transatlantic Perspectives on Immigrant Political Incorporation.* Ithaca, N.Y.: Cornell University Press.

Hoefer, Michael, Nancy Rytina, and Bryan C. Baker. 2011. *Estimates of the Unauthorized Immigrant Population Residing in the United States: January 2010.* Washington, D.C.: U.S. Department of Homeland Security.

Hollifield, James F. 2000. "The Politics of International Migration: How Can We 'Bring the State Back In?'" In *Migration Theory: Talking Across Disciplines,* edited by C. B. Brettell and J. F. Hollifield. New York: Routledge.

———. 2004. "The Emerging Migration State." *International Migration Review* 38(3): 885–912.

Holzer, Harry J. 2011. "Immigration Policy and Less-Skilled Workers in the United States: Reflections on Future Directions for Reform." In *Immigrants in a Changing Labor Market: Responding to Economic Needs,* edited by Michael Fix, Demetrios G. Papademetrious, and Madeleine Sumption. Washington, D.C.: Migration Policy Institute

Hondagneu-Sotelo, Pierrette. 1994. *Gendered Transitions: Mexican Experiences of Immigration*. Berkeley: University of California.

———. 2001. *Doméstica: Immigrant Workers Cleaning and Caring in the Shadows of Affluence*. Berkeley: University of California Press.

Hout, Michael. 2012. "Social and Economic Returns to Higher Education in the United States." *Annual Review of Sociology* 38: 379–400.

———. 2015. "A Summary of What We Know about Social Mobility." *Annals of the American Association of Political and Social Science* 657(1): 27–36.

Hsin, Amy, and Yu Xie. 2014. "Explaining Asian Americans' Academic Advantage over Whites." *Proceedings of the Academy of Political Science* 111(23): 8416–23.

Huff, James O. 1986. "Geographic Regularities in Residential Search Behavior." *Annals of the Association of American Geographers* 76(2): 208–27.

Human Mortality Database. 2013. University of California, Berkeley (USA) and Max Planck Institute for Demographic Research (Germany). Accessed August 25, 2013. http://www.mortality.org or www.humanmortality.de.

Humphreys, J.S., and J.S. Whitelaw. 1979. "Immigrants in an Unfamiliar Environment: Locational Decision-Making under Constrained Circumstances." *Geografiska Annaler. Series B, Human Geography* 61(1): 8–18.

Hutton, Will, and Anthony Giddens. 2000. *Global Capitalism*. New York: The New Press.

Hwang, Sean-Shong, and Steve H. Murdock. 1998. "Racial Attraction or Racial Avoidance in American Suburbs?" *Social Forces* 77(2): 541–66.

Iceland, John. 2009. *Where We Live Now: Immigration and Race in the United States*. Berkeley: University of California Press.

———. 2013. *Poverty in America: A Handbook*. 3rd ed. Berkeley: University of California Press.

Iceland, John, and Rima Wilkes. 2006. "Does Socioeconomic Status Matter? Race, Class, and Residential Segregation?" *Social Problems* 53(2): 248–73.

Inglehart, Ronald. 1997. *Modernization and Postmodernization: Cultural, Economic, and Political Change in 43 Societies*. Princeton, N.J.: Princeton University Press.

Inglehart, Ronald, and Christian Welzel. 2005. *Modernization, Cultural Change, and Democracy: The Human Development Sequence*. Cambridge, N.Y.: Cambridge University Press.

Jachimowicz, Maia, and Kevin O'Neil. 2006. "Practices and Policies for Immigrant Integration in the United States." In *Europe and Its Immigrants in the 21st Century: A New Deal or a Continuing Dialogue of the Deaf?* Edited by Demetrios G. Papademetriou. Washington: Migration Policy Institute.

Jasso, Guillermina. 2014. "The Social Psychology of Immigration and Inequality." In *Handbook of the Social Psychology of Inequality*, edited by Jane D. McLeod, Edward J. Lawler, and Michael L. Schwalbe. New York: Springer. Accessed May 28, 2015. doi:10.1007/978-94-017-9002-4_23.

Jaynes, Gerald D., and Robin M. Williams. 1989. *A Common Destiny: Blacks and American Society*. Washington, D.C.: National Academies Press.

Jiménez, Tomás R. 2010. *Replenished Ethnicity: Mexican Americans, Immigration, and Identity*. Berkeley: University of California Press.

Jiménez, Tomás R., and David FitzGerald. 2007. "Mexican Assimilation: A Temporal and Spatial Reorientation." *Du Bois Review* 4(2): 337–54.

Jiménez, Tomás R., and Adam L. Horowitz. 2013. "When White Is Just Alright: How Immigrants Redefine Achievement and Reconfigure the Ethnoracial Hierarchy." *American Sociological Review* 78(5): 849–71.

Johnson, Kevin R., and Bernard Trujillo. 2011. *Immigration Law and the U.S. Border: ¿Sí Se Puede?* Tucson: University of Arizona Press.

Jonassen, Christen T. 1949. "Cultural Variables in the Ecology of an Ethnic Group." *American Sociological Review* 14(1): 32–41.

Jones-Correa, Michael. 2005. "Bringing Outsiders In: Questions of Immigrant Incorporation." In *The Politics of Democratic Inclusion*, edited by Christina Wolbrecht and R. E. Hero. Philadelphia, Pa.: Temple University Press.

Jones-Correa, Michael, and Els de Graauw. 2013. "The Illegality Trap: The Politics of Immigration and the Lens of Illegality." *Daedalus* 142(3): 185–98.

Joppke, Christian. 2005. *Selecting by Origin: Ethnic Migration in the Liberal State.* Cambridge, Mass.: Harvard University Press.

———. 2010. *Citizenship and Immigration.* Malden, Mass.: Polity Press.

Julian, T., and R. Kominski. 2011. "Education and Synthetic Work-Life Earnings Estimates." *American Community Survey Briefs* ACS-14 (September). Washington, D.C.: U.S. Census Bureau.

Kandel, William, and Grace Kao. 2001. "The Impact of Temporary Labor Migration on Mexican Children's Educational Aspirations and Performance." *International Migration Review* 35(4): 1205–31.

Kandel, William, and Douglas S. Massey. 2002. "The Culture of Mexican Migration: A Theoretical and Empirical Analysis." *Social Forces* 80(3): 981–1004.

Kantrowitz, Nathan. 1973. *Ethnic and Racial Segregation in the New York Metropolis: Residential Patterns among White Ethnic Groups, Blacks, and Puerto Ricans.* New York: Praeger.

Kao, Grace, and Marta Tienda. 1995. "Optimism and Achievement: The Educational Performance of Immigrant Youth." *Social Science Quarterly* 76(1): 1–19.

Kao, Grace, Elizabeth Vaquera, and Kimberly Goyette. 2013. *Education and Immigration.* Malden, Mass: Polity Press.

Kasinitz, Philip, John H. Mollenkopf, Mary C. Waters, and Jennifer Holdaway. 2008. *Inheriting the City: The Children of Immigrants Come of Age.* New York: Russell Sage Foundation.

Keely, Charles B. 1971. "Effects of the Immigration Act of 1965 on Selected Population Characteristics of Immigrants to the United States." *Demography* 8(2): 157–69.

Keller, Ursula, and Kathryn Harker Tillman. 2007. "Post-secondary Educational Attainment of Immigrant and Native Youth." *Social Forces* 87(1): 121–52.

Kim, Ann H., and Michael J. White. 2010 "Panethnicity, Ethnic Diversity, and Residential Segregation." *American Journal of Sociology* 115(5): 1558–96.

King, Miriam, Steven Ruggles, J. Trent Alexander, Sarah Flood, Katie Genadek, Matthew B. Schroeder, Brandon Trampe, and Rebeccaa Vick. 2010. "Integrated Public Use Microdata Series, Current Population Survey: Version 3.0" [machine-readable database]. Minneapolis: University of Minnesota.

King, Robert D. 1997. "Should English Be the Law?" *Atlantic Monthly* 279(4): 55–64.

Kivisto, Peter, and Thomas Faist. 2010. *Beyond a Border: The Causes and Consequences of Contemporary Immigration.* Thousand Oaks, Calif.: Pine Forge Press.

Kling, Rob, Spencer Olin, and Mark Poster. 1991. *Postsuburban California: The Transformation of Orange County since World War II*. Berkeley: University of California Press.

Kloosterman, Robert, Joanne Van Der Leun, and Jan Rath. 1999. "Mixed Embeddedness: (In)formal Economic Activities and Immigrant Business in the Netherlands." *International Journal of Urban and Regional Research* 23(2): 252–66.

Koopmans, Ruud, Paul Statham, Marco Giugni, and Florence Passy. 2005. *Contested Citizenship: Immigration and Cultural Diversity in Europe*. Minneapolis: University of Minnesota Press.

Kossondji, Sherrie A., and Deborah Cobb-Clark. 2002. "Coming Out of the Shadows: Learning about Legal Status and Wages from the Legalized Population." *Journal of Labor Economics* 20(3): 598–628.

Krivo, Lauren J., and Robert L. Kaufman. 2004. "Housing and Wealth Inequality: Racial-Ethnic Differences in Home Equity in the United States." *Demography* 41(3): 585–605.

Kroneberg, Clemens. 2008. "Ethnic Communities and School Performance among the New Second Generation in the United States: Testing the Theory of Segmented Assimilation." *Annals of the American Academy of Political and Social Science* 620(November): 138–60.

Kulu, Hill, and Nadja Milewski. 2007. "Family Change and Migration in the Life Course: An Introduction." *Demographic Research* 17(19): 567–90.

Kymlicka, Will. 1995. *Multicultural Citizenship*. Oxford, U.K.: Oxford University Press.

Lamont, Michèle. 1992. *Money, Morals, and Manners: The Culture of the French and the American Upper-Middle Class*. Chicago, Ill.: University of Chicago Press.

———. 2000. *The Dignity of Working Men*. New York: Russell Sage Foundation.

Landale, Nancy S., R. S. Oropesa, and Aggie J. Noah. 2014. "Immigration and the Family Circumstances of Mexican-Origin Children: A Binational Longitudinal Analysis." *Journal of Marriage and the Family* 76(1): 24–36.

Lareau, Annette. 2011. *Unequal Childhoods: Race, Class, and Family Life. A Decade Later*. 2nd ed. Berkeley: University of California Press.

Leach, Mark A., and Frank D. Bean. 2008. "The Structure and Dynamics of Mexican Migration to New Destinations in the United States." In *New Faces in New Places: The Changing Geography of American Immigration*, edited by Douglas S. Massey. New York: Russell Sage Foundation.

Lee, Ericka. 2002. "The Chinese Exclusion Example: Race, Immigration, and American Gatekeeping, 1882–1924." *Journal of American Ethnic History* 21(3): 36–62.

Lee, Jennifer, and Frank D. Bean. 2004. "America's Changing Color Lines: Race/Ethnicity, Immigration, and Multiracial Identification." *Annual Review of Sociology* 30: 221–42.

———. 2010. *The Diversity Paradox: Immigration and the Color Line in 21st Century America*. New York: Russell Sage Foundation.

Lee, Jennifer, and Min Zhou. 2013. "Frames of Achievement and Opportunity Horizons: Second-Generation Chinese, Vietnamese, and Mexicans in Los Angeles." In *Immigration, Poverty, and Socioeconomic Inequality*, edited by David Card and Steven Raphael. New York: Russell Sage Foundation.

Legewie, Joscha, and Thomas A. DiPrete. 2012. "School Context and the Gender Gap in Educational Achievement." *American Sociological Review* 77(3): 463–85.

Lesthaeghe, Ron. 2010. "The Unfolding Story of the Second Demographic Transition." *Population and Development Review* 36(2): 211–51.

Lesthaeghe, Ron J., and Lisa Neidert. 2006. "The Second Demographic Transition in the United States: Exception or Textbook Example?" *Population and Development Review* 32(4): 669–98.

———. 2009. "U.S. Presidential Elections and the Spatial Pattern of the American Second Demographic Transition." *Population and Development Review* 35(2): 391–400.

Li, Wei. 2009. *Ethnoburb: The New Ethnic Community in Urban America.* Honolulu: University of Hawai'i Press.

Lichter, Daniel T. 2013. "Integration or Fragmentation? Racial Diversity and the American Future." *Demography* 50(2): 359–91.

Lieberson, Stanley. 1963. *Ethnic Patterns in American Cities.* New York: Free Press.

———. 1980. *A Piece of the Pie: Blacks and White Immigrants since 1880.* Berkeley: University of California Press.

Light, Ivan. 2006. *Deflecting Immigration: Networks, Markets, and Regulation in Los Angeles.* New York: Russell Sage Foundation.

Lipset, Seymour Martin, ed. 1990. *American Pluralism and the Jewish Community.* New Brunswick, N.J.: Transaction Publishers.

Logan, John R. 2014. "Diversity and Inequality: Recent Shocks and Continuing Trends." In *Diversity and Disparities: American Enters a New Century,* edited by John R. Logan. New York: Russell Sage Foundation.

Logan, John R., Brian J. Stults, and Reynolds Farley. 2004. "Segregation of Minorities in the Metropolis: Two Decades of Change." *Demography* 41(1): 1–22.

Logan, John R., Wenquan Zhang, and Richard D. Alba, 2002. "Immigrant Enclaves and Ethnic Communities in New York and Los Angeles." *American Sociological Review* 67(2): 299–322.

López, David E., and Ricardo D. Stanton-Salazar. 2001. "Mexican Americans: A Second Generation at Risk." In *Ethnicities: Children of Immigrants in America,* edited by R.G. Rumbaut and A. Portes. New York: Russell Sage Foundation.

Los Angeles Almanac. 2014. "Historical Median Home Sales Prices in Southern California by County, 1982–2008." Accessed October 4, 2014. http://www.laalmanac.com/economy/ec37.htm.

Lozano-Ascencio, Fernando. 1993. "Bringing It Back Home: Remittances to Mexico from Migrant Workers in the United States." Monograph Series 37. San Diego: University of California, Center for U.S.-Mexican Studies.

Luhmann, Niklas. 1998. *Observations on Modernity.* Stanford, Calif.: Stanford University Press.

Maloutas, Thomas. 2004. "Segregation and Residential Mobility: Spatially Entrapped Social Mobility and Its Impact on Segregation in Athens." *European Urban and Regional Studies* 11(3): 195–211.

Mansoor, Ali, and Bryce Quillin. 2006. *Migration and Remittances: Eastern Europe and the Former Soviet Union.* Washington, D.C.: World Bank.

Marcelli, Enrico A. 2004. "From the Barrio to the 'Burbs? Immigration and the Dynamics of Suburbanization." In *Up Against the Sprawl: Public Policy and the Making of Southern California,* edited by Jennifer Wolch, Manuel Pastor Jr., and Peter Dreier. Minneapolis: University of Minnesota Press.

Mare, Robert. D. 1997. "Differential Fertility, Intergenerational Educational Mobility, and Racial Inequality." *Social Science Research* 26(3): 263–91.

———. 2011. "A Multigenerational View of Inequality." *Demography* 48(1): 1–23.

Mare, Robert D., and Huey-Chi Chang. 2006. "Family Attainment Norms and Educational Stratification in the United States and Taiwan: The Effects of Parents' School Transition." In *Mobility and Inequality: Frontiers of Research in Sociology and Economics,* edited by S. L. Morgan, D. B. Grusky, and G. A. Fields. Stanford, Calif.: Stanford University Press.

Marrow, Helen B. 2011. *New Destination Dreaming: Immigration, Race, and Legal Status in the Rural American South.* Stanford: Stanford University Press.

Marsden, Peter V., ed. 2012. *Social Trends in American Life: Findings from the General Social Survey since 1972.* Princeton, N.J.: Princeton University Press.

Marshall, T. H. 1950. *Citizenship and Social Class and Other Essays.* Cambridge, U.K.: Cambridge University Press.

Marteleto, Letícia, Denisse Gelber, Celia Hubert, and Viviana Salinas. 2012. "Educational Inequalities among Latin American Adolescents: Continuities and Changes over the 1980s, 1990s, and 2000s." *Research in Social Stratification and Mobility* 30(3): 352–75.

Martin, Philip L. 2004. "The United States: The Continuing Immigration Debate." In *Controlling Immigration: A Global Perspective,* edited by W. A. Cornelius, T. Tsuda, P. L. Martin, and J. F. Hollifield. Stanford, Calif.: Stanford University Press.

———. 2009. *Importing Poverty? Immigration and the Changing Face of Rural America.* New Haven, Conn.: Yale University Press.

Martin, Susan F. 2011. *A Nation of Immigrants.* New York: Cambridge University Press.

Massey, Douglas S. 1979. "Effects of Socioeconomic Factors on the Residential Segregation of Blacks and Spanish Americans in U.S. Urbanized Areas." *American Sociological Review* 44(6): 1015–22.

———. 1985. "Ethnic Residential Segregation: A Theoretical Synthesis and Empirical Review." *Sociology and Social Research* 69(3): 315–50.

———. 1987. "Do Undocumented Migrants Earn Lower Wages than Legal Immigrants? New Evidence from Mexico." *International Migration Review* 21(2): 236–74.

———. 1999. "Why Does Immigration Occur? A Theoretical Synthesis." In *The Handbook of International Migration: The American Experience,* edited by Charles Hirschman, Philip Kasinitz, and Josh DeWind. New York: Russell Sage Foundation.

———. 2013. "America's Immigration Policy Fiasco." *Daedalus* 142(3): 5–15.

———. 2014. "Why Migrate? Theorizing Undocumented Migration." In *Hidden Lives and Human Rights in the United States: Understanding the Controversies and Tragedies of Undocumented Immigration,* edited by L. A. Lorentzen, vol. 1. Santa Barbara, Calif.: Praeger.

Massey, Douglas S., Rafael Alarcón, Jorge Durand, and Humberto Gonzáles. 1987. *Return to Aztlan: The Social Process of International Migration from Western Mexico.* Berkeley: University of California Press.

Massey, Douglas S., Joaquin Arango, Graeme Hugo, Ali Kouaouci, Adela Pellegrino, and J. Edward Taylor. 1993. "Theories of International Migration: A Review and Appraisal." *Population and Development Review* 19(3): 431–66.

———. 1998. *Worlds in Motion: Understanding International Migration at the End of the Millennium*. New York: Oxford University Press.

Massey, Douglas S., and Nancy A. Denton. 1987. "Trends in the Residential Segregation of Blacks, Hispanics, and Asians: 1970–1980." *American Sociological Review* 52(6): 802–25.

———. 1988. "Suburbanization and Segregation in U.S. Metropolitan Areas." *American Journal of Sociology* 94(3): 592–626.

———. 1989. "Residential Segregation of Mexicans, Puerto Ricans, and Cubans in Selected U.S. Metropolitan Areas." *Sociology and Social Research* 73(2): 73–83.

Massey, Douglas S., Jorge Durand, and Nolan J. Malone. 2002. *Beyond Smoke and Mirrors: Mexican Immigration in an Era of Economic Integration*. New York: Russell Sage Foundation.

Massey, Douglas S., and Kristin E. Espinosa. 1997. "What's Driving Mexico-U.S. Migration? A Theoretical, Empirical, and Policy Analysis." *American Journal of Sociology* 102(4): 939–99.

Massey, Douglas S., and Julia Gelatt. 2010. "What Happened to the Wages of Mexican Immigrants? Trends and Interpretations." *Latino Studies* 8(3): 328–54.

Massey, Douglas S., and Kerstin Gentsch. 2011. "Labor Market Outcomes for Legal Mexican Immigrants Under the New Regime of Immigration Enforcement." *Social Science Quarterly* 92(3): 875–93.

———. 2014. "Undocumented Migration and the Wages of Mexican Immigrants." *International Migration Review* 48(2): 482–99.

Massey, Douglas S., and Brendan P. Mullan. 1984. "Processes of Hispanic and Black Spatial Assimilation." *American Journal of Sociology* 89(4): 836–73.

Massey, Douglas S., and Karen A. Pren. 2012a. "Origins of the New Latino Underclass." *Race and Social Problems* 4(1): 5–17.

———. 2012b. "Unintended Consequences of U.S. Immigration Policy: Explaining the Post-1965 Surge from Latin America." *Population and Development Review* 38(1): 1–29.

Massey, Douglas S., Jacob S. Rugh, and Karen A. Pren. 2010. "The Geography of Undocumented Mexican Migration." *Mexican Studies/Estudios Mexicanos* 26(1): 120–52.

Massey, Douglas S., and Magaly Sanchez R. 2010. *Brokered Boundaries: Constructing Immigrant Identity in Anti-Immigrant Times*. New York: Russell Sage Foundation.

Massey, Douglas S., and J. Edward Taylor. 2004. "Back to the Future: Immigration Research, Immigration Policy, and Globalization in the Twenty-first Century." In *International Migration: Prospects and Policies in a Global Market*, edited by Douglas S. Massey and J. Edward Taylor. Oxford, U.K.: Oxford University Press.

Mayer, Christopher J., and Karen Pence. 2008. *Subprime Mortgages: What, Where, and to Whom?* Working Paper 14083. Cambridge, Mass.: National Bureau of Economic Research. Accessed October 1, 2014. http://www.nber.org/papers/w14083.

Mayer, Karl Ulrich. 2009. "New Directions in Life Course Research." *Annual Review of Sociology* 35: 413–33.

McConnell, Eileen Diaz. 2013. "Who has Housing Affordability Problems? Disparities in Housing Cost Burden by Race, Nativity, and Legal Status in Los Angeles." *Race and Social Problems* 5(3): 173–90.

McCutcheon, A. L. 1996. "Multiple Group Association Models with Latent Variables: An Analysis of Secular Trends in Abortion Attitudes, 1972–1988." *Sociological Methodology* 26: 79–111.

McKeever, Matthew, and Stephen L. Klineberg. 1999. "Generational Differences in Attitudes and Socioeconomic Status among Hispanics in Houston." *Sociological Inquiry* 69(1): 33–50.

Meara, E. R., S. Richards, and D. M. Cutler. 2008. "The Gap Gets Bigger: Changes in Mortality and Life Expectancy, by Education, 1981–2000." *Health Affairs* 27(2): 350–60.

Menjívar, Cecilia. 2000. *Fragmented Ties: Salvadoran Immigrant Networks in America*. Berkeley: University of California Press.

———. 2002. "The Ties That Heal: Guatemalan Immigrant Women's Networks and Medical Treatment." *International Migration Review* 36(2): 437–66.

———. 2006. "Liminal Legality: Salvadoran and Guatemalan Immigrants' Lives in the United States." *American Journal of Sociology* 111(4): 999–1037.

Merton, Robert K. 1957. *Social Theory and Social Structure*. Glencoe, Ill.: The Free Press.

Meuleman, Bart. 2009. "The Influence of Macro-Sociological Factors on Attitudes Toward Immigration in Europe: A Cross-Cultural and Contextual Approach." Leuven, Bel.: Katholieke Universiteit Leuven, Faculteit Sociale Wetenschappen, Centrum voor Sociologisch Onderzoek. Accessed May 30, 2015. https://lirias.kuleuven.be/bitstream/123456789/244575/1/PhD_Bart-Meuleman2009.pdf.

Michielin, Francesca, and Clara H. Mulder. 2008. "Family Events and the Residential Mobility of Couples." *Environment and Planning A* 40(11): 2770–90.

Minnesota Population Center. 2011. *Integrated Public Use Microdata Series, International: Version 6.1* [machine-readable database]. Minneapolis: University of Minnesota.

Mitchell, Mark, and Dave Russell. 1996. "Immigration, Citizenship and the Nation-State in the New Europe." In *Nation & Identity in Contemporary Europe*, edited by Bryan Jenkins and Spyros A. Sofos. London, U.K.: Routledge.

Mittelbach, Frank G., and Joan W. Moore. 1968. "Ethnic Endogamy: The Case of Mexican Americans." *American Journal of Sociology* 74(1): 50–62.

Mize, Ronald L., and Grace Peña Delgado. 2012. *Latino Immigrants in the United States*. Malden, Mass.: Polity Press.

Modood, Tariq. 2007. *Multiculturalism: A Civic Idea*. Cambridge, U.K.: Polity Press.

Montejano, David. 1987. *Anglos and Mexicans in the Making of Texas, 1836–1986*. Austin, Tex.: University of Texas Press.

Montserrat, Guibernau, and John Rex. 2010. *The Ethnicity Reader: Nationalism, Multiculturalism, and Migration*. Cambridge, U.K.: Polity Press.

Morgan, Edmund. 1975. *American Slavery, American Freedom: The Ordeal of Colonial Virginia*. New York: Norton.

Morgan, Stephen L., and Dafna Gelbgiser. 2014. "Mexican Ancestry, Immigrant Generation, and Educational Attainment in the United States." *Sociological Science* 1(September): 397–422.

Motomura, Hiroshi. 2006. *Americans in Waiting: The Lost Story of Immigration and Citizenship in the United States*. New York: Oxford University Press.

———. 2014. *Immigration Outside the Law*. New York: Oxford University Press.

Murdie, Robert, and Sutama Ghosh. 2010. "Does Spatial Concentration Always Mean a Lack of Integration? Exploring Ethnic Concentration and Integration in Toronto." *Journal of Ethnic and Migration Studies* 36(2): 293–311.

Muthén, Bengt O. 2001a. "Latent Variable Mixture Modeling." In *New Developments and Techniques in Structural Equation Modeling,* edited by G. A. Marcoulides and R. E. Schumacker. Mahwah, N.J.: Lawrence Erlbaum.

———. 2001b. "Second-Generation Structural Equation Modeling with a Combination of Categorical and Continuous Latent Variables: New Opportunities for Latent Class/Latent Growth Modeling." In *New Methods for the Analysis of Change,* edited by A. Sayer and L. M. Collins. Washington, D.C.: American Psychological Association.

———. 2002. "Beyond SEM: General Latent-Variable Modeling." *Behaviormetrika* 29: 81–117.

Muthén, Bengt O., and Linda K. Muthén. 2000. "Integrating Person-Centered and Variable-Centered Analyses: Growth Mixture Modeling with Latent Trajectory Classes." *Alcoholism: Clinical and Experimental Research* 24(6): 882–91.

Myers, Dowell. 2007. *Immigrants and Boomers: Forging a New Social Contract for the Future of America.* New York: Russell Sage Foundation.

———. 2013. "How Do the 50 States Rank on Child Loss?" PopDynamics. Los Angeles: University of Southern California, Sol Price School of Public Policy. Accessed on September 12, 2013. http://www.usc.edu/schools/price/research/popdynamics/research-children.html.

Myers, Dowell, and Seong Woo Lee. 1996. "Immigration Cohorts and Residential Overcrowding in Southern California." *Demography* 33(1): 51–65.

National Research Council. 2011. *Budgeting for Immigration Enforcement: A Path to Better Performance.* Edited by Steve Redburn, Peter Reuter, and Malay Majmundar. Committee on Estimating Costs of Immigration Enforcement in the Department of Justice. Committee on Law and Justice, Division of Behavioral and Social Sciences and Education. Washington, D.C.: National Academies Press.

Nee, Victor, and Hilary Holbrow. 2013. "Why Asian Americans Are Becoming Mainstream." *Daedalus* 142(3): 65–75.

Ngai, Mae M. 2004. *Impossible Subjects: Illegal Aliens and the Making of Modern America.* Princeton, N.J.: Princeton University Press.

Nguyen, Mai Thi. 2004. "The Self-Segregation of Asians and Hispanics: The Role of Assimilation and Racial Prejudice." *Race and Society* 7(2): 131–51.

Noam, Kris R., and Susan K. Brown. 2013. "Children and Language Shift: Factors Affecting English Usage at Home among U.S. Immigrant Groups." Paper presented at the 2013 annual meeting of the Population Association of America. New Orleans, La., April 13.

Oropesa, R. Sal, and Nancy S. Landale. 2009. "Why Do Immigrant Youths Who Never Enroll in U.S. Schools Matter? School Enrollment among Mexicans and Non-Hispanic Whites." *Sociology of Education* 82(3): 240–66.

Orrenius, Pia M., and Madeline Zavodny. 2015. "The Impact of Temporary Protected Status on Immigrants' Labor Market Outcomes." *American Economic Review: Papers and Proceedings* 105(5): 1–6.

Ortega, Alexander N., Sarah M. Horwitz, Hai Fang, Alice A. Kuo, Steven P. Wallace, and Moira Inkelas. 2009. "Documentation Status and Parental Concerns about Development in Young U.S. Children of Mexican Origin." *Academic Pediatrics* 9(4): 278–82.

Osypuk, Theresa L., Ana V. Diez Roux, Craig Hadley, and Namratha R. Kandula. 2009. "Are Immigrant Enclaves Healthy Places to Live? The Multi-ethnic Study of Atherosclerosis." *Social Science & Medicine* 69(1): 110–20.

Ottaviano, Gianmarco I. P., Giovanni Peri, and Greg C. Wright. 2013. "Immigration, Offshoring, and American Jobs." *American Economic Review* 103(5): 1925–59.

Ovink, Sarah M. 2014. " 'They Always Call Me an Investment': Gendered Familism and Latino/a College Pathways." *Gender and Society* 28(2): 265–88.

Papademetriou, Demetrios G. 2006. *Europe and Its Immigrants in the 21st Century: A New Deal or a Continuing Dialogue of the Deaf?* Washington, D.C.: Migration Policy Institute.

Parekh, Bhiku C. 2006. *Rethinking Multiculturalism: Cultural Diversity and Political Theory.* New York: Palgrave.

Park, Julie, Dowell Myers, and Tomás R. Jiménez. 2014. "Intergenerational Mobility of the Mexican-Origin Population in California and Texas Relative to a Changing Regional Mainstream." *International Migration Review* 48(2): 442–81.

Park, Robert E. 1926. "The Urban Community as a Spatial Pattern and Moral Order." In *The Urban Community,* edited by Ernest W. Burgess. Chicago, Ill.: University of Chicago Press.

Park, Robert E., and Ernest W. Burgess. 1921. *Introduction to the Science of Sociology.* Chicago, Ill.: University of Chicago Press.

———. 1969. *Introduction to the Science of Sociology.* 3rd ed. Chicago, Ill.: University of Chicago Press.

Parrado, Emilio A., and Chenoa Flippen. 2005. "Migration and Gender among Mexican Women." *American Sociological Review* 70(4): 606–32.

Passel, Jeffrey S., and D'Vera Cohn. 2009. "A Portrait of Unauthorized Immigrants in the United States." Washington, D.C.: Pew Research Center.

———. 2011. "Unauthorized Immigrant Population: National and State Trends, 2010." Washington, D.C.: Pew Hispanic Center.

Passel, Jeffrey S., D'Vera Cohn, and Ana Gonzalez-Barrera. 2012. "Net Migration from Mexico Falls to Zero—and Perhaps Less." Washington, D.C.: Pew Research Center.

———. 2013. "Population Decline of Unauthorized Immigrants Stalls, May Have Reversed." Washington, D.C.: Pew Hispanic Center.

Passel, Jeffrey S., D'Vera Cohn, and Molly Rohan. 2014. *Unauthorized Immigrant Totals Rise in 7 States, Fall in 14.* Washington, D.C.: Pew Hispanic Center.

Passel, Jeffrey S., Jennifer Van Hook, and Frank D. Bean. 2004. "Estimates of the Legal and Unauthorized Foreign-Born Population for the United States and Selected States, Based on Census 2000." Immigration Studies White Papers. Washington: U.S. Bureau of the Census and Sabre Systems Statistical and Demographic Analyses. Accessed May 17, 2009. http://www.sabresystems.com/sd_whitepapers_immigration.asp.

Passel, Jeffrey S., and Karen A. Woodrow. 1984. "Geographic Distribution of Undocumented Immigrants: Estimates of Undocumented Aliens Counted in the 1980 Census, by State." *International Migration Review* 18(3): 642–71.

Peach, Ceri. 2005. "The Ghetto and the Ethnic Enclave." In *Desegregating the City: Ghettos, Enclaves, and Inequality,* edited by David P. Varady. Albany: State University of New York Press.

Penninx, Rinus, Karen Kraal, Marco Martiniello, and Steven Vertovec. 2004. *Citizenship in European Cities: Immigrants, Local Politics, and Integration Policies.* Aldershot, U.K.: Ashgate.

Perdue, Theda, and Michael G. Green. 2007. *The Cherokee Nation and the Trail of Tears.* New York: Viking.

Perez, Anthony Daniel, and Charles Hirschman. 2009. "The Changing Racial and Ethnic Composition of the U.S. Population: Emerging American Identities." *Population and Development Review* 35(1): 1–51.

Pérez, William. 2012. *Americans by Heart: Undocumented Latino Students and the Promise of Higher Education.* New York: Teachers College Press.

Perlmann, Joel, and Roger Waldinger. 1997. "Second Generation Decline? Immigrant Children, Past and Present: A Reconsideration." *International Migration Review* 31(4): 893–922.

Pessar, Patricia R. 1999. "The Role of Gender, Households, and Social Networks in the Migration Process: A Review and Appraisal." In *The Handbook of International Migration: The American Experience,* edited by Charles Hirschman, Philip Kasinitz, and Josh DeWind. New York: Russell Sage Foundation.

Pfeiffer, Deirdre. 2012. "Has Exurban Growth Enabled Greater Racial Equity in Neighborhood Quality? Evidence from the Los Angeles Region." *Journal of Urban Affairs* 34(4): 347–71.

Piore, Michael J. 1979. *Birds of Passage: Migrant Labor and Industrial Societies.* New York: Cambridge University Press.

Plyler v. Doe, 457 U.S. 202 (1982).

Pong, Suet-ling, and Lingxin Hao. 2007. "Neighborhood and School Factors in the School Performance of Immigrants' Children." *International Migration Review* 41(1): 206–41.

Portes, Alejandro. 1974. "Return of the Wetback." *Society* 11(3): 40–46.

———. 1999. "Immigration Theory for a New Century: Some Problems and Opportunities." In *The Handbook of International Immigration: The American Experience,* edited by Charles Hirschman, Philip Kasinitz, Josh DeWind. New York: Russell Sage Foundation.

Portes, Alejandro, and Robert L. Bach. 1985. *Latin Journey: Cuban and Mexican Immigrants in the United States.* Berkeley: University of California Press.

Portes, Alejandro, Cristina Escobar, and Renelinda Arana. 2008. "Bridging the Gap: Transnational and Ethnic Organizations in the Political Incorporation of Immigrants in the United States." *Ethnic and Racial Studies* 31(6): 1056–90.

Portes, Alejandro, Patricia Fernández-Kelly, and William Haller. 2005. "Segmented Assimilation on the Ground: The New Second Generation in Early Adulthood." *Ethnic and Racial Studies* 28(6): 1000–40.

Portes, Alejandro, and Rubén G. Rumbaut. 2001. *Legacies: The Story of the Immigrant Second Generation.* Berkeley: University of California Press.

———. 2006. *Immigrant America: A Portrait.* 3rd ed. Berkeley, Calif.: University of California Press.

Portes, Alejandro, and Saskia Sassen-Koob. 1987. "Making It Underground: Comparative Material on the Informal Sector in Western Market Economies." *American Journal of Sociology* 93(1): 30–61.

Portes, Alejandro, and E. Vickstrom. 2011. "Diversity, Social Capital, and Cohesion." *Annual Review of Sociology* 37: 461–79.

Portes, Alejandro, and Min Zhou. 1993. "The New Second Generation: Segmented Assimilation and Its Variants." *Annals of the American Academy of Political and Social Science* 530(1): 74–96.

Potochnick, Stephanie R., and Krista M. Perreira. 2010. "Depression and Anxiety among First-Generation Immigrant Latino Youth: Key Correlates and Implications for Future Research." *Journal of Nervous and Mental Disease* 198(7): 470–77.

Price, Marie, and Lisa Benton-Short. 2008. "Migrants to the Metropolis: The Rise of Immigrant Gateway Cities." Syracuse, N.Y.: Syracuse University Press.

Rabe, Birgitta, and Mark Taylor. 2009. "Residential Mobility, Neighbourhood Quality and Lifecourse Events." Working Paper Series 2009-28. Essex, U.K.: Institute for Social and Economic Research.

Raftery, Adrian E. 1995. "Bayesian Model Selection in Social Research." *Sociological Methodology* 25: 111–63.

Ramakrishnan, S. Karthick. 2004. "Second-Generation Immigrants? The '2.5 Generation' in the United States." *Social Science Quarterly* 85(2): 380–99.

———. 2013. "Incorporation versus Assimilation: The Need for Conceptual Differentiation." In *Models of Immigrant Political Incorporation,* edited by Jennifer Hochschild, Jacqueline Chattopadhyay, Claudine Gay, and Michael Jones-Correa. Oxford, U.K.: Oxford University Press.

Ramakrishnan, S. Karthick, and Irene Bloemraad. 2008. *Civic Hopes and Political Realities: Immigrants, Community Organization, and Political Engagement.* New York: Russell Sage Foundation.

Rapino, Melanie A., and Alison K. Fields. 2013. "Mega Commuters in the U.S.: Time and Distance in Defining the Long Commute, Using the American Community Survey." Paper presented at the fall conference of the Association for Public Policy Analysis and Management. Washington, D.C.: November 7–9, 2013. Accessed September 9, 2013. http://www.census.gov/hhes/commuting/files/2012/Paper-Poster_Megacommuting%20in%20the%20US.pdf.

Reed, Deborah, Laura E. Hill, Christopher Jepsen, and Hans P. Johnson. 2005. *Educational Progress Across Immigrant Generations in California.* San Francisco: Public Policy Institute of California.

Reibel, Michael, and Moira Regelson. 2007. "Quantifying Neighborhood Racial and Ethnic Transition Clusters in Multiethnic Cities." *Urban Geography* 28(4): 361–76.

Reichert, Joshua S. 1981. "The Migrant Syndrome: Seasonal U.S. Wage Labor and Rural Development in Central Mexico." *Human Organization* 40: 56–66.

Reitz, Jeffrey G., Raymond Breton, Karen Kisiel Dion, and Kenneth L. Dion. 2009. *Multiculturalism and Social Cohesion: Potentials and Challenges of Diversity.* New York: Springer.

Rex, John. 1997. "The Ethnicity Reader: Nationalism, Multiculturalism, and Migration." In *The Concept of a Multicultural Society,* edited by G. Montserrat and J. Rex. Cambridge, U.K.: Polity Press.

Richardson, John G. 1980. "Variation in Date of Enactment of Compulsory School Attendance Laws: An Empirical Inquiry." *Sociology of Education* 53(3): 153–63.

Ritzer, George. 2011. *Sociological Theory.* 8th ed. New York: McGraw-Hill.

Rivera-Batiz, Francisco L. 1999. "Undocumented Workers in the Labor Market: An Analysis of the Earnings of Legal and Illegal Mexican Immigrants in the United States." *Journal of Population Economics* 12(1): 91–116.

Roberts, Bryan R. 1995. "Socially Expected Durations and the Economic Adjustment of Immigrants." In *The Economic Sociology of Immigration,* edited by A. Portes. New York: Russell Sage Foundation.

Roberts, Bryan R., and Augustín Escobar Latapí. 1997. "Mexican Social and Economic Policy and Emigration." In *At the Crossroads: Mexico and U.S. Immigration Policy,* edited by F. D. Bean, R. O. de la Garza, B. R. Roberts, and S. Weintraub. New York: Rowman and Littlefield.

Roberts, Bryan R., Reanne Frank, and Fernando Lozano-Ascencio. 1999. "Transnational Migrant Communities and Mexican Migration to the U.S." *Ethnic and Racial Studies* 22(2): 238–66.

Rocco, Raymond A. 1996. "Latino Los Angeles: Reframing Boundaries/Borders." In *The City: Los Angeles and Urban Theory at the End of the Twentieth Century,* edited by Allen J. Scott and Edward W. Soja. Berkeley: University of California Press.

Roche, Kathleen M., Sharon R. Ghazarian, and Maria Eugenia Fernandez-Esquer. 2012. "Unpacking Acculturation: Cultural Orientations and Educational Attainment among Mexican-Origin Youth." *Journal of Youth and Adolescence* 41(7): 920–31.

Romo, Ricardo. 1983. *East Los Angeles: History of a Barrio.* Austin: University of Texas Press.

Rosenbaum, Emily, and Samantha Friedman. 2007. *The Housing Divide: How Generations of Immigrants Fare in New York's Housing Market.* New York: New York University Press.

Rosenfeld, Michael J. 2002. "Measures of Assimilation in the Marriage Market: Mexican Americans, 1970–1990." *Journal of Marriage and the Family* 64(1): 152–62.

Ross, Stephen L., and Margery Austin Turner. 2005. "Housing Discrimination in Metropolitan America: Explaining Changes Between 1989 and 2000." *Social Problems* 52(2): 152–80.

Rossi, Peter H. 1980. *Why Families Move.* 2nd ed. Beverly Hills, Calif.: Sage Publications.

Rowland, Donald T. 2008. *Demographic Methods and Concepts.* New York: Oxford University Press.

Ruggles, Steven, J. Trent Alexander, Katie Genadek, Ronald Goeken, Matthew B. Schroeder, and Matthew Sobek. 2010. *Integrated Public Use Microdata Series.* Version 5.0 [machine-readable database]. Minneapolis: University of Minnesota.

Rugh, Jacob S., and Douglas S. Massey. 2010. "Racial Segregation and the American Foreclosure Crisis." *American Sociological Review* 75(5): 629–51.

Rumbaut, Rubén. 2004. "Ages, Life Stages, and Generational Cohorts: Decomposing the Immigrant First and Second Generations in the United States." *International Migration Review* 38(3): 1160–205.

———. 2006. "The Making of a People." In *Hispanics and the Future of America,* edited by Marta Tienda and Faith Mitchell. Washington, D.C.: National Academies Press.

Rumbaut, Rubén G., Frank D. Bean, Leo Chavez, Jennifer Lee, Susan K. Brown, Louis DeSipio, and Min Zhou. 2004. "Immigration and Intergenerational Mobility in Metropolitan Los Angeles (IIMMLA)." Ann Arbor, Mich.: Interuniversity Consortium for Political and Social Research [distributor]. Accessed July 1, 2008. doi:10.3886/ICPSR22627.v.1.

Rumbaut, Rubén G., Douglas S. Massey, and Frank D. Bean. 2006. "Linguistic Life Expectancies: Immigrant Language Retention in Southern California." *Population and Development Review* 32(3): 447–60.

Sampson, Robert J. 2012. *Great American City: Chicago and the Enduring Neighborhood Effect.* Chicago, Ill.: University of Chicago Press.

Sampson, Robert J., and John H. Laub. 2005. "A Life-Course View of the Development of Crime." *Annals of the American Academy of Political and Social Science* 602(1): 12–45.

Sampson, Robert J., Jeffrey D. Morenoff, and Felton Earls. 1999. "Beyond Social Capital: Spatial Dynamics of Collective Efficacy for Children." *American Sociological Review* 64(5): 633–60.

Sampson, Robert J., Jeffrey D. Morenoff, and Thomas Gannon-Rowley. 2002. "Assessing 'Neighborhood Effects': Social Processes and New Directions in Research." *Annual Review of Sociology* 28(1): 443–78.

Sánchez, George J. 1993. *Becoming Mexican American: Ethnicity, Culture, and Identity in Chicano Los Angeles, 1900–1945.* New York: Oxford University Press.

Sanders, Jimy M., and Victor Nee. 1987. "Limits of Ethnic Solidarity in the Enclave Economy." *American Sociological Review* 52(6): 745–73.

Sassen, Saskia. 1988. *The Mobility of Labor and Capital: A Study in International Investment and Labor Flow.* New York: Cambridge University Press.

———. 1991. *The Global City: New York, London, and Tokyo.* Princeton, N.J.: Princeton University Press.

———. 1995. "Immigration and Local Labor Markets." In *The Economic Sociology of Immigration,* edited by A. Portes. New York: Russell Sage Foundation.

———. 2000. *Cities in a World Economy.* 2nd ed. Thousand Oaks, Calif.: Pine Forge Press.

Schnell, Izhak, and Moshe Harpaz. 2005. "A Model of a Heterogeneous Neighborhood." *GeoJournal* 64(2): 105–15.

Segura, Denise A. 1994. "Working at Motherhood: Chicana and Mexican Immigrant Mothers and Employment." In *Ideology, Experience, and Agency,* edited by E. N. Glenn, G. Chang, and L. R. Forcey. New York: Routledge.

Sewell, William H., Jr. 1992. "A Theory of Structure: Duality, Agency, and Transformation." *American Journal of Sociology* 98(1): 1–29.

Sharp, Gregory, and John Iceland. 2013. "The Residential Segregation Patterns of Whites by Socioeconomic Status, 2000–2011." *Social Science Research* 42(4): 1046–60.

Sidanius, James. 1999. *Social Dominance: An Intergroup Theory of Social Hierarchy and Oppression.* Cambridge, U.K.: Cambridge University Press.

Simmel, Georg. 1923. *Soziologie.* Leipzig, Ger.: Duncker and Humblot.

Sisk, Blake. 2013. "Playing Catch-up: Legalization and the Occupational Mobility Trajectories of Unauthorized Latin American Immigrants." Paper presented at the annual meeting of the American Sociological Association, New York, August 10–13.

Smith, James P. 2003. "Assimilation Across Latino Generations." *American Economic Review* 93(2): 315–19.

———. 2005. "One More Embrace, Then Slam the Door." *Los Angeles Times.* May 1, M3.

———. 2006. "Immigrants and the Labor Market." *Journal of Labor Economics* 24(2): 203–33.

Smith, Robert C. 2002. "Gender, Ethnicity, and Race in School and Work Outcomes of Second-Generation Mexican Americans." In *Latinos: Remaking America,* edited by M. M. Suárez-Orosco and M. M. Paez. Berkeley: University of California Press.

Smith, Robert Courtney. 2006. *Mexican New York: Transnational Lives of New Immigrants.* Berkeley: University of California Press.

———. 2013. "Mexicans: Civic Engagement, Education, and Progress Achieved and Inhibited." In *One Out of Three: Immigrant New York in the Twenty-first Century,* edited by Nancy Foner. New York: Columbia University Press.

———. 2014. "Black Mexicans, Conjunctural Ethnicity, and Operating Identities: Long-Term Ethnographic Analysis." *American Sociological Review* 79(3): 517–48.

Soehl, Thomas, and Roger Waldinger. 2012. "Inheriting the Homeland? Intergenerational Transmission of Cross-Border Ties in Migrant Families." *American Journal of Sociology* 118(3): 778–813.

Solari, Claudia D., and Robert D. Mare. 2012. "Housing Crowding Effects on Children's Wellbeing." *Social Science Research* 41(2): 464–76.

Solinger, Dorothy J. 1999. *Contesting Citizenship in Urban China: Peasant Migrants, the State, and the Logic of the Market.* Berkeley: University of California Press.

South, Scott J., and Kyle Crowder. 1997. "Escaping Distressed Neighborhoods: Individual, Community, and Metropolitan Influences." *American Journal of Sociology* 102(4): 1040–84.

South, Scott J., Kyle Crowder, and Erick Chavez. 2005a. "Exiting and Entering High-Poverty Neighborhoods: Latinos, Blacks, and Anglos Compared." *Social Forces* 84(2): 873–900.

———. 2005b. "Geographic Mobility and Spatial Assimilation among U.S. Latino Immigrants." *International Migration Review* 39(3): 577–607.

Soysal, Yasemin Nuhoglu. 1994. *Limits of Citizenship: Migrants and Postnational Membership in Europe.* Chicago, Ill.: University of Chicago Press.

Stark, Oded. 1991a. "Migration Incentives, Migration Types: The Role of Relative Deprivation." *Economic Journal* 101(408): 1163–78.

———. 1991b. *The Migration of Labor.* Cambridge, U.K.: Basil Blackwell.

Stark, Oded, and J. Edward Taylor. 1989. "Relative Deprivation and International Migration." *Demography* 26(1): 1–14.

Stephens, Nicole M., Stephanie A. Fryberg, and Hazel Rose Markus. 2012. "It's Your Choice: How the Middle-Class Model of Independence Disadvantages Working-Class Americans." In *Facing Social Class: How Societal Rank Influences Interaction,* edited by S. T. Fiske and H. R. Markus. New York: Russell Sage Foundation.

Stiglitz, Joseph E. 2012. *The Price of Inequality: How Today's Divided Society Endangers Our Future.* New York: W. W. Norton.

Suárez-Orozco, Marcelo M., and Carola Suárez-Orozco. 1995. "The Cultural Patterning of Achievement Motivation: A Comparison of Mexican, Mexican Immigrant, Mexican American, and Non-Latino White American Students." In *California's Immigrant Children: Theory, Research, and Implications for Educational Policy,* edited by Rubén G. Rumbaut and Wayne Cornelius. La Jolla, Calif.: Center for U.S.-Mexican Studies.

Suárez-Orozco, Carola, Hirokazu Yoshikawa, Robert T. Teranishi, and Marcelo M. Suárez-Orozco. 2011. "Growing Up in the Shadows: The Developmental Implications of Unauthorized Status." *Harvard Educational Review* 81(3): 438–73.

Swencionis, Jillian K., and Susan T. Fiske. 2013. "More Human: Individuation in the 21st Century." In *Humanness and Dehumanization,* edited by P. Bain, J. Vaes, and J.-P. Leyens. New York: Psychology Press.

Swidler, Ann. 1986. "Culture in Action: Symbols and Strategies." *American Sociological Review* 51(2): 273–86.

———. 2000. *Talk of Love: How Culture Matters*. Chicago, Ill.: University of Chicago Press.

Taeuber, Alma F., and Karl E. Taeuber. 1967. "Recent Immigration and Studies of Ethnic Assimilation." *Demography* 4(2): 798–808.

Tafoya-Estrada, Rosaura. 2004. "The Unintended Consequences of Patriarchy: Mexican Immigrant Culture and Education among the Second Generation." Master's thesis, Sociology Department, University of California, Irvine.

———. 2008. "Gendered Incorporation Experiences: A Multi-generational Study of Mexican American Employment and Education." Ph.D. diss., Sociology Department, University of California, Irvine.

Taylor, J. Edward, Joaquin Arango, Graeme Hugo, Ali Kouaouci, Douglas S. Massey, and Adela Pellegrino. 1997. "International Migration and National Development." *Population Index* 62(2): 181–212.

Taylor, Paul. 2014. *The Next America: Boomers, Millennials, and the Looming Generational Showdown*. New York: PublicAffairs.

Telles, Edward E., and Vilma Ortiz. 2008. *Generations of Exclusion: Racial Assimilation and Mexican Americans*. New York: Russell Sage Foundation.

Telles, Edward, Mark Q. Sawyer, and Gaspar Rivera-Salgado. 2011. "Just Neighbors? Research on African American and Latino Relations in the United States." New York: Russell Sage Foundation.

Terriquez, Veronica. 2014. "Trapped in the Working Class? Prospects for the Intergenerational (Im)Mobility of Latino Youth." *Sociological Inquiry* 84(3): 382–411.

Thomas, William I., and Florian Znaniecki. 1927. *The Polish Peasant in Europe and America*. Vol. 2. New York: Knopf.

Tiebout, Charles M. 1956. "A Pure Theory of Local Expenditures." *Journal of Political Economy* 64(5): 416–24.

Tienda, Marta. 1991. "Poor People and Poor Places: Deciphering Neighborhood Effects on Poverty Outcomes." In *Macro-Micro Links in Sociology*, edited by Joan Huber. Newbury Park, Calif.: Sage Publications.

Tienda, Marta, and Faith Mitchell. 2006. "E Pluribus Plures or E Pluribus Unum?" Introduction to *Hispanics and the Future of America*, edited by Marta Tienda and Faith Mitchell. Panel on Hispanics in the United States. Washington, D.C.: National Academies Press.

Tienda, Marta, and Susana M. Sánchez. 2013. "Latin American Immigration to the United States." *Daedalus* 142(3): 48–64.

Todaro, Michael P., and Lydia Maruszko. 1987. "Illegal Migration and U.S. Immigration Reform: A Conceptual Framework." *Population and Development Review* 13(1): 101–14.

Tolbert, Charles M., Patrick M. Horan, and E. M. Beck. 1980. "The Structure of Economic Segmentation: A Dual Economy Approach." *American Journal of Sociology* 85(5): 1095–16.

Tran, Van C., Susan K. Brown, and Jens Schneider. 2012. "Neighborhoods and Perceptions of Disorder." In *The Changing Face of World Cities: The Second Generation in Western Europe and the United States*, edited by Maurie Crul and John Mollenkopf. New York: Russell Sage Foundation.

Ueda, Reed. 1998. "The Changing Face of Post-1965 Immigration." In *The Immigration Reader*, edited by D. Jacobson. Malden, Mass.: Blackwell Publishers.

US2010. 2013. Spatial Structures in Social Sciences. Providence, R.I.: Brown University. Accessed September 5, 2013. http://www.s4.brown.edu/us2010/SegSorting/Default.aspx.

U.S. Bureau of the Census. 2000a. DP-1. "Profile of General Demographic Characteristics: 2000." Data Set: Census 2000 Summary File 1 (SF-1). Washington: U.S. Department of Commerce. Accessed May 31, 2015. http://www.census.gov.

———. 2000b. DP-2. "Profile of Selected Social Characteristics: 2000." Data Set: Summary File 3 (SF-3). Washington: U.S. Department of Commerce. Accessed May 31, 2015. http://www.census.gov.

———. 2010. DP-1. "Profile of General Demographic Characteristics: 2010" Data Set: Summary File 1 (SF-1). Washington: U.S. Department of Commerce. Accessed May 31, 2015. http://www.census.gov.

———. 2013. "International Program, International Data Base." Washington: U.S. Department of Commerce. Accessed September 12, 2013. http://www.census.gov/population/international/data/idb/informationGateway.php.

U.S. Bureau of Labor Statistics. 2011. "Labor Force Statistics from the Current Population Theory." Washington: U.S. Government Printing Office. Accessed July 26, 2011. www.blss.gov/eps/#date.

———. 2012. "Employees on Nonfarm Payrolls by Major Industry Sector, 1962 to Date." Establishment Data, Historical Employment, Table B-1. Washington: U.S. Bureau of Labor Statistics. Accessed June 1, 2015. http://www.bls.gov/webapps/legacy/cesbtab1.htm.

U.S. Department of Commerce. 2010a. "Population Estimates." Washington: Bureau of the Census. Accessed May 2, 2013. http://www.census.gov/popest/data/historical/index.html.

———. 2010b. "Gross Domestic Product." Washington: Bureau of Economic Analysis. Accessed March 3, 2013. http://www.bea.gov/national/index.htm#gdp.

_____. 2012. "United States Trade Representative Annex I." Accessed May 11, 2013. http://www.ustr.gov/sites/default/files/Annex1.pdf.

U.S. Department of Health and Human Services. 2010. "Vital Statistics." Centers for Disease Control and Prevention, National Center for Health Statistics. Accessed June 1, 2015. http://www.cdc.gov/nchs/vitalstats.htm.

U.S. Department of Homeland Security. 2003. *2002 Yearbook of Immigration Statistics*. Washington: U.S. Department of Homeland Security, Office of Immigration Statistics.

———. 2009. *2008 Yearbook of Immigration Statistics*. Washington: U.S. Department of Homeland Security, Office of Immigration Statistics.

———. 2011. *2010 Yearbook of Immigration Statistics*. Washington: U.S. Department of Homeland Security, Office of Immigration Statistics.

———. 2012. *2011 Yearbook of Immigration Statistics*. Washington: U.S. Department of Homeland Security, Office of Immigration Statistics.

———. 2014. *2013 Yearbook of Immigration Statistics*. Washington: U.S. Department of Homeland Security, Office of Immigration Statistics.

U.S. Department of State, Bureau of Consular Affairs. 2011. "Mexico Family Preference Cut-off Dates from FY1992–2010." Accessed January 12, 2012. http://www.travel.state.gov/content/visas/english/law-and-policy/bulletin.html.

U.S. Immigration and Naturalization Service. 1987. *Statistical Yearbook of the U.S. Immigration and Naturalization Service, 1986.* Washington: U.S. Government Printing Office.

———. 1994. *1993 INS Yearbook.* Washington, D.C.: U.S. Government Printing Office.

———. 1999. *Statistical Yearbook of the U.S. Immigration and Naturalization Service, 1998.* Washington: U.S. Government Printing Office.

Valletta, Rob, and Leila Bengali. 2013. "What's Behind the Increase in Part-Time Work?" Federal Reserve Board of San Francisco Economic Letter. August 13. Accessed October 18, 2014. http://www.frbsf.org/economic-research/publications/economic-letter/2013/august/part-time-work-employment-increase-recession/.

van de Kaa, Dirk, J. 2001. "Postmodern Fertility Preferences: From Changing Value Orientation to New Behavior." *Population and Development Review* 27(Suppl: Global Fertility Transition): 290–31.

Van Hook, Jennifer, and James D. Bachmeier. 2013. "Citizenship Reporting in the American Community Survey." *Demographic Research* 29(1): 1–32.

Van Hook, Jennifer, James D. Bachmeier, Donna Coffman, and Ofer Harel. 2015. "Can We Spin Straw into Gold? An Evaluation of Immigrant Legal Status Imputation Approaches." *Demography* 52(1): 329–54.

Van Hook, Jennifer, and Frank D. Bean. 2009. "Immigrant Welfare Receipt: Implications for Immigrant Settlement and Integration." In *Immigrant Welfare Receipt: Ten Years after Welfare Reform,* edited by M. Fix. New York: Russell Sage Foundation.

Van Hook, Jennifer, Frank D. Bean, James D. Bachmeier, and Catherine Tucker. 2014. "Recent Trends in Coverage of the Mexican-Born Population of the United States: Results from Applying Multiple Methods across Time." *Demography* 51(2): 699–726.

Van Hook, Jennifer, and Jennifer E. Glick. 2007. "Immigration and Living Arrangements: Moving Beyond Economic Need Versus Acculturation." *Demography* 44(2): 225–49.

Vang, Zoua M. 2012. "The Limits of Spatial Assimilation for Immigrants' Full Integration: Emerging Evidence from African Immigrants in Boston and Dublin." *Annals of the American Academy of Political and Social Science* 641: 220–46.

Vasquez, Jessica M. 2011. *Mexican Americans Across Generations: Immigrant Families, Racial Realities.* New York: New York University Press.

———. 2014. "Gender Across Family Generations: Change in Mexican American Masculinities and Femininities." *Identities: Global Studies in Culture and Power* 21(5): 532–50.

Vernez, Georges. 1993. "Mexican Labor in California's Economy." In *The California-Mexico Connection,* edited by A. F. Lowenthal and K. Burgess. Stanford, Calif.: Stanford University Press.

Vertovec, Steven, and Susanne Wessendorf. 2010. *The Multiculturalism Backlash: European Discourses, Policies, and Practices.* New York: Routledge.

Villarreal, Andrés, and Erin R. Hamilton. 2012. "Rush to the Border? Market Liberalization and Urban- and Rural-Origin Internal Migration in Mexico." *Social Science Research* 41(5): 1275–91.

Wagmiller, Robert L., Jr., Mary Clare Lennon, Li Kuang, Philip M. Alberti, and J. Lawrence Aber. 2006. "The Dynamics of Economic Disadvantage and Children's Life Chances." *American Sociological Review* 71(5): 847–66.

Waldinger, Roger. 1996. "From Ellis Island to LAX: Immigrant Prospects in the American City." *International Migration Review* 30(4): 1078–86.

———. 2001. *Strangers at the Gates: New Immigrants in Urban America.* Berkeley: University of California Press.

———. 2011. "Immigration: The New American Dilemma." *Daedalus* 140(2): 215–25.

———. 2013. "Crossing Borders: International Migration in the New Century." *Contemporary Sociology: A Journal of Reviews* 42(3): 349–63.

Waldinger, Roger, and Michael I. Lichter. 2003. *How the Other Half Works: Immigration and the Social Organization of Labor.* Berkeley: University of California Press.

Waldinger, Roger, Nelson Lim, and David Cort. 2007. "Bad Jobs, Good Jobs, No Jobs? The Employment Experience of the Mexican American Second Generation." *Journal of Ethnic and Migration Studies* 33(1): 1–5.

Wallerstein, Immanuel. 1983. *Historical Capitalism.* New York: Verso.

Warner, W. Lloyd, and Leo Srole. 1945. *The Social Systems of American Ethnic Groups.* New Haven, Conn.: Yale University Press.

Waters, Mary. 1990. *Ethnic Options: Choosing Identities in America.* Berkeley: University of California Press.

———. 2010. "Second Generation Advantages: Recasting the Debate." In *Helping Young Refugees and Immigrants Succeed: Public Policy, Aid, and Education,* edited by G. Sonnert and G. Holton. New York: Palgrave Macmillan.

Waters, Mary C., and Philip Kasinitz. 2013. "Immigrants in New York: Reaping the Benefits of Continuous Immigration." *Daedalus* 142(3): 92–106.

Weber, Max. 1968. *Economy and Society.* Berkeley: University of California Press.

Weintraub, Sidney. 2010. *Unequal Partners: The United States and Mexico.* Pittsburgh, Pa.: University of Pittsburgh Press.

White, Katherine J. Curtis. 2002. "Declining Fertility among North American Hutterites: The Use of Birth Control Within a Dariusleut Colony." *Biodemography and Social Biology* 49(1–2): 58–73.

White, Michael J., and Jennifer E. Glick. 1999. "The Impact of Immigration on Residential Segregation." In *Immigration and Opportunity: Race, Ethnicity, and Employment in the United States,* edited by F. D. Bean and S. Bell-Rose. New York: Russell Sage Foundation.

———. 2009. *Achieving Anew: How New Immigrants Do in American Schools, Jobs, and Neighborhoods.* New York: Russell Sage Foundation.

Wilkerson, Isabel. 2010. *The Warmth of Other Suns.* New York: Knopf Doubleday.

Wilkes, Rima, and John Iceland. 2004. "Hypersegregation in the Twenty-first Century." *Demography* 41(1): 23–36.

Wojtkiewicz, Roger A., and Katharine M. Donato. 1995. "Hispanic Educational Attainment: The Effects of Family Background and Nativity." *Social Forces* 74(2): 559–74.

Woodrow-Lafield, Karen. 2014. "Undocumented Migration: Magnitude and Characteristics." In *Hidden Lives and Hidden Rights in the United States: Understanding the Controversies and Tragedies of Undocumented Migration, Volume I, History, Theory, and Legislation,* edited by Lois Ann Lorentzen. Santa Barbara, Denver, and Oxford: Praeger Books.

Woodward, C. Vann. 2001. *The Strange Career of Jim Crow.* 1995. Reprint, New York: Oxford University Press.

Wright, Matthew, and Irene Bloemraad. 2012. "Is There a Trade-off Between Multiculturalism and Socio-Political Integration? Policy Regimes and Immigrant Incorporation in Comparative Perspective." *Perspectives on Politics* 10(1): 77–95.

Wright, Richard, Mark Ellis, and Virginia Parks. 2005. "Re-Placing Whiteness in Spatial Assimilation Research." *City & Community* 4(2): 111–35.

Wright, Richard A., Mark Ellis, and Michael Reibel. 1997. "The Linkage Between Immigration and Internal Migration in Large Metropolitan Areas in the United States." *Economic Geography* 73(2): 234–54.

Wuthnow, Robert. 1987. *Meaning and Moral Order.* Berkeley: University of California Press.

Yang, Philip Q. 1995. *Post-1965 Immigration to the United States: Structural Determinants.* Westport, Conn.: Praeger.

Yinger, John. 1995. *Closed Doors, Opportunities Lost: The Continuing Costs of Housing Discrimination.* New York: Russell Sage Foundation.

Yoshikawa, Hirokazu. 2011. *Immigrants Raising Citizens: Undocumented Parents and Their Young Children.* New York: Russell Sage Foundation.

Yu, Zhou, and Dowell Myers. 2007. "Convergence or Divergence in Los Angeles: Three Distinctive Ethnic Patterns of Immigrant Residential Assimilation." *Social Science Research* 36(1): 254–85.

Zelinsky, Wilbur, and Barrett A. Lee. 1998. "Heterolocalism: An Alternative Model of the Sociospatial Behaviour of Immigrant Ethnic Communities." *International Journal of Population Geography* 4(4): 281–98.

Zhou, Min. 2009. *Contemporary Chinese America: Immigration, Ethnicity, and Community Transformation.* Philadelphia, Pa.: Temple University Press.

———. 2011. *The Accidental Sociologist in Asian American Studies.* Los Angeles, Calif.: UCLA Asian American Studies Center Press.

Zhou, Min, and Carl L. Bankston III. 1998. *Growing Up American: How Vietnamese Children Adapt to Life in the United States.* New York: Russell Sage Foundation.

———. 2001. "Family Pressure and the Educational Experience of the Daughters of Vietnamese Refugees." *International Migration* 39(4): 133–51.

Zolberg, Aristide R. 1999. "Matters of State: Theorizing Immigration Policy." In *The Handbook of International Migration: The American Experience,* edited by C. Hirschman, P. Kasinitz, and J. DeWind. New York: Russell Sage Foundation.

———. 2006. *A Nation by Design: Immigration Policy in the Fashioning of America.* New York: Russell Sage Foundation.

Zsembik, Barbara A., and Daniel Llanes. 1996. "Generational Differences in Educational Attainment among Mexican Americans." *Social Science Quarterly* 77(2): 363–74.

Index

Boldface numbers refer to figures and tables.

geographical differences, in educational orientation and attainments, 63–65
German immigrants, 25
Germany: immigration policies, 227n110
Glazer, Nathan, 23, 24, 43
globalization, 161, 170–71
Gordon, Milton, 22
Great Depression, 59
Great Recession, 141–42, 165, 173
Grebler, Leo, 48
Greenman, Emily, 70, 71
gross domestic product (GDP), 173
Guatemalan immigrants, 199
Guzman, Ralph, 48

H1B visas, 162
H2A visas, 162
H2B visas, 162
Hagan, Jacqueline, 28, 167
Hall, Matthew, 70, 71
Haller, William, 27
Hart-Celler Act of 1965, 165–66
health outcomes, neighborhood effects, 120
Hernández-León, Rubén, 28, 172
high school dropouts, 174
high school graduation rates, 131, 132–33, 135, **136**, 141, 174
higher education. *See* college education
Hirschman, Charles, 35
Hispanics: CPS identification, 62; definition of, 5, 6; labor market outcomes, 115–17; in Los Angeles, 120–21; spatial integration patterns, 123–25. *See also* Mexican Americans
historical-family-generation, definition of, 58–60
Hochschild, Jennifer, 37
Hoefer, Michael, **163**
home ownership, 138–41
Homeland Security, U.S. Department of, **163, 164**
housing market, 123
Hsin, Amy, 49–50

human-capital theory, 170
Hutterites, 18

IIMMLA (Immigration and Intergenerational Mobility in Metropolitan Los Angeles). *See* Immigration and Intergenerational Mobility in Metropolitan Los Angeles (IIMMLA)
immigrant settlement policies, 29
immigration and immigrant policy: border enforcement, 71, 167, 183, 197; Bracero Program, 34, 59, 165, 181; implications and recommendations, 194–98; quota abolishment, 165–66; research considerations, 1–2. *See also specific laws*
Immigration and Intergenerational Mobility in Metropolitan Los Angeles (IIMMLA): description of, 199–200; fertility, 155; income, 105–17; integration impact of unauthorized status on women, 186; language, 147–50; latent class analysis, **218**; schooling, 61–62, 64–65, 68, 78–88, 93, 95–105; second-generation incorporation indicators, **202, 203, 204**; spatial integration, 125–41; third-generation comparison, 11
Immigration and Naturalization Act of 1965, 165–66
Immigration Reform and Control Act (IRCA) of 1986, 8, 69, 70, 169, 195
inclusionary places, 37–38
income: and educational attainment, 68; gender differences, 105–17, 118; generational differences, 105–17, 118, 186–87; importance of analysis to policy makers, 67; and unauthorized status, 185–86
income maximization, 167
incorporation, definition of, 17
Indian immigrants, **164**
inequality, 168